LIFE ABOVE THE CLOUDS

LIFE ABOVE THE CLOUDS

Philosophy in the Films of
TERRENCE MALICK

edited by
Steven DeLay

Published by State University of New York Press, Albany

© 2023 State University of New York

All rights reserved

Printed in the United States of America

No part of this book may be used or reproduced in any manner whatsoever without written permission. No part of this book may be stored in a retrieval system or transmitted in any form or by any means including electronic, electrostatic, magnetic tape, mechanical, photocopying, recording, or otherwise without the prior permission in writing of the publisher.

For information, contact State University of New York Press, Albany, NY
www.sunypress.edu

Library of Congress Cataloging-in-Publication Data

Name: DeLay, Steven, 1986– editor.
Title: Life above the clouds : philosophy in the films of Terrence Malick / [edited by] Steven DeLay.
Description: Albany : State University of New York Press, [2023] | Includes bibliographical references and index.
Identifiers: LCCN 2022025224 | ISBN 9781438492117 (hardcover : alk. paper) | ISBN 9781438492131 (ebook) | ISBN 9781438492124 (pbk. : alk. paper)
Subjects: LCSH: Malick, Terrence, 1945—Criticism and interpretation. | Malick, Terrence, 1943—Philosophy. | Philosophy in motion pictures.
Classification: LCC PN1998.3.M3388 L55 2023 | DDC 791.43023/3092—dc23/eng/20220906
LC record available at https://lccn.loc.gov/2022025224

10 9 8 7 6 5 4 3 2 1

In memory of Remington Dahl

Contents

List of Films Directed by Terrence Malick — xi

List of Illustrations — xiii

Preface — xv
    Robert Sinnerbrink

Acknowledgments — xxi

Malickian Cinema at the Intersection of Art and Philosophy:
An Introduction — 1
    Steven DeLay

Part I. Cinematic Experience as Ethical Reflection and Spiritual Exercise

Chapter 1
"Find Your Way from Darkness to Light": Cinema as
Spiritual Exercise — 25
    Jonathan Scott Lee

Chapter 2
Terrence Malick's Cosmic Cinema — 47
    Manuel "Mandel" Cabrera Jr.

Chapter 3
"Why Should I Be Good If You Aren't?" The Problem of the
Moral World in *The Tree of Life*   63
    James D. Reid and Candace R. Craig

Chapter 4
Performativity and Transformative Experience:
Terrence Malick's Mysticism   91
    Rico Gutschmidt

Part II. Mystery, Evil, Creation: Framing the "Big Questions"

Chapter 5
Life-Time: Mystery in *The Tree of Life*   107
    David R. Cerbone

Chapter 6
Not One Power, But Two: Dark Grounds and Twilit Paradises
in Malick   127
    Jussi Backman

Chapter 7
Tending God's Garden: Philosophical Themes in *The Tree of Life*   147
    Naomi Fisher

Part III. Explorations of Image and Voiceover

Chapter 8
Sotto voce: Inscription as Voiceover in Malick's *Days of Heaven*   165
    Fred Rush

Chapter 9
The Melancholic Image in *Days of Heaven*   179
    Keith Jacobs and Jeff Malpas

Contents | ix

Chapter 10
Terrence Malick's Ephemeral and Eternal Images: Deleuze,
Time-Image, and Montage   197
   James Lorenz

Chapter 11
Malick's Cartesianism, or the Ghost by the Machine   221
   Enrico Terrone

Chapter 12
Love Is Smiling through All Things: Jean-Luc Marion,
Simone Weil, and the Visual Style of Terrence Malick   237
   Joel Mayward

Chapter 13
Let Me Not Pretend: The Promise of Beauty in *To the Wonder*   257
   Steven Rybin

Part IV. The Pursuit of Freedom and Transcendence

Chapter 14
Platonic Myths of Eros in *Knight of Cups* and *Song to Song*   279
   Matthew Strohl

Chapter 15
The Alien God Behind the Camera: A Gnostic Viewing of
Terrence Malick's Cinema, especially *Knight of Cups*   299
   Lee Braver

Chapter 16
A Hidden Life of Love: Sacrifice in Malick's Cinematographic
Philosophy   319
   Katerina Koci and Martin Koci

Chapter 17
Bleeding Hearts: Edith Stein, Franz Jägerstätter, and Martyrdom   337
   Donald Wallenfang

Chapter 18
Authoritarianism and the Authoritarian Personality:
Malick's Tragedy of Disobedience   355
    David Benjamin Johnson

Chapter 19
"But I Am Free!" Malick on Freedom and Transcendence   375
    Daniel Layman

List of Contributors   393

Index   401

Films Directed by Terrence Malick

Badlands, Warner Brothers, 1973
Days of Heaven, Paramount Pictures, 1978
The Thin Red Line, 20th Century Fox, 1998
The New World, New Line Cinema, 2005
The Tree of Life, Fox Searchlight Pictures, 2011
To the Wonder, Magnolia Pictures, 2012
Knight of Cups, Broad Green Pictures, 2015
Voyage of Time, Broad Green Pictures, 2016
Song to Song, Broad Green Pictures, 2017
A Hidden Life, Fox Searchlight Pictures, 2019
The Way of the Wind, in production

Illustrations

Figure 8.1	Days of Heaven	172
Figure 9.1	Melancholia I	187
Figure 10.1	Late Spring	203
Figure 10.2	The Tree of Life	207
Figure 10.3	The Thin Red Line	208
Figure 10.4	The Tree of Life	209
Figure 10.5	Days of Heaven	213
Figure 10.6	The New World	215
Figure 10.7	A Hidden Life	216
Figure 11.1	The Thin Red Line	230
Figure 11.2	The Thin Red Line	230
Figure 12.1	Days of Heaven	249
Figure 12.2	The Thin Red Line	249
Figure 12.3	The New World	249
Figure 12.4	The Tree of Life	251
Figure 13.1	To the Wonder	263
Figure 13.2	To the Wonder	271
Figure 13.3	To the Wonder	274

Preface

ROBERT SINNERBRINK

One of the challenges facing philosophically inclined film theorists is how to approach writing about a filmmaker whose work both invites and resists narrative interpretation—films that eschew character development or clear narrative plotlines in favor of mood, gesture, voiceover, and imagery. Terrence Malick is just such a filmmaker, having long enjoyed—or suffered from—the reputation of being a reclusive and unconventional cineaste, a "maverick" auteur who manages to maintain an independent artistic vision while attracting and working with some of the biggest stars in Hollywood. Many also describe him as a uniquely "philosophical" filmmaker, which raises the question as to what one means by calling films "philosophical."[1] In Malick's case, these questions are especially pertinent. As a former student of Stanley Cavell, scholar and translator of Heidegger, Malick famously abandoned the path of academic philosophy to pursue a career in cinema. His remarkable oeuvre, which has flourished since the release of his 2011 Palme d'Or–winning work *The Tree of Life*, has attracted a growing body of scholarship. Several volumes have been published over the past two decades, many of which focus on the philosophical and ethical dimensions of his work.[2] Despite Malick's widespread critical acclaim, the difficulty of writing about Malick's films continues to challenge those struck by their aesthetic beauty and philosophical resonances. How should one write about films that many describe as philosophical, ethical, or religious? And how can one write about these films in ways that do justice to them as works of art? For Malick's work raises questions about the relationship between aesthetic experience, critical reflection, and theoretical interpretation in ways that few other filmmakers can match.

The authors assembled in this book have admirably taken up this challenge: to write about Malick's films as artistic works that are simultaneously philosophically or ethically significant. A glance at the critical literature on Malick reveals that authors tend to adopt one of two strategies to meet this challenge: either (1) narrative interpretation and/or thematic analyses or (2) formalist analyses of aesthetic features and/or cinematic techniques.[3] Both approaches raise the question of cinematic style and the role of aesthetic experience in our understanding of film: there is the relationship between aesthetic experience and cinematic style but also that between cinematic style and narrative meaning and/or thematic understanding. We assume that aesthetic experience, cinematic style, and narrative meaning are related, but precisely how this works in Malick's films is left mostly unexamined. These issues become pressing in the "film and philosophy" approach that many scholars have brought to Malick, an approach that engages in philosophical interpretation and ethical reflection in response to singular works of art.[4] The challenge is to do this in a manner that does justice to Malick's films as both cinematic and philosophical works.

Here again observation yields two identifiable but polarized positions that we might call the philosophical approach versus formalist approach. According to the former, Malick's films are best interpreted through the lens of philosophical theory (Heideggerian, existentialist, phenomenological, Deleuzian, etc.). According to the latter, Malick's films demand formalist analysis of cinematic style and technique to account for their distinctive aesthetic effects (which therefore rejects philosophical readings).[5] One common criticism of the philosophical approach is that it neglects to acknowledge or analyze the films' aesthetic features, and thus it fails to clarify how aesthetic style shapes and communicates narrative meaning and critical reflection. A contrasting criticism of the aestheticist or formalist approach is that it brackets the (narrative) meaning of the films' aesthetic features or stylistic techniques, leaving us with technical but empty formalist analyses of indeterminate significance. These difficulties become acute in Malick's case because of the aesthetically distinctive features of his films: their repeated use of specific cinematic techniques coupled with an elliptical narrative and meditative style. His films not only emphasize subjective experiences of mood, for example, but also explore philosophical or metaphysical themes precisely through the use of mood, composition, music, and visual style. Consequently, the risks of both aesthetic reductionism and empty formalism loom large for the unwary critic.

As remarked, one common complaint about philosophical approaches to Malick is that they fall prey to what Thomas Wartenberg calls the "imposition objection": that philosophical critics do not reveal inherent or intended philosophical meanings but "read" these into such films via the lens of their own preferred theoretical frameworks.[6] When faced with the imposition objection, philosophers of film typically defend their approach either by arguing for cases of demonstrable intention on the part of filmmakers or by stressing the hermeneutic interplay between filmmaker and critic as how meaning is articulated.[7] The difficulties one faces in dealing with Malick's films are thus considerable. He famously refuses, for example, to articulate his intentions or provide support for particular interpretations, so the question of artistic intention remains open and ambiguous (and the few public comments available concerning Malick's attitude toward this question suggest that he remained skeptical that "one can film philosophy").[8] Hence, there is a strong reliance on Malick's philosophical background coupled with repeated emphases on his film's thematic elements (the role of voiceovers, nature imagery, and textual allusions become paramount in articulating these philosophical and ethical themes).

Here I would like to suggest an alternative approach to this problem, one exemplified by the chapters comprising this volume: namely, that film philosophers do not so much "impose" such meanings but rather turn to such philosophical approaches with the aim of articulating the kind of *aesthetic experience* that Malick's films can afford. The Heideggerian phenomenological account of "world," for example, offers a way of conceptualizing and understanding that (aesthetic, if not phenomenological) experience of world revealed or expressed in films like *Days of Heaven* or *The New World*. Even formalist critics who explore Malick's aesthetic style and cinematic techniques cannot help but fall back upon (philosophical) accounts of world to make sense of how and why Malick presents fictional worlds in particular ways.[9] On this view, the relationship between film and philosophy becomes a dialogue in which film invites a response from (philosophically receptive) viewers or elicits an aesthetically grounded experience that calls for philosophical and ethical reflection. This requires an attitude of hermeneutic openness to the kind of aesthetic and moral-philosophical experiences that Malick's films afford; it also requires attention to Malick's cinematic style and showing how it facilitates the aesthetic communication of meaning. It means, in short, accepting the film's "invitation" to reflect on the philosophical significance of the aesthetic experiences to which his films give rise.

To do so, however, requires time. It demands attention to one's experience of a film along with time for reflection about the meaning of these experiences. The question of time becomes more pressing for a philosophical appreciation of Malick's work, for there are many features of his films that are conducive to philosophical and ethical reflection but take time to acknowledge and comprehend. We could mention here, among other things, flowing camera movements and the mobility of shots expressing movement, vitality, and living nature; the use of voiceover to reveal individual subjectivity but also to broach broader ethical and metaphysical themes; and the pointed use of nature and landscape to frame human action and drama. There is the attenuation of narrative form in favor of mood, atmosphere, affect, and emotion; the artful use of music to heighten affect, mood, and emotional significance; and an emphasis on touch, hands, movement, bodily gesture, and facial expression. And there is the careful framing of the human body against nature and landscape (or modern architectural spaces); the use of textual (literary, historical, philosophical, religious) allusions in voiceovers and dialogue to frame individual characters as embodiments of particular modes of life; and existential reflections on love and belief in a world struggling with a diminution or narrowing of meaning. Taken together, these elements elicit an immersive yet reflective experience of inhabiting a historically specific sense of world with richly aesthetic qualities. This interweaving of elements—cinematic, aesthetic, historical-cultural, and philosophical—means that it takes time to process, reflect upon, and articulate these experiences in theoretical terms. This could be one reason for the curious fact that most, if not all, of Malick's films received mixed reviews, even quite negative ones, upon first release, even those that were later recognized as major cinematic achievements (such as *Badlands* [1973] and *The Tree of Life* [2011]).[10]

The chapters in this volume all attest to this complex mode of aesthetic reception and philosophical engagement with Malick's work. Steven DeLay's introduction situates Malick's filmmaking in the context of reflections on beauty in art, a topic that is still strangely neglected by most critical writing on Malick. He suggests that Malick's disappointment with contemporary (broadly analytic) philosophy offered one reason for his abandonment of philosophy in favor of cinema. Another is the importance of beauty in cinema as having moral and philosophical, as well as aesthetic, significance. Other contributors pick up this theme, weaving together reflections on the aesthetic dimensions of Malick's work with philosophical reflections on their existential meaning, moral dimensions, and religious significance. The latter is an important extension of the "film as philosophy" debate, which in Malick's case has focused primarily on thinkers such as Heidegger and Cavell but has also recently underlined the role of Kierkegaard as well as the influence of Christian theology and other religious traditions.[11] Among the topics addressed in the chapters that follow are cinema as spiritual practice, mysticism and transcendence, sacrifice and martyrdom, and conceptions of love both spiritual and religious, philosophical and moral. There are more recognizably philosophical, metaphysical, existential, and ethical topics such as Cartesianism, Platonic myths, transcendence, mystery and wonder, the promise of beauty, movement- and time-images, metaphysical dualism, the problem of the moral world, authoritarianism, and freedom. There are also detailed engagements with the aesthetic dimensions of Malick's work, exploring performance, beauty, voiceover, the melancholic image, and cinematic style. Together the authors weave a rich tapestry of concepts, references, and reflections that help us appreciate Malick's work as at once philosophical and religious, metaphysical and moral, existential and aesthetic. They deepen our understanding of the ways in which Malick's films illuminate our shared world, revealing it as both dark and light, troubled and transcendent—films with the power to help us appreciate the beauty of "all things shining."

Notes

1. See Thomas Deane Tucker and Stuart Kendall, eds., *Terrence Malick: Film and Philosophy* (New York: Continuum, 2011); and Robert Sinnerbrink, *Terrence Malick: Filmmaker and Philosopher* (London: Bloomsbury, 2019).

2. David Davies, ed., *The Thin Red Line: Philosophers on Film* (London: Routledge, 2009); Tucker and Kendall, *Terrence Malick: Film and Philosophy*; Steven Rybin, *Terrence Malick and the Thought of Film* (New York: Lexington Books, 2012); Sinnerbrink, *Terrence Malick: Filmmaker and Philosopher*.

3. There is also the "contextualist" approach, which situates Malick's work in relation to the history of contemporary American cinema, literary history, production practices, film theory traditions, and so on. See Hannah Patterson, ed., *The Cinema of Terrence Malick: Poetic Visions of America*, 2nd ed. (London: Wallflower Press, 2007); and Joshua Sikora, ed., *A Critical Companion to Terrence Malick* (Lanham, MD: Rowman and Littlefield, 2020).

4. See Rybin, *Terrence Malick and the Thought of Film*; Shawn Loht, "Film as Heideggerian Art? A Reassessment of Heidegger, Film, and His Connection to Terrence Malick," *Film and Philosophy*, 17 (2013): 113–26; and Sinnerbrink, *Terrence Malick: Filmmaker and Philosopher*. See Martin Rossouw, "There's Something about Malick: Film-Philosophy, Contemplative Style, and the Ethics of Self-Transformation," *New Review of Film and Television Studies* 15, no. 3 (May 2017): 279–98, for a critique of this approach. Rossouw argues that philosophers impose philosophical (often Heideggerian) interpretations on Malick in order to support their implicit claim that his films enact a transformational ethics.

5. For representative examples of these two approaches, see Marc Furstenau and Leslie MacAvoy, "Terrence Malick's Heideggerian Cinema: War and the Question of Being in *The Thin Red Line*," in *The Cinema of Terrence Malick: Poetic Visions of America*, 2nd ed., ed. Hannah Patterson (London: Wallflower Press, 2007), 173–85; and Richard Neer, "Terrence Malick's New World," *nonsite.org*, no. 2 (June 12, 2011). https://nonsite.org/terrence-malicks-new-world/.

6. See Rossouw, "There's Something about Malick"; and Neer, "Terrence Malick's New World."

7. See David Davies, "Terrence Malick," in *The Routledge Companion to Philosophy and Film*, eds. P. Livingston and C. Plantinga (London: Routledge, 2009), 560–80; Loht, "Film as Heideggerian Art?"; Sinnerbrink, *Terrence Malick: Filmmaker and Philosopher*.

8. In an early interview following the release of *Badlands*, Malick answered a question about his philosophical influences by stating, "I don't feel one can film philosophy." Quoted in James Morrison and Thomas Schur, *The Films of Terrence Malick* (Westport, CT: Praeger, 2003), 97.

9. See, for example, Neer, "Terrence Malick's New World."

10. The exception here is the *Thin Red Line*, which critics acknowledged as an existentially rich and artistically accomplished war movie but was also met with significant incredulity, bafflement, or derision when it was first released.

11. See Christopher B. Barnett and Clark J. Elliston, eds., *Theology and the Films of Terrence Malick* (London: Routledge, 2017).

Acknowledgments

I would like to express my deep gratitude to each of the contributors, without whom this set of chapters would not be what it is. I would particularly like to thank Jussi Backman, David Cerbone, Jonathan Lee, Jeff Malpas, and Fred Rush for their advice and guidance along the way. My thanks to George Leaman for so enthusiastically granting permission for me to print, in chapter 8, a revised version of Fred Rush's "*Sotto voce*: Inscription as Voiceover in Malick's *Days of Heaven*," originally published in *Film and Philosophy* in 2020. My thanks to Imogen Rivers, who kindly invited me to share an early version of the volume's introduction at the Oxford University Philosophy Society in November 2020. My thanks to the two reviewers for their very generous and helpful feedback and to Michael Campochiaro and Michael Rinella at SUNY for their support of the volume. Finally, above all, I owe thanks to Gabbie, with whom I have built a little nest above the clouds and who encouraged me to translate my longstanding fondness for Malick's films into print.

Malickian Cinema at the Intersection of Art and Philosophy

An Introduction

STEVEN DELAY

In a *Le Monde* interview with Yvonne Baby a year after the theatrical release of his second film *Days of Heaven* (1978), the American director Terrence Malick, then living in Paris, turns to the matter of his medium's capacity to transform the one who views it. As Malick explains, "For an hour, for two days, for longer, films can provoke little changes of heart, these changes which come back to the same thing: living better, loving more."[1] In this way, a work of cinema works on the very one who encounters it. In this respect, it does what any other work of art might. And when it does so, when a film exhibits the power to transform us profoundly, accomplishing more than what a mere commercial product or piece of entertainment can, accordingly demonstrating itself to be the work of art it is, could it thus be seen as a work of philosophy as well?

Now, what indeed besides beauty could more credibly account for this transformation? As Dietrich von Hildebrand says in his *Introduction to Aesthetics*, "There can be no doubt that beauty is one of the great sources of joy in human life."[2] A couple pages over, Hildebrand quotes no less an authority on the subject than Plato, who, as Hildebrand notes, recognizing beauty's significance for the development of our moral personality, says in the *Phaedrus*: "At the sight of beauty, the soul grows wings."[3] Art and philosophy, of course, historically have always had a close, if sometimes ambivalent, relationship. For philosophical thinking in the immediate wake of Kant, it was widely thought that art performs a redemptive vocation. Friedrich Nietzsche, for one, saw art as that which alone has the power to validate our suffering, to render sense of what would otherwise remain senseless and hence unjustified—"For it is only as an *aesthetic phenomenon* that existence and the world are eternally *justified*."[4] Before Nietzsche, Arthur Schopenhauer recognized art's power to afford the kinds of experiences that make life tolerable. Aesthetic experience, he was to note, delivers us from the ravages of desire, and, finding ourselves temporarily at rest from inner tumult, we experience a moment of tranquility before the beauty we behold: "We celebrate the Sabbath of the penal servitude of willing; the wheel of Ixion stands still."[5] For Schopenhauer, the unhappy reality articulated in his philosophical pessimism leads inexorably to the hunt for what can make existence endurable. Art comes to the rescue. His underlying idea is simple: the only relief we stand to find amid all of this world's suffering is in our experience of beauty, a fleeting refuge without which life itself would not be sufficiently tolerable.

For his own part, G. W. F. Hegel, whose philosophy Schopenhauer despised, also assigned art an exalted role in human existence. In Geist's historical evolution toward Absolute Knowing, art for Hegel is the sensuous expression of humanity's self-determination or freedom, the presentation of "ideal beauty."[6] As this short rollcall of names from the history of philosophy attests, a venerable tradition of thinkers has seen art as more than a means of escapism from the world but as tasked with the aim of revealing truth. Here, probably Martin Heidegger's philosophy of being is the example most likely to spring to mind. His famous essay on the origin of the work of art states that the artwork is capable of exemplifying the truth of being. For Heidegger, as with the others previously mentioned, art concerns beauty. As he says, beauty "is one way in which truth essentially occurs as unconcealment."[7] But what for him matters more than beauty per se is truth understood as ἀλήθεια ("unconcealedness"). As a work of unconcealment and thus truth, a work of art ensures "truth happens"[8] by setting up a world. In Heidegger's estimation, an artwork such as the temple of Delphi embodies a culture's fundamental understanding of the "Being of beings,"[9] of what a particular people (whether ancient Greek, medieval, modern, or technological) takes it to mean for an entity to *be* at all. Their various disagreements notwithstanding, for those belonging to this philosophical tradition, disputes are internal to a shared perspective for which art is far more than just an item of idle amusement or marginal experience. For Schopenhauer, Hegel, Nietzsche, and Heidegger (and others such as Friedrich Schiller), art discloses deep truths about the world and our standing within it.[10]

Against the laudatory role of art accorded by this line of philosophical thinking, naturally one may be tempted to cite Plato as a stark counterpoint. Does not the Platonic philosophy deride art, or at the minimum counsel that we turn a suspicious eye toward it? Rather than functioning as a work of truth, art is illusory or deceptive, so the objection goes, something that leads us into deception and illusion. This is what Book III of the *Republic* maintains of imitative poetry. For if, as Plato thinks, art is *mimêsis*, this is just to say that it is a replica of reality and so in some sense a work of illusion or untruth. It is at best a copy of the Idea (*eidos*). Thus, ontologically speaking, art is not a satisfactory substitute for the reality it aims to depict. In fact, by representing the visible and sensible world, the figurative arts such as painting and sculpture produce works twice removed from the intelligible world of the Idea. Accordingly, art for Plato concerns what amounts to a shadow world less real than the divine, invisible kingdom of the Forms. As the imitation of a sensible reality that is already itself derivative from the intelligible, art cannot be said to be a work of truth. Art traffics in the untrue.[11]

Platonism's dim opinion of artistic *mimêsis* is not merely an abstract concern. It enshrines for Western thought a fundamental distinction between appearance and being that frames a host of recurrent issues, some of which were directly brought to the fore later with the practical invention of photography. What, we may ask, exactly is a photograph? Obviously, a photograph is an image, but importantly, it is an image of something real: a person, a place, a thing, an event. The peculiar intentionality characterizing the photographic image intensifies the ontological concerns already at issue in Plato's account of artistic *mimêsis*. On the one hand, a photograph is itself something tangible and so in that respect just like the other physical objects we encounter in space. And yet, on the other hand, it is altogether different at the same time. Unlike even figurative paintings such as a portrait of Charlamagne or a seascape of Dieppe sailboats, photographs show the thing itself at the actual scene, as it were. In an authentic photo, the image (the physical item we hold in our hand or that hangs on the wall) makes appear what was absent (a dead loved one or an historical event); it makes present something in its absence.[12] The photo, in short, presents an image of reality and thereby inhabits a strange hinterland, straddling the classic Platonic division between appearance and being. The photographic image is not a mere semblance (for it replicates the physical reality it captures), nor is the reality it shows given in its bodily flesh (in *propria persona*, as Edmund Husserl's phenomenology would say).

These ontological puzzles to which photographs give rise lead again to the question of art generally: What is art? Or, more narrowly, is photography an art? From its inception, some critics held it was not. A photograph, they were adamant, is only a mechanical replication of reality. Hence, it is not an artwork. Art, so the thought goes, cannot simply imitate reality by replicating it mechanically. To be art it must possess inherent aesthetic qualities; it must be the work of creativity or inspiration. Related to this first so-called *reproduction objection* is another, the *redundancy objection*.[13] Why, someone may wonder, bother to copy reality mechanistically? Does not reality itself already suffice? Were art taken to be strictly mimetic, there evidently is no reason to create it, since at most it will produce what already existed. This threat of redundancy, so it seems, is particularly glaring with the case of photography, which is a breakthrough invention precisely because it enabled the duplication of reality for the first time. Its whole raison d'être is reproduction, which unavoidably entails redundancy. Whatever aims photography serves, this objection continues, it is not anything aesthetic. Photography is not art, so its critics conclude.

It is into the middle of this dispute over photography's relation to art that film entered upon its own invention. Understandably, many of the objections leveled against considering photography as an artform resurfaced with film. For if a photograph merely presents an image by way of the mechanical reproduction of reality, then how is film different? For, judged from a technological perspective focused on its material basis, is not the film medium also just a mechanistic sequence of moving pictures? If taking photographs were not an art form, how then could making motion pictures be so?

In response, classical film theory took up the challenge of explaining how (or indeed whether) film is art. If film was in fact an art, as the early silent-film theorists held that it was, what makes it so? As Rudolf Arnheim's 1933 classic *Film as Art* contends, it could be argued that the medium of film produces a divergence from the reality that it seeks to capture.[14] Arnheim, who was born in Alexanderplatz, came under the influence of the gestalt theory during his student years at the University of Berlin. Fittingly, the influence of the gestalt approach to perception is evident in his account of film's inherent aesthetic promise. "Perception is not a random collection of sensory data, but a structural whole," he said.[15] If the ordinary world of perception is configured in meaningful wholes, film itself accentuates such perceptual configurations. When the ordinary meaningful appearance of things is subverted or exaggerated, their latent expressive properties are brought into salience, he claimed. The symbolism of a film's scene can pronouncedly express the gestalt meanings we encounter in our everyday experience of seeing people, things, and events: serenity, fear, joy, evil. In keeping with the early twentieth-century Soviet theorists like Pudovkin, who held montage to be the artistic foundation of film (the "nerve of cinema," to use Sergei Eisenstein's phrase), Arnheim consequently contends that the stylization and manipulation of reality account for film's expressive, and hence aesthetic, qualities.

Arnheim's view of film as art can also be seen as an attempt to answer the earlier reproduction objection: film is not the straightforward mechanical reproduction of reality that its critics alleged, for in many ways, according to Arnheim, the medium actually distorts what it records. Such distortions, he claims, are not regrettable. To be sure, if judged by the standard of pure reproduction, the film image's inherent divergence from reality would be considered a limitation or a failure. But for Arnheim, these limitations endemic to the medium lay the foundation for the use of stylization, symbolism, and creative interpretation that are necessary for film to be art. Liberated from the constraints of banal reproduction, the film image can thus be an expressive, rather than just mechanistic, medium. For this same reason, film also is no longer strictly mimetic. It not only replicates reality but has the power to interpret it. So much, then, it would seem, for the corresponding redundancy objection.

Arnheim's expressivism does well to highlight film's aesthetic potential owing to its divergence from reality. Nevertheless, such a view shares an underlying assumption with those who denied that film is an art form, an assumption that may be challenged. Would acknowledging that film is a production of reality actually disqualify it as a work of art? Is it the case, as expressivism contends (and its opponents deny), that film must interpretively transform reality to be art? Or, to the contrary, might film's artistic power, along with what accordingly makes it a work of truth, reside in its ability not to alter reality stylistically but to bring unvarnished reality into clear and faithful viewing? Whereas Arnheim presumes that film must take a stylized or symbolic distance from normal perception in order to constitute art, might not film, by capturing faithfully what we do not usually notice about the everyday, serve as art?

This, perhaps, is the central thought animating André Bazin's own view of film as art. For the renowned early twentieth-century French film critic and theorist, art's mimetic power reconnects us to reality, attuning us to what is waiting to be encountered yet typically goes overlooked, ignored, or distorted. Rather than art creatively transforming reality, it seeks to transform us by initiating us into a thoroughgoing encounter with the world. In a way that will be recognizable to anyone familiar with the phenomenological tradition of philosophy, Bazin's realism maintains that a cinematic work, insofar as it is a true work of art, enacts a *reduction to the visible*. As is well known, the first Anglophone work of significance exploring the Bazinian theory of realist film was Stanley Cavell's *The World Viewed: Reflections on the Ontology of Film*. Cavell therein notes how film interrupts our "natural habitation within the world,"[16] in turn initiating something akin to what Husserl means when, in *Ideas I*, he speaks of the *epoché* neutralizing or suspending our "natural attitude."[17] Although it is a considerable oversimplification of the full complexity of Husserl's philosophical methodology, for present purposes it suffices to note that part of what Husserl means to accomplish with the *epoché* is to show that, without the necessary precautions, we are bound to distort the experiential facts when theorizing about the world around us. Prejudices and assumptions obscure what is there to be seen, and, in our contemporary technological world, a world that was already taking shape in Husserl's early twentieth-century Germany, this means a world wherein we habitually succumb to the temptation of interpreting everything from within a broadly naturalistic, or even scientific, perspective. Paradoxically, for Husserl, seeing what is there before us accordingly takes genuine effort and attention, since ordinarily the perceivable is distorted by ideology. Film's reduction to the visible, taken in the realist spirit of Bazin, attunes us to what is always already waiting to be encountered by showing us what the theoretical gaze would otherwise miss.[18] There is the further point, again recognized by Husserl, that anything we perceive in normal visual perception, whether it be a Parisian motorcycle or a Wisconsin barn, always admits of further perspectives beyond the one we have at any given moment or place—located as it is within a "horizon," the perceived thing is inexhaustible, and thus our experience of it remains ever "inadequate." Film, then, explores things from a perspective from which we are not typically either able or willing to do so, say, an extreme close-up of a murdered woman's eye (*Psycho* [1960]) or an aerial night view of the Los Angeles streets (Michael Mann's *Collateral* [2004]). Finally, by presenting things as purely as possible, or from unanticipated and unusual perspectives, this reduction to the visible transforms us, the ones encountering the same everyday world but now with closer attention and more care.

This Bazinian suggestion that art, especially painting, interrupts our experiential routine and draws our attention to what we had not noticed before is one for which Merleau-Ponty is famous. If the perceived world is the proper subject of art, he says, this is first because, as a matter of fact, we so infrequently see it truly. A Cézanne does not present us with something stylized beyond recognition. It shows us what we do not normally notice about something. This idea that art is art insofar as it highlights what we typically fail to see is also implied by Heidegger's observation that, in our inauthentic everyday mode of "practical *circumspection*,"[19] a mode of perceiving attuned to the task at issue, we accordingly see everything in our surrounding environment's "situation" in terms of its utility. Unsurprisingly, the aesthetic qualities of things largely elude us.

For instance, absorbed in the task of setting the dining table, I may fail to attend to the vase's sapphire blue, the sunlit curtain gently fluttering in the breeze, or the sweet melody of the bird singing its song on the oak branch outside the window. From the Bazinian perspective, a painting studying the vase, the window, or the oak with bird revives us from our perceptual slumber, reawakening us to what we had grown accustomed to ignoring. Capturing perceptual reality, film accordingly shows things as other than how they appear from the pragmatic, circumspective perspective in which we would ordinarily fail to see them.

By now, it is evident why Malick's films such as *Days of Heaven* and *The Tree of Life* employ the signature techniques for which they are so recognizable: long takes, deep focus, and medium-long shots. Utilizing seamless camera movement rather than editing, the resulting images draw our attention to things in the same way the phenomenologists described occurs with the work of art. Justifiably, then, in this respect, one can see Malick's films as exemplars of Bazinian realism. As Noël Carroll says, Malick and others such as Stan Brakhage and Werner Herzog "share an advocacy of the immediacy of experience, that is, an avowal of the possibility of experience—or, at least, of dimensions of experience—independent from routine, social modes of schematization. Indeed, all three regard normal practices of perceiving and of otherwise organizing the world—such as, most dramatically, language—as filters that exclude the whole, existing dimensions of qualities and feelings from our ken."[20] For anyone familiar with Malick's philosophical pedigree steeped in Heidegger, there is a great irony here. How unexpected that a technical invention like film would be the very thing to interrupt the technological "enframing" (*Gestell*) Heidegger takes to be responsible for barring access to the sheer presence of the world and its things. Of all things, it is a technological device that subverts the logic of technology![21]

What Carroll terms the *immediacy of experience*, we might call *presence*, a term connoting special significance in Heidegger's thought. What does it mean, not just for phenomenological philosophy but for Malick? Here, an anecdote concerning Malick's experience with the mindset of the ordinary language philosophy dominating Oxford in the 1960s is illustrative. At the time, there was a zeal to make everyday language the arbiter of philosophical disputes. The results were sometimes maddeningly comical. As Andrea Teuber recounts:

> Perhaps the best illustration of the deflationary aims of Oxford philosophy was the final exam questions set for the Schools in Philosophy at the end of Trinity Term around the time Terry and I were there. The question itself was simple enough: "Can there be absolutely nothing between two stars?" The answer that got the highest mark, was not the answer that took "nothing" to mean "absence of everything" or the answer that concluded that if there were absolutely nothing between two stars, the two would be one star, just one, but the answer that began with the question: "what if you were to ask me that if I were to drive up to Birmingham for the day, should I take a box lunch along? I would then say, 'Yes by all means please do, there's absolutely nothing between here and Birmingham,' so there can be absolutely nothing between two stars.'" Again: there is a prescribed use for the expression, "absolutely nothing" and in the ordinary language philosophy in vogue at the time, the prescribed use was a way to settle the question. Needless to say Terry and I were not happy with this, especially Terry.[22]

Presence, we thus can say, is a thing's meaning prior to (or independent of) the sheerly linguistic.[23] It would have been around the time of Teuber's anecdote that Malick's supervisor, the ordinary language philosopher

Gilbert Ryle, told Malick that he could not write a thesis on the concept of world in Wittgenstein, Heidegger, and Kierkegaard—such figures were not real philosophy, Ryle is reported to have said. After leaving Oxford as a result, Malick went off to teach philosophy at MIT. However, it proved to be a short stint. As Hubert Dreyfus recalls:

> [Malick] was teaching my Heidegger course at MIT at one point and got to the part on anxiety and discovered he wasn't experiencing anxiety, so he couldn't talk about anything. He just stared off into space for about ten minutes, making the class and me as his auditor at that point very nervous. So he gave up teaching that day and became a movie director because he felt that to teach Heidegger you had to actually be experiencing what Heidegger was talking about if you're going to do the phenomenology right.[24]

Thus began Malick's journey from academic philosophy into film.

Although it would be an oversimplification to reduce Malick's films to a "Heideggerian cinema," there are undeniable recurring themes in his films that lend themselves well to Heideggarian analysis. For example, as Division I of *Being and Time* observes, in inauthentic seeing, "one" (*das Man*) sees what "one" says. Malick's signature twist on Bazinian realism accordingly refocuses our attention on the presence of things. This approach achieves the aesthetic goal of dispelling the haze of unclarity that "idle talk" casts over the perceived. It gives new perspectives we had not enjoyed previously. And, above all, one might argue that it both appropriates and exemplifies an interesting philosophical thesis—namely, that there is more available in the world of perception than what we can articulate linguistically. By arguably showing us this dimension of prelinguistic meaning through film, whether deliberately or not, Malick has done a good bit of phenomenological philosophizing.

Hitherto, we have touched on the question of what art is, and with classical film theory we in turn explored how film can be considered an art. What, however, is to be said about the relation between film and philosophy? Following Stephen Mulhall, Robert B. Pippin, and others, Robert Sinnerbrink has identified three ways in which film can do philosophy, or be philosophical. First, there is *philosophy of film*, what film theorists such as Arnheim and Bazin examine, such as the nature of the film medium or image. Second, there is *film as philosophizing*, where films explore philosophical problems, themes, ideas, or figures. Third, there is *film in the condition of philosophy*, where films reflect upon their own conditions of possibility. It is with this third sense in mind that we note that film, which can interrupt our habits of perception to let the world be seen, exerts demands on our perceptual attention that are not merely aesthetic but ethical too. Even the simple fact that the world is in color should not be overlooked. When in *The New World* (2005) Pocahontas (Q'orianka Kilcher) asks John Rolfe (Christian Bale), "Why is the world colored?" we are struck by the perceptiveness of the question, for her way of putting it acknowledges the difficulty associated with beginning to conceive what might even look like a right answer.[25] Rolfe's reply, or better, non-reply, in the form of an almost bashful laugh, encapsulates the famous Wittgenstein adage ending the *Tractatus*: "What we cannot speak about we must pass over in silence."[26] In this scene, two of Malick's characters self-reflexively grapple with a recurring motif throughout Malick's films: that of experiencing oneself as being up against a mystery, the ineffable.

To return to Bazin, montage is condemned on ethical grounds for inviting passive spectatorship. It is wrong, so he argues, for a filmmaker to tell an audience what to think about what they see, and it is wrong to promote lazy viewing when a work of art should instead make demands of its viewers. For Bazin, one technique for challenging viewers is to rely on spatial realism, which induces active spectatorship. By employing shots that keep as much in focus as possible, the filmmaker allows viewers to explore and attend to whatever they so choose. The gaze is free. This freedom of the gaze, Bazin thinks, avoids the further pitfall of expressivism: montage's oversimplistic interpretation of reality. By suggesting just one meaning, expressivist film eliminates the ambiguity of perception and of existence. In contrast, realism respects not only the homogeneity of space but also its ambiguity.

The ambiguity of both the perceived world and the everyday circumstances characteristic of human existence calls for thinking. Malick's films, which are as able to show us the cosmic grandeur of the heavens above as the simple glory of a suburban front yard, enact a *reduction to the invisible*. Not only do they send us on an outward journey into the perceived world, but they send us on a pilgrimage into ourselves as well, into the depths of what Kierkegaard and Michel Henry call life's "inwardness" or "interiority." Now, V. F. Perkins's formalistic theory of film has reminded us that the successful film must uphold the value of organization. In doing so, it must consequently avoid the pitfall of lapsing into meandering, pretentious "idea-movies."[27] There is a concern that this happens in Malick, given some of his work's substantial departures from traditional Hollywood narrative structure (most notably *To the Wonder* [2012], *Knight of Cups* [2015], and *Song to Song* [2017]). Can such works be intellectually stimulating and ethically edifying, without succumbing to the worry Perkins flags? Audiences used to traditional narrative plots may not recognize it so immediately, but there is a story being told in such works. But to appreciate it, the viewer must engage. A case could be made that this is what great film-art should do. For although there is always the threat of a film taking itself too seriously, or of failing to live up to the content with which it attempts to grapple, there is the opposite concern too, that films increasingly have turned cinema into a commercial enterprise for popular storytelling of little substance. Though in its highest expression it is capable of being a great work of art, most commercial film has been reduced to something more resembling a cartoon or video game. If, thus, the Arnheimian-sounding slogan "nearer to nature, farther from art" is untrue, this is so because a great cinematic work, like any great artwork, invites us to search inside ourselves.

Here, the call of beauty cannot be overestimated. For when Malick himself states that the intention of *Days of Heaven* was to capture "absolute reality,"[28] this means, among other things, showing the beauty of creation. What could be mistaken for a pretentiousness on the part of the film in fact proves to be the opposite: far from being an instance of self-indulgent intellectualism, it is an at-once aesthetic and ascetic exercise in humility, a concerted exercise in subverting our perceptual habit of failing to submit to the real. With an eye toward returning once again to both Plato and Hildebrand, here the words of the French philosopher Jean-Louis Chrétien in *The Ark of Speech* are pertinent: "A rich tradition of thinking, which has developed in many ways, has seen in beauty a call, and has derived the word *kalos*, 'beautiful,' from *kalein*, 'to call.' But what is it is that calls, in beauty, and what does it call to or for? . . . Can it lead to God?"[29] This Platonic insight is translated into a distinctively Christian key when Hildebrand, like Chrétien, says, "The world of the beautiful and of art in particular represent a real voice of God."[30] For as Chrétien's meditation on beauty shows, all true human creativity, including art, comes in the form of a response to something that has already called it. In the case of art, first the artist must listen to beauty. Only then does inspiration happen. As Hildebrand comments, "At first it is the artist alone who sees these deeper worlds of beauty that are hidden in nature and in life; he is then able to realize them in a work of art in such a way that reveals them to people whose eyes do not penetrate as deeply as his. Every real work of art, beyond its own intrinsic worth, also has the function of unveiling nature and life as bearers of these worlds of beauty."[31] A description as apt for the filmmaker as it is for the painter, poet, musician, or sculptor! When cinema is art, as in Malick, it can accordingly assume a distinctively divine vocation. Occupying this role, Malick's films attest to this possibility—for in responding to the call of beauty, they make God perceptible, or if not quite that, at least God's presence felt. These are works at the thresholds of art and philosophy, "aesthetic theodicies" as it were, achievements of the human spirit affirming the goodness of existence even in light of the immensity of the world's evil and suffering. Here, the truth is profoundly simple—the best film, just as Malick says, is "something that strengthens you."[32]

Having set out some of the respects in which both the history of philosophy and classical film theory can inform and enrich our understanding and appreciation of Malick's films and the various metaphysical, spiritual, ethical, political, and aesthetic issues they raise, a concluding word should be said about this volume's contents. Opening part 1, "Cinematic Experience as Ethical Reflection and Spiritual Exercise," Jonathan Scott Lee's sweeping chapter offers an analysis of the familiar idea that Malick's films are somehow intended to serve as an injunction for self-reflection. Lee suggests that, whereas most commentators have interpreted Malick's films as works operating in an "indicative mood," the transformative power of his films is best understood when seen to be issued in what he calls the "subjunctive mood," a detail that serves to highlight how these films are akin to Pierre Hadot's notion of philosophy as a way life. Manuel Cabrera Jr.'s chapter, "Terrence Malick's Cosmic Cinema," concurs that Malick's films are transformative insofar as they are cosmic—that is to say, they aim to present the world in its full scope, in a way that calls us to reflect on our place within it. In doing so, however, such reflection is meant to disabuse us of our human narcissism, our anthropomorphic tendency to construe the world as being concerned with our own concerns. Malick, as Cabrera argues, instead gives us a view of the world that should serve to remind us that our ordinary humanistic perspective obscures the world as it subsists independently of our limited, and often rather myopic, focuses. If Cabrera is correct to note that Malick's cosmic focus counterbalances what would otherwise be an overly humanistic view of the world, James D. Reid and Candace R. Craig's " 'Why Should I Be Good If You Aren't?'

The Problem of the Moral World in *The Tree of Life*" delicately explores the manner in which the role of ethics and morality remain ineliminable, not only in our own everyday lives but in the cinematic moral universe of Malick's films. Thus, while it would be misleading to place human concerns above all others, it may well be equally mistaken to discount them altogether. Malick's view of the world, in short, is one that tries to appraise the value and dignity of human life within the larger scope of the world as a whole. As Rico Gutschmidt suggests in "Performativity and Transformative Experience: Terrence Malick's Mysticism," in light of the apparent ineffability and immensity of existence implicated by such a view, one might here justly speak of Malick's mysticism.

Part 2, "Mystery, Evil, Creation: Framing the 'Big Questions,'" further explicates and deepens the discussion of these issues by turning to the profound metaphysical and experiential themes centrally at stake in Malick's vision of the world and our place within it. David R. Cerbone, in "Life-Time: Mystery in *The Tree of Life*," accordingly turns our attention to the nature of time, highlighting how Malick's portrayal of events—at once both human and cosmic—produces a confrontation with the inherent mysteriousness of existence over which we ought to linger. If the previous chapters by Cabrera, Reid and Craig, and Cerbone all accentuate the paradox of existence, that our being-in-the-world is simultaneously beautiful and ugly, good and evil, joyous and painful, Jussi Backman's "Not One Power, But Two: Dark Grounds and Twilit Paradises in Malick" investigates this fundamental ambivalence in terms of Schelling's doctrine of evil, a view that assigns evil (and hence melancholy) a fundamental place as a basic principle of reality. Backman's suggestion at once deepens and complexifies the way in which Malick's films can be seen as exercises in "aesthetic theodicy," as Sinnerbrink has said. Inspired by Dostoevsky's own Christological view of the cosmos, in the section's last chapter, Naomi Fisher's "Tending God's Garden: Philosophical Themes in *The Tree of Life*," likens creation to God's garden. As Fisher observes, Malick's cinematic works can themselves be seen as seeds meant to occasion modes of transformative reflection and intuition (as epitomized by Kierkegaardian recollection) on our own part, something that might create goodness by inspiring us to emulate the childhood goodness we have recollected.

Lest it be mistakenly assumed that philosophical, ethical, spiritual, and aesthetic reflection on Malick's films could proceed without carefully considering the unique filmic qualities and techniques that enable such reflection, the chapters in part 3, "Explorations of Image and Voiceover," explore the role of image and voiceover in Malick's work. In the section's first chapter, "*Sotto voce*: Inscription as Voiceover in Malick's *Days of Heaven*," Fred Rush shows how Malick's early masterpiece pioneers a means of using written text presented visually as voiceover. As we shall see, a technique such as this opens up possibilities of depicting the human condition that would otherwise remain cinematically impossible. Developing what they term Malick's "poetics of melancholy," Keith Jacobs and Jeff Malpas's chapter "The Melancholic Image in *Days of Heaven*" offers an understanding of the film-image as itself melancholic, showing in turn how Malick depicts the melancholy not of the human experience only but of the very landscape itself, an observation that again underscores the underlying mysteriousness of the world, as emphasized earlier by Cerbone and Backman. If mystery, time, and creation are central to Malick's concerns, it stands to reason that his films would develop unique filmic techniques for imparting what that corresponding vision seeks to convey. In his chapter "Terrence Malick's Ephemeral and Eternal Images: Deleuze, Time-Image, and Montage," James Lorenz insightfully shows how Malick does precisely this, with recourse to image and montage.

If many of the volume's contributors emphasize the error of reducing Malick's oeuvre to a purely Heideggerian cinema, this is partly because Malick's films evince a recurring concern with subjectivity, with interiority, with the intimacy (even privacy) of the human mind and heart. In his chapter "Malick's Cartesianism, or the Ghost by the Machine," Enrico Terrone consequently proposes the provocative thesis that Malick's exploration of human interiority through voiceover can in some sense be said to be Cartesian, insofar as it disembodies the narrator who has taken up a spatial and temporal distance from the events he is recollecting—contrary, then, to what Gilbert Ryle famously said, there is indeed a "ghost in the machine," a fact fundamentally due to the presence of the very interiority (and an accompanying sort of retrospective epistemic privilege with regard to our pasts through memory), which certain strands of anti-Cartesian philosophy have denied but which the "film machine" captures. If, thus, it would be mistaken to overlook the significance of human interiority, it would also be misguided to emphasize the role of human thoughts, emotions, recollections, and memories alone. For as Joel Mayward notes in "Love Is Smiling through All Things: Jean-Luc Marion, Simone Weil, and the Visual Style of Terrence Malick," central to Malick's "spiritual cinematic" style is its depiction of love, a love that resides not only in the visible world but also within us, perhaps most paradigmatically in our potential relation to God. If so, what emerges is a view of human subjectivity that is not so much simply Cartesian but rather kenotic, as thinkers such as Simone Weil and Jean-Luc Marion have emphasized. At the same time, in good Bazinian fashion, Malick's spiritual cinematography elicits a kind of loving attention on our part that enables us to see aspects of the world that otherwise would be unseen, particularly the presence of the divine in the everyday. As Mayward accordingly notes, attending to what Malick's vision gives to be seen consequently entails a shift from *I* to "witness" (*la témoin*) (to borrow Marion's terminology), as we stand before a "saturated phenomenon" rather than an object subject to a complete concept or sufficient signification.[33]

In his chapter "Let Me Not Pretend: The Promise of Beauty in *To the Wonder*," Steven Rybin intriguingly exploits the richness of the theatrical notion of the image. In addition to its photographic or representational sense, there is also the ever-lurking connotational sense of pretense or illusion—after all, we understand that everyday social existence is characterized by the roles we perform, roles governed by various expectations and norms. For this reason, everyday social life is itself susceptible to becoming a mere performance, whereby we and others only present an image of ourselves, or pretend to be something we are not rather than being who we are. In a move that will consequently be familiar to those familiar with existentialist and phenomenological discussions of human authenticity, Rybin suggests that Malick's films explore the everyday tension between individualism and conformism through the relationship between actor and character exhibited in the films themselves.

Just as any analysis of Malick that overlooked the filmic qualities and techniques of his work would be incomplete, so too would it be unwise to ignore the social and political themes and implications of his work. The overt metaphysical, spiritual, ethical, and aesthetic issues and questions raised in his work bear such implications worth exploring. One way of summarizing Malick's preoccupations would be to say that they fall under the umbrella of transcendence—they are interested in exhibiting what it takes for us to reach self-understanding and self-knowledge in light of the nature of the world and one's place within it. Investigating the importance of memory and recollection (matters examined by Fisher, Terrone, and Rybin), Matthew Strohl's "Platonic Myths of Eros in *Knight of Cups* and *Song to Song*" and Lee Braver's "The Alien God Behind the Camera: A Gnostic Viewing of Terrence Malick's Cinema, especially *Knight of Cups*" each show that Malick's presentations of the pursuit of transcendence and individuation can be appreciated in terms of their deeply Platonic and Gnostic influences.[34] Central, too, to this pursuit of self-understanding is love, a theme readily apparent in Malick's most recent film, *A Hidden Life* (2019). In part, it certainly is possible to see the film as Malick's own attempt to reckon with his debt to Heidegger and his philosophy, given the latter's notorious involvement in Nazism. As Katerina Koci and Martin Koci show in their chapter "A Hidden Life of Love: Sacrifice in Malick's Cinematographic Philosophy," if there is in some sense a shift from a Heideggerian cinema to a Kierkegaardian cinema in Malick,[35] this is because love (as embodied between Franz and Fani Jägerstätter) takes center stage. Further exploring this theme of self-sacrifice rooted in love, Donald Wallenfang turns directly in "Bleeding Hearts: Edith Stein, Franz Jägerstätter, and Martyrdom" to the nature of martyrdom by showing how Malick's cinematic portrayal of Franz can be appreciated from a perspective considering not just Kierkegaard's philosophical influence but also that of Edith Stein, who herself was martyred. In light of the human condition as fraught with political violence and social upheaval, David B. Johnson's chapter "Authoritarianism and the Authoritarian Personality: Malick's Tragedy of Disobedience" accordingly explores the inherent tension in life between authenticity and conformism, this time with reference to our vexed relationship to authority as understood by the Frankfurt School. Finally, in the volume's final chapter, " 'But I Am Free!' Malick on Freedom and Transcendence," Daniel Layman continues the section's reflections on the meaning of the quest for transcendence and freedom by returning to themes explored at the volume's outset, suggesting that Malick's is a view according to which the resolution of such predicaments is spiritual. Although it is not a view of human political and social freedom Layman himself holds, for Malick, to be free is to find one's right orientation in the world by first finding oneself in God.

Of course, it almost certainly goes without saying that there is no substitute for experiencing the beauty of a Malick film in *propria persona*. It would be misguided for any written work, such as this one, to claim otherwise. Here, the written word's own work begins by acknowledging its comparatively humble task of responding to what the films themselves have given to be seen. As all true works of art do, these films invariably give much to think, and thus call forth speech. In reply, each chapter in this volume answers that call.

Notes

1. Terrence Malick, "Un entretien avec Terrence Malick, réalisateur de 'Days of Heaven' . . . Le paradis, entre les doigts." As Robert Sinnerbrink notes in his preface, after releasing *Badlands*, Malick said, "I don't feel one can film philosophy." It is entirely possible that Malick changed his mind as his filmmaking career progressed over the decades.
2. Hildebrand, *Beauty in the Light*, 81.
3. Hildebrand, 83.
4. Nietzsche, *The Birth of Tragedy out of the Spirit of Music*, §§ 5 and 24.
5. Schopenhauer, *The World as Will and Representation*, 196.
6. For one notable discussion of such beauty, see G. W. F. Hegel, *Aesthetics: Lectures on Fine Art*, Vols. I and II, trans. T. M. Knox (Oxford: Clarendon Press, 1975). For Hegel, of course, nature's beauty was of little significance in both his ethical and aesthetic theories. One might think that Hegel's startling lack of interest in natural beauty, which distinguishes him markedly from Kant and Schiller, is precisely what in part explains his aesthetic theory's unique capacity to account for the rise of abstractionism in modern art. For an essay addressing Hegel's foreseeing a shift from the sensuousness and the beautiful to the conceptual and the reflective, see Robert B. Pippin, "What Was Abstract Art (From the Point of Hegel)?" in *The Persistence of Subjectivity: On the Kantian Aftermath* (Cambridge: Cambridge University Press, 2005), 279–306. In the essay, Pippin mentions Kandinsky, Malevich, and Mondrain as three twentieth-century modern artists whose abstractionism takes painting itself to be at issue. Modern art, in this way, is somehow a self-conscious or self-reflexive exercise. For an opposing account that sees abstractionism as ultimately self-expressive rather than self-reflective, see Michel Henry, *Seeing the Invisible: On Kandinsky*, trans. Scott Davidson (London: Continuum, 2009). Henry's phenomenological conception of painting differs from not only the Hegelian understanding of art but also the Heideggerian. See Steven DeLay, "Disclosing Worldhood or Expressing Life? Heidegger and Henry on the Origin of the Work of Art," *Journal of Aesthetics and Phenomenology* 4, no. 2 (2017): 155–71.
7. Heidegger, "On the Origin of the Work of Art," 181.
8. Heidegger, 181.
9. Heidegger, 165.
10. For a work subtly highlighting the similarities between Schopenhauer's and Nietzsche's aesthetic responses to the problem of justifying suffering, see Julian Young, *Nietzsche's Philosophy of Religion* (Cambridge: Cambridge University Press, 2006). Hegel's philosophy of art, with its characteristic emphases on self-recognition, self-determination, and intersubjective intelligibility, crucially informs Robert B. Pippin's *Filmed Thought: Cinema as Reflective Form* (Chicago: Chicago University

Press, 2020). Pippin's exploration of what it means for a film itself to philosophize, to be a reflective form of thinking as such, is a question to which we shall turn shortly in this introduction when noting Malick's creative appropriation of André Bazin's work. Presently, it suffices to note that although Alfred Hitchcock receives more attention, Pippin's analysis examines Malick directly in chapter 9 of *Filmed Thought*, "Vernacular Metaphysics: On Terrence Malick's *The Thin Red Line*," an essay that readers will naturally find interesting. The Heideggerian view of art receives comprehensive treatment in Iain D. Thomson's *Heidegger, Art, and Postmodernity* (Cambridge: Cambridge University Press, 2011), with particular reference to ontotheology and technology, the latter of which we shall examine when discussing film's materiality as a mechanistic medium.

11. For an insightful account (with particular reference to Hegel and Nietzsche) of art's relation to philosophy in the postmodern condition resulting from Kant's critique of metaphysics, see Paul Miklowitz, *Metaphysics to Metafictions: Hegel, Nietzsche, and the End of Philosophy* (Albany: State University of New York Press, 1998). For an argument that art can in fact disclose truth, meeting the "Platonic Challenge" on its own terms, see Anthony Rudd, *Painting and Presence: Why Paintings Matter* (Oxford: Oxford University Press, 2023).

12. Robert Sokolowski provides an exceptional Husserlian investigation of the general problem of intentionality in *Introduction to Phenomenology* (Cambridge: Cambridge University, 2000), including an informative analysis of image consciousness and picture perception.

13. These turns of phrase are borrowed from Noël Carroll's *Philosophical Problems of Classical Film Theory* (Princeton, NJ: Princeton University Press, 1988), a marvelous analysis of classical film theory that includes, among other things, a fascinating study of the relation between photography and film.

14. Among other things, Arnheim mentions the following key items as central to the divergence between the film-image and reality: projection of solids upon a plane surface, reduction of depth, lighting and the absence of color (Arnheim is focused on early black-and-white silent film), delimitation of the image and distance from the object, and absence of the space-time continuum. See the section "Film and Reality," in Arnheim, *Film as Art*, 8–33.

15. Kleinman and Van Duzer, eds., *Rudolf Arnheim: Revealing Vision*, 2.

16. Stanley Cavell, *The World Viewed: Reflections on the Ontology of Film, Enlarged Edition* (Cambridge, MA: Harvard University Press, 1979), 180. That the film medium alters our ordinary and habitual stance to the world in the way Cavell states also explains why films interest us so much, why we feel drawn to viewing them, and why we enjoy going to the theater. To return to the earlier question, this observation is pertinent to the issue of whether film is art. Far from just mechanically duplicating reality (as many early film critics alleged), as the engrossing medium it is, film has the power to shape culture over time by creating stories and archetypes with whom the audience (and so the public)

comes to identify. The experience of going to the movies, thus, has led some to note that doing so is itself a kind of ritual, even a religious one. That film has this power to shape mass consciousness and culture is why someone like Plato was so concerned about the dangers of art—for Plato, the issue is not merely that the image concerns the visible and hence is "untrue" ontologically but that it is susceptible to being used for propaganda. It is, after all, possible to analogize entering the theater to the allegory of the cave: one sits inside the theater ("the cave") watching the projected images on the screen (the "shadows on the wall"). For a very interesting analysis of the symbolic power of film to influence culture by transforming audiences, see Jay Dyer, *Esoteric Hollywood: Sex, Cults and Symbols in Film* (Walterville, OR: TrineDay, 2016).

17. Edmund Husserl, *Ideas Pertaining to a Pure Phenomenology and to a Phenomenological Philosophy—First Book: General Introduction to a Pure Phenomenology*, trans. W. R. Boyce Gibson (New York: Collier Books, 1962), §§ 27–32.

18 As Walter Hopp says, phenomenology's quest for intelligibility leads to disclosing truths that are obvious (rather than surprising), yet this does not mean the insights are uninteresting. For example, when presented with any two external objects, we can ask which is farther from us, while such a question makes no sense for our own body parts, for my foot is as near to *me* as my hand. Hopp explains, "As a description of how we experience our own bodies in the vast majority of non-pathological cases, it's still obvious. Its obviousness, however, is of a distinctive kind. It's not obvious in the way that someone saying 'The phone's ringing' while the phone is ringing is obvious. Rather, its obviousness is more like the way a punch line of a joke or the answer to a riddle is obvious. It's obvious and insightful." Hopp, *Phenomenology*, xx. Malick's films are insightful in just this way, showing us the obvious but with insight. What Charles Taylor says in regard to realist painting in modernism can equally be said of realist cinema: "Realist painting can do what it does because of the crucial fact that painting can make us see things differently. Painting can bring to the fore patterns, lines of force, whole aspects of things, which are certainly there in our visual field but overshadowed, made recessive, by our normal way of attending to and apprehending things." Taylor, "Epiphanies of Modernism," in *Sources of the Self: The Making of the Modern Identity* (Cambridge, MA: Harvard University Press, 1989), 466–72.

19. Heidegger, *The Basic Problems of Phenomenology*, 163.

20. Carroll, *Interpreting the Moving Image*, 284.

21. For an especially judicious exploration of this paradox in its full Heideggerian context, see George Pattison, "In the Theater of Light: Toward a Heideggerian Poetics of Film," in *Theology and the Films of Terrence Malick*, eds. Christopher B. Barnett and Clark J. Elliston (New York: Routledge, 2017), 29–45.

22. Andrea Teuber, interview in *All Things Shining*, 131.

23. In the wake of Husserl, many phenomenological figures have challenged the "linguistic turn," most recently and notably Claude Romano in *At the Heart*

of Reason, trans. Michael B. Smith (Evanston, IL: Northwestern University Press, 2015). Jean-Yves Lacoste's *Thèses sur la vrai* (Paris: Presses universitaires de France, 2018) is another case in point. Those working in the Anglophone context have contributed to the effort also. Among the most notable examples is Frederick A. Olafson, *Heidegger and the Philosophy of Mind* (New Haven, CT: Yale University Press, 1987), which explores this domain of primal meaning through the lens of Heidegger's question of being, what Olafson terms "being *qua* presence." At the same time, there are of course those who have taken Heidegger in the opposite direction, casting him as a forerunner of the linguistic turn. See Ernst Tugendhat, *Traditional and Analytical Philosophy: Lectures on the Philosophy of Language*, trans. P. A. Gorner (Cambridge: Cambridge University Press, 1982). Considerable light can be shed on this presence with Jean-Luc Marion's conception of the "saturated phenomenon," as Joel Mayward's chapter in this volume shows.

24. Hubert Dreyfus, interview in *All Things Shining*, 112. If the influence of Heidegger's philosophy on Malick's filmmaking is well known, so too is the fact that Malick met Heidegger, although the extent of their personal relationship is unknown. It is a well-known fact, for instance, that Malick visited Heidegger at his hut in the Black Forest. While there, Malick is said to have received an autograph from Heidegger that Malick gave to his philosophy friend Paul Lee, which Lee subsequently lost. There is evidence suggesting that Malick may even have served for a time as Heidegger's personal driver. See, for example, Von Thilo Komma Pöllath, "Wer was Heidegger's Chauffer? Der stille Amerikaner," *Frankfurter Allgemeine*, February 2, 2021, https://www.faz.net/aktuell/feuilleton/debatten/war-terrence-malick-1970-heideggers-chauffeur-17207934.html. Thanks to Rico Gutschmidt for drawing my attention to this intriguing article.

25. One's mind turns to Frank Jackson's famous thought experiment concerning Mary, the brain scientist, who lives in a black-and-white room, with no experiential acquaintance with colors. The question arises: in possessing all the physical facts about color, might Mary be said to have the relevant information necessary to answer the question mystifying Pocahontas and Rolfe? The scene itself suggests not, Pocahontas and Rolfe are registering a primal wonder about the world of perception, something thus akin to David Chalmers's "hard problem," or even better, a kind of metaphysical awe evoked when facing the question "Why is there something rather than nothing?" Having what a neuroscience textbook says to hand would be neither here nor there. My thanks to Enrico Terrone for mentioning this connection to me.

26. Wittgenstein, *Tractatus Logico-Philosophicus*, proposition 7.
27. Perkins, *Film as Film*, 189.
28. Terrence Malick, interview in *All Things Shining*, 80.
29. Chrétien, *The Ark of Speech*, 79.
30. Hildebrand, *Beauty in the Light*, 55.
31. Hildebrand, 59.

32. Bruno, "Terrence Malick Talks Filmmaking."
33. Marion, *D'Ailleurs, la Révélation*, 255–59.
34. The strands of Gnostic influence (both cinematic and literary) apparent in Malick extend widely, even beyond Malick himself. When, for example, Strohl (in his chapter's discussion of *Song to Song*) examines Faye (Rooney Mara) reading William Blake's "Divine Image," one might call to mind Ridley Scott's *Blade Runner* (1982), which references Blake also. In the film, the replicant Roy Batty (Rutger Hauer) misquotes Blake directly. The fact that *Blade Runner* is itself a deeply Gnostic work (Tyrell [Joe Turkel], for instance, represents a kind of demiurge) is unsurprising, given that it was based on the Philip K. Dick novella *Do Androids Dream of Electric Sheep*? As Braver notes, Dick's fiction is useful for appreciating the Gnostic influences detectable in Malick.
35. To adduce but one illustrative example, in a very powerful scene in which Franz is still deciding whether or not to swear the oath to Hitler, the painter at the local church, Ohlendorf (Johan Leysen), says to Franz,

> What we do is just create . . . sympathy. We create. We create admirers. We don't create followers. Christ's life is a demand. You don't want to be reminded of it. So we don't have to see what happens to the truth. A darker time is coming . . . when men will be more clever. They won't fight the truth; they'll just ignore it. I paint their comfortable Christ, with a halo over his head. How can I show what I haven't lived? Someday I might have the courage to venture, not yet. Someday I'll—I'll paint the true Christ.

These lines are nearly verbatim quotations of passages from Kierkegaard's *Practice in Christianity*. Could it be that the aged painter's words are at one level a self-reference to Malick's own artistic career as a filmmaker? It is possible. The film on which he is working currently, *The Way of the Wind*, is a depiction of the life of Christ.

Bibliography

Arnheim, Rudolf. *Film as Art*. Berkeley: University of California Press, 1957.
Bruno, Christopher. "Terrence Malick Talks Filmmaking at a Rare Public Speaking Event." *Little White Lies: Truth & Movies*, October 27, 2016. https://lwlies.com/articles/terrence-malick-live-appearance-digital-filmmaking/.
Carroll, Noël. *Interpreting the Moving Image*. Cambridge: Cambridge University Press, 1998.
Chrétien, Jean-Louis. *The Ark of Speech*. Translated by Andrew Brown. New York: Routledge, 2004.

Heidegger, Martin. *The Basic Problems of Phenomenology*. Translated by Albert Hofstadter. Bloomington: Indiana University Press, 1982.

———. "On the Origin of the Work of Art." In *Martin Heidegger: Basics Writings*, edited and translated by David Farrell Krell, 139–212. London: Harper-Collins, 2008.

Hildebrand, Dietrich. *Beauty in the Light of the Redemption*. Steubenville, OH: Hildebrand Project, 2019.

Hopp, Walter. *Phenomenology: A Contemporary Introduction*. New York: Routledge, 2020.

Kleinman, Kent, and Leslie Van Duzer, eds. *Rudolf Arnheim: Revealing Vision*. Ann Arbor: University of Michigan Press, 1997.

Maher, Paul Jr. *All Things Shining: An Oral History of the Films of Terrence Malick*. Self-published, Vellum, 2018.

Malick, Terrence. "Un entretien avec Terrence Malick, réalisateur de 'Days of Heaven' . . . Le paradis, entre les doigts." Interview by Yvonne Baby. *Le Monde*, May 17, 1979. https://www.lemonde.fr/archives/article/1979/05/17/un-entretien-avec-terrence-malick-realisateur-de-days-of-heaven-le-paradis-entre-les-doigts_3054948_1819218.html.

Marion, Jean-Luc. *D'Ailleurs, la Révélation*. Paris: Bernard Grasset, 2020.

Nietzsche, Friedrich. *The Birth of Tragedy out of the Spirit of Music*. Translated by Walter Kaufmann. New York: Vintage Books, 1967.

Perkins, V. F. *Film as Film: Understanding and Judging Movies*. New York: Penguin Books, 1972.

Schopenhauer, Arthur. *The World as Will and Representation, Vols. I and II*. Translated by E. F. J. Payne. New York: Dover, 1969.

Wittgenstein, Ludwig. *Tractatus Logico-Philosophicus*. Translated by D. F. Pears and B. F. McGuinness. London: Routledge and Kegan Paul, 1961.

Part I

Cinematic Experience as Ethical Reflection and Spiritual Exercise

Chapter 1

"Find Your Way from Darkness to Light"

Cinema as Spiritual Exercise

JONATHAN SCOTT LEE

The films of Terrence Malick share characteristics that make them immediately recognizable and distinctive: their stunningly beautiful cinematography of the natural world, their meditative first-person voiceovers, their active (often handheld) camera work, their rich orchestral and choral soundtracks (generally built upon preexisting music), and their fragmented, episodic, and often nonlinear narrative structures. These characteristics make Malick's films difficult to process on a first viewing, and it is this difficulty that has helped to generate such a rich literature around his work. The films make it almost impossible for a viewer to remain passive: work must be done, and it is their quality of demanding some form of intellectual and emotional labor that I want to explore here.

To the extent that the films manifest what Robert Pippin has called a kind of "interrogative attention,"[1] they have proven themselves irresistible to philosophers, most of whom are quick to look for broadly philosophical themes that help to make Malick's kaleidoscopic works cohere. This work of deciphering is, to be sure, a necessary aspect of any attempt at interpretation of a work of art, and Malick's films—so deeply engaged with a number of fundamental philosophical questions—richly reward those who focus on the thematic (often narrative) dimension of the works. As

Martin Rossouw has noted, however, recent philosophical work on Malick has shifted toward formulating "how films can do philosophy in 'uniquely cinematic' ways."[2] For Pippin, this means that "interpretation is simply identical to fully experiencing a work as a work of art,"[3] and Rossouw emphasizes that most assessments of Malick now stress the dimension of ethical transformation: "His films not only move us to contemplation but potentially *transform* us to greater awareness, openness, and connection."[4] We see this perhaps most clearly in the work of Robert Sinnerbrink, who reads all of Malick's work as a kind of "cinematic ethics," exploring "the *aesthetic dimensions* of cinema as a way of evoking ethical experience and thereby expressing ethical meaning."[5]

However, even Sinnerbrink remains focused on Malick's films as complex systems of representation, and the viewer's self-transformation comes about (somehow) as a result of the way the films "express" an ethical world. As Rossouw remarks, "if readers hope to get from these philosophers an exact explanation of *how* Malick's style links up with particular transformational effects, they will be left disappointed."[6] To put the point another way, most philosophical commentators on Malick treat the films as though they exist in the *indicative* mood, simply declaring that "this is the way the world is" and offering this picture of the world as a stimulus for further philosophizing. In contrast, I want to argue that at least some of Malick's films exist in the *subjunctive* mood, proposing a possibility—"if the world were this way"—and sketching a template for the viewer's self-transformation based on this possibility.

To explore the different kinds of difficulty that Terrence Malick poses to his viewers and the different transformational templates or models that these kinds of difficulty offer, I will look briefly at three very different examples of his work: *Knight of Cups* (2015), *A Hidden Life* (2019), and *The Tree of Life* (2011).

༄

Knight of Cups[7] may be the least well received of Malick's films: Peter Bradshaw, writing in the *Guardian*, perhaps distills the explanation for the film's 37 percent approval rating on Rotten Tomatoes when he notes that Malick's style here "is stagnating into mannerism, cliche and self-parody," adding that "for every pinch of poetry, there are kilos of joyless, uninspired prose."[8] Sinnerbrink captures quite effectively what he describes as the film's "fragmentary, paratactic style" in an extended description of its opening minutes filled with vivid images of the decadent Hollywood life of Rick (Christian Bale), voiceover quotations from religious and philosophical texts, and a weighty musical score suggesting a mood of spiritual gravity.[9] To a much greater extent than any other Malick film, *Knight of Cups* pushes a highly experimental approach to filmmaking, an approach that comes across as deliberately obscure, difficult, and more than a little maddening. In addition to its ever-changing mélange of images, voiceover quotations, and music, on its surface the film structures its account of Rick's life as a screenwriter by means of a series of seven discrete episodes (following the opening minutes), each signaled by the name of a tarot card, with a final episode given the title "Freedom." However, the chronology of the different episodes is unclear, and any expectation of a relatively linear narrative is undermined by the fact that the final scene of the film seems to pick up where the initial scene left off. The action of the film begins in a desert setting, with Rick (in voiceover, as virtually always throughout the film) lamenting, "All these years, living the life of someone I didn't even know," while the film's action ends in the same desert setting, with Rick saying to himself, "Begin." This desert scene recurs elsewhere in the film—with Rick always dressed in the same clothes—suggesting that the other episodes bear some important relation to his experience in the desert, but nothing about this quasi-cyclical interplay of the distinct episodes is at all clear. In short, *Knight of Cups* is simply provocative in its difficulty.

The difficulty of the film is manifested by the radically different interpretations we see in its commentators. Richard Brody, for example, perceptively notes that "*Knight of Cups* is close to a first-person act of remembering, and the ecstatic power of its images and sounds is a virtual manifesto, and confession, of the cinematic mind at work." He goes further to argue that Malick has made "an angrily prescriptive film, the contention of which is: the bullshit of Hollywood lives is reflected in the bullshit of Hollywood films."[10] In contrast, Matt Zoller Seitz—in a wonderfully quirky review—urges the film's viewers to "accept that it's unfinished, open-ended, by design, because it's at least partly concerned with the impossibility of imposing meaningful order on experience, whether through religion, occult symbolism, mass-produced images and stories, or family lore."[11] Sinnerbrink, in turn, reads the film in close relationship with *To the Wonder* (2012) and *Song to Song* (2017) as presenting "the 'weightless' (groundless, shifting, and distracted) subjectivity defining much of our contemporary moral-cultural experience."[12] Elaborating this point, he writes that "scenes featuring multiple characters will sometimes background spoken dialogue in favor of inner meditation, deliberately mismatching image and sound to evoke their detached and distracted subjectivity" and adds that "this is a cinematic style expressive of characters failing to achieve authentic selfhood or lives grounded in the (finite and infinite) experience of love."[13] Sinnerbrink plausibly explores this theme of love—erotic, ethical, and spiritual—in terms derived from Søren Kierkegaard and sketches the ways in which *Knight of Cups*'s six episodes, focused on different women, reveal Rick's failure to find love because of his fundamental lack of a self.[14] However, his suggestion that Rick finally finds some sort of authentic peace with Isabel (Isabel Lucas) at the end of the film depends on understanding its episodic structure as essentially chronological, but this is difficult to reconcile with the quasi-cyclical character of the film's structure and with the fact that Isabel clearly appears in several different episodes without even being named (except in subtitles).

Brody, Seitz, and Sinnerbrink each capture something important about *Knight of Cups* as a representation of aspects of the contemporary world, and Sinnerbrink goes so far as to argue that the "weightless trilogy" powerfully evokes a sense of "mood—as revelatory and world-disclosing; as resensitizing our receptivity to the world and others—in ways that invite ethical reflection, or even a conversion of attitudes consistent with an ethic of self-transformation."[15] In so doing, these commentators remain within the domain of representation—of the indicative—but I would now like to explore how *Knight of Cups* can be experienced from the perspective of the subjunctive. What is the experience of Malick's viewer here? What does the film ask us to do?

I would begin with the observation that, throughout the film, the viewer is suspended between a third-person perspective and a first-person perspective: in the vast majority of the film's shots, Rick is present in the image and the dominant focus of the camera's attention; in shots where he is not in the image, the camera effectively takes Rick's position in the scene. The viewer can only experience the film, then, in some kind of fundamental relationship with Rick, but this relationship is curiously both subjective and objective, evoking the way in which the viewer's experience of their own being is necessarily both subjective and objective. In this way, *Knight of Cups* continually weaves and reweaves the viewer into its complex fabric: if the film works on us at all, it asks us to make some sense—intellectual and emotional—of this paradoxical condition. Central to the film's difficulty, then, is that it throws us mercilessly into Rick's chaotic life.

From the beginning, a notable aspect of this chaos is that it is punctuated with fragments of religious and philosophical texts. Indeed, the film opens with a non-diegetic voiceover intoning what is effectively the expanded title of *The Pilgrim's Progress* (1678), John Bunyan's allegory of the Christian life: "The Pilgrim's Progress from this World to That Which is to Come Delivered under the Similitude of a Dream: Wherein is Discovered the Manner of His Setting Out, His Dangerous Journey, and Safe Arrival at the Desired Country." With this, the film begins with the scene of Rick in the desert, which then quickly dissolves into images of children at play accompanied by a voiceover by Rick's father, Joseph (Brian Dennehy), giving a condensed version of *The Song of the Pearl*, best attested in the Gnostic text *The Acts of Thomas*. Fragments of the story of the pearl—a tale of a young knight whose father, the King of the East, sends him "west into Egypt, to find a pearl, a pearl from the depths of the sea"—recur throughout the film, reverberating in Rick's memory as well as in that of the viewer, and the film's countless images of water (the sea, swimming pools, and rivers) offer a visual reminder that the pearl is to be found in watery depths. Shortly after the film introduces Della (Imogen Poots) in its first tarot card episode, "The Moon," another non-diegetic voiceover quotes from the myth of Plato's *Phaedrus* 246a–253c, with its account of how the soul lost its wings when it took on an earthly body but sprouts these wings again when a beautiful body reminds the soul of the beauty it knew before its embodiment. After ending her brief liaison with Rick with the devastating observation, "I think you're weak. You don't want love. You want a love experience," Della offers Rick some advice: "Love and do what you like," adding that "A saint said that," alluding to Augustine. Much later in the film, at the beginning of the episode headed by the tarot card "Death," Rick and Elizabeth (Natalie Portman), a woman who has abandoned her husband for an affair with Rick, visit Christopher (Peter Matthiessen), a Zen teacher who offers a brief bit of wisdom that could itself be found in any number of spiritual texts: "I just teach this moment. Pay attention to this moment. Everything is there: perfect and complete, just as it is."

Whatever Rick makes (or fails to make) of all these fragments of philosophy, the viewer is encouraged by the film itself to take these philosophemes as guidelines for working with the apparent chaos of the experience of being human represented by the ever-shifting web of images and sounds, individuals, and incidents that constitutes *Knight of Cups*. Each of us, as we sink into the various beauties and terrors of Rick's Los

Angeles, is asked to see ourselves as a Knight of Cups, as someone who needs to learn that "the true imagination feeds on action rather than fantasy."[16] To move from fantasy to action requires that an individual find and/or create a self that is coherent and integrated, at least to some degree, and the first step in this process is the cultivation of attention. Without paying attention, one can never take the path of a pilgrim, one can never hope to find the pearl, one can never see heavenly beauty in an individual human being. What Rick lacks more than anything else is an ability to pay attention, and in this respect Christopher's Zen-inflected advice is aimed squarely at the viewer of Malick's film: pay attention to this moment. In paying attention to the moment—and the moments—of *Knight of Cups*, the viewer must also pay attention to the philosophical advice explicitly quoted in the film, using the metaphor of the pilgrim's path, the tale of the pearl, and the allegory of beauty reflected in Plato's account of the soul's wings as guidelines for achieving some sort of integrated self. Each of us is likely to do this work in different ways, but the film offers us a variety of philosophical exercises that will allow us to shape ourselves so that we can avoid the constant and repeated failures illustrated so graphically by Rick's life.

Limitations of space keep me from elaborating these ideas at length, but let me suggest one way in which *Knight of Cups* might help viewers begin to make sense of their own lives. If we let ourselves acknowledge that our life experience is not so different from Rick's—if we accept the subjunctive possibility that our world could be like Rick's—then we might want to look a little more into that story of the pearl that Rick's father told him as a child. If, after watching the film, we actively do a little research so as "to remember the pearl," we will find that the Gnostic *Song of the Pearl* suggests that the pearl sought by the son is both the son's soul (which he has temporarily lost) and the deity that saves his soul.[17] When Rick tells himself "Find your way from darkness to light," he seems to be urging us (as well as himself) to find a path of integration along which the individual caught up in worldly concerns ultimately achieves a kind of integration with a self that transcends the cares of this world. In this way, paying attention to this moment—not to a desired future or a remembered past—reveals not just a world that is "perfect and complete" but a self that in that moment is authentically integrated. Were Malick's film to launch us on the path of cultivating the present moment, *Knight of Cups* would succeed in helping us actively come to self-transformation.

My claim that some of Terrence Malick's films might fruitfully be approached as subjunctive templates for self-transformation is itself inspired by Pierre Hadot's provocative reappraisal of the ancient philosophical tradition. Hadot argues that we fail to grasp the genuine significance of Greco-Roman philosophy unless we recognize that philosophy for the ancient schools was understood as the art of living. Writing of the Stoics, for example, Hadot notes that they

> declared explicitly that philosophy, for them, was an "exercise." In their view, philosophy did not consist in teaching an abstract theory—much less in the exegesis of texts—but rather in the art of living. It is a concrete attitude and determinate life-style, which engages the whole of existence. The philosophical act is not situated merely on the cognitive level, but on that of the self and of being. It is a progress which causes us to *be* more fully, and makes us better.[18]

From this perspective, philosophy is not a discipline essentially devoted to theorizing, and all the explorations of epistemology, metaphysics, and ethics that are found in ancient philosophical texts are strictly subordinate to the question of how to live a good life.[19] A crucial implication of this fact is that "the philosophical work is always implicitly a dialogue. The dimension of the possible interlocutor is always present within it."[20] What this means is that works of philosophy should not be understood as existing primarily in the indicative mood: they are not essentially complex systems of representation describing the nature of the world and our place in it. Rather, philosophical writings exist more fully in the subjunctive mood, asking us to consider alternative ways that the world could be and, on the basis of these possibilities, sketching "spiritual exercises" that would have the potential to transform us and our relation to the world. I am suggesting, then, that Malick's films might better be approached as spiritual exercises in Hadot's sense than as cinematic representations of philosophical questions and doctrines. Thematic analyses of films such as *Knight of Cups* can be intellectually provocative and more or less persuasive, but such analysis cannot really capture the impact that the films have on viewers who take them to heart.[21]

Hadot's reorientation of our understanding of the philosophical tradition might seem a little abstract and even banal. However, his argument rests on a careful review of the wide variety of spiritual exercises to be found in the Greco-Roman tradition: these exercises are most apparent in Stoic and Epicurean texts—and perhaps it is for this reason that these Hellenistic schools have been relatively ignored by mainstream philosophical commentators—but they are also to be found in the dialogues of Plato and in the texts of later Platonists, perhaps most especially in the work of Plotinus. For my purposes here, the kinds of exercises Hadot discusses can be divided into three broad categories: (1) exercises that cultivate "attention" (*prosoche*) by means of "meditations" (*meletai*) that lead to some degree of "self-mastery" (*enkrateia*); (2) exercises that cultivate "conscience" (*metanoia*) by means of various "therapies of the soul" deepening the extent of self-mastery; and (3) exercises that cultivate "conversion" (*metastrophe*), a transformation of one's perspective from that of the isolated individual to that of the *kosmos* as a whole.[22]

We have already seen that *Knight of Cups* can be seen as nurturing in its viewer the work of attention, and the film does this by offering us a host of philosophemes for reflection: watching and listening to the film will immerse us in Rick's world, but it will also give us much upon which to meditate as we try to regain for ourselves the kind of self-mastery that Rick may never experience. If *Knight of Cups* works to cultivate our attention as a means toward achieving some degree of authenticity, *A Hidden Life* shows us how conscience can be deepened by means of a sense of gratitude toward the world just as it is, while *The Tree of Life* offers us a path toward conversion, a transformation of our very being in light of the inseparability of the individual and the universe.

A Hidden Life,[23] which at the time of writing is Malick's most recent film, is perhaps the most "traditional" of his works: while it retains all of the familiar hallmarks of his oeuvre (lush cinematography, intensely moving music, dynamic camerawork, and extensive voiceovers), the film also works with a rigorously linear plot and features a number of psychologically rich characters. In these respects, at least, *A Hidden Life* could not be more different from *Knight of Cups*. Like *Badlands* (1973) and *The New World* (2005), the film is very loosely based on actual historical figures, in this case the Austrian peasant Franz Jägerstätter, who refused to take the oath of allegiance to the Führer when he was conscripted for military service in

1943 and who was executed some months later for this act of courage.[24] The film traces in a fairly chronological way the relation of Franz (August Diehl) with his wife Fani (Valerie Pachner) in a stunningly beautiful mountain village (Radegund) before his conscription, the growing tension between the young couple and their fellow villagers as Franz's opposition to Hitler's war-making becomes apparent, Franz's imprisonment for failure to take the oath, and the series of events surrounding Franz in prison and Fani in the outside world, ending with Franz's execution and Fani's ongoing life in Radegund.

The difficulties that *A Hidden Life* poses its viewers paradoxically stem from its comparative clarity. On the one hand, the film's narrative has the inexorability of a Greek tragedy—within the film's first half-hour, Franz confides in his parish priest, Father Fürthauer (Tobias Moretti), "I can't serve. We're killing innocent people," thereby setting up his inevitable fate—but Malick allows the plot to develop over the course of a three-hour, emotionally wrenching film. On the other hand, while the film explores Franz's resolution and commitment through a series of dramatic interactions with other characters, the ultimate motivation for his courageous stand remains something of a mystery at the film's end.[25] It is the tension between the inexorability of Franz's fate and the psychological mystery of his resoluteness, as depicted by Malick, that makes *A Hidden Life* such a challenging film for its viewer.

Despite the inevitability that hangs over the film's narrative, the viewer's interest is continually renewed by the various hopeful possibilities about which Franz and Fani dream as Franz's conscription, arrest, and imprisonment loom in the background: Could he be exempted from military service as a farmer? Could his Catholic bishop make a case for him as a conscientious objector? Could Fani persuade Nazi administrators to have him released from prison? Could the war come to an end before Franz's execution? As each of these possibilities is ruled out, the viewer comes to feel more woven into the film's narrative, and we find ourselves more and more in something like Franz's shoes: as the film slowly unfolds, we are effectively asked what it would take for us to share his commitment to his ideals, what it would take for us to be people of conscience in an unforgiving and terrible world. The power of *A Hidden Life* as a spiritual exercise in this sense is reflected in the fact that these questions addressed to us become only more pressing even after the film's end.

Moreover, as the film unfolds its narrative, Franz's deep moral commitment is challenged by a series of characters, each of whom has plausible enough reasons for thinking that his course of action is wrong.

In his very first encounter with Franz, Father Fürthauer's response is blunt: "Don't you think you ought to consider the consequences of your actions? You'll almost surely be shot. Your sacrifice will benefit no one." When Franz takes his case to Bishop Fliesser (Michael Nyqvist), the bishop resignedly declares, "You have a duty to the fatherland. The church tells you so." Radegund's mayor (Karl Markovics), an enthusiastic convert to the Nazi cause, finally dismisses Franz, saying, "You're worse than them. Because they are enemies, but you are a traitor." In Franz's first interrogation after imprisonment, Captain Herder (Matthias Schoenaerts) asks, "Do you think your protest will change things? What purpose does it serve? Are you innocent?" Judge Lueben (Bruno Ganz), before sentencing Franz to death, asks, "Do you imagine that anyone outside this court will hear of you?" In each of these encounters, Franz himself is largely silent, although to the judge he explains, "I don't know everything. I have this feeling inside me that I can't do what I believe is wrong." In this way, *A Hidden Life* powerfully dramatizes the conflict between what Hegel calls "ethical life" (*Sittlichkeit*) and "morality" (*Moralität*), between those concrete rights and duties that are defined by an individual's social position at a given historical moment and the relatively abstract "good and evil attaching to his individual freedom."[26] It is precisely because the call of conscience so often runs counter to the clearly articulated expectations of our social roles that it is so difficult to cultivate the resoluteness that conscience demands. Franz's apparent inability to respond in a compelling way to his interlocutors suggests that we need to turn to other characters in our search for the exercises that might strengthen the call of conscience, and two such characters stand out: Waldland (Franz Rogowski), a friend from Franz's days of military training who ends up with him in Tegel Prison in Berlin, and Fani.

In the course of his training, Franz notes that Waldland is "always smiling," and he comes across as a good-natured jokester, always having fun. When the two friends meet up again in prison, Waldland remains surprisingly upbeat, his smile as winning as ever. "You know," he says, "even if it rains, the sun is shining. The sun shines on good and evil the same." In their final conversation, just before Franz's trial, Waldland shares with him a slightly wistful but joyous vision of the life he would have liked to have led. The scene begins with Waldland watching his warm, moist breath on the prison cell's window, a moving reminder of the fragile concreteness of life itself. Resting his head against the windowsill, he reflects, "I wish I'd had a wife. And a farm. And apple trees.

And a cherry tree. And maybe some grapes. We could do our own wine. White wine. And red wine. Red wine for the winter and white wine for the summer. We would not drink too much. We would pray and work. But sometimes, sometimes a little drink is good. Sometimes, we would go to church. And sometimes not. Sometimes we'd stay at home. And we'd make music." And with that, Franz and Waldland laugh and sing together in their cell. This scene, introducing the film's denouement, reminds us of the way that friendship can keep us grounded in the here-and-now of our lives. Waldland's vision is also surely a reminder to Franz that that for which Waldland longs is precisely the life that Franz has enjoyed. I'd like to suggest, then, that what Terrence Malick offers us here is a kind of spiritual exercise in gratitude: if the world were the way Waldland imagines it to be—and the world is, in fact, precisely this simple and beautiful—then we should be grateful for being able to share friendship in such a world. This gratitude, in turn, could provide the ground for a strengthening of conscience. Rather than hoping that a conscientious life will somehow allow us to satisfy the duties of our ethical life, our moral resoluteness finds its home in our giving thanks for the life that we have, no matter how fleeting that life may be.

If Waldland's role in *A Hidden Life* points us toward the value of friendship and gratitude in honing moral conscience, Fani's role is to remind us that conscience is also nurtured in the intimacies of love. In her letters to Franz and her conversations with her sister, Resie (Maria Simon), Fani sometimes expresses a confidence in God's will—"He won't send us more than we can bear," "A time will come when we know what all this was for. And there will be no mysteries about why we live"—but much more striking is the depth of her loving commitment to Franz. This commitment is tested again and again during Franz's months in prison, and Malick compellingly shows Fani to be at least as courageous and resolute as Franz. The film's emotional peak comes in Franz and Fani's final meeting, when she comes to Tegel Prison after he has been sentenced to death. To his question "Do you understand?" she nods and replies, "I love you. Whatever you do. Whatever comes. I'm with you. Always. Do what is right." The final words of the film are also Fani's, spoken as a voiceover after Franz's execution: "I'll meet you there. In the mountains." As the camera lingers on the mountains and waterfall that have come to shape the viewer's sense of the natural environment of Radegund, we are also inevitably struck by the echo of Franz's initial voiceover at the very beginning of the film, "We'll build our nest in the mountains." As tempting as it might be to understand Fani and Franz's love in terms of something like a Catholic faith in the divine, I think there is an even more powerful resonance with Waldland's gratitude for the simple joys of this life. Intimate love is itself a mode of gratitude, a recognition of the grace that is to be found in the here-and-now. And it is this grace that provides the foundation for a resolute moral conscience. *A Hidden Life*, then—experienced not as a depiction of Franz Jägerstätter's courageous life but as an exhortation to living conscientiously—urges us to cultivate friendship and love in this life, in this world of natural beauty and human suffering, as the path toward developing the moral steadfastness that makes a good life possible.

∽

Perhaps more than any other Malick film, *The Tree of Life*[27] has deeply divided both critics and audiences. The film's premiere at the Cannes Film Festival ended with cheers and jeers, even though it went on to win the Palme d'Or. Commentators generally admire the film's audacity and sheer technical accomplishment, although many remain baffled about its ultimate significance. Peter Bradshaw ends his enthusiastic review with the admission, "This film may not be for everyone, but it makes other movies and other movie-makers look timid and feeble. I am an evangelist for it."[28] David Sterritt admires "the courage Malick shows in organizing such an ambitious, personal film around themes that Hollywood rarely bothers to sniff at, much less explore," but he worries that Malick's "theology" taps into "a kind of American religiosity that specializes in affirming static traditions and shoring up reactionary mindsets."[29]

My own sense is that this divided reception stems directly from the fact that the film makes thematic readings almost inevitable, even though such readings completely sidestep the emotional impact of the film. The film opens, for example, with a quotation from Job (38:4-7)—"Where were you when I laid the foundation of the earth? . . . When the morning stars sang together and all the sons of God shouted for joy?"—immediately contextualizing everything that follows as a kind of meditation on the problem of human suffering in a world created by God. Indeed, the film's narrative core is a flashback of scattered childhood memories through which a successful architect, Jack (Sean Penn), tries to come to grips with a brother's death years before and with the suffering this death caused his mother. Immediately after the quotation from Job, however, the screen is filled with the flickering image of a Lumia projection by Thomas Wilfred[30]—an image that recurs periodically throughout the film—and this gives way to a voiceover by Jack: "Brother. Mother. It was they who led me to your door." Before any sort of narrative begins, we are introduced to Mrs. O'Brien (Jessica Chastain) who speaks in voiceover across a series of images that will become familiar in what follows: "The nuns taught us there were two ways through life: the way of nature and the way of grace. You have to choose which one you will follow." As the film's narrative unfolds, it becomes clear that the way of nature is reflected in the cynical life advice that Mr. O'Brien (Brad Pitt) gives to his sons, while the way of grace is embodied in the radiant screen presence of Mrs. O'Brien, whose life advice is encapsulated in a voiceover: "Help each other. Love everyone, every leaf, every ray of light." Thus, the theme of human suffering (a problem for most forms of theism) is instantly entangled with the distinctively Christian theme of grace, and we find ourselves confronting profound philosophical/theological questions in the first minutes of the film before we learn anything about its narrative course.

Focusing immediately on these grand philosophical questions and expecting *The Tree of Life* to develop a complex representation of the world in which these questions will be answered, the viewer is then confronted by a film that simply refuses to play by any of the rules of the classic narrative film. The central narrative of Malick's film begins in the 1960s with the O'Briens living in a very comfortable mid-century modernist home, when a telegram delivered to Mrs. O'Brien announces the death of one of her sons, and she collapses in abject grief. The scene rapidly shifts to the 2000s and a coldly elegant contemporary house, where Jack lights a candle in memory of his dead brother. In a series of brief discontinuous scenes intercut with what seem to be memories of his childhood, we then see Jack at work in a glass-sheathed skyscraper, apologizing to his father on the phone, and walking in a desolate desert landscape. This contemporary episode comes to an end with the return of the Lumia projection and Mrs. O'Brien in voiceover, "Was I false to you? Lord, why? Where were you?"

As if all of this were not sufficiently puzzling, *The Tree of Life* now shifts gears completely and spectacularly answers Mrs. O'Brien's question with a stunning seventeen-minute montage depicting the origin of galaxies, the beginning of life, a curious intimation of "compassion" in the interaction of two dinosaurs, and the asteroid impact that destroyed the age of dinosaurs. At this point, the central narrative of the film begins, shifting the viewer's attention to small-town Texas in the 1950s and the birth of the O'Briens' sons. For the next ninety minutes, Malick takes us through the course of Jack's boyhood as filtered by his memories of his mother, his father, his brothers, the streets and houses of his small town, and the woods, rivers, and sky of the town's natural setting. Many of the details here are autobiographical, but Malick disrupts any sense of linear time or causality by weaving scenes together in radically discontinuous ways and emphasizing the constant movement of Emmanuel Lubezki's stunningly radiant cinematography. Much has been written about the remarkable ways in which the heart of *The Tree of Life* manages simultaneously to evoke the particularity of an individual American boyhood of the 1950s and the universality of individuals having to find their identity within and beyond the constraints of their family's dynamics.[31] Equally remarkable may be the way this portion of the film shows the complete interdependence of knowing and feeling in the life of a child: scattered memories coalesce into powerful emotional responses, while obscure moments of ill-defined feeling prompt new cascades of fragmentary memories.

With a return to Jack's votive candle, *The Tree of Life* suddenly shifts gears a final time, its closing twelve minutes offering the viewer a vision of what Robert Sinnerbrink has aptly called "the shores of eternity."[32] We follow Jack and Mrs. O'Brien into a desert landscape of radiantly bright light, of sandy shores and sunbaked salt flats, where they encounter once again people from their past, including their earlier selves: Jack and his mother embrace as adults, adult Jack and his father walk together in deep empathy, and a scattering of children including the O'Brien boys in their youth run across the sands. To the luminous strains of the "Agnus Dei" from Hector Berlioz's *Grande Messe des Morts*, Mrs. O'Brien finds her lost son and ecstatically embraces him. At the end of a complex montage of frankly surreal scenes, we see Mrs. O'Brien and her late son at the door of the family's modest house, now reduced to its shell and situated on eternity's shores, where she kisses him goodbye. As Berlioz's choirs intone "Amen," Mrs. O'Brien speaks in a voiceover, "I give him to you. I give you my son," and we see her in the middle-distance walking into the radiance of a sunrise (or sunset). Following a quick series of shots from Jack's adult life, the film comes to an end with the image of the Lumia projection and the sound of wind, gulls, and waves.

It is surely not surprising that viewers of *The Tree of Life* might be left in a state of bewildered confusion simply by the film's vast shifts in subject matter and cinematic style. The viewer's deep difficulty holding the parts of the film together makes it clear that Malick's film should not be read in the indicative mood: it is not a representation of the way the world is but a subjunctive proposal of a possible way of relating to the world. To put this point in another way: it is fairly easy to read the film's structure as describing how an individual's life is both the outcome of the natural history of the universe (the way of nature) and a meaningful node in the unfolding of eternity (the way of grace).[33] However, learning to live in a way that holds these perspectives together remains terribly difficult, and I think the real power of *The Tree of Life* comes in the way that the scattered and fragmentary memories of Jack's childhood apparently help him to achieve a kind of consciousness of the universe as a whole and of his place within it. We see the development of this consciousness in the occasional voiceovers of Jack as an adult that punctuate the unspooling of his childhood memories:

> "You spoke to me through her. From the sky, the trees. Before I knew I loved you, believed in you."
> "I want to know what you are to see what you see."
> "Where were you? You let a boy die. You'll let anything happen?" (Addressed both to Mr. O'Brien and to God.)
> "How do I get back where they are?"
> "What was it you showed me? I didn't know how to name you then, but I see it was you. Always you were calling me."
> "Father. Mother. Always you wrestle inside of me. Always you will."

In this way, the film provides its viewers with a template for the self-transformation of their lives. Against the background of an essentially naturalistic and scientific understanding of nature, what patterns of significance can I find in the sometimes faint, sometimes vivid, but always shifting memories of my life? With the objective distance that scientific understanding affords and with the temporal distance that characterizes memory, how can we make sense of our lives? What apparently insignificant flash of memory might finally provide a key to a grasp of the whole? And once I achieve some kind of consciousness of the meaningfulness of the universe as a whole, how might this lead me to change the way I live?

My approach to *The Tree of Life* and to the other films I have considered in this chapter suggests that we not see in Malick's work anything like definitive answers to the questions that his works ask; rather, the films invite us to engage in spiritual exercises that might help us find answers to these questions for ourselves. *The Tree of Life* has, however, led some commentators to claim that Malick has presented us here with something like a set of theological teachings. We have already seen that David Sterritt has qualms about Malick's "theology," and Christopher Barnett argues in a provocative essay that the film is "*best* understood within the Christian mystical tradition."[34] In his sensitive and highly nuanced analysis of the film, Robert Sinnerbrink argues that *The Tree of Life* "shows how the lives of an ordinary family are embedded, yet also embraced, by a sublime vision of re-enchanted nature (and spirit) in which human joy and suffering have their place, where the religious problem of suffering finds an aesthetic response—an aesthetic theodicy."[35] In contrast, I would note that God is addressed regularly in the film but only in the mode of prayerful questioning.[36] While this may well imply that Malick is willing to assume the existence of God within the context of the film, such questioning does nothing to elaborate an account of the divine nature; there really is no clear theology present in the film, Christian or otherwise.[37] Nevertheless, the problem of human suffering hangs over the film with its opening words from the book of Job, and it seems impossible not to read *The Tree of Life* as engaging its viewers in the project of theodicy. But what kind of engagement in theodicy does the film invoke?

Sinnerbrink seems to maintain that "the sublimity of the cosmos"— so vividly reflected in the scenes of natural beauty that recur throughout Malick's work—itself justifies or makes up for the suffering found in the world, insofar as this sublimity evokes "what the young Nietzsche called an 'aesthetic affirmation of existence.'"[38] I would argue, however, that a process of profound spiritual training is needed to move from a recognition of the sublimity of the cosmos to any kind of acceptance of the existence of suffering: aesthetics in itself would seem to have no clear ethical bearing. I have already proposed that *The Tree of Life* offers us exercises by which we might seek to find patterns of meaning in the scattered fragments that make up the memories of our lives, patterns of meaning that can help each of us recognize how our lives are reflective of and integral to the unity of the cosmos. Building upon such an insight, how might we approach the problem of suffering?

Bearing in mind that we come to a realization of our unity with the whole of the cosmos through an examination of our memories, we might also realize that our own internal unity is inseparable from the complex patterning of our memories, with the consequence that every fragment of memory—no matter how pleasant or painful, profound or trivial—contributes to the sublime whole that is the cosmos. *The Tree of Life* effectively teaches us to say "Yes" to memory, no matter how difficult this is, as a necessary step on the path of spiritual self-transformation. To become able to affirm our memories even as we affirm the sublimity of the cosmos effectively constitutes a powerful form of conversion, a transformation of our perspective from that of an isolated individual to that of a self who has achieved a kind of integration with the cosmos.

There is, moreover, a productive paradox at the heart of this affirmation of memory: in saying "Yes" to each of our scattered memories, we place ourselves in a position to let go of the events in the past that precipitated those memories, to let them simply be what they were, quite apart from how they may have felt to us at the time. Affirmation makes letting go genuinely possible. The closing scene of *The Tree of Life* serves as a kind of parable of the power of this spiritual exercise: Mrs. O'Brien's act of kissing her late son goodbye on the shores of eternity is an affirmation of her memories, and this act of affirmation makes it possible for her to say, "I give him to you. I give you my son." We recognize in this moment a profound gesture of gratitude (and of grace) for the world just as it is.

This paradox—that affirmation of a memory allows us to let the object of that memory go—finds a fruitful resonance with the late work of Martin Heidegger. In a rethinking of his own earlier reflections on the essence of technology, Heidegger borrows a term from Meister Eckhart—*Gelassenheit* ("releasement")—to characterize a "comportment towards technology which expresses 'yes' and at the same time 'no,'" a way of living in the world that cultivates both an "openness to the mystery" and a "releasement towards things."³⁹ Rather than offering a philosophically argued justification for the existence of suffering in a world in which there is a God, Malick's film teaches how we might learn to practice the "releasement towards things" that is made possible by an "openness to the mystery." Rather than elaborating a theodicy, *The Tree of Life* offers us a path toward conversion, toward a perspective in which the individual and the universe are inseparable, a perspective from which there is no longer any need for a theodicy.⁴⁰

Much more could be said about Terrence Malick's films as examples of cinema as spiritual exercise, and much more could be said about the methodology that I have sketched in the course of this chapter. If my very preliminary attempt at what could be called a *subjunctive phenomenology* of the cinematic experience opens up new ways of thinking about these films, it would surely be productive to extend this mode of interpretation to the work of other filmmakers. Andrei Tarkovsky's *Solaris* (1972) or *Stalker* (1979) may well give up some of their mysteries were they approached from the perspective of their viewers' actual or possible experience.[41] Similarly, the experimental short films of Maya Deren—*Meshes of the Afternoon* (1943) and *Ritual in Transfigured Time* (1946)—demand modes of interpretation that go beyond considerations of narrative or thematic analysis.[42] Moreover, if my application to cinematic experience of Pierre Hadot's model of philosophy as spiritual exercise seems fruitful, it would be useful to consider the ways in which films provoke their viewers to engage in cultivating states of mind or virtues beyond attention, conscience, and conversion. In pursuing these various extensions of the arguments here, we would certainly come to a fuller realization of the possibility that cinema, like philosophy, is an "art of living."[43]

Notes

1. Pippin, "Vernacular Metaphysics," 269–75.
2. Rossouw, "There's Something about Malick," 280.
3. Pippin, *Philosophy by Other Means*, 9–10.
4. Rossouw, "There's Something about Malick," 281.
5. Sinnerbrink, *Terrence Malick*, 14–15.
6. Rossouw, "There's Something about Malick," 292.
7. *Knight of Cups*, directed by Terrence Malick (Broad Green Pictures, 2015), Blu-ray Disc.
8. Bradshaw, "*Knight of Cups* Review: Malick's Back!"
9. Sinnerbrink, *Terrence Malick*, 186–92.
10. Brody, "Terrence Malick's *Knight of Cups* Challenges Hollywood to do Better."
11. Matt Zoller Seitz, review of *Knight of Cups*.
12. Sinnerbrink, *Terrence Malick*, 164.
13. Sinnerbrink, 171.
14. Sinnerbrink, 192–93.
15. Sinnerbrink, 168.
16. Rachel Pollack, *Seventy-Eight Degrees of Wisdom*, 190.
17. Barnstone and Meyer, eds., *The Gnostic Bible*, 387.
18. Pierre Hadot, *Philosophy as a Way of Life*, 82–83.

19. Hadot, 104.
20. Hadot, 105.
21. To the best of my knowledge, the use of Hadot to explore cinema was introduced into the literature by Anne Eakin Moss. See Moss, "Cinema as Spiritual Exercise," especially 214–16.
22. See Hadot, *Philosophy as a Way of Life*, 84–96; and Hadot, *The Present Alone Is Our Happiness*, 87–97.
23. *A Hidden Life*, directed by Terrence Malick (Fox Searchlight Pictures, 2019), Blu-ray Disc.
24. The psychoanalyst Heinz Kohut devotes part of an important essay to Jägerstätter, arguing that he should be seen as an authentic martyr-hero and not as a psychotic. See Heinz Kohut, "On Courage."
25. In this respect, Malick departs significantly from what we know about the actual life of Franz Jägerstätter, who was beatified as a Catholic martyr by Pope Benedict XVI in 2007 precisely because his actions were grounded in his profound religious faith.
26. Hegel, *Reason in History*, 36–38, 45.
27. *The Tree of Life*, directed by Terrence Malick (Fox Searchlight Pictures and River Road Entertainment, 2011), Blu-ray Disc.
28. Peter Bradshaw, review of *The Tree of Life*, *Guardian*, July 7, 2011.
29. Sterritt, "Days of Heaven and Waco," 52.
30. For a very helpful account of Wilfred's work, see the comments of Dan Glass and Nick Gonda in *Terrence Malick: Rehearsing the Unexpected*, 329–31; and Sinnerbrink, *Terrence Malick*, 132.
31. See, for example, Richard Brody, "*The Tree of Life*: Roots and Shoots"; Roger Ebert, "The Blink of a Life, Enclosed by Time and Space"; Joe Balay, "How to Grow a Tree"; and Sinnerbrink, *Terrence Malick*, 125–26.
32. Sinnerbrink, *Terrence Malick*, 148.
33. See, for example, Sinnerbrink, *Terrence Malick*, 137–46.
34. Barnett, "Spirit(uality) in the Films of Terrence Malick," 23.
35. Sinnerbrink, *Terrence Malick*, 137–46.
36. Similarly, in the theatrical version of Malick's IMAX film, *Voyage of Time: Life's Journey* (2016)—a film that directly approaches the problem of suffering by looking at the entire history of the universe from its origin in something like the Big Bang to its end in something like a black hole—the narration (by Cate Blanchett) largely takes the form of prayerful questions addressed to the creator of the universe, "Mother." See *Voyage of Time: Life's Journey*, directed by Terrence Malick (IMAX Entertainment and Sophisticated Films, 2016), DVD.
37. The use of "Agnus Dei" from Berlioz's Requiem in the film's final minutes may seem to force a Christian reading of Malick's intent, but Berlioz himself was at best an agnostic. David Cairns notes, "The absence of God is the driving force behind the Requiem. That, deeper than all other motives, is why he had to write it.

The work conveys a poignant regret for loss of faith, a profound awareness of the need, the desperate need, to believe and to worship." See Cairns, *Berlioz—Volume Two: Servitude and Greatness*, 136.

38. Sinnerbrink, *Terrence Malick*, 146.

39. Heidegger, *Discourse on Thinking*, 54–55.

40. Barnett too stresses the importance of *Gelassenheit* in Malick's films, but he elaborates an overtly Christian, if mystical, approach. See Barnett, "Spirit(uality) in the Films of Terrence Malick," 18–24.

41. Tarkovsky himself opens his own book on filmmaking by quoting the responses (positive and negative) of viewers of his films. See Tarkovsky, *Sculpting in Time: Reflections on the Cinema*, 7–13.

42. See, for example, Keller, *Maya Deren*.

43. I owe a deep debt of gratitude to Daniel Teplow, whose bibliographic research and enthusiastic conversation about the films of Terrence Malick helped me bring this chapter to completion. Daniel's participation in this research project was made possible by the generous support of a faculty-student collaborative research grant from Colorado College.

Bibliography

Balay, Joe. "How to Grow a Tree: Wonder and (Re)presentation in Terrence Malick's *The Tree of Life*." *Journal of Asia-Pacific Pop Culture* 1, no. 2 (2016): 227–38.

Barnett, Christopher B. "Spirit(uality) in the Films of Terrence Malick." *Journal of Religion and Film* 17, no. 1 (2013): 1–33. https://digitalcommons.unomaha.edu/jrf/vol17/iss1/33/.

Barnstone, Willis, and Marvin Meyer, eds. *The Gnostic Bible*. Boston: Shambhala, 2003.

Bradshaw, Peter. "*Knight of Cups* Review: Malick's Back! With the Least Interesting Spiritual Crisis in History." *Guardian*, February 8, 2015. https://www.theguardian.com/film/2015/feb/08/knight-of-cups-review-film-terrence-malick-christian-bale.

———. Review of *The Tree of Life*. *Guardian*, July 7, 2011. https://theguardian.com/film/2011/jul/o7/the-tree-of-life-review.

Brody, Richard. "Terrence Malick's *Knight of Cups* Challenges Hollywood to Do Better." *New Yorker*, March 7, 2016. https://www.newyorker.com/culture/richard-brody/terrence-malicks-knight-of-cups-challenges-hollywood-to-do-better.

———. "*The Tree of Life*: Roots and Shoots." *New Yorker*, May 22, 2011. https://www.newyorker.com/culture/richard-brody/the-tree-of-life-roots-and-shoots.

Cairns, David. *Berlioz—Volume Two: Servitude and Greatness, 1832–1869*. Berkeley: University of California Press, 1999.

Ebert, Roger. "The Blink of a Life, Enclosed by Time and Space." https://rogerebert.com/reviews/the-tree-of-life-2011.
Hadot, Pierre. *Philosophy as a Way of Life*. Edited by Arnold I. Davidson. Translated by Michael Chase. Oxford: Blackwell, 1995.
———. *The Present Alone Is Our Happiness: Conversations with Jeannie Carlier and Arnold I. Davidson*. 2nd ed. Translated by Marc Djaballah and Michael Chase. Stanford: Stanford University Press, 2011.
Hegel, G. W. F. *Reason in History: A General Introduction to the Philosophy of History*. Translated by Robert S. Hartman. Upper Saddle River, NJ: Prentice-Hall, 1997.
Heidegger, Martin. *Discourse on Thinking*. Translated by John M. Anderson and E. Hans Freund. New York: Harper and Row, 1966.
Hintermann, Carlo, and Daniele Villa, eds. *Terrence Malick: Rehearsing the Unexpected*. London: Faber and Faber, 2015.
Keller, Sarah. *Maya Deren: Incomplete Control*. New York: Columbia University Press, 2015.
Kohut, Heinz. "On Courage." In *Self Psychology and the Humanities: Reflections on a New Psychoanalytic Approach*, edited by Charles B. Strozier, 5–50. New York: W. W. Norton, 1985.
Moss, Anne Eakin. "Cinema as Spiritual Exercise: Tarkovsky and Hadot." In *Refocus: The Films of Andrei Tarkovsky*, edited by Sergey Toymentsev, 209–24. Edinburgh: Edinburgh University Press, 2021.
Pippin, Robert B. *Philosophy by Other Means: The Arts in Philosophy and Philosophy in the Arts*. Chicago: University of Chicago Press, 2021.
———. "Vernacular Metaphysics: On Terrence Malick's *The Thin Red Line*." *Critical Inquiry* 39, no. 4 (Winter 2013): 247–75.
Pollack, Rachel. *Seventy-Eight Degrees of Wisdom: A Tarot Journey to Self-Awareness*. Newburyport, MA: Weiser Books, 2019.
Rossouw, Martin P. "There's Something about Malick: Film-Philosophy, Contemplative Style, and Ethics of Transformation." *New Review of Film and Television Studies* 15, no. 3 (2017): 279–89.
Seitz, Matt Zoller. Review of *Knight of Cups*. https://www.rogerebert.com/reviews/knight-of-cups-2016.
Sinnerbrink, Robert. *Terrence Malick: Filmmaker and Philosopher*. London: Bloomsbury Academic, 2019.
Sterritt, David. "Days of Heaven and Waco: Terrence Malick's *The Tree of Life*." *Film Quarterly* 65, no. 1 (2011): 52–57.
Tarkovsky, Andrey. *Sculpting in Time: Reflections on the Cinema*. Translated by Kitty Hunter-Blair. Austin: University of Texas Press, 1987.

Chapter 2

Terrence Malick's Cosmic Cinema

Manuel "Mandel" Cabrera Jr.

Humanistic vs. Cosmic Storytelling

One of the aims of narrative art is the depiction of place. There are, for example, the settings of stories; along with character, theme, plot, and so on, setting is one among the standard list of storytelling elements. However, a setting is often viewed as merely the stage on which the main attractions—the affairs of the story's characters—unfold. As it's sometimes put, the engine of storytelling is drama, which fundamentally concerns characters' desires. Thus, setting in an important sense has the lower billing. Of course, drama is next to impossible without setting. After all, it's the environments in which characters find themselves that arouse, frustrate, and fulfill their desires, so it's largely through characters' dynamic interaction with settings that dramatic arcs can unfold. However, important as settings are, they're often seen as containers—vessels in the service of delivering to us the true heart of a story: the lives and times of its characters.

This view gives us one approach to a common sensibility about storytelling we might call *narrative humanism*. As this sensibility would have it, the role of narrative art is fundamentally to tell our stories. Its special magic lies in dramatizing human struggles to clarify and express our viewpoints on the world, as well as to put them into action. It's natural, then, for creators and audiences of a humanistic bent to hold, if only implicitly, that characters are storytelling's proper focus—stand-ins, as it were, whose perspectives we can inhabit to achieve insight into our own. Thus, as I put it previously, settings are simply the stages on which characters do what we need them to do, and any story that attempts to go beyond this mandate goes off the rails in doing so.

I call this view humanistic because it's part and parcel of a humanistic view of the world at large. A humanist in this broader sense regards the world fundamentally as the venue in which we lead our lives. Everything about us is caught up in the all-consuming project of figuring out how to conduct our existence—what to do, be, believe, and feel. Nothing can matter except in terms of how it bears on this endeavor. We are all, in this sense, die-hard narcissists. Not, of course, because we can't rise above individual self-interest but rather in the sense that it's in terms of the existence of beings like us that anything has significance. The world, in a real sense, is our world. We alone, members of an elite designated class (human beings, persons, rational natures, subjects, or what have you), are the protagonists of any stories about what's meaningful in it. Things outside this class are at best supporting players, and the world itself is simply the grand stage on which we lead our lives so that nothing in it can matter except in terms of stories that are fundamentally ours.

Humanism in this broader sense has been one of the dominating sensibilities of modern Western culture. It has, in fact, percolated so deeply that its advocates often brush off any alternative as intellectually backward or tautologically false. Of course, it hasn't been without its detractors as well, including among those who've rebelled against narrative humanism. From modernist attempts to reach beyond the bounds of human sense-making through a radical break from expressive conventions to speculative fiction's explorations of utterly alien forms of existence and worldly possibilities remote from human concerns to environmental fiction's efforts to see the world as filled with living presences rather than mere objects for our interpretation and manipulation, many creators have envisioned the world non-humanistically—often only to be accused of intellectual posturing, escapism, or vulgar mysticism.

What other approaches to storytelling could there be, though? Breaking with narrative humanism doesn't entail abandoning all concern for characters and their struggles. One could thus adhere to the tenet that drama is essential to storytelling without embracing the humanist view. Instead, perhaps the best examples of an alternative approach lie in the great storytelling traditions of religion, myth, and folklore, in which we often find what we might call *cosmic* storytelling. While stories of this sort usually contain characters—human, nonhuman, inhuman, divine—their ultimate subject matter isn't so much the dramas of such characters as it is the story-world itself, which more often than not is absolutely unbounded.

When we talk about the world of a story, what we're describing is simply things as portrayed by that story. Story-worlds, though, are usually partial. In the world of *Hamlet*, there are various objects and people, both real (Denmark) and fictional (Claudius). Various events (e.g., Ophelia's drowning) occur, and various things (e.g., that Rosencrantz and Guildenstern are companions) are the case. We can, of course, quibble over details. For example, since it happens "off stage," does *Hamlet* actually portray Ophelia's death? However, some things are certain. Donald Trump isn't in the world of *Hamlet*. Bugs Bunny eats no carrots there, nor does the universe contain any phlogiston. Such things are simply not portrayed by the play. Most works of narrative art are like this: they focus on portraying certain bits of the world and not others. And, although what a work portrays isn't the be-all and end-all of its significance, it's certainly a crucial part of what makes it tick.

In cosmic storytelling, though, we find all-encompassing story-worlds. Whereas the world of *Hamlet* is Denmark of the late Middle Ages, the world of a cosmic story is the cosmos itself—not just this or that locale, but all of it. More than this, though, cosmic stories make such unbounded story-worlds their primary focus. Of course, they typically lavish a great deal of attention on their characters. After all, as creators and audiences, we have a keen interest in these peculiar story elements since they're most like us. Nevertheless, while cosmic stories are about their characters, they're in a more fundamental sense about their unbounded story-worlds. Implicit in them is always the message: this is the story of the world as a whole and everything in it, or this is an episode in that story. The story-world isn't significant insofar as it serves the characters' narratives. Rather, the latter are significant insofar as they serve the narrative of the story-world itself. In other words, the world isn't treated as simply the stage on which character stories unfold. Instead, what's being recounted is fundamentally something about *its* story, and events in characters' lives are simply aspects of that story.

The impulse to cosmic storytelling is certainly evident in works like the Bible, the Eddas, the Quran, the Upanishads, and any number of storytelling traditions that similarly recount cosmogonies and the grand sweep of universal history. However, this impulse also evident in many stories that don't attempt anything so comprehensive. We sense in such stories the ambition to say something, not just about the human world, or the human viewpoint on the world, but about the nature and character of the world at large. Indeed, this is why such works—especially those prized for their specifically religious significance—have often been accused of being primitive attempts at scientific cosmology. However, just as a work of fiction might give us an insightful portrait of Napoleonic Russia, Tehran, or a New York neighborhood without making any claim to literal accuracy in many or even most of its descriptions of these places, so cosmic stories can give us insight about the world as a whole without our having to see them as purporting to tread on the territory of history or science. They are, in this sense, works of world portraiture—works that, like so many other great portraits, can illuminate their subjects without pretending to be photographs or scientific diagrams.

Now, if a narrative humanist were to dismiss such works as flawed attempts at narrative art, this would of course be justifiably met by shocked incredulity. It would mean rejecting an alarmingly wide swathe of human storytelling—not to mention many of the most deeply cherished stories there are. Instead, then, people with narrative humanist instincts have often opted to view cosmic stories in humanistic terms. Perhaps using some banal sentiment like "all stories are really about the human condition," they might prize cosmic stories for their insights into a culture's worldview or for how they dramatize human concerns using powerful cosmic metaphors. Both are worthy aspirations. However, this way of reading cosmic stories misses something crucial about their significance. In doing so, it risks lapsing into anachronism and chauvinism, blind to the historical specificity of its own way of looking at storytelling—the product of a distinctively modern, Western humanist worldview. A great deal of human storytelling has been driven by the sense not that the world is a human world, *our* world, but that human stories are simply threads in the tapestry of the world's story—threads whose significance depends on their place therein.

Malick between Humanism and the Cosmic

Terrence Malick's cinema provides a remarkable case study in the interplay between humanistic and cosmic storytelling and, ultimately, in what cosmic stories can be in a contemporary world suffused by humanistic skepticism that there are world stories to tell at all rather than simply human ones.

In his earliest phase—the Malick of *Badlands* and *Days of Heaven*—we find films that comfortably lend themselves to humanistic readings. The beauty and uncanniness of the nonhuman world figures prominently in them—for example, in Malick's famed wide shots of majestic landscapes and intimate close-ups of animals and plants. However, both seem entirely focused on their main characters: in each case, destitute lovers who flee into the American wilderness to escape their own past violence. And, indeed, both are narrated entirely from character viewpoints: those, specifically, of young girls dragged through harrowing circumstances, observing yet finally moving past them. As a result, the depiction of the nonhuman world in these films can easily be seen exclusively in terms of how it serves the characters' stories. The sublime views we get of the endless plains of South Dakota and Montana or of Texas wheat fields at golden hour become, for example, grand canvasses on which the characters project their longings: the childish fantasies of rebellious autonomy à la James Dean in Kit (Martin Sheen) and Holly (Sissy Spacek) of *Badlands* or the urgent desire to escape poverty in Bill (Richard Gere) and Abby (Brooke Adams) of *Days of Heaven*. Or the disturbing shots of animal corpses early in *Badlands* become expressions and portents of human indifference to life, and the locust plague in *Days of Heaven* becomes a stunning image of divine judgment—a figurative expression of and penalty for human desperation and folly.

Once Malick returns to filmmaking after a twenty-year hiatus, though, he produces two films—*The Thin Red Line* and *The New World*—of immensely expanded scope. This is true, of course, in the sense that they have far larger budgets and leave behind small-scale stories of star-crossed lovers on the lam to tackle world historical events. Beyond this, though, in these films the nonhuman world becomes a more central preoccupation both for the camera and the characters.

For example, for much of *The Thin Red Line* we're kept within a claustrophobic bubble of tension—the one that the American soldiers carry with them as they attempt to seize Guadalcanal from Japanese forces. As a result, we're trapped alongside them, feeling with them as they feel. Yet, the film is also replete with moments in which the larger world pierces through this bubble—often, at just those moments when the men of C Company, and thus we, feel the most penned in by its walls. For example, just before the film's first battle sequence, hidden marksmen shoot and kill two men pressing forward on a hill so that their bodies fall and disappear into the windswept grass. Rather than sustaining the resulting intensity by pitching us straight into the skirmish that follows, the camera lingers for a few moments to watch the swaying green of the hill burst forth as the sun emerges from behind a cloud. Then, once the battle begins, as if its attention has now been partially drawn away from the human arena, the camera is periodically distracted from the violent chaos, pausing to witness the squirming of a snake before two soldiers, a baby bird struggling on the ground, the closing of a touch-me-not leaf as a soldier brushes it with his fingers. We, along with the soldiers, glimpse the world that stretches beyond the boundaries of human concerns, one in which the irreducibility to the drama of war unfolding within it belies the sense, for those caught up in that drama, that human conflicts swallow anything and everything.

Paired with this cinematography, *The Thin Red Line* makes prominent use of voiceovers, just as in Malick's 1970s films. However, rather than being assigned to a single character, they're distributed among a number of them. In some cases, the voiceovers highlight how someone's private struggle with themselves stands in stark contrast with their public face. Colonel Tall (Nick Nolte) stews on his resentments, self-loathing, and ambition while outwardly projecting bluster and paternal affection to his men. Or, in a poignant scene, Private Doll (Dash Mihok) reels in stunned despair at having shot a man dead—"worst thing you can do . . . worse than rape"—at the very moment he's boasting of the kill to his comrades. In other cases, a character expresses the ideals that drive them in voiceover, only to have those ideals dashed by circumstances: for example, Private Bell (Ben Chaplin) doting on the image of his wife (Miranda Otto) to anchor himself within war's tumult, even as she's already fallen in love with another man or Private Witt (Jim Caviezel) hoping that he'll face death with the same equanimity that his mother did, which he betrays by pointlessly precipitating his own death when captured by a group of Japanese soldiers.

Among this unusual plurality of voiceovers, the most important one is that of an otherwise minor character, Private Edward P. Train (John Dee Smith), which not only frames the entire film at its beginning and end but serves as a kind of head to the chorus of voices. Diegetically, Train speaks very little in the film: most notably, once early on, confessing his abject fear of battle to Sergeant Welsh (Sean Penn) on the eve of their arrival at Guadalcanal and once near the end, expressing guarded optimism about the future as they're departing it. And strikingly, his voiceovers don't accompany these moments, or even his appearances on-screen. Instead, they speak about the events of the film from a distance. Rather than dwelling on his own private experiences or struggles, Train, like the camera, bears witness to what is unfolding around him but labors to place it in its cosmic context.

That is, many of the other characters see themselves as cosmic outsiders caged within a hostile world. For some, this means they're left with no other recourse than to grapple with the world like some perpetual foe, just in order to survive.[1] Others cling to the prospect of escaping the world's savagery by looking to an otherworldly presence.[2] Despite the opposition between these two kinds of views, they share something crucial in common: the sense that the world, taken on its own, is barren of hope, meaningfulness, divinity—that these can only come from some source that transcends it.

In contrast, Train's voiceovers are led over the course of the film toward a view that is pantheistic in tenor. To begin with, where his fellow soldiers see only local, human struggles—struggles with oneself, struggles with the world, warfare among armies and nations—Train sees a "war in the heart of nature" of which individual and collective human struggles are simply manifestations, a war internal to nature's workings rather than one between a fallen world and some redemptive force beyond it. And he questions it, wondering if the world itself is just a battle between heterogeneous forces. "Why does nature vie with itself, the land contend with the sea?" he asks in the film's first lines. "Is there an avenging power in nature? Not one power, but two?" Often, this questioning is expressed using a Celan-esque ambiguous "you" to address himself and the viewer as much as nature or the divine: "Who's doing this? Who's killing us, robbing us of life and light, mocking us with the sight of what we might have known? Is this darkness in you, too? Have you passed through this night?"

The other character with whom Train's voiceovers are most closely linked is Witt. The film's opening minutes introduce an AWOL Witt leading an idyllic existence among Melanesian natives while Train's voice speaks, thereby forging this link—one so tight, in fact, that these voiceovers are often mistaken for being Witt's. Later, the film makes productive use of the link when Witt offers in voiceover the beginnings of the answer Train himself will end up offering to his own questions: "Maybe all men got one big soul who everybody's a part of. All faces of the same man. One big self. Everyone looking for salvation by himself, each like a coal drawn from the fire." From this viewpoint, the distinctions among individuals melt away, and each character's private struggles can be seen as those of a single, unified humanity. Indeed, it's in light of Witt's realization here that his death becomes all the more tragic. In the final accounting, he's killed due to a sense of opposition to his fellow human being that exceeds all reason. Essentially, he commits suicide, attempting to shoot Japanese soldiers who are clearly begging him to simply surrender.

At the end, then, it's Train who takes up the insight expressed by the now dead Witt and extends it, striving to see in things the answer to his own line of questioning: "Darkness and light, strife and love. Are they the workings of one mind? The features of the same face? Oh, my soul. Let me be in you now. Look out through my eyes. Look out at the things you made. All things shining." In these words, the transindividual human soul is united with the divine, and with nature itself as its expression, its "workings." Train's own soul becomes this single "mind" or "face," not in the sense that he as an individual is the whole of the creative divine but rather in the sense that he along with everything else is just another expression of it. Train's pleas, then, are at once addressed to himself, to us, and to the divine principle of which he's simply one local embodiment. He pleads to see everything—"darkness and light, strife and love"—not as the contention of opposed forces but rather in their divine unity: "all things shining."

In *The New World* we find the same cinematographic preoccupation with extra-human nature, as well as characters contending in voiceover with the human place in the cosmos. The titular "new world" is, of course, what the film's would-be colonizers call the Americas. However, it also marks the guiding question of John Smith's and Pocahontas's voiceovers, which dominate the film—a variation on Train's line of questioning in *The Thin Red Line*. Is finding a "new world"—the realization of one's hopes and ideals, a true haven—a matter of abandoning an old, "fallen" world or of seeing something new, something beautiful and divine, in the world in which one already finds oneself?

Smith's principal flaw lies in his clinging to the former view. He sees in the Americas a pristine, innocent land that can be crafted into such a new world—human society built again from the ground up in a decisive break from the old world's oppression and corruption. Precisely because of his attachment to this image, though, he ultimately fails to embrace Pocahontas's love and his own better self. While he's held captive by the Powhatans, he briefly recognizes that the new world isn't something to be built from scratch but found in the world as it already is. Once he returns to the bickering and squalor of the nascent Jamestown, though, these experiences seem like they'd been nothing more than a dream, and he falls into a despair that is simply the mirror image of his own former idealism, convinced that he can only fail at building a new world because he's inescapably infected with the old world's depravity. In the throes of this despair, he flees from love, thinking himself unworthy of it—just another putrid symptom of the old world's disease.

In contrast, in her voiceovers Pocahontas addresses the world around her as "Mother"—nature in unity with the divine. She longs for contact with this mother: "How shall I seek you? Show me your face." Yet she does so in full confidence that it already suffuses the entirety of the world around her: "You fill the land with your beauty. You reach to the end of the world." For her, the divine is "the great river that never runs dry," immanent in anything and everything. Her spirit is shaken numerous times: when her loyalties are divided between Smith and her father; when Smith departs Virginia without even telling her; when she's deceived, on Smith's instruction, into thinking he's dead; and finally when the Jamestown colonists exile her people from their land. However, none of this shakes her conviction in the all-pervasiveness of the maternal divine. Where Smith sees himself as torn between two worlds, one profane and the other divine, Pocahontas sees a love "unbound by limits," a love "like pain" but no less divine because of it. Where Smith sees only the absence of divinity in the barbarity of his compatriots, she sees her "mother" there as well: "We can enter you, question you," she says to this mother even as her people's villages burn. As with Train, Pocahontas sees "all things shining": the divine unity of nature and of humanity in and with nature. At the end, she feels this unity with particular vividness. "Oh, Mother," she says in the film's final lines. "Now I know where you live." The message is clear: she lives everywhere. The human world, the human viewpoint, with all its strife and division, is just one expression of the divine.

In these ways, Malick's first two post-hiatus films push past humanistic concerns. In both, while the camera endeavors to show us not only the human drama but what lies beyond it, what cannot be reduced to it, the characters struggle between seeing themselves as expressions of the cosmos on the one hand and uncomprehending, vulnerable strangers to it on the other. It's these characteristics that have often inspired critics to call *The Thin Red Line* and *The New World* "existentialist" or "religious" films. They seem to address the question of how to go on in the face of a world that strikes us as "absurd" and/or "fallen" specifically by dramatizing the lives of characters who struggle with such questions. Yet precisely because of this, one might retort that while they're indeed films that tackle cosmic themes, this is only because they're telling the stories of characters who do so, thus highlighting something about the human story, one of its fundamental predicaments—the trials and tribulations of feeling lost in a seemingly indifferent, hostile, or depraved universe. However, in Malick's next film, *The Tree of Life*, we find a decisive turn away from humanistic and toward cosmic storytelling. That is, the film itself, and not just its characters, turns its attention to the whole of the cosmos and attempts to situate human existence as simply one of its manifestations.

Malick Goes to Outer Space

Malick's earlier cinematographic fixations on the nonhuman world seem positively timid in comparison to *The Tree of Life*. The focal character in the film's human story is Jack O'Brien (Sean Penn), whom we see in his jaded middle age in twenty-first-century Houston but also as a child (Hunter McKracken) suffering through growing pains in small-town central Texas in 1956.[3] At the opening, we're presented with this story's defining event: the death of Jack's brother R. L. (Laramie Eppler) in 1968 at nineteen. Then, the film jumps back and forth in time, recounting the grief of their parents (Brad Pitt and Jessica Chastain) in the aftermath of R. L.'s death, its impact on Jack's life decades later, and, most of all, its background in the family's early history, which the film surveys at length from the parents' courtship to their departure from Waco in the 1950s when their sons are still children.

However, Malick notoriously pulls back from this intimate human drama for a substantial portion of the film. After introducing R. L.'s death as well as the various time frames for the O'Briens' story, the film takes a nearly twenty-minute detour into the history of the cosmos. It begins quite literally at the beginning then gradually zooms in on our tiny corner of the universe. We see the birth of the universe, the congealing of gases into stars and planets, and the formation of Earth. Then, major developments in the history of terrestrial life, from its first stirrings in volcanic pools to the evolution of single-celled and then multicellular organisms to the ascendancy of dinosaurs and finally to the K–T extinction event that eliminated most life on Earth sixty-six million years before humans emerged. Then later, near the film's end, there's another sequence depicting Earth's final destiny: the death of the sun and of all terrestrial life with it. Between these two large-scale events, of course, the entire history of humanity unfolds—a blip in the course of universal history. Appropriate to this, the film puts the bulk of its human story between these two cosmic sequences: a blip, so to speak, within a blip, even though it occupies most of the runtime.

What to make of such sequences? They certainly strike some viewers as tiresome—for example, those prone to impatience at anything that "doesn't advance the story." For them, these sequences seem like long, pointless detours. However, the notion that they don't contribute to the story presupposes something about what that story is. For many, it will go without saying that it's the human story—that of Jack O'Brien and his family. But this is exactly the expectation about films and stories in general that *The Tree of Life* ostentatiously defies. That is, it's better understood as a film whose story precisely is the history of the universe, one that dwells, of course, on certain aspects of that story—the role of one young man's death in his family's lives—but the history of the universe nonetheless.

To accept this odd suggestion, though, we must understand this: if the film's scope is really this broad, why would it approach its subject matter with such a striking emphasis on much more discrete, local matters? The first thing to notice is that such emphases are rather common in cosmic stories. We find it, for example, in the most influential piece of cosmic storytelling in the Western tradition: the Bible, which, after briefly recounting the story of creation and of humanity's early history, devotes the vast majority of its pages to the origins and history of the nation of Israel. Of course, one might retort that this emphasis is simply due to the fact that in the world story that the Bible recounts, Israel occupies a central place—the chosen of God and the root from which his universal messiah eventually springs. In contrast, *The Tree of Life* posits no grand world historical role for the O'Briens. By any measure, they're portrayed as an unremarkable family in an unremarkable corner of Earth. However, rather than constituting a real objection to the film's being a cosmic story, this simple fact is instead the key to understanding what kind of cosmic story it is.

The film, in fact, hints from the very start at its ambitions. It begins with an epigraph from Job 38:4–7: "Where were you when I laid the foundations of the earth? . . . When the morning stars sang together and all the sons of God shouted for joy?" This, one of the book's most famous passages, is also the pivot around which its structure revolves. Job, a man who's suffered ultimate loss, has been pleading to be told, by anyone who'll listen, why he's been subjected to such torment. The only answer, though, that those around him have to offer is that he's being punished for some unknown sin—the sentence of divine justice. Deeply unsatisfied by this, he longs to "return to the days when God was my guardian" and finally demands for God himself to "state his case before me."[4] When a voice comes from out of a whirlwind to respond, though, it offers no justifications. Instead, it continues in the vein of the above passage, taken from the speech's opening. It speaks of nature's dazzling wonders—as if by demanding that his life be justified by the order of nature, Job is asking the wrong questions about that order.

The wrong questions in what sense, though? Of course, one traditional religious reading is that there is indeed a cosmic order of the kind Job seeks—one in the context of which his suffering is just—but that it's neither his place to question it nor within his power to grasp it. However, there's no hint of such an order in the whirlwind speech itself. The notion that there is such an order is based on a reading that situates the book in an overall interpretation of the unique compilation of disparate texts we call the Bible. The whirlwind speech, taken on its own, never claims that a providential order renders Job's suffering just: it doesn't address the details of Job's life at all and chastises Job's friends for having offered that answer. Instead, it speaks of the world at large, sparking, through a series of questions about it, Job's recognition of the depths of his own failure to understand it.

In terms of the present themes, Job is a kind of ur-humanist. His folly doesn't lie in his agonizing grief. Who could blame him for this? Instead, it lies in his conviction, presupposed in his expression of this grief, that the world is the stage on which his existence unfolds, and thus it must be ordered in the service of making sense of that existence. Because of this conviction, Job can't understand what story he's in, so to speak. The universe seems senseless because it doesn't offer him the sense he seeks, so he demands clarification from the divine storyteller—creation's author. When the whirlwind responds, though, it undermines his entire viewpoint on the world around him. It speaks of the violence, power, and awesomeness of nature, not to defend it but to highlight repeatedly not only that Job doesn't comprehend it but also that it isn't about him—about us—at all. In doing so, the whirlwind reorients him away from a humanistic and toward a cosmic perspective. At the end, he realizes that he isn't in *his* story, not fundamentally. He isn't the main character even in his own life, but rather he is one element in the story of the cosmos.

The Tree of Life stages a similar confrontation between humanistic and cosmic perspectives. However, rather than doing so from within the viewpoints of its characters, it stages this confrontation primarily for the viewer. In each of the three time frames for the O'Briens' story, we find characters who, like Job, try to comprehend the world in human terms, asking why it treats us as it does. Upon R. L.'s death in 1968, Mrs. O'Brien asks those around her why this happened and finds their conventional platitudes hollow and contemptible. Longing for death in order to be with her son, she demands of God, or perhaps the world itself: "What did you gain?" and "Was I false to you?"[6] Twelve years earlier, young Jack raises similar questions, disturbed by a child's drowning death and other glimpses of human frailty as well as by his own childhood travails: a father who lashes out from bitterness and anger and the stirrings of the same tendencies in himself. And again, in the 2000s, the adult Jack is a successful architect who nevertheless walks dejectedly through his luxurious life, feeling like he's "just bumping into walls," still dwelling on his brother's death and on how the "world's gone to the dogs . . . people are greedy, keep getting worse."

The film's cosmic sequences serve as a response to such questioning and bafflement. However, this response is not, as in *The Thin Red Line* and *The New World*, delivered by a character. Nor, indeed, is there even any explicit indication that it's for any character's benefit: none of them encounters a voice from a whirlwind or anywhere else or explicitly responds to these sequences. Rather, the status of cosmic sequences as a response is suggested exclusively through montage. Thus, it's us as viewers to whom they're directed much more than any of the characters. In other words, the film itself shifts registers and takes up a cosmic perspective, hence the tendency for these sequences to seem like narrative ruptures. For audiences whose sensibilities are trained to expect all stories to be character stories, and who think of the cosmic perspective as the province of science rather than art, the film seems to puts its story on pause for a time and morph into something like a nature documentary. However, instead of serving to convey scientific knowledge, *The Tree of Life*'s cosmic sequences are exercises in world portraiture, dragging viewers out of their default humanistic stance toward storytelling and casting its character's stories as subplots in a grander narrative.

What narrative, though? What world story is the film trying to tell? We see planets and living things brought into being, existing, destroying, and destroyed; we see animals living, suffering, and dying, consuming others but also giving them reprieve. In other words, these sequences weave the history of human living, suffering, violence, and grace into a universal history replete with the same things, a story in which the O'Briens' lives—and by extension, ours—are just a few among the many threads. Like the whirlwind speech in Job, they offer not so much an answer to the characters' questions but a challenge to their asking of such questions at all—to the narcissism of demanding for the world's story to simply be ours, to have an order dictated by human concerns.

Now, such a response can of course seem deeply unsatisfying. What troubles the film's characters, again like Job, is what's traditionally called the problem of evil. This problem is often posed in theistic terms, but the heart of it lies in this simple question: Why does the world contain evil? By dismissing the posing of this problem, it might be thought, one dismisses the significance of suffering itself. However, the question is asked in a very specific spirit. It doesn't seek just any old explanation for evil. Causal explanations, for example, don't answer it, and this is because it seeks justifications. In other words, implicit in it is a specific demand: for the world to be ordered like a legal case, prepackaged to appease us as the case's judges.

But one of the central themes in *The Tree of Life*, just like in its precursor in the book of Job, is that taking suffering seriously requires making no such demand. The characters who do so are obviously lost—lost in anxious self-involvement. We feel for their suffering and the suffering of others that prompts it, and no less so because that suffering leads them astray. However, the film challenges us to escape this very human form of lostness: the tendency to cry out to God, the gods, or nature itself and narcissistically ask, "Why us, why me?" It challenges us, that is, to seek and to tell cosmic stories without attempting to see the world as designed to satisfy human longings and concerns.

What could such stories be, though? How do we see the world as one whose story is meaningful without seeing it as simply the stage for our lives? What could this story's themes even be if we don't insist that they be driven by our local concerns? The film offers no easy answers: its cosmic sequences are mute, without handholding narration, merely showing us nature as it was and is. In taking such a cosmic perspective, it can strike many viewers as backward because it breaks from the current humanistic consensus. However, in depriving us of any easy answers about what such a break can mean, it is absolutely contemporary. It opens a door to world beyond humanism but doesn't attempt to dictate to us any list of directions for where to go once we exit it.

Conclusion

As I've told the tale, *The Tree of Life* represents a culmination of tendencies implicit in Malick's earlier work—specifically, his distinctive embrace of cosmic concerns. His next four films contain the traces of that film's dramatic change of perspective. In *Voyage of Time*, for example, we find an entire feature-length film made in the mode of *The Tree of Life*'s cosmic sequences: something akin to a hybrid nature and anthropological documentary but with a dramatic arc structured by a rhythm of existential and philosophical questions about the world as a whole rather than by any drive to informativeness, let alone any character stories. In the three narrative films he made after *The Tree of Life*—*To the Wonder*, *Knight of Cups*, and *Song to Song*—we find films again focused on character stories. However, they're crafted almost entirely out of the kinds of footage typically reserved for establishing shots, rapid montages, and scene transitions, and auditorily they are suffused by murmured voiceovers that are often given equal weight with environmental sounds, as if Malick were intent on finding a way to withdraw from the usual narrative dynamics of human drama and embed the characters' actions and thoughts in the teeming flow of worldly events in which human dramas are just eddies. With *A Hidden Life* (2019), Malick returned to more conventional—albeit masterful—narrative film. However he proceeds from this point, *The Tree of Life* represents a benchmark in an already remarkable body of work—one that taps into premodern, cosmic sensibilities in a distinctively contemporary way.

Notes

1. For example, while relieving Captain Staros (Elias Koteas) of his command, Tall seemingly out of nowhere muses, "Look at those vines, the way they twine around the trees, swallowing everything. Nature's cruel, Staros." This is as if to claim that his self-serving and craven punishment of Staros is simply an act of nature: Tall taking advantage of its cruelty to his own ends. Or we have Welsh's ongoing dialogue with Witt (Jim Caviezel), in which the former expresses his sense of needing to shield himself from a world in which everyone is inescapably trapped. For example, near the end of the film, the words of his new commander

Captain Bosche (George Clooney) inspire utter contempt in Welsh: "Everything a lie. Everything you hear, everything you see. So much to spew out. They just keep coming, one after another. You're in a box, a moving box. They want you dead, or in their lie. Only one thing a man can do: find something that's his; make an island for himself."

2. For example, we have Staros's pleas to God in prayer on the eve of battle: "Are you here? Let me not betray you. Let me not betray my men. In you I place my trust." And there are Bell's visions of his wife, Marty, idealized as a kind of angelic figure, and his vow not to taint the almost monastic purity of his relationship with her by so much as speaking to another woman.

3. Precise dates are not given in the film. These years are based on the original screenplay (from which, it should be noted, the final film departs considerably). Compare Malick, *The Tree of Life*, 1.

4. Mitchell, ed., *The Book of Job*, 69, 75.

5. Although these words seem explicitly directed toward God, in the original screenplay Mrs. O'Brien's questioning is suggested to be directed to nature as much as toward God: "Where is God? Where was he then? Nature gives no answer, whispers not a word." Malick, *The Tree of Life*, 3.

Bibliography

Malick, Terrence. *The Tree of Life*. Unpublished film script. 2007. https://indiegroundfilms.wordpress.com. Accessed October 6, 2019.

Mitchell, Stephen, ed. *The Book of Job*. New York: Harper Collins, 1987.

Chapter 3

"Why Should I Be Good If You Aren't?"
The Problem of the Moral World in *The Tree of Life*

JAMES D. REID AND CANDACE R. CRAIG

Terrence Malick's films have an uncanny ability to make things appear, to draw our attention to things as they show up, in light and in darkness (at times to draw our attention to the very light itself within which the things of this world shine), and to illuminate moments of joy and affirmation and episodes of despair, distraction, or grief. His films do not merely make isolated things apparent (films are always revealing things in some sense, within the space of the medium), but they make the viewer aware of the importance of their *being* apparent and probe their relation to an elusive whole within which they obscurely, elusively find themselves placed—a whole at times natural, at times cultural and political—and in a way that makes the relationship between the cultural, the political, or the social and the natural a problem. And they make this larger context apparent even when it appears lacking for one or more of his often-disoriented characters. His work seems to gesture toward and somehow to reveal the larger world(s) within which whatever action can be discerned within his loosely plotted narratives needs to be set, sometimes at the expense of the individuals whose lives his films are ostensibly portraying. And this seems, not without reason, to place his work in relation to the philosophical achievement of Martin Heidegger, who made the world and what he called our "being-in-the-world" central problems for philosophy.[1]

But Malick's cinematic interest in the problem of world, a staple in the philosophical literature devoted to his films, is often conflated with a related but distinct ambition to create a "Heideggerian cinema." The reasons for this, tethered to Malick's intellectual biography, have been repeated so often that it would be tiresome to rehearse them in detail here (e.g., Malick's studies with Cavell at Harvard; a planned dissertation on the concept of world in Kierkegaard, Heidegger, and Wittgenstein at Oxford; a teaching stint at MIT; a translation of Heidegger's *Vom Wesen des Grundes*), all of which invite the philosophically informed critic to see Malick's turn to cinema as a case of pursuing philosophical questions by other means, to present Heideggerian perspectives on the nature of the world in the medium of film.[2]

Malick's films do appear to reflect Heideggerian concerns about the world in a way that might be described as broadly phenomenological, and we try to do some justice to the Heideggerian dimension of *The Tree of Life* in this chapter. Malick's unconventional techniques—the frequent use of meditative voiceover, gesturing toward overarching interpretation and questioning, the long shots of a nature apparently indifferent to human concern, the unusual employment of music[3]—can be seen as efforts to make visible the troubled context of significance that Heidegger calls "world" and to remind us that whatever action his films might be said to reveal needs to be situated in the larger, more elusive spaces of meaning that envelop and often eclipse the words and deeds of their characters.

But if Malick's films explore such heady philosophical questions, it is not always clear what we gain by thinking about the problems they address along exclusively Heideggerian lines.[4] There are characteristics of his work, from *The Thin Red Line* to *A Hidden Life*, that fail to show up within a narrowly Heideggerian framework, aspects that we have come to think can only be adequately addressed along distinctively moral lines without sustained parallel in Heidegger's ontological musings. And there are reasons to think that with *The Tree of Life* Malick is expressing on film a quiet farewell to the figure who dominated the academic pursuits of his youth, a gesture that looks even more like an official break in *A Hidden Life*, which outlines a moral road not taken by the fundamental ontologist and Nazi sympathizer during the National Socialist Revolution.[5] At the very least, Malick is making certain sorts of moral experience central to an account of what the world can be said to be. Moral concerns are not marginal or arbitrary features of the world(s) we inhabit and that Malick's films tirelessly explore, but open onto fundamental features of whatever meaning the world might be said to have.[6]

What we hope to show in what follows, then, is that *The Tree of Life* is not merely about the world in some general ontological sense (although it is this too), but a sustained exploration of certain problems of the *moral* world that Heidegger too often failed to take seriously enough. Malick's fifth feature-length film is a careful study of the formation and the fragility of a moral vision of the universe threatened by death (which is no mere occasion to become authentic, on one reading of Heidegger's account of our relation to death) and the experience of unjustified suffering (not my own death and my own suffering but the deaths and sufferings of others), and one that challenges us to think about the sources of moral commitment, the experiences that undermine our faith in a moral worldview, and the possibility of regaining lost confidence in our moral vocation and a devotion to communities of ethical concern. *The Tree of Life* may not be an example of anti-Heideggerian cinema, but it addresses issues to which Heidegger was notoriously blind.[7]

The Tree of Life opens with an epigraph drawn from the book of Job (38:4, 7), not read in voiceover but presented as text: "Where were you when I laid the foundations of the earth? . . . When the morning stars sang together, and all the sons of God shouted for joy?" Why does the film begin in this way? What has Malick omitted? His decision invites us to reread the book of Job in view of what the quotation both elides and implies about the importance of the biblical response to the problem of suffering.[8]

The passage comes near the end of the biblical text: nothing of Job's misery enters the passage (the sufferings of the O'Brien family will serve the film's purpose), the long discussion between Job and his friends is passed over, and most of the Lord's badgering insistence upon Job's ignorance is ignored. Gone is the Lord's rather irritating enumeration of everything Job does not understand (*The Tree of Life* is a film about the pursuit of knowledge and understanding, in our view). Gone is Job's self-loathing repentance ("Behold, I am vile" in 40:4, "I abhor *myself*, and repent in dust and ashes" in 42:6), perhaps signaling that self-abasement before a superior power is unsatisfying. And gone, too, is Job's reward in 42:10 ("also the Lord gave Job twice as much as he had before"), as if to deny an interpretation of human existence built on an easy scheme of punishment and reward. What remains are two questions that the film will pursue throughout, questions concerning the origin of all things and the prospect of joy that some form of understanding might bring, inviting us to read what follows as a revision of the book of Job, with the O'Brien family taking the place of the biblical figure and his family, with discussions on the meaning of the death of R. L. (Laramie Eppler) replacing the long conversations between Job and his three friends that occupy much of the biblical account, and the culminating vision of Jack's reconciling affirmation of his life in this world as a moral agent serving as a substitute for Job's material reward.[9]

A more conventional filmmaker might have gone straight to the creation sequence and told a more straightforward tale of how we get from the beginning of things to the present, before introducing us to the O'Brien family and their conflicts and experiences. *The Tree of Life* famously subverts conventional narrative form. Instead, Malick gives us compressed, decontextualized scenes of grief and a glimpse of Jack (Sean Penn) in present-day Houston, preceded by images of a young Mrs. O'Brien (Jessica Chastain) followed by slices of the O'Brien family's life with voiceover (Mrs. O'Brien's) on the ways of nature and grace, itself an answer that appears to echo Job: the nuns who instructed her "taught us that no one who loves the way of grace ever comes to a bad end." And all of this is accompanied by the sounds of John Tavener's "Funeral Canticle," presaging the theme of mortality and sustained briefly into the announcement of R. L.'s death. The creation account comes, then, only after the human stakes of revisiting questions about the origin of the world have been announced.

The creation sequence, which we discuss at some length below, brings us back to the O'Briens and into Waco, Texas, in the 1950s with an image of a snake slithering through the water. So begins the human story, from the beginning this time around. If Job opens the film, setting out the stakes, if the creation sequence rewrites the account in Genesis in scientific guise, the beginnings of family life echo visions of the fall from Eden. Some of the earliest images have an almost mythical quality, as if we are glimpsing life in a primordial garden. We see a woman and children dressed in white. We are shown an open book on a table, its pages blank, a *tabula rasa* upon which the lines of human experience and suffering have yet to be written. A child is shown swimming up toward a door in a house underwater, an image of our aqueous beginnings. The first question we should ask is, What does a coming-of-age story set in Texas in the 1950s have to do with larger philosophical questions about the nature of the world?

On one level (palpably Heideggerian), Malick is depicting a specific, richly particularized world of human experience, perhaps with the ambition of drawing attention to the facticity of the things his characters encounter—*this* house, *this* dining room, *this* moment on Halloween or the Fourth of July, a family dinner accompanied by the sounds of Brahms (and a specific recording of the final movement of Symphony no. 4), an obscure image in an attic with a giant that combines recollection with fantasy— an image that evokes the possibility that other, more mysterious beings loom in the secret recesses of an otherwise canny home. A comparatively unique universe of middle-class life in America toward the middle of the last century is opening up to the viewer. (We only learn where the film is set by fleeting glimpses of place-names on automobiles.) On this plane, the major arc of the film looks like a record, perhaps a celebration of the contingencies that define its characters and the world they inhabit, and a celebration that film is uniquely able to capture—the fragmented nature of our earliest experiences and the fragments that form our recollections of earliest childhood. Balls rolling without cause or reason, an empty chair sliding across the floor, a mother floating above the earth.

Malick's vignettes, however, also have a typical character (also still consistent with Heidegger's thought). The film's scenes disclose the general *kinds* of experiences that *one* might pass through, a reflection of general truths about childhood and the world of human engagement within the particular contexts on display throughout *The Tree of Life*. In this respect, the film confronts us with a series of isolated but exemplary experiences—learning what things are to be called (crocodile, kangaroo, etc., or what the young Jack [Hunter McCracken] calls "original words"), being told where God lives (in the sky, for Mrs. O'Brien), coming to recognize ourselves in a mirror ("Me," the young Jack at one point declares). There are efforts to shield the young from less pleasant facts about the world. There are stories read before bed. There are visions of the natural background of life—suns setting over paradigmatic childhood activity, rivers in which children play, trees to climb, forests to wander in—and depictions of things in nature that require assistance to flourish, the trees and grasses that must be watered, the gardens that need weeding. Voyages into the unknown happen under the sheets at night, with flashlights and dreams of outer space. And all of this raises questions about what it is like, and what it might mean, to be cast into a world of parents and siblings, grandparents, friends, neighbors, and strangers, to become a member of *this particular* community. It is an archetypal account of one's coming to learn what the world is and a reminder that, at a certain stage in human development, we have no original or originating world but this—the stuff of childhood, in all its density, shown when things really seemed to matter, before they began to settle into routines that blunt our capacity to care.

All of this is philosophically important, especially in relation to the Creation arc that, as we noted above, serves as a prelude to the fuller human story. Although Malick nods toward Freudian theory (Jack appears to suffer from an Oedipal complex), there are lessons that transcend the merely psychological dimension of analysis, gesturing toward how we ought to think about the very world itself. The world is not, or at least not only, what shows up within the context of natural scientific inquiry (a point Malick could have learned from early Heidegger, too). The universe of population III stars, nebulae, and galaxies is not more real than the world of dinner tables and music, nightlights and bedtime rituals, spelling tests and swimming pools, slamming screen doors, and nature itself as the beauty of a sunset or the cooling element of water on a hot summer afternoon. More fundamentally, we don't have access to the world of scientific objectivity if we haven't been initiated into a world of human interests and concerns. Among the principal achievements of our introduction to the world is the growth of care in relation to things we are encouraged to consider to be worthy of our concern. We learn throughout childhood what kinds of things (and persons) there are and what sorts of claims they make on us.

The viewer does not have to work very hard to make sense of any of this. All that is required is a capacity to place such episodes within a narrative framework. But Malick's ability to capture the abundance of childhood and its initiating power is astonishing, and this feature of the film surely accounts for some of the first appreciative reviews of it, prompting the late Roger Ebert to write, in his last review shortly before his death, "I don't know when a film has connected more immediately with my own personal experience. In uncanny ways, the central events of *The Tree of Life* reflect a time and place I lived in, and the boys in it are me. If I set out to make an autobiographical film, and if I had Malick's gift, it would look so much like this."

What could degenerate into sentimentality, however, is saved by the moral seriousness of Malick's exploration of childhood. *The Tree of Life* is also a probing study of the nature, formation, and possible conditions of a fragile *moral* worldview. The film's longest arc does not merely explore the reasons enabling us to affirm our lives in a world of loss or to probe the conditions of our capacity for belief in it.[10] There are lots of potential answers to that question—the pull of the aesthetic, for example, is clearly present in the film (the "life is beautiful" motif). The film also wrestles pervasively with the conditions of being able to assent to a world of moral responsibility in spaces of meaning we share with those who have claims upon us. Suffering and death are figured throughout as distinctively moral problems in a register far more Kantian than Heideggerian.[11]

The film asks: What must we believe about the world (or, more deeply, how must the world reveal itself, beyond what we explicitly think or believe) for certain moral commitments to be possible and sustained, despite pressures that tempt us to a life "beyond good and evil"? This is not a question for moral psychology alone but about how the world itself shows up as a context of fragile moral norms. The moral life requires enabling conditions of its realization in concrete human existence, in a struggle against forces that breed cynicism. And the threat of moral nihilism is real: morality might prove a lie (the Nietzschean thread, anticipated by Thrasymachus in Plato's *Republic*) imposed upon us by those in power to keep us in line.

On a prevalent view of what morality requires (call it Kantian), our initiation into the moral world is inseparable from our becoming aware of a peculiar fact about us. It requires the dawning of an awareness that does not merely add another object to an expanding list of objects in the universe but places what exists (all of it, the very universe itself) in a distinctive light. When it comes, a certain space of possibility is revealed, or a way of standing toward the possible. The moral life demands, in short, an experience and an acknowledgment of our finite freedom, a lesson that Malick shows Jack learning throughout the family romance.

Certain episodes, words, and lessons that the viewer is likely to find morally salient cannot be said to be true for Jack at a certain stage in his development—his mother's firm "No" as two-year-old Jack (Finnegan Williams) is about to throw a toy at her and the infant R. L. (John Howell), the instruction from his father (Brad Pitt) on property and the invisible boundaries that shouldn't be crossed, a similar lesson in limits to be respected supplied by a reading of *Peter Rabbit*. The world innocent Jack encounters is full of boundaries from the start, but something needs to happen before his relation to them becomes morally relevant for him. Before this occurs, Jack is like Malick's cleverly-filmed rabbit moving innocently through the O'Brien family's vegetable garden. Sometimes, at an early stage of his moral formation, Jack responds to a barrier reactively, recoiling as if from an obstacle brutely encountered in the world.

Nor is the bare awareness of important differences between good and bad behavior enough. Young Jack's first voiceover—"Mother. Make me good"—betrays a confusion about *how* one becomes good, one repeated at a slightly more advanced level when he prays for help in the work of becoming and being good. The advance from wanting to be *made* good to wanting help in *doing* good is a subtle but important shift toward a stronger sense of moral responsibility, but it still lacks a fuller sense of self-ascription.

The proper world of morality reveals itself to Jack only when he takes himself to be an agent. It is not easy to depict this dawning in film, although the use of voiceover in combination with the representation of action surely helps. The pivotal moments come in consecutive chapters of *The Tree of Life* called (in the Criterion edition) "Experiments" and "Mrs. Kimball" (Savannah Welch), the first of which shows Jack making mischief with several boys in the neighborhood but in a way marked by hesitancy (an awareness, perhaps, that what's about to happen depends upon what he decides to do), and the second of which depicts a deepening awareness of the power to cross boundaries marked by both shame and a consciousness of the power of freedom to set things in motion. It is easy to moralize against throwing stones through windows or sending frogs into the sky hitched to a bottle rocket. But Malick refuses to turn these scenes into fodder for complacent condemnation. There are, as young Jack himself asserts, things we need to learn, things that can only be known

"Why Should I Be Good If You Aren't?" | 71

when we look, when we observe the transformations introduced into the world on our own initiative. The life of discovery is itself an embodiment of our freedom.

After stealing a garment from Mrs. Kimball's bedroom and discarding it in the river, Jack asks in voiceover: "What have I started? What have I done?" The real world of moral struggle has begun, including the prospect of angry defiance ("I'm gonna do what I want," he informs his mother), explicit betrayals of trust, and deepening anguish over choices made (in voiceover, "What I want to do I can't. I do what I hate"). The moral "I" has entered the landscape of Jack's behavior, transforming his world, or his sense of and orientation toward the world, and reflected in an important linguistic shift from the passive "me" in Jack's earlier pleas to the "I" of responsible agency.

There is another dimension of the overarching moral theme central to Malick's story, also of Kantian provenance, perhaps mediated by *The Brothers Karamazov* in the figure of Ivan.[12] Jack's discovery of his own agency and his entry into the moral universe are tied to the revelation of certain characteristics of the world that raise questions about the very place of morality in the order of events and the role of religious belief in moral commitment itself. This is arguably the central (religious, moral) theme of the film, crystallized in the death of R. L. but brought into focus in several key episodes within the family romance. If this is a movie about the coming-to-be of agency, it is also a film about the limits of what we can do and being haunted by the specter of a divine agent who is either indifferent or worse. There is something unsettling in the discovery of the terrible power of freedom itself. At least as unsettling is the discovery that, in the overall scheme and order of things, it may not really matter. The death of R. L. is set into a scene even more potentially shattering, occasioning the loss of trust in the value of the very world where moral agency finds itself thrown, prompting the question, "Why be moral?"

Middle-aged Jack traces his own break with God to adolescence, during a time when he registers unexplained or undeserved suffering—a young man with conspicuous physical deformities, a mangy dog, a three-legged dog, and the spectral eyes of an abject prisoner (Christopher Ryan). After Jack and his brothers endure Mr. O'Brien's guided tour of wealthy white neighborhoods and his success stories of the men who inhabit them, they travel to the poor end of town to buy BBQ brisket. Here, Jack scans the impoverished surroundings with a look of awed pity. Suffering is everywhere, and his father's advice seems to capture a worry about the moral universe: "You can't be too good" or people will take advantage of you. If Jack had another voiceover here, it might have asked, "Were they too good?" But it is not until after the drowning of the boy (Tyler Thomas) at the pool that Jack wonders, "Was he bad?" and directly questions the notion of a divine protector: "Where were you? You let a boy die. You'll let anything happen." Only his father comes to the rescue, a man of fierce will and action who attempts almost divinely to breathe new life into the boy's lungs. It is no accident that Malick's musical choice for this scene is Mahler's "Titan," which accompanies a low angle shot of Mr. O'Brien rising to the occasion like a demigod. But even Mr. O'Brien's most robust efforts are not enough, and the community is abandoned to mourn a life cut unspeakably short. Jack's mind wanders to other misfortunes in his circle, a house devoured by fire, the permanent burn scars on the back of a friend's head, a truck emitting clouds of DDT, and a flock of ebullient children rushing blindly into its billows. Jack submits his fiercest challenge to God in this context: "Why should I be good if you aren't?"

༄

Jack's question could also be addressing his father, whom he takes to be a hypocrite, revealing the close connection between moral norms and their embodiment in parental paradigms and reminding us of the opening contrast between the ways of nature and grace, encouraging us to read the two chief figures in Jack's moral education in its light.

There are Mr. O'Brien's lessons in discipline and self-control, but they come from someone whose vision of worldly success lives at the expense of moral conscientiousness. And there is a compelling moral orientation represented by Mrs. O'Brien, but one that Jack has come to associate with vulnerability, possibly with despair. The chief question confronted by the young Jack concerns which of these two ways of life is better or whether some combination of the two is more suitable.

The differences between the two figures are visible (and audible) throughout and stand at the center of most commentaries on the film, with Jack's mother often taken to be the moral hero of the tale, understandably. Mrs. O'Brien shields two-year-old Jack from disturbing facts about the world, protects her boys from enduring harm, is more playful and spontaneous, and is more responsive to what the world has to offer than her husband. Her moral lessons are delivered in the reading of bedtime stories, a more imaginative and compelling approach to childhood education than Mr. O'Brien's authoritarian commands, which are there to be obeyed without question.[13] (His table-talk reminds us of God's response to Job.) In a pivotal scene, accompanied by the sounds of Kancheli's "Morning Prayers," the boys see her giving a prisoner water to drink, a paradigmatic act that shows her capable of caring for the heartsick and the poor. She can be firm, but she is almost always revealed to be loving and forgiving, lessons especially relevant to Jack's accumulating evidence that the innocent and the outcast are unprotected by the alleged divinity that fashioned our world, sees all things, and shapes our ends.

Mr. O'Brien's combative approach to a world that "lives by trickery" is more consistent with a vision of the will imposing itself upon a world in which, in his own words, "you can't be too good" if you want to succeed. His is a world of self-made individuals, some of whom succeed and others who get taken advantage of by those less troubled by moral scruples, a world in which "You make yourself what you are. You have control over your own destiny," and such biblical advice as "Turn the other cheek" is silly. Instead, you should strike at your opponent when he least expects it (*vide* his sparring advice to his children). Always suspicious, he pits himself against his sons, whose clumsy, fumbling utterances appear to him as acts of defiance. A flickering gardening scene encapsulates Mr. O'Brien's approach to the world and its fundamental importance: "Got to get it by the root."

But against easy moralizing dichotomies, Mr. O'Brien's controlling hands, the very organs of his will, are also shown playing Bach on the organ and Mozart on the piano, indications of the facile nature of a philosophy of letting go that some might associate with his wife. (The role of hands throughout cannot be overestimated, hands that grip in an effort to control, hands that point and gesture toward higher things, hands running under water, hands christening the newborn and placed on the infirm, hands that paint and play guitar, hands of surrender.) His parable over the grill on Toscanini, who once recorded a piece sixty-five times and still proclaimed, "It could be better," isn't misguided. If nothing great is achieved without passion, nothing great is accomplished without discipline. We have it on Nietzsche's authority that the realization of essential things on earth requires obedience: "this always brings and has brought about something that makes life on earth worth living—for instance: virtue, art, music, dance, reason, intellect—something that transfigures, something refined, fantastic, and divine."[14] Whatever limits viewers are likely to see in Mr. O'Brien's vision of authority, self-discipline, and self-command, including the importance of gaining control over the natural world itself, it has its serious philosophical proponents. He's in good intellectual company among defenders of the will and suspicions facing passivity and emotional responsiveness to the world throughout the Western intellectual tradition. And the watery element of a fluctuating reality that Mrs. O'Brien appears to embody is also the threatening force that Mr. O'Brien alone tries to avert.

Of course, such mixed messages cause Jack to wrestle with himself, although he is not wrong to admit that he resembles his father more than his mother. In a pregnant exception, which anticipates the vision of a deeper, more encompassing community with which the film comes (close to) an end, we see Jack place his hand tenderly on the boy burned in the house fire. It arrives shortly after R. L. has forgiven him for betraying his trust, prompting the young Jack to muse (in voiceover): "What was it you showed me? I didn't know how to name you then. But I see it was you. Always you were calling me." Who calls? God? His brother? It could just as well be the spirit of love, compassion, and forgiveness.

Middle-aged Jack nonetheless more consistently resembles his father in earlier scenes, moving through rigid, sterile environments. Both men are steely, like the structures within which they've grown accustomed to moving. Jack seems to have become the type of man his father taught him from early on to revere, a great outward success rooted in stubborn individuality, perhaps tempered by a commitment to the importance of providing for that small community within the larger community that we call the family. And this internalization is clearly unsatisfying to the elder Jack, whose emptiness in adult life appears to set the entire recollection of childhood in motion.

But Mrs. O'Brien's voiceover reveals a neatly compartmentalized spiritual view of the ways of nature and grace, which insists that those who live by the latter never come to a bad end and concludes with a solemn promise to God (all to the sounds of Tavener's "Funeral Canticle"): "I will be true to you. Whatever comes." But it comes, of course, in the form of a telegram. Her promise is tested by the unexpected death of R. L., and there is evidence that she died still grieving for her dead son, disoriented and disengaged.[15] (The introduction of Nietzsche in this context raises questions about the willfulness of submission, the vanity of humility, and the egotism of a moral commitment that expects to be well paid—all of which places Mrs. O'Brien in a less flattering if more natural light.)

In any event, Malick unsettles any easy identification of one character with the central voice or moral example of the whole, a whole that always remains elusive.[16] Although Mr. O'Brien appears to have a change of heart toward the end, it is worth reminding ourselves that appreciating the glory of what surrounds us doesn't support a family. And his subsequent success, revealed by a spacious, finely furnished, window-walled house in the late 1960s, suggests that his willful resilience has paid off in some sense after all, if only financially. The search for an authorial voice in Malick's films ignores his commitment to what Hannah Arendt called the condition of *plurality*, which assumes an almost metaphysical importance in Malick's work, as if to say that the diversity of perspectives is part and parcel of what the world itself is and shows. And both figures could be said to possess visions that lead to nihilism—passive on the part of Mrs. O'Brien, active on the part of her husband.

On this view, no moral hero of the story clearly emerges. There are only three voiceover speakers throughout this narrative arc: father, mother, and son, the former two of which "wrestle inside" the last. This line, which occurs late, is arguably central to the entire childhood narrative. What Malick gives us are not tidy moral conclusions but scenes of moral instruction, some in the form of words (chiefly Mr. O'Brien's), others in the shape of deeds. The tidy distinction between the two ways is precisely what this stretch of the film appears to question. It is hardly a statement of thesis, which the remainder of what we see is somehow meant to confirm. Like the passage from Job, the two ways play an investigative role, not a position we should take to be normative for what follows. What looks like a declaration quickly becomes a question, and a question that the film refuses to answer directly. As the car rolls away from the house in Waco, we wonder what vision of the moral life Jack will go on to embrace. And despite the powerful words of Mrs. O'Brien (in voiceover, her last before Eternity)—"The only way to be happy is to love. Unless you love, your life will flash by. Do good to them. Wonder. Hope."—the film doesn't allow us to settle on her vision.

Jack's questions facing suffering and loss, his parents' competing visions of the good, and the potential emptiness of modern life are not merely local worries but open onto ultimate questions about the beginnings of things. The stakes of the film are not merely psychological but tend toward what we might call metaphysical musings. How do our local, particular concerns fare in light of our perspectives on first and last things and everything in between? In one of his boldest moves, as we noted previously, Malick's longstanding preoccupation with the problem of getting things started, clearly on display in *The New World* but also central to the more Kierkegaardian tale of the aesthetic life in *Knight of Cups*, takes shape as a creation story that throws us back to the very beginnings of time itself, prompting us to ask about its bearings on the moral themes in play throughout the more human-centered stretches of the story.

The creation sequence comes right after we see Mrs. O'Brien walking through the woods in silent lamentation over the death of R. L., looking skyward toward the place she associates later in the film (but earlier in the film's timeline) with God's home. The sky is notably cloudy. The divine radiance has fled. She closes her eyes, and we cut to black. As if to remind us of the context of grief that brings us to this visual history of time, we hear Mrs. O'Brien (in voiceover), after an artistic play of light (a Lumia) reappears, "Lord. Why? Where were you?"[17] We are thrown back to the biblical text with which *The Tree of Life* opens, as Mrs. O'Brien asks the Lord the very question He had put to Job, as if the vision we are about to see is meant both to answer the Lord and to provide the human drama to come with a context no smaller than the cosmos as a whole. But her second question ("Where were you?") sounds only after the Lumia has vanished, implying that God is unlikely to make an appearance in what follows, at least not the biblical being who speaks to his creatures out of the whirlwind.

It isn't obvious that the vision of beginnings answers Mrs. O'Brien's questions. It would be disappointing if it did. There is no hand of God fashioning the universe or dividing the waters, no commanding voice decreeing "Let there be . . . ," no mighty spirit hovering over the face of the deep. The *why* itself is wonderfully multivalent, a large, searching question that carries us beyond any simple search for causes. Mrs. O'Brien could be asking, "Why did you allow my son to die?" But the question could also be taken in a vaster, more metaphysical direction, echoing

Leibniz: Why does anything exist at all? If we probe the scenes in search of reasons, we are likely to be disappointed. Regarding the deaths of those we love, no answer is offered; we are given nothing more than further examples of destructiveness woven into the foundations of things. There is movement from the simpler to the more complex, but this is a far cry from the sort of teleological explanation of the development of galaxies, solar systems, and living beings that the *why* in some theological and philosophical settings seems to be seeking.

And yet, this is no scientific documentary on the history of the universe either. It both frames and is framed by the human context of the family, set in motion by the experience of grief and saturated with the tokens of human cares and concerns. The bulk of what Dan Glass calls the "astrophysical domain" (from the first appearance of light to the formation of our solar system) unfolds to the sounds of Preisner's "Lacrimosa." This story of beginning is interwoven with the human voice (we hear the hushed words of both Mrs. O'Brien and Jack at crucial moments) and musical accompaniments redolent of death (John Tavener's "Resurrection in Hades" and Berlioz's *Requiem*, as well as the Preisner), reminders that our interest in origins, even in its scientific shape, is anchored in care and responsive to human needs. Even scientific accounts of the genesis of the cosmos have a narrative structure. At the very least, the creation arc supplies natural conditions for the things we find valuable. If this stretch of the film is meant to justify anything, it appears to be neither God nor the universe but our own brief and seemingly insignificant lives.

It is tempting to say that Malick begins his creation sequence with the Big Bang, but for important scientific and cinematic reasons, this can't be right. What we are probably being granted is a cinematic vision of what Volker Bromm (the University of Texas at Austin physicist whom Malick's team consulted) calls "first light," the moment when the universe first became illuminated, the very moment when the possibility of self-showing entered the world. Call this the Heideggerian moment where Malick is celebrating both the belated emergence of the world's ability to be seen and the birth of a condition of his own art as a filmmaker.

More relevant to the moral issues at stake throughout, we eventually find ourselves on a beach, in anticipation of the eternity sequence where members of Jack's past congregate. A graceful plesiosaurus studies a gash on its flank, signaling a primitive stage of self-awareness, made possible or occasioned by the experience of pain. The dinosaur catches sight of itself suffering, the wound an invitation to self-scrutiny. The dinosaur and a low-angle shot of a team of hammerhead sharks followed by the ominous passing of a gigantic stingray open onto the unsettling reality that life feeds upon itself. The water now includes blood, flowing through the circulatory systems of animals and animated by the pumping, sometimes bleeding heart.

We find additional signs of awareness expressed on a higher plane in subsequent scenes, the first in the creation sequence to suggest a rudimentary narrative structure. We see a parasaurolophus lying incapacitated on a rocky riverbed, perhaps the same dinosaur we just saw romping through the forest, when a dromiceiomimus approaches and forcefully steps on its head. On a first viewing, we expect the carnivore to follow its rawer instincts, reminiscent of *Jurassic Park*, but we are surprised when it repeatedly touches the herbivore's head with increasing curiosity, almost gentleness. It hesitates in a seeming moment of indecision and ultimately spares its life.

It is hard to know what precisely to make of this ambivalent scene. Berlioz's *Requiem* begins to sound as Mrs. O'Brien's voiceover continues: "Light of my life. I search for you. My hope. My child." It looks like an early expression of empathy on the part of a primitive creature. In the eyes of several commentators, it represents the birth of compassion or mercy in the pre-human world,[18] but this is certainly more than the film itself shows. A moment of hesitation is all we see, perhaps an anticipation of the human capacity to deliberate and choose. That the "merciful" dinosaur's head is not shown at the moment of decision is surely relevant, a visual indication that nothing like thought is to be read into the scene. It is a pregnant moment, and one that anticipates some of what comes in the family romance. The dinosaur's increasingly gentle use of its foot is particularly suggestive, an anticipation of hands placed on the heads or backs of others in sympathy, friendship, and forgiveness, forecasting a view according to which life in the absence of something like love and compassion is merely one in which "shit happens."

But at the cosmic level, it is difficult to shake the sense that things do just happen. A note of contingency sounds through the music of cosmic unfolding, a sense strengthened by the fragmented episodes of the long sequence centered on the O'Brien family. The earth is burgeoning beautifully when an asteroid is shown rotating serenely through space, Kubrick-like,[19] before it strikes a fertile earth, throwing debris into the air and causing massive tidal waves to surge over the land, bringing an end to the dinosaurs' 180-million-year reign. Whatever the dromiceiomimus achieved, it was a beginning that soon came to an end.

This need not detract from the beauty of what we see. Nor should it weaken the sense of awe that comes from the recognition that this thing *here* and *now* is the fruit of eons of countless dicey happenings; that each of us is, if not miraculous, at least an astonishing product of an unfathomable series and concatenation of events; that our capacity for moral concern is a late development bound up with and somehow made possible by an almost endless chain of events. In some respects, or for some of us, the senses of awe and wonder are likely to increase when we eliminate the divine watchmaker or demiurge or miraculous interventionist from our conceptions of how things (including morality itself) get started in this world of breathtaking spatiotemporal proportions.

Stories about beginnings are often tied to tales of how things end. If we live and act *in medias res*, we strain toward an understanding of what came before us and what might be to come, envisioning even the end of all things in the death of stars and planets and the collapse of the very universe itself. In another bold move, Malick offers us an eschatological vision as *The Tree of Life* draws to a close that no reading of the film can afford to ignore. It is all so odd that any interpretation cannot help but be tentative. This so-called Eternity sequence is central to the development of an understanding of the film's philosophical potential and what (if anything) it might have to contribute to the morality theme. A few preliminary words on what we see and hear are therefore in order.

We see Jack in his contemporary setting, sunk in thought, apparently indifferent to the reality that surrounds him. He rides an ascending elevator before the camera cuts to and pans upward in a tall, narrow canyon of wavy red and purple ribbons. We hear "Brother" in voiceover. He hesitates before a door set in a desert landscape before crossing the threshold to follow a young female guide on the other side.

What comes next is a sequence of images too obscure to reduce to any easy narrative configuration, set against imagistic suggestions that all of this is happening against the background of a dying sun, leaving us with a parched earth through which a molten river courses and glows in the darkness. The atmosphere's sepia tones run with clouds that streak rather than billow. Jack whispers, "Keep us." There is a long pause. "Guide us. To the end of time." We hear instruments striking the first chords of the sonorous laments of Berlioz's *Requiem*. Young Jack beckons: "Follow me."

There are figures lighting candles in the darkness and entering the light, corpses wrapped tightly in linen lying supine on a grassy lawn, pueblo-style homes clustered in the distance, then a ladder leaning against an archway. There are images of a grave from below and a woman stretching down toward the viewer, and images of a bride-to-be lying corpse-like on a metal mattress frame soon shown standing as if suddenly resurrected from the dead.

All of this seems to be leading toward some sort of reunion on Jack's part with the figures of his youth (conspicuously his childhood friend with the burn scar), on a shore with mountains visible in the distance and water splitting on a shoal, the elder Jack prepared to kneel in the sand to embrace an obscure woman's bare feet. There are cuts to the family tree of the O'Brien's home in Waco and R. L. playing with a flashlight at bedtime. Jack gives R. L. to his ecstatic parents before easing both his brother and his mother onto salt flats and toward a distant mountain chain. Mrs. O'Brien, accompanied by a young woman and a girl, raises her hands heavenward to the sounds of Berlioz's chorus singing "amen" and says, "I give him to you. I give you my son." No sooner does our gaze lift toward the heavens than it returns to the earth, where a multitude of buoyant sunflowers sway gently in the breeze. Berlioz's chorus descends in a meditative decrescendo of the closing word: amen.

Back in Houston, the elevator falls rapidly, interrupted by a low-angle shot of the tree extending from the yard at the base of Jack's office tower. Jack is shown looking up toward the sky and turning about as if disoriented. He suddenly seems to get his bearings and smiles faintly. Something in the distance draws his gaze at eye level. In the concluding shot, a suspension bridge spans the water between two shores. The credits begin to roll to the sounds of "Welcome Happy Morning."

What are we to make of all this? What, if anything, does this culminating chapter have to do with the morality theme we've been tracking throughout?

The images pull the viewer in several interpretive directions. Critics sympathetic to Malick's vision tend to locate the sequence within a narrowly Christian frame of reference,[20] a move that seems justified by the "Agnus Dei" of Berlioz's stirring *Grande Messe des morts* (1837) that runs throughout much of what the camera gives us to see. But Malick's imagery is not so easy to place and is suggestive enough to resonate both within and beyond the boundaries of Christian faith. Some of the more overt religious interpretations risk reducing a poignant image to a transparent symbol. The ladder leaning against the archway, the sky visible through its rungs and the sun radiating through it, has been read as an allusion to Jacob's Ladder (Gen. 28:10–19).[21] But our glimpse of the ladder in *The Tree of Life* is truncated. We don't see it "set up [squarely] on the earth," and its reach is far beneath the lofty heavens of its biblical counterpart. We see nothing like angels "ascending and descending on it." And the film carries no promise that Jack's seed will be spread like dust in all directions. Beyond asserting a commonplace (ladders are symbols of transcendence), it is hard to know what interpretive work this affiliation of image with biblical text is supposed to do. If we are attentive to cinematic detail and care about the world at stake in the film, we are just as likely to be reminded of the ladder set against the tree in the O'Briens's yard in Waco, as if the middle-aged Jack were weaving a vision of eternal life out of the materials of his own childhood, as though echoing the elegiac poet's assertion in Rilke's *Duineser Elegien* that fate or destiny (*Schicksal*) is nothing but "the density of childhood [*das Dichte der Kindheit*]."[22] Part of what makes *The Tree of Life* so powerful is its capacity to exceed the narrow bounds of our partisan conceptions of it.

The expulsion from the Eden of Waco, Texas eventually leads Jack to an unsatisfying life in the city, the place where his personal vision of eternity forms. In a prelude of sorts, we are given images of the city from above, in Jack's office, and in the ascending elevator, suggesting a Platonizing ambition to see things from on high, more steadily and in the whole. But what Jack envisions outside the Platonic cave is not a world of unchanging forms, glimpsed by a solitary knower in a land of eternal truth; what he beholds or fashions for himself is a community of sorts. Before Jack walks through the doorway in the first of several desert landscapes after a woman with dark hair (a personage named Guide [Jessica Fuselier] in the film credits, but one we might associate with the figures of Lament in Rilke), he utters "Brother" in voiceover, reminding us of the central problem of the film, the Rilkean one of "those who died young," now set within the larger context of a cosmos of moral concern. The vision of reality Jack appears to be fashioning for himself is woven of love and longing. If the film's creation story gives us reality as the correlate of scientific objectivity, albeit one in which we are encouraged to see our own meaningful lives set, the vision of reality on display here is clearly the work of love in the face of death.

In Malick's version, not only the death of the beloved but the death of life on earth as we know it should be confronted. The importance of coming to grips with the loss of the cosmic background of our existence— the emergence of which we witnessed in the creation sequence—is made visible in the images of the death of our star that prefaces the resurrection and reunion sequences that follow, as if to ask, What power could love and moral commitment possibly have in the face of a loss so complete? Echoing the title and theme of another film released in the same year, this is what we might call the *Melancholia*-moment of *The Tree of Life*. Could anything be said to matter in light of the prospect of absolute annihilation (a loss so total that it threatens our moral and erotic investments)? No fantasies of lineage (cultural, political, familial) seem to withstand the disquieting thought that nothing is built to last, not even the planetary context of our existence.

Whatever answer the film can be said to imply, it has something to do with the renewing power of recollection, a resurrection of the dead in the spaces of memory, a gathering of the past in the visionary imagination, and an overcoming of time and death itself in poetic figuration. The major narrative arc of the film has prepared us for a retrieval that brings the figures of Jack's youth, and (just as importantly) those that we haven't encountered in the film so far, into an intense present on the shoal of time. Transcendence is just the integration of time on Earth, no longer one thing after another but a gathering of what passes, and seems so insignificant as it comes and goes, into a coherent whole. In this (reconfigured) world, a dead bride comes to life again as our memories of those who left us do when we recall their importance in the density of the past. The waters that signify what comes and goes beat against the sandbank of memory, in the midst of which the overwhelming waters of oblivion are still there as a reminder. The wind still ruffles the hair of the remembered mother, dressed in evergreen. Darkness still descends upon eternity. Candles still need lighting. The mighty cataract asserts itself as a moving image of eternity, of our being cast into watery uncertainty. The mask of pretense falls into the waters signifying everlasting flux.

There is nothing static in this image of reunion, what the cynical viewer might dismiss as a wishful fantasy of community. In a higher sense, everyone and everything has been united from the beginning. What Jack has come perhaps finally to acknowledge is his belonging to a moral community of mutually dependent individuals whose place in his life, however contingent, should be met with gratitude. A community no longer made up of antagonists in the struggle for self-assertion but a vast community potentially united in loving embrace.[23]

But there is another aspect of Jack's vision that tells a story of reclaimed agency, bordering on the heretical, at least from a conventionally religious (chiefly Christian) point of view. His vision is tied, both visually and sonically, to the loss of brother and mother. It is important that both are released into the vast white plain of eternity, the watery element having given way to salty remains and the solid mountain range visible in the distance. But Jack is, crucially, an active participant in the landscape of lament. His task seems to be to redeem both deaths in a reconciling vision that places his own agency at the center, as if he alone can do what an absent or silent god could not or would not accomplish. He finds R. L., as he was shown in the childhood sequences, on the shores and gives him to his parents, allowing Mr. and Mrs. O'Brien to reclaim their own agency in letting R. L. go, as if he himself has answered their prayers. Of course, none of this is literally happening. His mother is merely imagined to be reconciled to the death of her beloved son. But it is important that he makes himself an active participant in the loss, an agent in the overcoming of death in a vision that brings the dead (and those who survived the final departure of those who matter most) together for one last embrace.

For religious poets like John Donne, there is always the promise of heaven. But for someone like Jack, whose faith in traditional religious dogma has become untenable, who has the modern benefit (if it can be called that) of understanding the origins of the earth, another way of contending with the fact of death is necessary. Donne's famous insistence that "death too shall die" is not likely to inspire moral action. It is for Jack (for us) to address undeserved suffering and to honor the gifts that earthly life has to offer in the midst of mortality. No blind obedience to inscrutable power, no anticipation of reward, but acting without expectation of worldly success in light of the claims others make upon us—this constitutes morality in a deeper sense.

On this perishing earth amidst beings that suffer and die, it is the human task to appreciate what endures within fragile and fleeting life, to celebrate those we love, and to notice what is remarkable and inspiring about their pure or titanic spirits. There is enough earthly glory to celebrate without having to imagine a more glorious heaven beyond, and enough to do in this life without having to worry about what we might do in another. In this respect, Malick departs from the (literalizing) Kantian vision of what Nietzsche dismissed as just another world behind the scenes, where the morally upright will be granted both further opportunity for moral improvement and a reward for unrecognized good behavior in this unjust world of ours.[24]

If the eternity sequence begins with a Platonizing gesture toward worlds beyond, it ends with Jack returning to this world (also, to be sure, a Platonic motif), brought down from the heights on a commonplace elevator, at first looking slightly bewildered, then gently smiling. His gaze finally settles at eye level. Has he reconciled the two ways of nature and of grace in the parental figures who wrestle always within him? The willingness to accept what comes with the resolve that makes moral responsibility and concern possible? His mother's fragile love of the world with his father's realism and strong agency? Wonder in the face of the glory of what shows and work toward the realization of a better world? Not just to be good, as if this were a divine dispensation, but to become good, perhaps to make a heaven out of what others found a hell?

There is no way of answering these questions, nor does Malick give concrete advice on how one ought to live. The moral register of his films refuses the moralizing advice. With the possible exception of *A Hidden Life*, on the plight of a Nazi dissenter where the moral stakes are stark and for the most part clear (barring certain utilitarian calculuses that the film explores in painful detail), Malick's films operate on a more fundamental plane than this. In this respect, they remain on what Heidegger would call *ontological* terrain, if one still figured in moral terms.

The final image of a bridge inspires confidence, perhaps reflecting the discovery of some fruitful soil between stream and stone or a link between the domains of nature and grace, but endings in Malick's films never really end anything: a bridge between cityscapes suspended over a river, no more. Jack is still there, an architect in Houston, the end he's envisioned only the intimation of a fresh start. We are given to think that Jack has achieved some reconciling vision of the world, but we are left as the credits roll (to the sound of "Welcome Happy Morning," which appears in the musical credits without the comma, as an injunction rather than an address) to wonder what this new beginning might mean. The meaning of setting out is never clear when we begin. Its significance comes late, always only in retrospect, as we reflect upon the vicissitudes and fates of our decisions, sufferings, and deeds (the entire film could be said to be about this painful fact). In the end, there is no everlasting place of rest, no secure life above the clouds. Our visions of what was and what will be are always of the here-and-now, uncertain and searching and calling for us to make of them what we can and within communities to be inhabited with greater vigilance, recollective force, and moral concern.

Notes

1. We have argued for the importance of cinematic depictions of world in the work of a rather different filmmaker, and one without Malick's philosophical education and background in Reid and Craig, *Agency and Imagination in the Films of David Lynch*.

2. See especially Furstenau and MacAvoy, "Terrence Malick's Heideggerian Cinema"; and, more recently, Loht's "Film as Heideggerian Art?" Cavell himself blazed the trail in the 1979 foreword to an expanded edition of *The World Viewed: Reflections on the Ontology of Film*, noting that the mode of beauty of the images in *Days of Heaven* "somehow invokes a formal radiance which strikes me as a realization of some sentences from Heidegger's *What Is Called Thinking*," xv, and that the film itself contains "a metaphysical vision of the world," xiv.

3. For a helpful discussion of the role of music in *The Tree of Life* framed by the Heideggerian interest in the phenomenon of the world, see James Wierzbicki's *Terrence Malick: Sonic Style*. There are a few worrisome mistakes, however, including misattributed songs. It is, importantly, not the first movement of Gorecki's 1976 Symphony no. 3 that we hear when Mrs. O'Brien is reminiscing with her sons but the second (the words of which come from a child addressing its parents), and the piece that Mr. O'Brien is shown on the piano playing with R. L. on the guitar is Couperin's "Les Barricades Mystérieuses," a piece about boundaries, which we hear in other contexts.

4. There are echoes of Emerson in the voiceovers of *The Thin Red Line*, borrowings from Dostoyevsky and Kierkegaard and problems of Kantian provenance on display in *The Tree of Life*, and references to Christian texts and traditions throughout Malick's more recent films that carry the viewer considerably beyond the sphere of Heideggerian influence. Sinnerbrink, for example, has drawn attention to the importance of Kierkegaard's distinction between aesthetic and ethical modes of existence throughout the so-called Weightless Trilogy that could justify classifying these films as instances of a Kierkegaardian cinema.

5. If we had more space, it would be worthwhile to document a few of the anti-Heideggerian moments that come forward in Malick's films after *The Tree of Life*. To mention one very subtle detail, which appears to have gone unnoticed in the literature to date: the character of Neil in *To the Wonder*, an existential failure on many levels (and a film ostensibly anchored, along with *The Tree of Life*, in Malick's own life), is shown (very briefly) casting a copy of Joan Stambaugh's

translation of *Sein und Zeit* to the side of his bed, perhaps in frustration, in the midst of serious romantic difficulties, as if to say that Heidegger's magnum opus is of no use, that it fails to address some of our weightier questions about love and interpersonal commitment.

6. John McAteer approaches the film as a meditation on religious morality that parallels Job's plight and centers on the problem of evil in "The Problem of the Father's Love in *The Tree of Life* and the Book of *Job*." And Shawn Loht argues that the film takes a philosophical position on human flourishing, holding that "an argument in environmental ethics emerges from the tale the film tells of the history of earth, nature, and life" in Loht, "Film as Ethical Philosophy, and the Question of Philosophical Arguments in Film." Our moral reading remains religiously neutral, although we acknowledge that religious issues are in play throughout.

7. We don't mean to deny that Heidegger's ontology has any ethical significance. In *Heidegger's Moral Ontology*, Reid has developed an interpretation of Heidegger's early thought that places normative and ethical concerns at the center. But Heidegger tends to privilege Aristotelian over Kantian paradigms, at least during the early period (1919–1927).

8. As far as we know, the only reading of the film that makes the ellipses relevant to an interpretation of the epigraph is John Bleasdale's "*The Tree of Life* and Death" in *The Way of Nature and the Way of Grace*.

9. We agree here with Marc Furstenau who sees the film as a rejection of the wrathful God of Job and an expression of sympathy with the family whose story he is telling. If the book of Job is a denigration of the human, then "Malick, like [Harold] Bloom, seems to prefer a more humane description of earthly existence." "Technologies of Observation," 66.

10. This is the broad thesis of Sinnerbrink's discussion of the film in *Terrence Malick: Filmmaker and Philosopher*, chap. 4: "Cinema as Ethics: *The Tree of Life*."

11. On this score, we disagree with Leslie MacAvoy, who relegates the moral problems the film confronts to the nonphilosophical level, in favor of the truly philosophical concern with "the meaning and purpose of existence." "Suffering and Redemption: A Nietzschean Analysis of *The Tree of Life*," 195. If the problem of undeserved suffering is not truly philosophical, then a substantial part of Kant's moral philosophy would have to be dismissed as an unphilosophical intrusion into his thought. Kant's reflections, which would, if we had space, be worth bringing out more explicitly, can be found in the discussion of the highest good in the *Critique of Practical Reason*, which places at the center the problem of unmerited suffering and our empirical sense that the world itself is inhospitable to the demands of morality.

12. For the influence of the novel, see Handley, "Faith, Sacrifice, and the Earth's Glory in Terrence Malick's *The Tree of Life*."

13. We should note, however, that Mrs. O'Brien's bedtime stories include Kipling's *The Jungle Book* (1894), which include anecdotes that seem to be about the importance of law and order.

14. Nietzsche, *Beyond Good and Evil*, 78.

15. Some of the more powerful episodes in the film show Mrs. O'Brien struggling to make sense of the death of her son. Early on, we hear her walking down the street, whispering, "My son. I just want to die, to be with him." Moments later, in a quick cut, we hear her uttering Christian commonplaces, suddenly interrupted by the more passionate "What did you gain?" The last time we see Mrs. O'Brien, in the probable chronological order of events, she appears to be still unreconciled to the death of her son. This comes, importantly, just before the Eternity sequence, which suggests that she never quite recovered her faith and sets the stage for Jack's own reconciling vision.

16. In Malick's 2007 screenplay, Mr. O'Brien is painted in a much less flattering and, in some respects, multidimensional light than in the theatrical version (e.g., his reflections on the death of his own father). Our chapter concerns the 2011 theatrical release, which we take to stand on its own, against a strong temptation on the part of readers to read screenplays as authoritative texts, at times going as far as to substitute them for the film itself. The recent Criterion edition provides another text, so to speak, but Malick himself saw it as a distinct film rather than as an extended cut.

17. The Lumia, a play of reddish light, flame-like, appears at the start of the film and at its end. The image is from Thomas Wilfred's *Opus 161* (1965). Its meaning is controversial. Leithart sees it in a literalizing frame of mind as the God "to which Jack and Mrs. O'Brien pray." Leithart, *Shining Glory*, 31. John Bleasdale writes that the lights "represent an absence, a marker for the God-shaped hole at the center of the narrative, a shifting, elusive, screensaver God." Bleasdale, *"The Tree of Life* and Death," 130. And in his essay "Seeing the Light in *The Tree of Life*" from the same volume, William Rothman notes, in connection with Jack's opening voiceover, that the Lumia "gives no sign of being responsive to this man's words," 47. It seems more like an enigma that opens and closes an enigmatic film. Like the White Whale in *Moby-Dick*, it is an occasion to project what meanings we are disposed to discover in, or to project upon, the filmic image. It is, perhaps, important for a filmmaker with philosophical ambitions that the thing itself is a work of art in light.

18. See Sinnerbrink, *Terrence Malick*, 145. However, Leithart expresses this view far more boldly and with less nuance in *Shining Glory*, 59.

19. This is more than a contingent resemblance, as Douglas Trumbull, who worked with Kubrick on the special effects in *2001: A Space Odyssey*, is listed in the film credits as visual effects consultant.

20. Leithart, *Shining Glory*, 84.

21. Sinnerbrink makes this unsupported connection in passing in *Terrence Malick*, 147.

22. Although Rilke's influence on Malick's vision cannot be demonstrated, the apparent echoes of the *Duino Elegies* are striking. Both *The Tree of Life* and the Elegies center on the death of the young; both associate cityscapes with death, despair, and unreality; both explore the roles of mothers and fathers in the development of a poetic vision of more reconciled life; and both culminate in an almost otherworldly but celebratory vision of the dead and dying in what Rilke's poetic narrator calls a "landscape of lament."

23. In his 2007 script, Malick envisions a community assembled in these final scenes that embraces everyone who ever lived.

24. Again, see Kant's argument for what many view as conventional religious belief in the second *Critique*.

Bibliography

Bleasdale, John. "*The Tree of Life* and Death." In *The Way of Nature and the Way of Grace: Philosophical Footholds on Terrence Malick's The Tree of Life*, edited by Jonathan Beever and Vernon W. Cisney, 123–38. Evanston, IL: Northwestern University Press, 2016.

Cavell, Stanley. *The World Viewed: Reflections on the Ontology of Film*. 2nd ed. Cambridge, MA: Harvard University Press, 1979.

Furstenau, Marc. "Technologies of Observation: Terrence Malick's *The Tree of Life* and the Philosophy of Science Fiction." In *The Way of Nature and the Way of Grace: Philosophical Footholds on Terrence Malick's The Tree of Life*, edited by Jonathan Beever and Vernon W. Cisney, 59–88. Evanston, IL: Northwestern University Press, 2016.

Furstenau, Marc, and Leslie MacAvoy. "Terrence Malick's Heideggerian Cinema: War and the Question of Being in *The Thin Red Line*." In *The Cinema of Terrence Malick: Poetic Visions of America*. 2nd ed., edited by Hannah Patterson. New York: Wallflower Press, 2007.

Handley, George B. "Faith, Sacrifice, and the Earth's Glory in Terrence Malick's *The Tree of Life*." *Angelaki* 19, no. 4 (2014): 79–93.

Kant, Immanuel. *Critique of Practical Reason*. Translated by Mary Gregor. Cambridge: Cambridge University Press, 2015.

Leithart, Peter J. *Shining Glory: Theological Reflections on Terrence Malick's Tree of Life*. Eugene, OR: Cascade Books, 2013.

Loht, Shawn. "Film as Ethical Philosophy, and the Question of Philosophical Arguments in Film—A Reading of *The Tree of Life*." *Film and Philosophy* 18 (2014): 164–83.

---. "Film as Heideggerian Art? A Reassessment of Heidegger, Film, and His Connection to Terrence Malick." *Film and Philosophy* 17 (2013): 113–36.

MacAvoy, Leslie. "Suffering and Redemption: A Nietzschean Analysis of *The Tree of Life*." In *The Way of Nature and the Way of Grace: Philosophical Footholds on Terrence Malick's The Tree of Life*. 2nd ed., edited by Jonathan Beever and Vernon W. Cisney, 195–212. Evanston, IL: Northwestern University Press, 2016.

McAteer, John. "The Problem of the Father's Love in *The Tree of Life* and the Book of Job." *Film and Philosophy* 17 (2013): 137–50.

Nietzsche, Friedrich. *Beyond Good and Evil*. Edited by Rolf-Peter Horstmann and Judith Norman. Translated by Judith Norman. Cambridge: Cambridge University Press, 2003.

Reid, James D. *Heidegger's Moral Ontology*. Cambridge: Cambridge University Press, 2019.

Reid, James D., and Candace R. Craig. *Agency and Imagination in the Films of David Lynch: Philosophical Perspectives*. Lanham, MD: Lexington Books, 2020.

Rothman, William. "Seeing the Light in *The Tree of Life*." In *The Way of Nature and the Way of Grace: Philosophical Footholds on Terrence Malick's The Tree of Life*, edited by Jonathan Beever and Vernon W. Cisney, 195–212. Evanston, IL: Northwestern University Press, 2016.

Sinnerbrink, Robert. *Terrence Malick: Filmmaker and Philosopher*. London: Bloomsbury, 2019.

Wierzbicki, James. *Terrence Malick: Sonic Style*. New York: Routledge, 2020.

Chapter 4

Performativity and Transformative Experience

Terrence Malick's Mysticism

RICO GUTSCHMIDT

It has often been pointed out that Terrence Malick is strongly influenced by Heidegger's philosophy. He studied philosophy and worked on a PhD thesis on the concept of world in Kierkegaard, Heidegger, and Wittgenstein. He did not finish the thesis, but he translated Heidegger's *The Essence of Reasons* and it is rumored that he even worked as Heidegger's chauffeur in the late 1960s.[1] One of the reasons Malick started a career as a filmmaker was that he realized, while teaching a class on Heidegger at MIT, that he could not convey Heidegger's philosophy unless both he and his students experienced the moods Heidegger talks about. Heidegger himself points out frequently that his philosophy can only be understood against the background of certain philosophical experiences that he wanted to evoke through his particular philosophical style. There is, thus, a strong performative dimension in Heidegger's philosophy, and it seems very plausible to interpret Malick's films as attempts to convey Heidegger's philosophy with the help of cinematic means. This is indeed a widespread interpretation.

Heidegger's philosophy, in turn, was strongly influenced by mysticism, particularly by Meister Eckhart. Mysticism has a similar problem. It cannot simply put forward its claims on a theoretical level but can only be fully understood through personal experiences. Therefore, mysticism also proceeds performatively and aims at evoking a form of experiential understanding, which particularly applies to Eckhart. It is this aspect of Eckhart's mysticism that influenced Heidegger the most.[2] Both mysticism and Heidegger's philosophy can be interpreted as performatively aiming at transformative experiences that yield a new way of being and seeing.

What I want to show in this chapter is that Terrence Malick's films can also be interpreted along these lines. While the performative dimension in mysticism and Heidegger is bound to textual and rhetorical means, Malick employs cinematic means that aim at similar experiences. Moreover, I will argue that Malick's films do not just attempt to illustrate or convey Heidegger's philosophy but that they aim performatively at evoking transformative experiences that go beyond Heidegger and should rather be linked to mysticism in more general terms. My claim, in short, is that there are important points of overlap among mysticism, Heidegger, and Malick with regard to performativity and transformative experience.

With respect to this very general claim about Terrence Malick's mysticism, I will approach his films from a rather detached point of view. I am not going to interpret any particular film philosophically or analyze the details of Malick's cinematic means. This has been done quite often already. Instead, in what follows, I will briefly discuss mysticism in terms of performativity and transformative experience and apply this interpretation to Eckhart and Heidegger. Then, with references to Robert Sinnerbrink's recent book on Malick, I will turn to Malick's cinematic style and argue that it can also be understood in the light of this interpretation.[3]

Mysticism, Performativity, and Transformative Experience

There are many ways of interpreting mysticism philosophically.[4] On my reading, the best way to understand mystical experience is through its relation to negative theology. I will briefly note in what follows that negative theology can be understood as attempting to evoke the experience of mystical union by performatively undermining our understanding of God or the absolute. It is important to highlight that this is an experience of non-understanding. On my reading, negative theology can evoke experiences of non-understanding also underneath the level of mystical union, for example in terms of certain moods or feelings of being.[5] What these experiences of non-understanding have in common is that they can be transformative in yielding a new perspective on the world. There are many forms of mystical experience, but I think that they can be understood to a great extent in these terms.

Negative theology, broadly understood, claims that God or the absolute is beyond human comprehension and can only be approached by negation, that is to say, by the study of what God is not. However, claiming that God is beyond human comprehension is self-defeating since this claim appears to constitute a comprehensible proposition about God. This problem establishes a paradox at the center of negative theology. On my reading, the key to resolving this paradox is that negative theology is not committed to contending a negative claim about our knowledge of God, which would indeed be self-defeating. Instead, negative theology can be conceived of as a practice that performatively undermines our putative knowledge of God.

Indeed, for most of its protagonists, negative theology is not aiming at a negative theoretical statement about God but at an experiential understanding of God's incomprehensibility that is achieved through the practice of negation. Nicholas of Cusa, for example, famously argued that we understand God through our non-understanding. More precisely, Cusa is not claiming by way of a theoretical statement that God would be incomprehensible. Instead, he employs textual and rhetorical means to yield an experiential understanding that he describes as learned ignorance, or *docta ignorantia*. This form of understanding is linked to a new attitude, as Hans Blumenberg points out: "But the Cusan's procedure sees an essential difference between muteness and falling silent. The language and system of metaphor that he developed for *docta ignorantia* do not represent a state of knowledge but a praxis, a method, a path to a certain sort of attitude."[6]

Proceeding from this, I think that the practice of negative theology can be understood as evoking the experience of failing to think the absolute. This experience is transformative since it engenders an attitude of wonder with respect to the mystery of existence. Even more, the experience is not just personally but also epistemically transformative.[7] The new attitude is related to an experiential understanding of the incomprehensibility of the absolute. We fail to think the absolute, yet the experience of this failure does not end in brute ignorance but in learned ignorance.[8] For Cusa, this notion describes a new attitude that is attained through the experiential understanding of God's incomprehensibility.[9] On my reading, Cusa's concept of God "showing Godself to us as incomprehensible"[10] can thus be interpreted as referring to the epistemically transformative experience of the failure to grasp the absolute. Consequently, in line with Blumenberg's interpretation I think that negative theology is a practice, a via negativa, that is, a path to a new attitude.

The practice of negative theology refers not only to the theological notion of God but also to the philosophical problem of the totality of the world. Neoplatonism, for example, asks for the totality and the origin of everything that exists. The metaphysical quest for this absolute leads to paradoxes. For Plotinus, everything emanates from the One, but the One itself is beyond comprehension since every concept attributed to the One would bring the One under the twofold structure of attribution and thus contradict its unitary structure.[11] However, Plotinus's texts should not be understood as stating at the theoretical level that the One would be inconceivable. Instead, the texts show the incomprehensibility of the One performatively through a radical dialectic of negation.[12] In the end, this performance aims at the mystical experience of the One, the *henosis*, yielding a form of experiential understanding that goes beyond thinking and is thus called hyper-noesis.[13] On my reading, the practice of the negative theology of the One starts with the theoretical problem of the absolute in terms of the totality and the origin of everything that exists and becomes entangled in this problem in such a way that the failure of the attempt to grasp this totality and its origin evokes an epistemically transformative experience. The epistemic value of this experience consists in an experiential understanding that is linked to an attitude of wonder that acknowledges the mystery of existence.

The paradox of negative theology can thus be resolved: instead of incoherently claiming that the absolute is beyond human comprehension, negative theology evokes a transformative experience that occasions a new attitude. This experience can have different forms and ranges from certain moods or feelings of being to the strong experience of mystical union. In addition, I think that many forms of mystical experiences can be understood as experiences of non-understanding with respect to the mystery of existence. This interpretation of mysticism in terms of negative theology was elucidated here with references to Plotinus and Cusa but can be fruitfully applied to many other protagonists of negative theology. Eckhart, for example, was strongly influenced by Plotinus, and Heidegger, in turn, was strongly influenced by Eckhart.[14] As I will show, the films of Terrence Malick can also be interpreted along similar lines, which might be due in part to the influence of Heidegger. Beyond the question of heritage, however, there are strong structural analogies in the works of Eckhart and Heidegger in terms of performativity and transformative experience that I will now briefly discuss. In the next part, I will show that these analogies can also be found in Malick's films.

To begin with, Reiner Schürmann points to the performative aspect of Eckhart's thought. He refers to Eckhart's sermon on poverty, where Eckhart says at the beginning, "So long as you do not equal this truth about which we now want to speak, you cannot understand me." At the end of the sermon, Eckhart argues, "Those who cannot understand this speech should not trouble their hearts about it. For, as long as man does not equal this truth, he will not understand this speech." When Eckhart speaks of detachment, he makes a similar point: "There are many people who do not understand this. That is not surprising to me. Indeed, whoever wants to understand this has to be very detached and raised above all things."[15] According to Schürmann, this strongly resembles Heidegger: "To understand poverty one must be poor. To understand detachment one must be detached. In Heidegger, to understand the turn, one must oneself turn about. To understand authentic temporality, one must exist authentically."[16] For Schürmann, this dimension of Heidegger's thought constitutes a "practical a priori" that can be found throughout Heidegger's philosophy.[17] Schürmann also claims that Heidegger is strongly influenced by Eckhart in this respect.[18]

Occasionally, Heidegger himself points to this performative dimension of his philosophy. In the lecture course of the winter term 1929–1930, he characterizes his method of formal indication as follows: "For this we need to reflect upon the thoroughgoing character of philosophical concepts, namely that they are all formally indicative concepts. That they are indicative implies the following: the meaning-content of these concepts does not directly intend or express what they refer to, but only gives an indication, a pointer to the fact that anyone who seeks to understand is called upon by this conceptual context to undertake a transformation of themselves into their Dasein."[19] In 1962, he argues in a seminar on his talk "Time and Being" that his philosophy can only be understood through certain experiences and that he thus aims at evoking such experiences:

> The experimental quality of the seminar was thus twofold: on the one hand, it wanted to point directly at a matter which in accordance with its very nature is inaccessible to communicative statements. On the other hand, it had to attempt to prepare the participants for their own experience of what was said in

terms of an experience of something which cannot be openly brought to light. It is thus the attempt to speak of something that cannot be mediated cognitively, not even in terms of questions, but must be experienced.[20]

Obviously, he tries to fulfil this task with the help of his neologisms, wild metaphors, and poetical experiments.[21]

Eckhart, too, not only argues that a personal relatedness to the contents of his instructions is needed to be able to understand them but also tries to evoke such personal relatedness through his sermons and writings. With Schürmann's concept of the practical a priori in the background, which Schürmann established with respect to Eckhart and Heidegger, Ian Alexander Moore discusses Eckhart's performative approach.[22] He argues that "Eckhart deploys such strategies as dialectic, paradox, and deliberate mistranslation in order to cultivate his listeners and readers for the experience of releasement."[23] Like Schürmann, Moore observes that Heidegger's philosophy is shaped by a practical a priori, and that he was strongly influenced by Eckhart in this way.[24]

However, while Eckhart aims at experiencing union with God, Heidegger rather refers to the transformative power of moods, such as anxiety. As noted earlier, the mystical union is an extreme version of the transformative experience of negative theology, which can also be understood in terms of moods or feelings of being. Both Eckhart and Heidegger performatively expose our fundamental non-understanding, be it with respect to God or with respect to Heidegger's notion of being, which leads through different kinds of transformative experience to an attitude that acknowledges the mystery of existence. Both Eckhart and Heidegger speak of an attitude of releasement in this respect, and Heidegger explicitly links this attitude to an "openness to the mystery."[25] Thus, their approaches fit into the philosophical interpretation of mysticism in terms of negative theology that I have outlined. Moreover, Mailck's films can also be interpreted along these lines.

Terrence Malick's Mysticism

Although Malick's films are certainly influenced by Heidegger and deal with Heideggerian themes, they belong to the wider context of mysticism that was sketched out previously. Malick might have been inspired to his version of mysticism by Heidegger, but he goes beyond Heidegger both methodologically and thematically. Next to Heidegger, it is well known that Malick is familiar with Kierkegaard and Wittgenstein. Kierkegaard's performative method of indirect communication, which is closely related to Heidegger's method of formal indication and Kierkegaard's existential understanding of faith, might have influenced Malick. Similar to the philosophical interpretation of negative theology, Wittgenstein points to "the mystical" with respect to the incomprehensibility of the origin of everything that exists: "Not how the world is, is the mystical, but that it is."[26] Not least, Malick took classes under Paul Tillich in the 1960s at Harvard and might have been influenced by Tillich's existential account of faith. In line with negative theology, for Tillich "absolute faith" is based on "the God above the God of theism."[27] Be that as it may, my claim here is that Malick's films can be interpreted in terms of performativity and transformative experience and seem to aim at evoking an attitude that acknowledges the mystery of existence.

To begin with, in his 1969 translator's introduction to Heidegger's *The Essence of Reasons*, Malick highlights what Schürmann later called the practical a priori in Heidegger's philosophy. In order to understand this philosophy, we must have a personal relatedness to its contents. In the words of Malick, "If Heidegger resorts to his own peculiar language, it is because ordinary German does not meet his purposes; and it does not because he has new and different purposes. If we cannot educate ourselves to his purposes, then clearly his work will look like nonsense."[28] He is thus fully aware of the performative dimension of Heidegger's philosophy, and it seems that he wants to educate the viewer of his films in a similar way. Obviously, Malick's films are not just telling stories or displaying characters but are rather confronting the viewer with fundamental aspects of the human condition. However, they are not just illustrating certain philosophical ideas but seem to incorporate a specific way of doing philosophy. Heidegger argues that philosophy should be done in the same way as poetry or art. Through the medium of cinema, Malick seems to be doing philosophy poetically.

With respect to certain Heideggerian themes, Stanley Cavell points out in the foreword to the second edition of *The World Viewed* that Malick "has indeed found a way to transpose such thoughts for our meditation."[29] In more general terms, Stephen Mulhall argues that film can be conceived of as a particular form of doing philosophy. For Mulhall, it is not just that certain ideas can be transposed for our meditation but that film can reflect upon philosophical concerns on its own via cinematic means and can thus itself be thought of philosophizing.[30] In a paper about Malick's *The Tree of Life*, John Caruana similarly explicates such cinematic thinking with respect to Deleuze as follows: "Cinema thinks in its own terms: in and through images. In relation to this cinema, philosophy must learn to see and listen carefully without superimposing its own conceptual and logical expectations. For Deleuze, the thinking in question is cinema's capacity to disrupt routinized perception while making possible unanticipated ways of seeing."[31] With this background in mind, Caruana argues that *The Tree of Life* "is an invitation for the viewer to change, to adopt a different attitude toward life."[32] Along these lines, I think that the notion of cinematic thinking can be interpreted as performatively inducting and entangling the viewer into a process of considering philosophical issues through cinematic means, which may lead to experiential forms of insight. Similar to the case of mysticism that I discussed in the first section, such insights might not be propositional but rather might be linked to epistemically transformative experiences that are induced by cinematic thinking. In his philosophical interpretation of Malick's films, Sinnerbrink, for example, points to such experiences: "Malick's films elicit and evoke forms of experience that often invite metaphysical reflection or prompt one to seek comprehension by having recourse to philosophical reflection."[33]

Malick's particular cinematic means have often been analyzed and are nicely summarized by Sinnerbrink: "flowing, mobile camera movements; the use of natural light; non-scripted performances aiming at authenticity and spontaneity; a fragmentary, episodic, audiovisually driven narrative; the interpolation of abstract image sequences; the use of intimate, reflective, prayer-like voiceovers; borrowed dialogue referencing literary, philosophical and religious sources; an artful sequencing of music to set mood and allude to aesthetic, cultural and theological themes."[34] In particular, the voiceover does not just comment on the story or provide insights into the character's state of mind but rather offers thoughts that go beyond the story and asks general questions concerning the human condition. This can be seen as a form of philosophical meditation. It does not provide answers but rather asks questions and thereby entangles the viewer in the process of philosophizing, which, together with the other cited cinematic means, might evoke philosophically significant transformative experiences. Sinnerbrink, for example, speaks of a "transformation of our ways of apprehending the world"[35] in this context.

Such transformation can happen with respect to different aspects of the human condition. Malick's films touch on many issues, including the problem of human finitude and mortality, different aspects and different kinds of love, the beauty and the cruelty of nature, the nature and meaning of war and violence, the problem of the appearance of evil, different problems of morality, and, over and above, religiosity and spirituality. In his 2019 film *A Hidden Life*, Malick focuses on responsibility and guilt. Many of these themes go beyond Heidegger's philosophy. As I have noted already, however, a crucial problem that stands in the background of mysticism and negative theology is the metaphysical quest for the totality and the origin of everything that exists. This problem is presented brilliantly in Malick's *Voyage of Time*, which links the origin of the universe to our contemporary world by showing the history of the evolution of the universe and the earth with great images and a meditative voiceover. This can have the effect of making the viewer perceive our contemporary world differently. Through the film, one sees it against the background of the incomprehensible origin of everything that exists, which can induce an attitude of wonder that acknowledges that we are part of something that is beyond our comprehension. In *The Tree of Life*, Malick presents a short version of the history of the origin and evolution of the universe and links it to the birth of a child and to everyday life in a suburban American neighborhood in the 1950s, which can also have the effect of making the viewer perceive everyday life as being part of an incomprehensible totality.

This can be seen as a mystical transformation even though it does not imply the experience of mystical union. Mysticism, after all, can be interpreted in terms of transformative experiences leading to a new attitude that acknowledges the mystery of existence. Here Sinnerbrink argues that Malick's films are "evoking experiences of wonder and perplexity, grace and confusion, or immanence and transcendence."[36] A corresponding transformation can be understood, for example, as a transformation of one's mood or feeling of being. Sinnerbrink again speaks of the "poetic evocation of mood through image montage, camera movement and non-linear narration"[37] and argues that "the most productive way of approaching Malick's later films . . . is as evoking moods—joy, wonder, anxiety, restlessness, boredom, longing—inviting sensuous immersion and meditative contemplation."[38] In this context, he highlights the transformative power of Malick's films.[39]

The mystery of existence, then, can be acknowledged particularly through transformative experiences of non-understanding. Malick's films can evoke such experiences with respect to all of the previously mentioned themes. They do not offer answers to the questions they raise, but rather they involve the viewer in an open process of reflection and philosophizing, which may lead to an attitude that acknowledges our fundamental non-understanding of crucial aspects of the human condition. Instead of inducing despair, the acknowledgement of such non-understanding can lead to an attitude of wonder, which, quite plausibly, is what Malick is aiming at. There is no solution to the riddle of existence but an attitude that acknowledges the riddle in terms of a mystery. In *The Tree of Life*, Malick advocates an attitude of wonder that Mrs. O'Brien, one of the central characters of the film, calls the "way of grace." *The Thin Red Line*, a film that reflects on war and violence, ends with the following narration: "Look out through my eyes. Look out at the things you made. All things shining." For Sinnerbrink, "with these final words . . . we are returned to the finite world, now illuminated by wonder."[40] All things shine even in the face of war and violence. This can be understood as the result of acknowledging the incomprehensibility of these aspects of the human condition. Appositely, the soundtrack of *The Thin Red Line* extensively uses Charles Ives's "The Unanswered Question."

Though it might initially have appeared hyperbolic, given an appreciation of the influence of mystical non-understanding in his cinematic vision, Malick can accordingly be said to quite literally make all things shine in his films. In the case of *The Tree of Life*, Sinnerbrink notes, "Almost every outdoor shot in the film, for example, displays the setting sun, in the background yet shining brilliantly through trees, radiating across faces, a benevolent eye illuminating the everyday world."[41] This use of natural light, particularly during the "magic hour" of sunset, can be found in many of Malick's later films. In my view, Malick wants to show that the everyday world can be perceived against the background of the mystery of existence. This mystery, I think, comes to light through experiences of fundamental non-understanding with respect to the absolute or to the origin of the totality of everything that exists. But the mystery of existence can also be experienced in everyday contexts, as they are part of an incomprehensible totality. Malick's films, thus, attempt to make the viewer perceive the mystery of the everyday in this sense.

The notion of the mystery of the everyday is also discussed in theology and philosophy of religion. Here Richard Kearney, for instance, speaks of "epiphanies of the everyday."[42] Kearney argues "against the Grand Metaphysical Systems that construed God in terms of formal universals and abstract essences"[43] and claims that we should focus instead on the "eschaton dwelling in each unique, material instant, no matter how lowly or profane."[44] In everyday contexts, Kearney describes forms of non-understanding in terms of a breakdown of everyday practices that lead to the transformative experience of seeing the world differently: "Some breaking down or breaking away from our given lived experience is necessary, it seems, for a breakthrough to the meaning of that same experience, at another level, one where we may see and hear otherwise."[45] As he notes, this process can happen in a moment, in an "eschatological instant": "For the eschatological instant is the one (and it is potentially every moment) in which we receive the gift of the world anew. The same world, of course, but refigured."[46] This strongly resembles Sinnerbrink's reading of Malick's films: "Malick shares a conviction in the mythopoetic power of cinema to reveal reality anew, to transfigure the everyday, to illuminate the world and nature with a revelatory power that inspires belief."[47] As already mentioned, Caruana points out with respect to Deleuze that cinematic thinking and particularly Malick's films have the "capacity to disrupt routinized perception while making possible unanticipated ways of seeing."[48] Such effect can be achieved by Malick's meditative form of questioning our understanding of central aspects of the human condition without giving answers, which can indeed lead to "some breaking down or breaking away from our given lived experience" in Kearney's sense.

Consequently, Malick's films, it seems to me, belong to the venerable tradition of mysticism that tries to evoke such epiphanies. On my reading, mysticism performatively undermines our understanding of God, the absolute, or the origin of the totality of everything that exists, while the corresponding transformative experience of non-understanding also affects our perspective on the everyday world. While mysticism is bound to textual and rhetorical means, Malick employs cinematic means to a similar end. His films performatively involve the viewer in an open-ended process of philosophizing that might evoke transformative experiences yielding an attitude of wonder, which acknowledges the incomprehensibility of the human condition and, thereby, the mystery of existence. With such an attitude, the world is perceived as a miracle. All things shining. It is in this sense that I think it just to speak of Terrence Malick's mysticism.

Notes

1. Komma-Pöllath, "Wer war Heideggers Chauffeur? Der stille Amerikaner."
2. Compare Schürmann, *Heidegger on Being and Acting*, 235; and Moore, *Eckhart, Heidegger, and the Imperative of Releasement*, 92.

3. See Sinnerbrink, *Terrence Malick*.
4. Compare e.g., Stace, *Mysticism and Philosophy*.
5. Here compare Ratcliffe, *Feelings of Being* for the notion of feelings of being.
6. Blumenberg, *The Legitimacy of the Modern Age*, 490.
7. The connection between personally and epistemically transformative experience is discussed in Paul, *Transformative Experience*, 5–15.
8. For a more detailed exposition of this interpretation of negative theology in terms of transformative experience, see Gutschmidt, "Skeptizismus und negative Theologie," 23–41.
9. Nicholas of Cusa, *Selected Spiritual Writings*, 91.
10. Cusa, 127.
11. Plotinus, *The Enneads*, V, 1, 4, 5–13.
12. Plotinus, III, 8, 10, 28–31.
13. Plotinus, VI, 9, 17.
14. For example, compare Caputo, *The Mystical Element in Heidegger's Thought*; and Moore, *Eckhart, Heidegger, and the Imperative of Releasement*.
15. These citations are quoted from Schürmann, *Heidegger on Being and Acting*, 235–36.
16. Schürmann, 236.
17. Schürmann, § 40.
18. Schürmann, 235.
19. Heidegger, *The Fundamental Concepts of Metaphysics*, 297.
20. Heidegger, *On Time and Being*, 26.
21. The performative dimension of Heidegger's philosophy is discussed, for example, in Ciminio, *Phänomenologie und Vollzug. Heideggers performative Philosophie des faktischen Lebens*.
22. Moore, *Eckhart, Heidegger, and Releasement*, 81–90.
23. Moore, 38.
24. Moore, 92.
25. Heidegger, *The Essence of Reasons*, 55.
26. Wittgenstein, *Tractatus Logico-Philosophicus*, 6.44.
27. Tillich, *The Courage to Be*, 190.
28. Heidegger, *The Essence of Reasons*, xvii.
29. Cavell, *The World Viewed*, xv.
30. Mulhall, *On Film*, 85–103.
31. Caruana, "Repetition and Belief," 69–86.
32. Caruana, 70.
33. Sinnerbrink, *Terrence Malick*, 12.
34. Sinnerbrink, 117.
35. Sinnerbrink, 168.
36. Sinnerbrink, 16.
37. Sinnerbrink, 163.

38. Sinnerbrink, 168.
39. See previous note 38.
40. Sinnerbrink, 48.
41. Sinnerbrink, 135.
42. Kearney, "Epiphanies of the Everyday," 3.
43. Kearney, 4.
44. See previous note 43.
45. Kearney, 16.
46. Kearney, 15.
47. Sinnerbrink, *Terrence Malick*, 159.
48. Caruana, "Repetition and Belief," 69.

Bibliography

Blumenberg, Hans. *The Legitimacy of the Modern Age*. Translated by Robert M. Wallace. Cambridge, MA: MIT Press, 1983.
Caputo, John D. *The Mystical Element in Heidegger's Thought*. New York: Fordham University Press, 1986.
Caruana, John. "Repetition and Belief: A Kierkegaardian Reading of Malick's *The Tree of Life*." In *Immanent Frames: Postsecular Cinema between Malick and von Trier*, edited by John Caruana and Mark Cauchi, 69–86. Albany: State University of New York Press, 2018.
Cavell, Stanley. *The World Viewed: Reflections on the Ontology of Film*. 2nd ed. Cambridge, MA: Harvard University Press, 1995.
Cimino, Antonio. *Phänomenologie und Vollzug. Heideggers performative Philosophie des faktischen Lebens*. Frankfurt: Klostermann, 2013.
Cusa, Nicholas. *Selected Spiritual Writings*. Translated by H. Lawrence Bond. New York: Paulist Press, 1997.
Gerson, Lloyd P., ed. *The Enneads*. Translated by George Boys-Stones, John M. Dillon, Llyod P. Gerson, R. A. H. King, Andrew Smith, and James Wilberding. Cambridge: Cambridge University Press, 2019.
Gutschmidt, Rico. "Skeptizismus und negative Theologie. Endlichkeit als transformative Erfahrung." *Deutsche Zeitschrift für Philosophie* 67, no. 1 (2019): 23–41.
Heidegger, Martin. *Discourse on Thinking*. Translated by John M. Anderson and E. Hans Freund. New York: Harper and Row, 1966.
———. *The Essence of Reasons*. Translated by Terrence Malick. Evanston, IL: Northwestern University Press, 1969.
———. *The Fundamental Concepts of Metaphysics*. Translated by William H. McNeill and Nicholas Walker. Bloomington: Indiana University Press, 1995.
———. *On Time and Being*. Translated by Joan Stambaugh. Albany: State University of New York Press, 1972.

Kearney, Richard. "Epiphanies of the Everyday: Toward a Micro-Eschatology." In *After God: Richard Kearney and the Religious Turn in Continental Philosophy*, edited by John P. Manoussakis, 3–20. New York: Fordham University Press, 2006.
Komma-Pöllath, Thilo. "Wer war Heideggers Chauffeur? Der stille Amerikaner." *Frankfurter Allgemeine Zeitung*, February 22, 2021. https://www.faz.net/aktuell/feuilleton/debatten/war-terrence-malick-1970-heideggers-chauffeur-17207934.html.
Moore, Ian A. *Eckhart, Heidegger, and the Imperative of Releasement*. Albany: State University of New York Press, 2019.
Mulhall, Stephen. *On Film*. 3rd ed. London: Routledge, 2016.
Paul, Laurie A. *Transformative Experience*. Oxford: Oxford University Press, 2014.
Ratcliffe, Matthew. *Feelings of Being: Phenomenology, Psychiatry and the Sense of Reality*. Oxford: Oxford University Press, 2008.
Schürmann, Reiner. *Heidegger on Being and Acting: From Principles to Anarchy*. Bloomington: Indiana University Press, 1987.
Sinnerbrink, Robert. *Terrence Malick: Filmmaker and Philosopher*. London: Bloomsbury, 2019.
Stace, Walter T. *Mysticism and Philosophy*. London: St. Martin's Press, 1961.
Tillich, Paul. *The Courage to Be*. New Haven, CT: Yale University Press, 1952.
Wittgenstein, Ludwig. *Tractatus Logico-Philosophicus*. Translated by Charles K. Ogden. London: Routledge, 1981.

Part II

Mystery, Evil, Creation: Framing the "Big Questions"

Chapter 5

Life-Time

Mystery in *The Tree of Life*

DAVID R. CERBONE

The pure "that it is" shows itself, but the "whence" and the "whither" remain in darkness.

—Martin Heidegger, *Being and Time*[1]

Cinematic Mystery

I want to begin with what I take to be one of the more apparent and accessible mysteries at work in *The Tree of Life*. This first mystery is really a kind of interpretive puzzle concerning the structure of the film. I know from teaching the film that first-time viewers find *The Tree of Life* baffling. There are many reasons for this—its whispered voiceovers; its cryptic imagery, such as the recurring flame and the door in the desert; and, of course, dinosaurs—but what is most disorienting is the way the viewer is whipsawed back and forth, through and across different temporal frameworks, often within relatively short periods of viewing-time. Consider the opening of the movie: the first character we see (and hear) is the mother (Mrs. O'Brien [Jessica Chastain]), although we don't really know this yet. We hear her adult voice in the voiceover but see her as a little girl, who we can gather grew up on a farm, close to nature and in the care of a loving and protective father. The film then cuts quickly to scenes of Mrs. O'Brien as a wife and mother, outside with her husband and three boys (insofar as the film will later settle into a conventional narrative structure, these characters at this point in time will be the focus of that narrative). These snippets of life in what we will later learn is Waco, Texas, give way to an older Mrs. O'Brien receiving a telegram that we might guess—but will only later confirm—is news of the death of the middle son, R. L (Laramie Eppler). (That the news is delivered by telegram—as well as the age of R. L. at the time of death—leads many to conclude that he was killed in Vietnam; however, the guilt and recrimination that accompany the boy's death, especially on the part of Mr. O'Brien [Brad Pitt], plus the facts of Malick's own life—namely that his own brother committed suicide—point in another direction.) Finally, in these opening scenes, we also see Jack (Sean Penn)—the oldest of the three O'Brien boys—as a middle-aged man leading what looks to be a high-powered professional life, although nothing about this outward success translates into any appearance of happiness or contentment.

So within just a few minutes, we have traversed multiple generations over a period of somewhere between fifty and seventy-five years. The traversal is quick and abrupt and understandably disorienting the first time through: most of the descriptions I provided above of these vignettes are unavailable to the first-time viewer, as they only become so in retrospect as identities and relationships are more clearly delineated. Already, this is a lot to take in and make sense of, but we are then thrown an even funkier temporal curveball: twenty minutes into the film, the frame of reference shifts from an intergenerational perspective to a far more cosmic point of view, as we follow, in the manner of an IMAX nature film, nothing less than the formation of Earth and the emergence of life. We see Earth take shape as a planet, watch volcanoes erupt and lava cool, and witness the development of life from simple one-cell organisms to the flourishing of first sea and then terrestrial creatures, culminating with the appearance and extinction of the dinosaurs. Whereas the first twenty minutes gave us somewhere between fifty and seventy-five years (a branch or two of a family tree), the next twenty gives us billions (the tree of life writ large).

Roughly the first third of the movie thus presents us with a number of interpretive challenges, all of which concern the temporal structures Malick has adumbrated in these opening sequences. We have the challenge of understanding the fragmentary, far-from-linear manner in which the

O'Brien family has been introduced. (We will, to be sure, get a somewhat more linear presentation of the family's formation, but the family portrait throughout will be piecemeal and episodic.) Beyond this challenge, we then confront the issue of how to understand the shift to the more cosmic perspective twenty minutes in. What are we supposed to make of this shift? How does the story of life's emergence and flourishing hang together with the microscale story of the O'Briens's trials and tribulations? Of course, at the most basic level, we can say that the cosmic temporal perspective contains the O'Briens, as their saga is but a fraction of a fraction of a blink in the billions of years the nature sequence depicts. But what is the point of drawing our attention to that containment? Beyond it just being true that what happens to the O'Briens is part of what happens on Earth more generally, what is the point of being encouraged to see it that way?

I want to suggest here—and will explore over the course of this chapter—that Malick's unconventional use of temporal structures[2] serves to delineate a series of mysteries. These mysteries are not separate or isolated but are connected such that reflection upon one naturally leads, or gives way, to another. In so giving way, the scale of the mystery increases but in a manner that continues to encompass the prior mystery. We can think of these mysteries as something like a set of nesting boxes,[3] but where, contrary to the usual order of grappling with such sets, we are encouraged to work our way from the smallest box at the center out to the largest. The order of the boxes is not exactly reversed, however: that there are larger "boxes" is readily apparent at the very outset of the film, as the first fragments of the O'Brien story are framed first by an epigraph from the book of Job and second by Mrs. O'Brien's voiceover, which contrasts the "way of nature" and the "way of grace." These first gestures indicate that what we will see of the O'Briens's story should indeed be seen as a small box within a larger set. I want to note here and will continue to emphasize that by "working our way," I do not mean anything like solving the mysteries to which Malick calls our attention. We confront with each "box" a mystery, which leads in turn to a further mystery, but in being so led, we do not thereby come to possess a series of solutions; quite the contrary, as each subsequent mystery only reinforces the mysteriousness of whatever was contained in the prior, smaller box.

That solving any mysteries thrown at us by *The Tree of Life* is beside—indeed, contrary to—the point reflects the continued influence of Heidegger's philosophy on Malick's filmmaking (Malick's deep engagement with Heidegger's philosophy is well documented and will not be rehearsed here).

Two concepts in particular bear mentioning as touchstones: Heidegger's coinage of the notion of *thrownness* in *Being and Time*, which anticipates the appeal explicitly to *mystery*. The latter term appears at least as early as the 1931 essay "On the Essence of Truth"[4] and reappears throughout many of his later essays and addresses, perhaps most notably in the first part of the *Gelassenheit* volume, a memorial address in honor of the composer Conradin Kreutzer.[5] In both cases, Heidegger adduces these concepts not to point a way toward their overcoming—getting back behind one's thrownness or penetrating the mystery of being—but to encourage their acknowledgment as ineliminable features of our finite existence. In a late essay—"The Principles of Thinking"—Heidegger refers to "the dark" as "the secret mystery of what is light." Rather than try to illuminate that darkness, thereby dispelling the mystery, Heidegger recommends a more difficult course, namely, "to keep the dark pure and clear, to preserve it from admixture with a brightness that does not belong to it and to find the only brightness that does."[6] I have no idea if Malick was familiar with this passage, but I will nonetheless suggest that we see *The Tree of Life* as using the luminosity of film as a means of striving for what Heidegger recommends here: keeping the dark pure and clear, protecting it from stray and misleading light.

Mnemonic Mystery

"Tell us a story from before we can remember," one of the O'Brien boys asks at bedtime. Although met with a particular story—the parents' flight in a vintage airplane taken as a graduation present—the child's request points toward a more general lesson concerning the reach of memory. On the whole, *The Tree of Life* has a recollective structure. Each nesting box is "opened" through an effort to recall what precedes one's present experience and condition. The "one's" here can be substituted for in more than one way, as we can think of the film internally as depicting Jack's attempt to recover his origins or, more externally, as Malick's. Beyond Jack and Malick, the mnemonic structures are generic and so allow for the substitution of pretty much anyone.[7] All of us have life stories coupled with limited memories, and so whatever stories we might muster through recollection to tell about ourselves will always be embedded in stories that extend beyond any such recollections. In each case, the activity of recollection is shaped by structures that ineluctably funnel back to a common past (the dinosaurs precede any and all of us), and so in each case, such recollections will enlist the imagination, along with the testimony of others and more mute forms of evidence, as what lies in the past is indeed "a story from before we can remember."

The vicissitudes of memory—its dynamic, creative, and distorting dimensions—have been well-documented through empirical studies, but the aspects of memory at issue in *The Tree of Life* do not require a clinical perspective to be confirmed or appreciated. The film instead offers a perspective available through phenomenological reflection, which again underscores the indefinite substitutability with respect to the structures it delineates.[8] Consider the activity of recounting one's own life story. Such efforts are occasional (even those among us who "dwell in the past" do not spend all their time constructing recollective narratives) and occasioned, prompted or triggered, sometimes by a question or request ("Tell me about your childhood"), a commemorative event (birthday, *Jahrzeit*, anniversary, etc.), or sometimes just idle musing. What occasions the activity of recollection can also be more motivated, as it may be prompted by a problem or issue such as a recurring or resurfacing conflict (usually involving family) or an event in one's past to which one repeatedly returns (often with feelings of shame, resentment, or guilt). As occasional and especially as occasioned by something in particular, recollection is fragmentary and episodic: when we recollect our lives, we do not remember them whole but only bits and pieces. Just what resurfaces is largely involuntary: although we may make deliberate efforts to remember things about our past, what actually "comes to mind" will do so mostly of its own accord and typically not in any tidy linear order. We tend to find our memories skipping around among events from various times in our lives, linked by various associative chains that can imbue those times with added significance, but we also sometimes fix—and fixate—upon a more particular period in greater detail, which may come to be regarded as especially formative, pivotal, or otherwise determinative. While we can impose some order on the jumble of memories that bubble up—arranging them in a rough earlier-later structure—what is recalled very often has a kind of archetypical and nostalgic structure where various actual events from one's past are compressed or condensed into unspecifiable but representative scenes. I might, for example, vividly recall on some occasion childhood trips to the beach, but it will not be identifiable as a particular trip on a particular day in a particular year. As nostalgic, its content is no specific trip to the beach but only a kind of proxy or placeholder for all of the many times I went to the beach throughout my childhood in southern California.[9] This does not make the memory inaccurate exactly—I really did go to the beach throughout my childhood—but rather heightens its significance by indicating something about my past that appears worthy of condensation into a nostalgic archetype (e.g., representing the carefree nature of my youth, where my current life—with all its adult cares and concerns and distance from the ocean—may be understood as a kind of fall or decline).

Recounting one's life—engaging in the activity of recollection—is part of the ongoing activity of making sense of one's life: understanding who I am consists in large part of grappling with questions of where I come from and what sorts of things happened that led to my being where I am now. Everyone has a life story, although that story may remain largely latent, not so much forgotten as simply unremembered. The task of recollection becomes more pressing when things do not make sense, where there are questions about who one is that feel especially vexing or troubling. The recollective structure of *The Tree of Life* crystallizes around Jack. Insofar as the film offers a narrative present, this is represented by Jack in middle age, and so what we see of the O'Briens's life in Waco is presented from middle-aged Jack's point of view and as occasioned by Jack's present (middle-aged) situation. That present situation is only lightly sketched, but I think we can safely gather a number of things from what little we see: as mentioned above, Jack in middle age is a high-powered professional, ensconced in a glass-and-metal tower that contrasts starkly with the environs of his Waco childhood (the same can be said for his sleek, modernist home), but Jack is clearly unhappy despite the outward appearance of success. His malaise is both general—"The world is going to the dogs"—and also specific. What we see of his interactions with his wife and several women at work suggest estrangement and perhaps infidelity. We will also come to see in Jack's marriage the continuation of a pattern that extends back to his childhood in Waco, as the wife resembles—is the same "type" as—both the little girl the young Jack follows home from school and the neighbor whose lingerie he steals. The one scene we get of Jack at home shows him waking and still groggy; by the scene's end, he is dressed for work but pauses to light a candle at his kitchen counter. Coupled with the phone conversation with his father shortly thereafter, I think it is safe to infer that the candle is lighted in commemoration of R. L., most likely to mark either his birthday or the anniversary of his death. This, more than anything else about Jack's current situation, triggers and drives his recollection, as the key elements of the recollective narrative are Jack's relation to R. L. and both boys' relation to their mother and father, with understandably special emphasis on Jack's particular struggles with Mr. O'Brien (even if what Jack most wants to understand is what led to the death of his brother, he cannot help but drift back to his own issues and frustrations). The childhood scenes are structured to reflect their memorial status: fleeting and fragmentary, without a precise temporal order, bits of remembered experiences interwoven with stretches of Jack's life (infancy, the birth of his brother) that he could not possibly remember but has probably been told about so often that they blend almost seamlessly with his own recollections. The memories include largely nostalgic moments with representative status—primal scenes of conflict and insight, symbolic moments of triumph or frustration—that have come to be imbued with heightened significance ("the time when" that stands out as emblematic of a relationship or typifies a much more extended pattern of action and interaction). Insofar as there is a dateable period, Jack's memories zero in on what he takes to be pivotal moments in his life and the life of his family: the final stretch of their life in Waco, which are also the waning moments of Jack's childhood, and thus what we can think of as a bounded "chapter" in the family's life as well as Jack's own (this "closing of the chapter" is further emphasized in the later, extended version, where the family's moving is also the occasion for Jack's being sent to boarding school and thus separated from the family).

Jack's recollections can thus be understood as driven by a desire to understand both his present situation (how did he come to be who he finds himself to be now?) and the more troubling events in his life that clearly continue to haunt him, especially the death of his younger brother. His recollections are thus directed toward his origins—his coming to be with *these* parents, within *this* family animated by *this* dynamic, in *this* place, among *these* people, and so on—that might somehow provide answers to the questions that beset him. This endeavor is not exactly futile, as recollection allows for, but in no way guarantees, the discernment of patterns and chains of events that allow for answering at least some *why* questions. For example, what we see—what Jack recollects—of his childhood allows us (and him) to see his marriage as the continuation of a pattern of attraction to girls and women of a certain "type," who are dark-haired and dark-eyed and may thus be seen as a kind of rejection of, or recoil from, his fair, red-headed mother. So if Jack asks himself, "Why was I attracted to *her* (my now-wife)?" he can answer that question by locating this one relationship in the broader pattern that recollection allows him to discern. Notice, though, that there is something unsatisfying—if not outright illusory—about such an explanation, as it only serves to shift the *why* question. We can think of the shift as moving back down the chain of events—"Sure, I was attracted to my wife because she resembles my next-door neighbor growing up (or looks like the first girl I had a crush on)"—which only invites the *why* question all over again: "Why, of all the girls in my elementary school, was I attracted to her?" Alternatively, we can think of the *why* question as shifting in level, to asking about the pattern as a whole: "Why am I attracted to women of this type?" While there is a sense of gaining some explanatory purchase by locating particular events and episodes in larger patterns, of tracing later events and episodes back to earlier ones, in each case, something still functions as a kind of given; while what functions as a given in one explanation can then be the thing to be explained, at some point the effort will come to be abandoned. Rather than yielding a final authoritative explanation that provides satisfaction, one comes to see that the process trails off into the unfathomable past.[10]

Making sense of one's own life through recollection can thus be seen to be doubly mysterious. The piecemeal, fragmentary, limited nature of memory assures that there are aspects of one's life that are destined to remain opaque. As temporally extended, one's own life is unsurveyable with anything approaching completeness. *The Tree of Life* is admittedly a long movie, but what it presents of Jack's life in Waco is only a small sliver of his entire life story (and presenting it in its entirety is not an option, both because of the time involved and because it is not entirely clear what "in its entirety" means here). Yet even if it were more or less completely surveyable, what would then be available would still generate *why* questions that point beyond one's life as a whole. In *Being and Time*, Heidegger remarks that human existence is structured such that "it never comes back behind its thrownness in such a way that it might first release this 'that-it-is-and-has-to-be' from *its being*-its-self and lead it into the 'there.'"[11] Jack cannot get outside of being Jack; he cannot attain mastery over his identity by fully recovering his origins, which means that there are aspects of himself—and of events in his life—that he can never fully understand in the sense of coming to possess satisfying explanations. Recollection allows for the arranging and rearranging of those aspects and events—of locating and relocating them within various patterns and chains—but the feeling of insight this kind of activity provides quickly gives way to new questions, new pools of darkness (as whatever is recalled and arranged will always point to stories "from before we can remember.") As *The Tree of Life* so artfully illustrates, the mystery of existence begins at home. But it hardly ends there.

Cosmic Mystery

We have so far moved about within the smallest of the nesting boxes *The Tree of Life* offers, but there are intimations already of some of the ways that such an exploration points beyond the confines of that box. Answers to *why* questions about one's own existence generate chains consisting of further *why* questions, whose answers generate further *why* questions, and so on. I am this way because of these features of my childhood, my childhood had this shape because of choices my parents made and events that befell them, my parents made those choices because of the kind of people they are, they are the kind of people they are because of their childhood, and so on. Numerous such chains can be generated and just how events fall into patterns and hook together with other aspects or features of one's life can change over time (the meaning of various events can alter dramatically in light of how one's life continues), but all of them point toward a past that precedes the life at issue: my parents came before me, their parents came before them, and so on. Even if we remain on the plane of human, existential temporality, "my time" can be seen to be embedded in a broader temporal horizon (even the smallest of the nesting boxes at issue in *The Tree of Life* is not really a single box) that already ensures that I will be a mystery to myself, that questions about who I am, what I have done, and what has happened to me will only generate more questions rather than definitive answers. Any individual life is embedded in a broader intergenerational structure, as the opening scenes of *The Tree of Life* already indicate and later sequences only reinforce. But that entire temporal horizon points to a further, broader horizon, as all of humanity is itself embedded in an even broader temporal structure. The image of the tree of life indicates as much, as all of humanity resides somewhere in the upper "branches," with an abundance of surrounding branches and massive trunk (and with the entire tree rooted in something nonliving). Malick attunes us to the presence and importance of these larger boxes at the very outset of the film with the epigraph from the book of Job that frames the film as a whole, along with the voiceover accompanying the scenes from Mrs. O'Brien's childhood where an adult Mrs. O'Brien rehearses the contrast between the ways of nature and the ways of grace. Although not exactly separate boxes, I will consider each of these in turn and their role in deepening the sense of life's mystery. Doing so will help us to make fuller sense of the initially baffling structure of the film.

The Mystery of Suffering (Job)

Apart from the opening epigraph, there are further explicit references to the Job story woven into the O'Brien narrative: after the funeral for R. L., the grandmother, in an almost cringeworthy attempt at consolation, cites the near-cliché line, "The Lord gives and the Lord takes away," and later in the film, the family attends a Sunday sermon that centers on the story of Job. Apart from these explicit references, there are numerous elements in the film that serve as touchstones for reflection on the meaning of the Job story: the crippled man we see during a downtown outing where the boys had been amusing one another by staggering and stumbling down the street; the marginal but recurring appearances of the neighbor boy whose house burned down and whose head bears the scars of the fire; the drowning of a boy during a summer outing; Mr. O'Brien's failures and frustrations, despite what he perceives as his efforts to be a good person; and, most prominently, the premature death of R. L.

Central to the book of Job is the attempt to make sense of suffering, to find the reasons for why things happen as they do, especially when those things are traumatic or tragic. The story's protagonist had been living a fortunate life replete with material comforts and a thriving family. Job is faithful and obedient to God, which encourages the idea that his wealth was a kind of reward for his piety: as a good person, Job deserved the various riches he had accrued. But as is well known, the story of Job centers on the misfortunes he suffers, which include the sudden death of his wife and all of his children (along with their families), the loss of all his worldly possessions, and his affliction with boils and other maladies. It is natural—indeed, almost unavoidable—to seek reasons for this dramatic change in fortune: we (and, of course, Job) feel there must be an explanation that somehow justifies Job's torment (the unavailability of any such explanation only serves to heighten his suffering). When Job receives counsel from Bildad, Zophar, and Elihu, their speeches all point toward some hidden failing on Job's part—a secret lack of piety, a buried impropriety—that accounts for why God has turned on him. What is striking about the book of Job is its rejection of such moralizing accounts of the vicissitudes of fortune. We know, reading the narrative, that none of what his reprovers say by way of explanation is legitimate: Job has not done anything to deserve what has befallen him (which also means that he really did not do anything special to merit his initial good fortune either). Indeed, given how the story is framed, if anything explains Job's suffering, it is that God allowed Satan to torment him. Such torment is connected to a bet between God and Satan over whether Job's piety is solely a result of the good fortune he had until then enjoyed.

That this explanation is itself a kind of illusion emerges in the story's most dramatic episode: God's speaking to Job from out of a whirlwind. The epigraph for the film is taken from Job 38:4–7, which marks the beginning of God's speech to Job. On-screen, the passage has been condensed to just the first line and the final two. The whole passage reads as follows (in a slightly different translation): "Where were you when I laid the earth's foundation? Tell me, if you understand. Who marked off its dimensions? Surely you know! Who stretched a measuring line across it? On what were its footings set, or who laid its cornerstone—while the morning stars sang together and all the angels shouted for joy." These verses can be understood as the beginning of a long rebuke to Job's quest to understand his plight. The implied answers to God's questions are, of course, that Job was not present at the laying of the earth's foundation, did not mark off its dimensions, and did not stretch a measuring line. Job knows nothing of such things. God is thus reminding Job here of the vastness of the Creation, against which his particular sufferings appear as miniscule. The reminder is offered not so much to diminish or make light of Job's suffering (knowing that others are in pain, have been in pain, and have endured far worse pains does not, just like that, make *my* pain go away); instead, it situates that suffering in a vast chain of events into which Job has no insight. God continues the cited verses by recounting the details of the Creation following the formation of Earth, emphasizing the many forms of life He has made, including all manner of wondrous beasts. The point is not just that Job is one instance of one type of living thing among a vast array of others and so is not in any way the center of the universe. Rather, the idea here is that whatever might serve to explain Job's plight is not something that God can make available to Job. Why Job suffers, why Job had to suffer, is not something God could possibly explain to Job. True, the angels "shouted for joy" at the Creation, which attests to the essential goodness of there being something rather than nothing, but how such shouts for joy can prefigure all the pain and misery that life offers is something only God and the angels can understand. Even if Job were to occupy our perspective, those of us reading the story, it would not help. True, Satan singled out Job for the purpose of his wager with God and that is why the particular calamities that befall him do so just then, but that still leaves the questions of why Job was singled out, why Satan and God chose to wager (why would anyone, angel or mortal, make a wager with God?), why just then when Job happened to be around, and so on. Insofar as there is an explanation, only God is privy to it, but it is not as though God is keeping a secret from Job (as though He could tell Job and chooses not to). Whatever God has by way of explanation is not something He could share with Job, since nothing that really served as an explanation is something that Job could possibly understand.[12] He would have had to be witness to the Creation from the get-go; he would have to take it all in and hold it all together in a way that allowed him to see just where his predicament fits. But he cannot do that; none of us can. Only God can do that, which is precisely what God is reminding Job about from out of the whirlwind. Even if God managed to assure Job that his suffering was necessary—indeed, that all suffering is necessary—that might provide something by way of consolation, but it would not provide any insight as to why suffering is necessary. If the fact of suffering is mysterious, then its necessity is equally so.

With God's speech to Job, there is thus a pivot from the particulars of Job's afflictions to the vastness of the Creation, a dramatic shift in scale from what is now delineated as micro—the sufferings of one man and his family—to the macro writ large. The shift in *The Tree of Life* at the twenty-minute mark can thus be understood as recapitulating the pivot that takes place in the book of Job. Given the details of God's speech—his recitation of the order of Creation—it is hard not to see the Job story as central to what Malick refers to with the extended nature sequence, as there too we get a recounting of the Creation. In a sense, we can see Malick as one-upping God: whereas God can only recount in words what Job was not present to see, Malick is able to show the wonders of life's emergence and development in, as we say, magnificent technicolor detail. It is as though we are placed in the perspective that God described to Job as unavailable. The illusion of the nature sequence in *The Tree of Life* is thus twofold: first, we are, of course, not really bearing witness to the Creation, even indirectly via the medium of film, as whatever footage Malick has assembled is either derived from events happening on Earth now (recent volcano eruptions, etc.) or constructed through cutting edge film technology. Second, and more importantly, bearing witness in this manner provides only an illusory sense of advantage over Job (we can add to this the illusion that we are in any way one-upping God). For one thing, getting (re-created) glimpses of the Creation does not really put us any closer to a God's-eye point of view. Perhaps seeing it in real time would get us a little closer, but seeing things that way is only a super-human rather than truly divine perspective. So we are still no better off than Job in terms of being present at the events God recounts. More than that, being shown what is only described to Job does nothing to equip us with any further explanations when it comes to the misfortunes that beset the O'Briens and other characters in the film. Situating what happens to the O'Briens against the backdrop of Creation only intensifies the mystery of their lives taking the shape they do. Understanding, even notionally, that there is an explanatory chain extending back from the death of R. L. to the dinosaurs and beyond provides next to nothing by way of insight into R. L.'s death. Saying, "R. L. died at age nineteen (rather than twenty, twenty-one, twenty-two, etc.) because of the dinosaurs" lands with a kind of empty thud, compounding rather than alleviating any sense of mystery.

The Mysteries of Nature and Grace

Malick's use of the Job story reinforces the mysteriousness of life—of one's own life and, more generally, of the fact of there being life at all—that emphasizes the mysteriousness of suffering and misfortune. It is natural—perhaps even inevitable—to emulate Job's quest for understanding, to want to know not just why there is suffering but why I suffer in just these ways on these occasions. Unlike a theodicy that aims to provide a justification for suffering, the Job story turns any such aim aside: God will not provide any such justification because He cannot make such things understood to the likes of us. While we might come to acknowledge the inevitability of suffering—to see the fact of there being life at all as necessitating suffering—this will not help us to understand the particular forms suffering takes and the particular patterns of suffering that accrue. By emphasizing suffering's mysteriousness, *The Tree of Life* eschews such forms of understanding.

There is life; there is suffering. Both are essentially mysterious. Where does that leave us? *The Tree of Life* is framed most broadly by the epigraph from the book of Job, which presages the broadest nesting box, that is, the cosmic perspective that encompasses life on Earth as a whole in accordance with the perspective of God's speech from out of the whirlwind. But the opening scenes of the film already suggest different ways of acknowledging that broadest box, different ways of moving about within those most general parameters. These are the ways of nature and grace that Mrs. O'Brien recounts in the initial voiceover that accompanies scenes of both her childhood and the childhood of her three sons. Mrs. O'Brien presents these ways as having been taught to her by the nuns in her school in the form of a choice: the nuns said, "You have to choose which way you'll follow." The way of nature is presented as an orientation toward things that is self-centered and self-concerned: "Nature wants only to please itself." Others, for the way of nature, are there to serve the self and to be "lorded over" whenever possible. Given the vicissitudes of life—the ebb and flow of fortune and misfortune—the way of nature fosters resentment and bitterness in the face of suffering: "It finds reasons to be unhappy." These reasons are coupled with a kind of failure on the part of the way of nature, a willful closure to the splendors and beauty of the world: "It finds reasons to be unhappy when all the world is shining around it . . . when love is smiling through all things." The way of grace, by contrast, is open to this shining of the world and attuned to the love that smiles "through all things." Grace is both receptive and responsive. We can think of grace as involving a kind of acceptance with respect to the sufferings of the world, but such acceptance has to be understood neither as a kind of sullen acquiescence (the posture of the way of nature in defeat), nor as simple passive complacency (rose-tinted glasses in the midst of a dark-hued world).

Mrs. O'Brien's recounting of the two ways ends with the nun's reassurance that "no one who loves the way of grace ever comes to a bad end." The film then cuts to her receiving the news of R. L.'s death. Malick's harsh juxtaposition forecloses any easy argument in favor of the way of grace in the sense of offering any kind of protective insulation from the misfortunes of the world. It would, after all, be graceless to follow the way of grace out of a sense that one will be "better off" for doing so. To be motivated only by what makes one better off is itself emblematic of the way of nature. There cannot in this way be an argument in response to the question, "Why follow the way of grace?"[13] Anyone who poses that question is not properly attuned to be receptive to the surrounding world as offering love and beauty as opposed to simply opportunity and risk. Love and beauty will for that person be indulgences, further sources of pleasure and gratification. There is no answer to the *why* question that can serve as a motivating reason for choosing grace over nature if what motivates are reasons geared to one's self-interest. That there is grace—that grace can be chosen—is a kind of paradox, a further mystery at issue in *The Tree of Life*. It is paradoxical because the choice of grace is posed within the natural world—within nature—and yet is a fundamentally unnatural choice. As the name suggests, the way of nature comes naturally, emerging out of the natural drive for self-preservation: what contributes to this self-preservation is sought as a good, while what detracts is shunned. Even where there is "selfless" behavior in the natural world—actions that appear to involve self-sacrifice—these too can be understood according to a kind of natural economy, as fostering the preservation of the species rather than the individual creature.

Malick illustrates the paradox of grace in one of the strangest scenes in *The Tree of Life*, which we see near the end of the long nature sequence that interrupts and situates the O'Brien story. The scene depicts a predatory dinosaur (a velociraptor) coming upon a sickly and struggling herbivore (most likely a parasaurolophus) in the shallows of a stream. For the velociraptor, the encounter is an ideal opportunity, as it offers abundant calories without having to expend any more energy than would be required to tear apart and devour its prey: no chasing, no long death struggle, no real risk of failure. Rather than the expected carnage, we instead see the velociraptor pause, first placing and then lifting its taloned foot from the head of the parasaurolophus. This moment of hesitation gives way to the velociraptor opting not to kill and eat its would-be prey. It instead moves slowly away from the struggling creature and then disappears down the bank of the stream. The scene is puzzling, to say the least. Indeed, the scene is wildly implausible in terms of depicting anything that might have actually happened in the age of the dinosaurs. Not only do velociraptors most likely lack the cognitive wherewithal to make such complex choices involving concepts such as mercy, forbearance, and selflessness, but the predator's actions simply make no sense given the life of a predator. A velociraptor does not forgo easy calories; it does not show pity or display kindness toward potential prey; doing so is radically and fundamentally contrary to its nature.[14]

I think that such a reaction is part of Malick's point in including such a peculiar scene.[15] He chooses to construct such an obviously premature moment of grace in order to highlight its inevitable prematurity: if the dinosaurs are too soon for something like grace—for qualities like pity, mercy, charity, and kindness—to make an appearance, when exactly would the right time be? If we insist, as is tempting, that grace could only emerge with the advent of human beings—fully linguistic creatures who clearly do have the cognitive wherewithal for concepts like hope, pity, mercy, and self-sacrifice—that still means, indeed requires, that there was a changeover at some point, that space somehow opened up for something beyond what comes naturally via the way of nature. Replace the velociraptor with an early human being out on the hunt: we still confront the paradox of foregoing the opportunity presented by the struggling creature. There is still a mystery at the heart of that choice, of there being a choice at all in the face of the pressure to survive.

Coda: *The Tree of Life* and *The Thin Red Line*

The way of nature and the way of grace are two different orientations toward the world, two different "paths" through one and the same world. As confronting a common world, both are confronted with the same facts, including the fact of suffering. But as a different way of responding to suffering, the way of grace transforms the world confronted by the way of nature: where the latter finds reasons for resentment and bitterness, the former finds occasions for beauty and love. There are perhaps the same facts for both, but the shift from one to the other involves a rearrangement of the facts that shows them in a new light. Here we confront another mystery, of how one and the same world could appear in such a different light.[16] Consider something perhaps a little less mysterious: puzzle pictures such as the duck-rabbit made famous by Wittgenstein in his later philosophy. Here too we see the same picture—one and the same assemblage of lines on paper—and yet the picture is wholly transformed: now a duck, now a rabbit, and never both at the same time. And in each case, whether the duck or the rabbit, it is perceived as being out there, rather than any kind of subjective image hidden away in the mind. The same holds with the two different ways: Mr. O'Brien, an embodiment in many ways of the way of nature, really sees reasons for disappointment and really experiences setbacks and frustrations, thereby "missing the glory," as he chastises himself later in the film. Seeing things otherwise will appear unintelligible, just as someone who only sees the rabbit will not really understand how it can be a duck as well. But the way of grace too will find it odd, if not baffling, that someone could fail to see the beauty of the world, could miss the way "love is smiling through all things." Shining and smiling are no less visible than suffering and hardship: in each case, one feels oneself in the presence of genuine features of the world rather than in possession of a mere "interpretation."

That one and the same world can be seen in such radically different ways renders the world mysterious, since it is not clear how that could be so. Viewed one way—as the realm of nature—grace seems unintelligible, impossible; viewed another way—as the realm of grace—the way of nature becomes unthinkably brutish and deplorable. I have confined my remarks in this chapter to Malick's grappling with the mysteries of existence in *The Tree of Life*. Our current mystery—how is grace possible in the natural world—is one among many the film explores. If we figure that mystery in terms of a Gestalt shift—a figure that provides a name for the mystery rather than a solution—we can, by looking beyond *The Tree of Life* to other work by Malick, get a sense of just how deep the mystery runs. While in *The Tree of Life*, nature provides the duck to grace's rabbit so that the possibility of that kind of goodness is a mystery, in the earlier *The Thin Red Line*, the valence of the figures is reversed: there, nature is inherently good, happy, and serene, and the question becomes how that came to be tainted with the presence of evil. Nature in *The Thin Red Line* is naturally graceful, balanced, and harmonious, and while it is easy to say that it is through the agency of human beings—our willful striving, our warring ways—that anything is evil, it is not so easy to say how that came to be: we, no less than anything else, came to be within the natural world even while no longer feeling a part of it.[17] Taken together, the two films are a Gestalt switch of a Gestalt switch, presenting the world and its life as indeed "a riddle, wrapped in a mystery, inside an enigma."[18]

Notes

1. Heidegger, *Being and Time*, 173/134.
2. There is a third temporal perspective at work in the film, which is intimated at various points and then presented in more detail in the last fifteen minutes of the film. These are the beach scenes, which might be understood as offering a kind of post- or extra-temporal perspective, a vision of the afterlife. That the rules of terrestrial chronology are not in play is shown in the way characters are present—and present to one another—at different stages of their lives. Such commingling of temporal stages allows for consolation and atonement. The middle-aged Jack and the older O'Brien father can, for example, offer apologies

to the young R. L., while the mother is able to find peace and comfort in their reunion. The status of this vision of eternity within the film is not entirely clear to me. Is Malick positing an afterlife? Should these images be taken literally? (And what would it mean to take them literally?) I won't try to answer these questions, but I'll note two things about these sequences. First, while these scenes appear to depict a kind of freedom from the forms of suffering at issue in the film as a whole, at the same time it is clear that in this suffering-free, extra-temporal setting, nothing happens. The characters simply mill about on the shore (the shores of eternity), reuniting and parting, presumably to reunite and part again and again. This suggests that the cost of foregoing suffering is the loss of the vibrance and dynamism of terrestrial life, which throws us back to the questions I'll be exploring at length in this chapter. Second, that the shores of eternity sequence ends by returning to Jack in middle age, released from his glass-and-steel tower into the light of day, lends to it a sense of fantasy, a longing on Jack's part for what is only a magical form of reconciliation and repair. If this is correct, then it is not really a third temporal perspective alongside the two main frameworks the film explores.

3. The structure of *The Tree of Life* thus brings to mind Winston Churchill's 1939 remark concerning action on the part of Russia, namely, that it "is a riddle, wrapped in a mystery, inside an enigma."

4. See Heidegger, "On the Essence of Truth," especially § 6.

5. See Heidegger, *Discourse on Thinking*, especially 55–57.

6. Martin Heidegger, "The Principles of Thinking." All citations from 56. I am indebted to Kate Withy for drawing this passage to my attention.

7. In the preface to the 2007 script for *The Tree of Life*, Malick writes: "The 'I' who speaks in this story is not the author. Rather, he hopes that you might see yourself in this 'I' and understand this story as your own." Terrence Malick, "The Tree of Life: A Screenplay by Terrence Malick" Writers Guild of America, June 25, 2007, https://indiegroundfilms.files.wordpress.com/2014/01/tree-of-life-the-jun-25-07-1st.pdf. This prefatory remark attests to the generic nature of the structures at issue in the film and their allowing—indeed encouraging—indefinite substitutability.

8. Unlike, say, a film such as *Memento*, whose protagonist suffers from a pathological loss of all but the shortest form of short-term experiential or episodic memory.

9. Here I am indebted to Crowell, "Spectral History: Narrative, Nostalgia, and the Time of the I," 83–104, which offers a careful analysis of the difference between straightforward, event-specific recollection and more nostalgic forms, which involve what I'm referring to here as condensation and symbolically affective significance.

10. In this paragraph (and more generally), I draw upon Kate Withy's "Situation and Limitation," 61–81. See especially section 3: her example of a "chatty"

acquaintance who persists in asking *why* questions is in the background of my discussion here.

11. Heidegger, *Being and Time*, 330/284.

12. We might well wonder here how something could "serve as an explanation" and yet be something "we could not understand," since what it is for something to be an explanation crucially involves its providing understanding. This last idea suggests that God is not exactly withholding an explanation from Job, as though God has one but cannot share it with Job; rather, God's words are meant to convey that there just is no explanation, which is again to say that we are here in the presence of a mystery. I am indebted to Maria Balaska for pressing me on this point.

13. We might consider here another nun, whose grace so stunned a young Raimond Gaita. See Gaita, *A Common Humanity*. Faced with incurably mentally ill patients at a mental hospital—lifers who "had no grounds for self-respect insofar as we connect that with self-esteem; or, none which could be based on qualities or achievements for which we could admire or congratulate them" (17)—the nun, unlike even the best-intentioned doctors in the hospital, showed in every interaction with the patients that they were for her fully her equals in stature and dignity. Gaita recounts the story in part for us to marvel at it but also to suggest that we see immediately the nun's goodness; as immediately evident, why the nun does what she does requires no further argument or list of reasons. At the same time, Gaita does not want us to lose sight of the mysteriousness of such immediately evident goodness. We can see that what the nun does—her orientation toward the patients—embodies pure goodness, but without fully knowing or understanding how that is possible. By *mystery*, Gaita means "something which no powers of understanding can penetrate, not because it is so difficult that even God would be perplexed, but because the mystery of good and evil is not contingent on our limited cognitive powers" (39). What Gaita says here reinforces my suggestion in the previous note regarding the difficulties attending the notion of an explanation that is in principle unavailable. God, of course, is not perplexed, but to say that *God only knows* (as we sometimes do) is just another way of saying that it is—and will forever be—a mystery.

14. While sharks who forgo eating fish make for good comic fare in *Finding Nemo*, part of the humor consists in just how cartoonish the conceit is. Real sharks that opted out of preying on other fish would not last very long at all.

15. I read some time ago, while first preparing to teach *The Tree of Life*, an online post that included remarks from one Malick's editors, who reported Malick's telling him that the whole point of the scene is to illustrate the emergence of something like the way of grace. I have been unable to track down the post again.

16. Such a mystery is perhaps part of what leads Wittgenstein to say, in the *Tractatus*, "The world of the happy man is a different one from that of the unhappy man." The world, he says, must "wax and wane as a whole." But this is

no less mysterious—how can two people occupy different worlds by dint of their attitude toward it?—and so really just transposes the mystery into a different key. See Wittgenstein, *Tractatus Logico-Philosophicus*, 6.43.

17. However, as Steven DeLay reminded me, *The Thin Red Line* opens with a crocodile menacingly entering the water, most likely in search of prey. It is difficult not to see the crocodile as menacing and so as a reminder that nature—with or without us—is a place of violence and danger.

18. I would like to thank Maria Balaska, Henry Cerbone, Randall Havas, Sean Kelly, Fredrik Westerlund, and Kate Withy for comments and discussion of earlier drafts of this chapter. Thanks to Steven DeLay for comments but also for providing the occasion for me to try to work out my thoughts about this wonderfully mysterious film.

Bibliography

Crowell, Steven. "Spectral History: Narrative, Nostalgia, and the Time of the I." *Research in Phenomenology* 29, no. 1 (1999): 83–104.

Gaita, Raimond. *A Common Humanity*. New York: Routledge, 2002.

Heidegger, Martin. *Being and Time*. Translated by John Macquarrie and Edward Robinson. New York: Harper and Row, 1962.

———. *Discourse on Thinking*. Translated by Joan Stambaugh. New York: Harper and Row, 1966.

———. "On the Essence of Truth." In *Pathmarks*, edited by William McNeill. Cambridge: Cambridge University Press, 1998.

———. "The Principles of Thinking." In *The Piety of Thinking*, translated by James G. Hart and John C. Maraldo. Bloomington: Indiana University Press, 1976.

Withy, Kate. "Situation and Limitation: Making Sense of Heidegger on Thrownness." *European Journal of Philosophy* 22, no. 1 (2014): 61–81.

Wittgenstein, Ludwig. *Tractatus Logico-Philosophicus*. Translated by D. F. Pears and B. F. McGuinness. London: Routledge and Kegan Paul, 1961.

Chapter 6

Not One Power, But Two

Dark Grounds and Twilit Paradises in Malick

Jussi Backman

Eden Lies About Us Still: Malick's Melancholy

One of the most persistent themes of Terrence Malick's cinematic works, from *Badlands* to *A Hidden Life*, is the irruption of forces of chaos and destruction—aggression, violence, war, and armed conquest—into pristine settings of peace and harmony, typically the rural homestead or a native community, portrayed as fostering simple domestic bliss, familial love, and a delicate balance with the natural environment. Malick has never made an attempt to conceal the biblical dimensions of this theme. The Eve and Adam of *Badlands*, Holly (Sissy Spacek) and Kit (Martin Sheen), rebel violently against a domineering father figure and the spiral of violence thereby commenced banishes them from their Edenic refuge in the badlands of Montana. Similarly, in *Days of Heaven*, violent crime drives the lovers Abby (Brooke Adams) and Bill (Richard Gere) to the prairies of northern Texas where their pretense to be siblings and their plot to marry Abby to the wealthy farmer (Sam Shepard) reproduces the triangle between Sarai, Abram, and Pharaoh (Gen. 12:10–20); even here, treachery and murder bring about a plague of locusts and further banishment. Both celebrations of idealized love and natural beauty take place against a bellicose background: Kit is a Korean War veteran; *Days of Heaven* ends with troops departing for World War I. In *The Thin Red Line*, it is war itself—the Guadalcanal campaign marking the decisive turning point in the Pacific theater of World War II—that makes a full-frontal intrusion into the idealized life of the native Solomon Islanders, at least as perceived by the daydreaming Private Witt (Jim Caviezel), convinced that he has "seen another world." *The New World* recounts the first stages of the invasion of Virginia by the English colonists, convinced (in the words of Captain Newport) they are an "advance guard" sent to conquer the "Eden [that] lies about still" as a "great inheritance" handed to them by God. In *The Tree of Life*, the innocence of a 1950s childhood in small-town Texas summoned up in flashbacks is breached by the harshness of the protagonist's father, fleeting experiences of terrible accidents and marginalized members of the community, the protagonist's own occasional violent impulses, and finally the traumatic loss of a brother, contrasted with an alienated adult life amid the urban desert of contemporary capitalism. In Malick's romantic interlude trilogy—*To the Wonder*, *Knight of Cups*, and *Song to Song*—the focus is on the tensions between selflessness and self-centeredness, loving commitment and fleeting passions, and spiritual simplicity and worldly temptations. Finally, in *A Hidden Life*, it is the Nazi military machine that encroaches upon the simple, close-knit, and devout rural life of the Upper Austrian village, threatening Franz Jägerstätter (August Diehl) and his family with conscription.

Malickian cinema is thus permeated by a deep-seated melancholy, a tragic sense of conflict between harmony and chaos. Malick's variations of the expulsion from Eden narrative also involve a tangible sense of loss; in these films, the most lyrical visions of beauty invariably have the feeling of flashbacks from something long past. Yet it would be simplistic to conclude—as many will be quick to do—that what is expressed here is nostalgia, an elegiac longing for the unspoiled American Midwest, the "natural" way of life of Pacific islanders or Native Americans, or the middle-class small-town suburbia of the 1950s as pasts that have once actually been present as such. Precisely the palpably stylized, even schematic aesthetics of Malick's scenery, bemoaned by some as artificial or shallow, should act as a pointer to the fact that what we are being shown are not so much recollections as idealized (re)constructions—sublimity, serenity, and joy in abstraction extracted from their ordinary everyday intertwining with banality, anguish, and suffering. Malick's most exalted visualizations are intermittently interrupted and punctuated by fleeting and abortive traumatic moments, such as the explosions of warfare, suffering, death, and heartbreak interspersed among the breathtaking and meditative Pacific scenery in *The Thin Red Line* or the brief glimpses of domestic strife, illness, exclusion, and malice with an abrupt, abortive, even suppressed or censored feel that interlace the blissful childhood images of *The Tree of Life*. It is essential to note that without the contrast provided by these rupturing intrusions of, let us say simply, evil—but in its widest sense that includes the metaphysical (imperfection), physical (suffering), and moral (sin) dimensions distinguished by Leibniz[1]—the Malickian visions of goodness and beauty—again in the widest sense of the classical *agathon* and *kalon* as "appropriate" and "perfect"—would appear vacuous and pointless indeed.

In what follows, I will look at the profound philosophical and theological dimensions of this core Malickian topic. I will first briefly recapitulate the main strategies through which the Western intellectual tradition has sought to tackle the problem of the presence of evil in its various forms in nature, understood as the work of a metaphysically perfect, omnipotent, and benevolent creator—a problem generally referred to since Leibniz as the problem of theodicy. I argue that if there is a consistent philosopheme running through Malick's word—omitting here the thorny wider discussion of whether this is really the proper way to read cinema philosophically—it is most akin to the radical approach to evil adopted by F. W. J. Schelling in his essay on human freedom: the possibility of evil is not to be understood in terms of a privation or lack but as a positive and inescapable consequence of a dark and chaotic "ground" of creation against which perfection, harmony, and light can first appear as such.[2] Detached from its traditional theological framing, the Schellingian idea of ground subsequently resonates in Heidegger's phenomenological and hermeneutic model of an irreducible background dimension involved in all meaningful and intelligible givenness, a notion by which Malick is known to have been directly influenced. I will then return to examine more closely instances of this relational dynamic of foreground and background, of light/harmony/goodness in its intertwining with darkness/chaos/evil, in Malick's central cinematic works.

Dark Grounds: Evil in the Tradition and Its Schellingian Transformation

As Nietzsche's *On the Genealogy of Morals* reminds us, evil as we tend to understand it today is primarily a Judeo-Christian concept.[3] Classical antiquity was mainly concerned with what Leibniz labels the "metaphysical" aspect of evil—or rather, badness or baseness (*to kakon*)—with regard to which moral vice (*kakia*) as a base disposition of the soul is only derivative. Evil in this sense is the ontological deficiency that constitutes the gap between the ideal and the real; for the Neoplatonic synthesis of the Platonic and Aristotelian traditions, evil hinges on the role of materiality (*hylē*) as the measureless (*ametros*) element, as darkness (*to skotos*) lacking the intelligible structure and articulation bestowed by the pure light of the Ideas. Evil is the mute and chaotic dimension of being.[4] It is only within the theological framework of creation that the existence of evil—moral and physical as well as metaphysical—becomes the fundamental problem of why a perfect and omnipotent being would bring about an imperfect world. The main resources for tackling this issue provided by scripture itself are the narrative of the Fall in Genesis 3 to account for the origin of moral evil (and of morality itself) in terms of human freedom of choice and self-will and the book of Job to account for physical evil, inexplicable and unjust misfortune, and suffering through the inscrutability of divine designs.

The Gnostic movements of the first two centuries CE simply disconnected the transcendent redeeming divinity entirely from the sordidness of the material cosmos, seen in Neoplatonic terms as a distant emanation, given shape by an inferior Demiurge of the initial and absolute divine unity. The Manichaean religion, which influenced certain Christian sects, taught a more radical dualism between a spiritual sphere of good and light and a material sphere of evil and darkness. Battling these heretic orientations, both of which were deemed profoundly incompatible with scripture, gave the fundamental impetus for the theological agenda of the early Christian Church Fathers. Anti-Gnostic and anti-Manichaean efforts also brought about the radicalized doctrine of a creation ex nihilo: matter itself was created in an act preceded by absolute nothingness.[5] When evil can no longer be relegated to the realm of materiality, it can no longer be a positive feature of nature at all; instead, evil must be accounted for as a mere privation of goodness and perfection, *privatio boni*, due to the necessarily finite character of created nature and the created will, which had become permanently corrupted and predisposed to evil as a consequence of original sin.

The account of evil as mere negativity, privation, and corruption without a positive substance is the traditional approach of Christian theology, most influentially elaborated by Augustine.[6] Human sinfulness is also ultimately based on lack and finitude: in contrast to the divine will, the finite human will does not naturally will the universal good—which, in late medieval voluntarism, is increasingly understood to be good *because* God wills it[7]—but is tempted to choose a particular and individual good over the universal. This derivation of moral imperfection from metaphysical finitude still orients Kant's doctrine of "radical" evil as the human inclination to exempt oneself from the universal requirements of the moral law.[8]

Another central strategy, in many ways a systematic reconstruction of the traditional theological teaching, is found in certain early modern rationalistic systems in which evil is reduced to an epiphenomenon or aspect of a systematic totality that, considered as a whole, is completely harmonious. The most influential version of this approach is the metaphysical "optimism" elaborated in Leibniz's 1710 essay on theodicy and famously ridiculed in Voltaire's *Candide* (1759). Out of all possible finite worlds, Leibniz argues, the perfectly good creator will choose the one that is maximally good, but even this world cannot be perfect, since God alone is perfect. Even the best of all possible worlds will thus include aspects of deficiency, not as positive and substantial features but rather as epiphenomena. Were sin and suffering removed from the world we actually inhabit, it could not thereby be a better world for it would not be the world that God has in fact chosen and that, by that very token, must be optimal.[9]

In brief, the Western speculative tradition, while compelled to face the reality of evil in the sense of imperfection, suffering, and moral depravity, consistently denied these phenomena positive substance. The gradual rejection, in the nineteenth century, of the systems of German idealism as the last great heirs of this tradition, finally opened the door to the complete trivialization of evil. In Nietzsche's genealogical reading, the very concepts of good and evil arose in a specific historical constellation of power, in the great moral "slave revolt" against the ancient "aristocratic" value-system of nobility and baseness; like all values and countervalues, "evil" is simply a perspectival construction subservient to certain power interests and one that has now outlived its usefulness.[10] Post-Nietzschean thought has, accordingly, largely disavowed the concept of evil along with the concept of sin as superfluous. "Evil" has become a largely metaphorical psychological expression for extreme instances of disregard for shared moral norms or the dictates of fundamental empathy, evoked in the context of genocides, serial killers, and true crime documentaries. Hannah Arendt's concept of banal evil remains among the rare attempts to update the predominantly Kantian framework of contemporary ethics to accommodate the novel totalitarian forms of destruction and terror encountered by the twentieth century.[11]

However, at the threshold of this post-evil era lies an entirely exceptional phase in the philosophical history of evil: an extraordinary and often overlooked intensification of evil as an inherently positive metaphysical concept. This we find in the work of Schelling, in many ways the last of the German idealists and a prequel to Nietzsche. Schelling's first work, his 1792 master's thesis, was devoted to a study of the origin and nature of evil, imbued with the German idealist faith in the rational and moral progress and development of the human spirit,[12] and he continued to address the issue in his later philosophy of nature. His principal work on the topic, and one of his most influential works overall, is his 1809 treatise *Philosophical Investigations into the Essence of Human Freedom*, colloquially known as the *Freiheitsschrift*, the freedom essay. The basic problem for Schelling here is whether and to what extent the system philosophy of idealism is compatible with freedom. In principle, it is, in an idealist system for which the primal and absolute form of spiritual being is *will*.[13] Such a system, for Schelling, can simultaneously be characterized as a pantheism, in the sense that it sees all being as comprised within an absolute being, a primal will.[14] The key problem is the fact that freedom cannot be understood as mere formal lack of determination or compulsion; "the real and vital concept" of freedom is a positive capacity for both good and evil.[15] A real system of freedom would thus have to accommodate evil within the primal will itself, within the absolute or "divine" substance. None of the traditional strategies that present evil as mere deficiency or privation are truly capable of accounting for a free choice between good and evil as two positive alternatives. In a true system of freedom, there must thus be a certain split, difference, or distinction within the primal and absolute being itself.

In the dynamic system that Schelling is proposing, the primal and absolute being is will, but there is no will without becoming, as willing necessarily involves a striving from somewhere toward something.[16] There must thus be a difference between the actuality that is strived for and the ground (*Grund*) from out of which it emerges, in Schelling's terms, between existence (*Existenz*) and the ground of existence, yet both must somehow also be comprised within the being of the absolute substance. The ground of God's existence must be within God, yet "it is not God considered absolutely, that is, in so far as he exists"; it is "inseparable [*unabtrennliches*], yet still distinct [*unterschiedenes*], from him."[17] In Schelling's tortuous phrasing, the ground is "that which in God himself is not *He Himself*,"[18] in other words, that which God's existence inseparably involves but which is not identical with it. In Schelling's romantic nature-philosophy (*Naturphilosophie*), which seeks to combine idealism and realism in having the ideal emerge from the real rather than reducing the real to the ideal, nature is the dark, chaotic, and material ground from which and against which light, harmony, and ideal order are differentiated in an organic teleological development. "Nature in general is everything that lies beyond the absolute being [*Seyns*] of absolute identity."[19] Nature is the dimension involved by divine being that is not divinity *qua* divinity—the ground from out which the primal will strives toward the actualization of an ideal existence and against which light and harmony can manifest themselves. "Without this preceding darkness creatures have no reality; darkness is their necessary inheritance."[20]

The distinction between God's existence and the ground of this existence is the key to Schelling's distinction between good and evil. Just as light and harmony can only reveal themselves against darkness and chaos, goodness as the orientation of the divine will can only manifest itself against the possibility of an evil will,[21] that is, against the existence of particular and individual wills that are not driven by a mere instinctual striving from darkness to light but have an understanding and consciousness that enables them to distinguish between divine existence and its ground, between light and dark, and thus to make a free choice between them. The individual human "self-will" (*Selbstwille*) is capable of inverting and perverting the order between ground and existence and of willing the ground in its own right, the material and sensual particularities of nature in themselves rather than the divine universal harmony, which they merely background.[22] That there are evil acts of willing is a necessary condition for goodness to reveal itself,[23] yet individual wills are never compelled to either evil or good; they choose freely. Evil is a dark canvas against which goodness can appear. Because, in Schelling's system of freedom, "God is a life, not merely a being [*Seyn*]"[24]—darkness, chaos, and evil are indispensable dimensions, conditions, and effects of light, harmony, and goodness and inextricably intertwined with them. To use the scriptural metaphor, it is only after losing the state of innocence and attaining knowledge of the difference between good and evil that Eve and Adam can truly become conscious of God's goodness. "This is the sadness [*Traurigkeit*] that clings to all finite life: and, even if there is in God at least a relatively independent condition, there is a source of sadness in him that can, however, never come into actuality, but rather serves only the eternal joy of overcoming. Hence, the veil of dejection [*Schwermuth*] that is spread over all nature, the deep indestructible melancholy [*Melancholie*] of all life. Joy must have suffering, suffering must be transfigured in joy."[25]

Schelling, the last of the German Idealists, not only provided us with one of the most radical accounts of evil but was also one of the last great Western philosophers to tackle the problems of evil and theodicy within their traditional theological framework. Even during his lifetime, Schelling had the opportunity to witness how this framework and these problems gradually became obsolete and he himself turned into a living monument of a bygone age of speculative metaphysics. Heidegger, one of the few twentieth-century thinkers to give Schelling a decisive role in modern thought, makes the surprising statement that "Schelling is the truly creative and boldest thinker of this whole age of German philosophy . . . to *such* an extent that he drives German Idealism from within right beyond its own fundamental position."[26] Only two years after the apex of German idealism in Hegel's *Phenomenology of Spirit* (1807), Schelling's freedom essay bursts the whole project apart: the distinction between the existence of God and its ground ultimately makes the kind of system sought by German idealism—an order that would refer all of being, reality as a whole, back to self-consciousness as a unifying absolute point of reference—impossible.[27] When the absolute becomes dependent on a background that is not simply identical with the absolute, the absolute can no longer be absolute, in the literal sense of being "absolved" of any constitutive dependencies upon anything beyond itself—it precisely becomes inextricably embedded in a context that stretches beyond it.

For Heidegger, this account of the irreducible context-embeddedness of all being was precisely the decisive moment in Schelling's thought, a discovery that, although Schelling himself never realized it, transgresses the fundamental premises not only of German idealism but of the entire Western metaphysical search for absolute points of reference as a whole. Already in his early work, Heidegger himself appropriates the Schellingian concept of ground as a pathway for approaching the radical contextuality and relationality of being, particularly in his 1929 essay "On the Essence of Ground." Here, expanding on the project of *Being and Time*, he articulates, in heavily Schellingian terms,[28] the human Dasein's manner of making sense of beings through "transcending" the immediately given toward a temporally dimensional background-context of meaning as "freedom for ground."[30] Dasein understands things by "grounding" them, in the sense of placing them into a wider context, a network of references that always transcends that which is immediately present, and this contextualization is precisely the essence of human freedom. Heidegger thus detaches Schelling's account of human freedom as the capacity to orient oneself toward the "dark ground" of existence from its theological framework and presents this freedom as constitutive for all human access to meaningfulness in general.[30]

Leviathan in Paradise: Malick and Evil

It is well-known biographical fact that Terrence Malick studied philosophy at Harvard with Stanley Cavell in the early 1960s; after a successful bachelor's thesis on Husserl and Heidegger and a personal interview with Heidegger during a visit to Germany, Malick embarked on graduate studies at Magdalen College, Oxford. However, due in part to disagreements with his advisor, Gilbert Ryle, over the proposed topic of his thesis—the concept of world in Kierkegaard, Heidegger, and Wittgenstein—he did not complete his Bachelor of Philosophy degree, and ultimately he abandoned the prospect of an academic career. He nonetheless continued to teach philosophy for some time at MIT as a stand-in for Hubert Dreyfus, and during this period he completed the first English translation of Heidegger's "Vom Wesen des Grundes," published in 1969 by Northwestern University Press in a bilingual edition of the text under the title *The Essence of Reasons*.

Because of this background, Malick's cinema is often seen as in some sense "Heideggerian," as incorporating overarching reflections on being or Heideggerian themes such as finitude or mortality.[31] There is no denying that the engagement with Heidegger's thought left clearly detectable marks on Malick's work; we may suppose that his translation effort reflects a particular significance for him of the themes of ground and freedom. Here, however, I propose a more mediating role of Heideggerian thought as a pathway for approaching fundamental questions inherent to the entire tradition; indeed, Malick seems, to a certain extent, to transpose the theme of ground back to its more traditional theological framework, thus approaching the Schellingian context from which Heidegger himself drew influence. With this, I am not suggesting that Malick has ever seriously engaged the work of Schelling, of which there is no evidence, or that his works should be seen as Schellingian on any level more profound than that of connotations.[32] Still, Schelling's freedom essay, with its insistence—

against the traditional view of evil as mere privation and corruption—on the positivity of evil and its indispensability as the dark background of the good, seems to me to provide particularly apt conceptual tools for interpreting the specific images of the interaction between good and evil, light and darkness, conveyed to us by Malick's core works.

The prominence of the problems of evil and theodicy in Malick, perhaps most explicit in *The Tree of Life*, has not escaped commentators.[33] Yet Malick's treatment of good and evil has often been read as a straightforward nostalgia for paradise lost, as "an Edenic yearning to recapture a lost wholeness of being, an idyllic state of integration with the natural and good,"[34] as a "reinvented myth of the Fall, filtered through a Vietnam-era political consciousness,"[35] or in terms of a reestablished "opposition between the world of nature as paradise and the world of modern human society as paradise lost"[36]—or simply as giving poetic expression to the inexplicable mystery of evil and suffering.[37] I prefer here to highlight the "war in the heart of nature" evoked by the opening voiceover of *The Thin Red Line*, attributed to Private Train, precisely as the constitutive and original conflictual interplay between good and evil, light and darkness, harmony and chaos. Nature is here not an immaculate Garden of Eden, but rather already "vies with itself" precisely because the "avenging power" in nature is, from the outset, "not one power, but two"—in Schellingian terms, on the one hand, nature as the dark chaotic ground, and on the other, the light, harmony, and unity ever striving to differentiate itself from this background.

The first thing we are shown in *The Thin Red Line* is, significantly, a crocodile—one possible translation of the biblical Leviathan, the "king over all that are proud" (Job 41:34), which God in his reply to Job holds out as an emblem of the humanly insuperable majesty of creation but also of its dark and blind brutality and monstrosity. The crocodile is also a descendant of the serpent that was already in Eden, cursed after the Fall and condemned to thereafter go upon its belly (Gen. 3:14). After that we see light sifting from above into the perpetual twilight of the tropical rainforest and also the vines, serpent-like, twining around the trees and "swallowing everything" as Colonel Tall (Nick Nolte) later points out to Captain Staros (Elias Koteas) to illustrate his crude point: "Nature's cruel," not intrinsically different from the human-made slaughter they are themselves engaged in. The following images showing the joyous and peaceful play of the Melanesian children on the beach and in the ocean—seen, as we are immediately made aware, through the adoring eyes of Private Witt, for whom they doubtless manifest "another world" transcendent to the bellicose one he is momentarily fleeing—should not deceive us as to the proper scriptural subtext. We are in an Eden that is already postlapsarian, one in which the serpent, the Leviathan, holds sway. Even Witt's ecstatic vision begins to falter at the moment his idealized conjecture—"Kids around here never fight"—is gently discredited by the native mother (Polyn Leona) (who admits to being afraid of Witt's "army" look): "Sometimes. Sometimes when you see them playing, they always fight."

A patrol boat arrives to snatch Witt from his AWOL cloud cuckoo land "where everything's gonna be ok" back to "this rock" that is "blowin' itself to hell as fast as everybody can arrange it" (Sergeant Welsh [Sean Penn]). The men of C Company—each driven, like the stock characters of a medieval morality play, by a single fundamental motive, Witt by his exalted longing, Tall by his Faustian personal ambition, Staros by his compassion for his men, Private Bell by his love for his wife—are promptly shipped off to the inferno of Guadalcanal to capture Henderson Airfield. The ensuing bloody scramble for the Japanese strongpoint at Hill 210 brings death for many and disillusionment for the rest: Staros is powerless to prevent the destruction of his company and is ultimately sent away by Tall as being "too soft." Bell is shattered by his wife's unexpected request for divorce. Witt returns from battle to see the native community in a transformed light, as marred by distrust, fear, aggression, and disease, before having his own "spark" put out in an ambush.

The everyman of *The Thin Red Line*—the representative of humanity as a whole, embodying Witt's reflection that "all men got one big soul who everybody's part of; all faces of the same man, one big self"—is the unremarkable and unassuming Private Train (John Dee Smith), a youth from the South whose only concerns are "dyin' and the Lord." It is Train's voice that is used in Malick's emblematic lingering voiceovers to convey the abstract universal questions at play in the human condition—essentially Job's questions to his creator—concerning the origin of evil ("This great evil. Where's it come from? How'd it steal into the world? What seed, what root did it grow from?"), its persistence ("Who's doing this? Who's killing us? Robbing us of life and light. Mocking us with the sight of what we might have known"), its purpose ("Does our ruin benefit the earth? Does it help the grass to grow or the sun to shine?"), and, finally, its compatibility with the absolute ("Is this darkness in you, too? Have you passed through this night?"). A Schellingian synthesis is attained in Train's concluding voiceover, in which "darkness and light, strife and love" are seen as inextricably intertwined "workings of one mind" or primal will to which individual human minds appear to be related, in Witt's expression, as "coals thrown from the fire." From this absolute viewpoint, it is the dark background itself that permits creation to shine forth: "Look out through my eyes. Look out at the things you made. All things shining." In the unadorned parlance put into the mouth of the actual character Train, this is captured perhaps even more efficiently: "It's gonna get a lot worse before it gets better."

Variations of these themes abound throughout Malick's mature work. In *The New World*, King James's colonists, like Columbus before them, find themselves in terrestrial paradise, primarily seen through the eyes of Witt's kindred spirit, the romanticizing professional adventurer John Smith (Colin Farrel), for whom the native Powhatan people—the "naturals"—are "gentle, loving, faithful, lacking in all guile and trickery." In this unspoiled wilderness, expropriated from these Rousseauian noble savages who, we are told, have "no jealousy, no sense of possession," the Jamestown pioneers are going to prepare the "new kingdom of the spirit" preached by Captain Newport (Christopher Plummer), "a land where man may rise to his true stature." These sentiments of wonder are reciprocated by the native Americans, in awe of the Europeans' ships and gunpowder. "A god he seems to me," says the adolescent Pocahontas (Q'orianka Kilcher) of John Smith, her first love. "There is no evil in you." In a magnificently evocative scene, her uncle Opechancanough (Wes Studi), brought to the Old World, wanders among the perfect geometrical order and harmony of Hampton Court gardens, speechlessly witnessing the Europeans' professed victory over nature and their human-made completion of creation yet failing to find in Europe "this 'God' they speak so much about." Mutual disillusionment is inevitable; Eden grows darker as the Jamestown colonists are beset by hunger and hardship, with the explosion of conflict the gentle and loving naturals soon come to be perceived as "naked devils," and the "true stature" of European humanity in the New World turns out to be violent conquest driven by the desire for gold. John Smith's love is treacherous; his consuming quest for paradise on earth ultimately drives him to abandon Pocahontas and "sail past his Indies," "killing the god" in Pocahontas who, in the end, finds happiness only in her mundane married life with Thomas Rolfe (Christian Bale).

What is tragically put to test in *The Tree of Life* is the protagonist's mother's (Jessica Chastain) naive faith that no one who loves "the way of grace," the way of humble and selfless love, "ever comes to a bad end"—but equal disappointment is met by his father's (Brad Pitt) tough-minded pursuit of "the way of nature" with its self-centered ambitions, as both of them are devastated by the loss of a son. What is fundamentally challenged here is the idea that nature and grace, distinguished since the early Church Fathers, are really two separate ways that can be kept apart.[38] The dark, chaotic, and blind forces of "nature"—inevitably involving destruction and suffering—and flickering moments of beauty, love, and purpose—unexpected and unwarranted "grace"—are shown to penetrate and intersperse each other both in the personal history of protagonist, Jack O'Brien (Michael Koeth/Finnegan William/Hunter McCracken/Sean Penn) (violent and aggressive impulses and callous selfishness alternating with love, reconciliation, and forgiveness) and in the cosmic history of the universe (the brutal instincts of the animal kingdom balanced with the harmony of the celestial bodies). The hand that gives is the hand that takes away, and both movements are meaningful only in this reciprocity.

The brutal summary of the core issue at stake is finally given to us in *A Hidden Life*: "He who created us, he created evil." But this line is pronounced by the devil's advocate, the attorney Herder (Matthias Schoenaerts), who quotes *Hamlet*: "Conscience makes cowards of us all." And yet this is the story of an entirely ordinary man, a simple and unassuming farmer whose life as a whole was by no means an unambiguous archetype of pure virtue—a conscientious objector who became remarkable solely by relying on his conscience alone, on the Socratic conviction that it is better to suffer injustice than to do it, at a time when individual conscience had all but become irrelevant. In normal times, Jägerstätter's life would indeed have remained entirely hidden and was distinguished up to the point of sainthood simply because its momentary spark of unrelenting personal rigor shone so brightly against the profound darkness, evil, and mass conformity of its day.

Conclusion: Twilit Paradises

In summary, what Malick's films present, when read from the Schellingian perspective I have proposed here, is not the traditional theological narrative of the Fall in the sense of a lapse from an original immaculate and paradisiacal state of nature through subsequent corruption and contamination by extrinsic evil. Eden lies about us still, but it is an Eden where the serpent, figuratively speaking, is always already present, where primeval innocence has always already been contaminated by the fruit of the tree of the knowledge of good and evil—which, in one exegetical tradition, is just another name or aspect of the tree of life, situated in the very midst of Eden.[39] Life as portrayed by Malick does not take place in the clarity of a noon without shadows but rather, in the words of Danforth in Arthur Miller's *The Crucible*, "in the dusky afternoon when evil mixed itself with good and befuddled the world."[40] It is only in such a twilit paradise that harmony, light, and goodness can ever appear against a murky background of chaos, darkness, and evil—and what Malick's cinema shows us is precisely this chiaroscuro, this interplay, this endless dialectic without synthesis. The deep-seated melancholy of Malickian cinema invoked above turns out to be "the deep indestructible melancholy of all life" described by Schelling: joy must have suffering, suffering must be transfigured in joy.[43]

Notes

1. Leibniz, *Œuvres philosophiques*, vol. 2, 97; Leibniz, *Theodicy*, 136.

2. I am thankful to Dr. Olli Pitkänen for the opportunity to supervise his magnificent doctoral dissertation, *The Possibility of a Metaphysical Conception of Evil in Contemporary Philosophy* (Jyväskylä: University of Jyväskylä, 2020), which decisively deepened my understanding of Schelling's radical approach to the problem of evil.

3. Nietzsche, *Zur Genealogie der Moral*, 780–81; Nietzsche, *On the Genealogy of Morals*, 19–20. For a comprehensive overview of the conceptual history of evil, see Marquard, "Malum I"; Schottlaender, "Malum II"; Arndt, "Malum III"; Schneider, "Malum IV"; Riesenhuber, "Malum V"; and Hügli, "Malum VI."

4. See Plotinus, *Enneads* 1.8.8.

5. Creation ex nihilo was first taught by the second-century theologian Tatian of Adiabene, and soon after him by Theophilus of Antioch and Irenaeus; see Köhler, "Schöpfung III."

6. See Augustine, *Enchiridion ad Laurentium*, 236; Augustine, *The Augustine Catechism*, 40–41.

7. See William of Ockham, *In librum primum Sententiarum ordinatio*, d48. q1; cf. Riesenhuber, "Malum V," 674–81.

8. For Kant on radical evil, see Kant, *Die Religion innerhalb der Grenzen der bloßen Vernunft*, 17–53; Kant, *Religion within the Boundaries of Mere Reason and Other Writings*, 45–73.

Not One Power, But Two | 141

9. Leibniz, *Œuvres philosophiques*, vol. 2, 88–89; *Theodicy*, 128–29.
10. Nietzsche, *Zur Genealogie der Moral*, 771–98; Nietzsche, *On the Genealogy of Morals*, 11–38.
11. See Arendt, *Eichmann in Jerusalem*.
12. Schelling, *Antiquissimi de prima malorum humanorum origine philosophematis Genes. III explicandi tentamen criticum et philosophicum*.
13. "In the final and highest judgment, there is no other being [*Seyn*] than will [*Wollen*]. Will is primal being [*Urseyn*] to which alone all predicates of being apply: groundlessness, eternality, independence from time, self-affirmation. . . . In our times philosophy has been raised up to this point by idealism." Schelling, *Philosophische Untersuchungen über das Wesen der menschlichen Freiheit und die damit zusammenhängen Gegenstände*, 350–51; and Schelling, *Philosophical Investigations into the Essence of Human Freedom*, 21 (translation modified).
14. Schelling, *Philosophische Untersuchungen*, 409–11; Schelling, *Philosophical Investigations*, 71–72.
15. Schelling, *Philosophische Untersuchungen*, 352; Schelling, *Philosophical Investigations*, 23.
16. Schelling, *Philosophische Untersuchungen*, 358–60; Schelling, *Philosophical Investigations*, 28–29.
17. Schelling, *Philosophische Untersuchungen*, 358; Schelling, *Philosophical Investigations*, 27.
18. Schelling, *Philosophische Untersuchungen*, 359; Schelling, *Philosophical Investigations*, 28.
19. Schelling, *Philosophische Untersuchungen*, 358; Schelling, *Philosophical Investigations*, 28 (translation modified).
20. Schelling, *Philosophische Untersuchungen*, 360; Schelling, *Philosophical Investigations*, 29.
21. Schelling, *Philosophische Untersuchungen*, 373–76; Schelling, *Philosophical Investigations*, 40–42.
22. Schelling, *Philosophische Untersuchungen*, 362–64, 389–94; Schelling, *Philosophical Investigations*, 31–33, 54–58.
23. Schelling, *Philosophische Untersuchungen*, 377–78; Schelling, *Philosophical Investigations*, 44.
24. Schelling, *Philosophische Untersuchungen*, 403; Schelling, *Philosophical Investigations*, 66 (translation modified).
25. Schelling, *Philosophische Untersuchungen*, 399; Schelling, *Philosophical Investigations*, 62–63.
26. Heidegger, *Gesamtausgabe*, vol. 42, 6; and Heidegger, *Schelling's Treatise on the Essence of Human Freedom*, 4 (translation modified).
27. Heidegger, *Gesamtausgabe*, vol. 42, 278–79; *Schelling's Treatise*, 161.

28. In "On the Essence of Ground," Heidegger does not discuss Schelling at length but points out the central importance of Schelling's freedom essay for the conceptual history of the problem of ground (*Grund*); Heidegger, "Vom Wesen des Grundes," 125; Heidegger, "On the Essence of Ground," 99. Heidegger taught his first seminar on Schelling's freedom essay during the preceding winter semester of 1927–28; Heidegger, *Gesamtausgabe*, vol. 86, 49–54, 529–48.

29. Heidegger, "Vom Wesen des Grundes," 163–75; Heidegger, "On the Essence of Ground," 125–35.

30. On this, see Backman, "Radical Contextuality in Heidegger's Postmetaphysics."

31. For discussions of the "Heideggerian" features of Malick's cinema, see Cavell, *The World Viewed*, xiv–xvi; Sinnerbrink, "A Heideggerian Cinema?"; and Sinnerbrink, *Terrence Malick*, 9–13, 40–44, 56, 65, 68, 70–71; Furstenau and MacAvoy, "Terrence Malick's Heideggerian Cinema"; Rhym, "The Paradigmatic Shift in the Critical Reception of Terrence Malick's *Badlands* and the Emergence of a Heideggerian Cinema"; Woessner, "What Is Heideggerian Cinema?"; Pattison, "In the Theater of Light"; and Barnett, "*Gelassenheit*."

32. A connection between Malick and Schelling has very rarely been brought up in commentaries; a notable exception is Warwick Mules's remark concerning the Schellingian dimensions of *The Thin Red Line*, namely, the insight that "nature grounds the possibility of both good and evil by withdrawing from them (as indifferent nature)." Mules, *With Nature*, 171–73.

33. See Mottram, "All Things Shining"; Leithart, *Shining Glory*, 10–16, 73–81; Manninen, "The Problem of Evil and Humans' Relationship with God in Terrence Malick's *The Tree of Life*"; and Scott, "Light in the Darkness."

34. Mottram, "All Things Shining," 15.

35. Streamas, "The Greatest Generation Steps Over *The Thin Red Line*," 143.

36. Silberman, "Terrence Malick, Landscape and 'What Is This War in the Heart of Nature?,' " 166.

37. Leithart, *Shining Glory*, 16.

38. On this, see Cisney, "All the World Is Shining, and Love Is Smiling through All Things." On the history of the theological opposition between nature and grace, see Peters, "Gnade."

39. On the trees of life and of the knowledge of good and evil, see Makowiecki, "Untangled Branches."

40. Miller, *The Crucible*, 76.

41. I thank Steven DeLay for the opportunity to contribute to this volume and for superb feedback and encouragement, and Olli Pitkänen for profoundly introducing me to Schelling's radical approach to the problem of evil. For financial support, I am indebted to my Academy of Finland research fellowship *Creation, Genius, Innovation: Towards a Conceptual Genealogy of Western Creativity* (decision number 317276).

Bibliography

Arendt, Hannah. *Eichmann in Jerusalem: A Report on the Banality of Evil* [1963]. 2nd ed. New York: Viking Press, 1964.
Arndt, Martin. "Malum III." In *Historisches Wörterbuch der Philosophie*, vol. 5, edited by Joachim Ritter and Karlfried Gründer, 665–67. Basel: Schwabe, 1980. https://doi.org/10.24894/HWPh.5254.
Augustine. *Enchiridion ad Laurentium*. In *Patrologia Latina*, edited by Jacques Paul Migne, vol. 40, 231–90. Paris: Migne, 1865.
———. *The Augustine Catechism: The Enchiridion on Faith, Hope, and Charity*. Translated by Bruce Harbert. Edited by Boniface Ramsey. New York: New City Press, 1999.
Backman, Jussi. "Radical Contextuality in Heidegger's Postmetaphysics: The Singularity of Being and the Fourfold." In *Paths in Heidegger's Later Thought*, edited by Günter Figal, Diego D'Angelo, Tobias Keiling, and Guang Yang, 190–211. Bloomington: Indiana University Press, 2020. https://doi.org/10.2307/j.ctvxcrxjn.13.
Barnett, Christopher B. "*Gelassenheit*: Spirit and Spirituality in the Films of Terrence Malick." In *Theology and the Films of Terrence Malick*, edited by Christopher B. Barnett and Clark J. Elliston, 99–114. New York: Routledge, 2017. https://doi.org/10.4324/9781315743158.
Cavell, Stanley. *The World Viewed: Reflections on the Ontology of Film*. 2nd ed. Cambridge, MA: Harvard University Press, 1979.
Cisney, Vernon W. "All the World Is Shining, and Love Is Smiling through All Things: The Collapse of the 'Two Ways' in *The Tree of Life*." In *The Way of Nature and the Way of Grace: Philosophical Footholds on Terrence Malick's The Tree of Life*, edited by Jonathan Beever and Vernon W. Cisney, 213–32. Evanston, IL: Northwestern University Press, 2016.
Furstenau, Marc, and Leslie MacAvoy. "Terrence Malick's Heideggerian Cinema: War and the Question of Being in *The Thin Red Line*." In *The Cinema of Terrence Malick: Poetic Visions of America*. 2nd ed., edited by Hannah Patterson, 179–91. London: Wallflower Press, 2007.
Heidegger, Martin. *Gesamtausgabe*. Vol. 42, *Schelling: Vom Wesen der menschlichen Freiheit (1809)* [1936], edited by Ingrid Schüßler. Frankfurt am Main: Klostermann, 1988.
———. *Gesamtausgabe*. Vol. 86, *Seminare: Hegel–Schelling* [1927–1957], edited by Peter Trawny. Frankfurt am Main: Klostermann, 2011.
———. "On the Essence of Ground." Translated by William McNeill. In *Pathmarks*, edited by William McNeill, 97–135, 367–72. Cambridge: Cambridge University Press, 1998.
———. *Schelling's Treatise on the Essence of Human Freedom*. Translated by Joan Stambaugh. Athens: Ohio University Press, 1985.

———. "Vom Wesen des Grundes" [1929]. In *Wegmarken*, edited by Friedrich-Wilhelm von Herrmann, 123–75. Vol. 9 of the *Gesamtausgabe*. Frankfurt am Main: Klostermann, 1976.

Hügli, Anton. "Malum VI." In *Historisches Wörterbuch der Philosophie*, vol. 5, edited by Joachim Ritter and Karlfried Gründer, 681–706. Basel: Schwabe, 1980. https://doi.org/10.24894/HWPh.5254.

Kant, Immanuel. *Die Religion innerhalb der Grenzen der bloßen Vernunft* [1793]. In *Kant's Gesammelte Schriften*, vol. 6, 1–202. Berlin: Reimer, 1907.

———. *Religion within the Boundaries of Mere Reason and Other Writings*. Translated and edited by Allen Wood and George Di Giovanni. Cambridge: Cambridge University Press, 1998.

Köhler, Johannes. "Schöpfung III." In *Historisches Wörterbuch der Philosophie*, vol. 8, edited by Joachim Ritter and Karlfried Gründer, 1395–99. Basel: Schwabe, 1992. https://doi.org/10.24894/HWPh.5419.

Leibniz, G. W. F. *Œuvres philosophiques*, edited by Paul Janet. Vol. 2, *Essais de théodicée* [1710]. 2nd ed. Paris: Alcan, 1900.

———. *Theodicy: Essays on the Goodness of God, the Freedom of Man and the Origin of Evil*. Translated by E. M. Huggard. Eugene, OR: Wipf and Stock, 2001.

Leithart, Peter J. *Shining Glory: Theological Reflections on Terrence Malick's Tree of Life*. Eugene, OR: Cascade Books, 2013.

Makowiecki, Mark. "Untangled Branches: The Edenic Tree(s) and the Multivocal WAW." *The Journal of Theological Studies* 71, no. 2 (2020): 441–57. https://doi.org/10.1093/jts/flaa093.

Manninen, Bertha A. "The Problem of Evil and Humans' Relationship with God in Terrence Malick's *The Tree of Life*." *Journal of Religion and Film* 17, no. 1 (2013). https://digitalcommons.unomaha.edu/jrf/vol17/iss1/34/.

Marquard, Odo. "Malum I." In *Historisches Wörterbuch der Philosophie*, vol. 5, edited by Joachim Ritter and Karlfried Gründer, 652–56. Basel: Schwabe, 1980. https://doi.org/10.24894/HWPh.5254.

Miller, Arthur. *The Crucible* [1953]. Oxford: Heinemann, 1992.

Mottram, Ron. "All Things Shining: The Struggle for Wholeness, Redemption and Transcendence in the Films of Terrence Malick." In *The Cinema of Terrence Malick: Poetic Visions of America*, 2nd ed., edited by Hannah Patterson, 14–26. London: Wallflower Press, 2007.

Mules, Warwick. *With Nature: Nature Philosophy as Poetics through Schelling, Heidegger, Benjamin and Nancy*. Bristol: Intellect, 2014.

Nietzsche, Friedrich. *On the Genealogy of Morals: A Polemic*. Translated by Douglas Smith. Oxford: Oxford University Press, 1996.

———. *Zur Genealogie der Moral: Eine Streitschrift* [1887]. In *Werke in drei Bänden*, vol. 2, edited by Karl Schlechta, 762–900. Munich: Hanser, 1954.

Pattison, George. "In the Theater of Light: Toward a Heideggerian Poetics of Film." In *Theology and the Films of Terrence Malick*, edited by Christopher

B. Barnett and Clark J. Elliston, 29–43. New York: Routledge, 2017. https://doi.org/10.4324/9781315743158.

Peters, Albrecht. "Gnade." In *Historisches Wörterbuch der Philosophie*, vol. 3, edited by Joachim Ritter, 707–13. Basel: Schwabe, 1974. https://doi.org/10.24894/HWPh.1378.

Pitkänen, Olli. *The Possibility of a Metaphysical Conception of Evil in Contemporary Philosophy*. Doctoral dissertation. Jyväskylä: University of Jyväskylä, 2020. http://urn.fi/URN:ISBN:978-951-39-8074-0.

Plotinus. *Plotini Opera*. Edited by Paul Henry and Hans-Rudolph Schwyzer. Vol. 1, *Enneades* [*The Enneads*] *I–III*. Leiden: Brill, 1951.

Rhym, John. "The Paradigmatic Shift in the Critical Reception of Terrence Malick's *Badlands* and the Emergence of a Heideggerian Cinema." *Quarterly Review of Film and Video* 27, no. 4 (2010): 255–66. https://doi.org/10.1080/10509200802350331.

Riesenhuber, Klaus. "Malum V." In *Historisches Wörterbuch der Philosophie*, vol. 5, edited by Joachim Ritter and Karlfried Gründer, 669–81. Basel: Schwabe, 1980. https://doi.org/10.24894/HWPh.5254.

Schelling, F. W. J. *Antiquissimi de prima malorum humanorum origine philosophematis Genes. III explicandi tentamen criticum et philosophicum* [1792]. In *Sämtliche Werke*, vol. 1, edited by K. F. A. Schelling, 1–40. Stuttgart: Cotta, 1856.

———. *Philosophische Untersuchungen über das Wesen der menschlichen Freiheit und die damit zusammenhängen Gegenstände* [1809]. In *Sämmtliche Werke*, vol. 7, edited by K. F. A. Schelling, 331–416. Stuttgart: Cotta, 1860.

———. *Philosophical Investigations into the Essence of Human Freedom*. Translated by Jeff Love and Johannes Schmidt. Albany: State University of New York Press, 2006.

Schneider, Helmut. "Malum IV." In *Historisches Wörterbuch der Philosophie*, vol. 5, edited by Joachim Ritter and Karlfried Gründer, 667–69. Basel: Schwabe, 1980. https://doi.org/10.24894/HWPh.5254.

Schottlaender, Rudolf. "Malum II." In *Historisches Wörterbuch der Philosophie*, vol. 5, edited by Joachim Ritter and Karlfried Gründer, 656–65. Basel: Schwabe, 1980. https://doi.org/10.24894/HWPh.5254.

Scott, Mark S. M. "Light in the Darkness: The Problem of Evil in *The Thin Red Line*." In *Theology and the Films of Terrence Malick*, edited by Christopher B. Barnett and Clark J. Elliston, 173–86. New York: Routledge, 2017. https://doi.org/10.4324/9781315743158.

Silberman, Robert. "Terrence Malick, Landscape and 'What Is This War in the Heart of Nature?'" In *The Cinema of Terrence Malick: Poetic Visions of America*, 2nd ed., edited by Hannah Patterson, 164–78. London: Wallflower Press, 2007.

Sinnerbrink, Robert. "A Heideggerian Cinema? On Terrence Malick's *The Thin Red Line*." *Film-Philosophy* 10, no. 3 (2006): 26–37. https://www.euppublishing.com/doi/epdf/10.3366/film.2006.0027.

———. *Terrence Malick: Filmmaker and Philosopher*. London: Bloomsbury, 2019.
Streamas, John. "The Greatest Generation Steps Over *The Thin Red Line*." In *The Cinema of Terrence Malick: Poetic Visions of America*, 2nd ed., edited by Hannah Patterson, 141–51. London: Wallflower Press, 2007.
William of Ockham. *Opera theologica*. Vol. 4, *In librum primum Sententiarum ordinatio*, edited by Girard Etzkorn and Francis Kelley. St. Bonaventure, NY: St. Bonaventure University, 1979.
Woessner, Martin. "What Is Heideggerian Cinema? Film, Philosophy, and Cultural Mobility." *New German Critique* 38, no. 2 (2011): 129–57. https://doi.org/10.1215/0094033X-1221803.

Chapter 7

Tending God's Garden

Philosophical Themes in *The Tree of Life*

Naomi Fisher

God took seeds from other worlds and sowed them on this earth, and raised up his garden; and everything that could sprout sprouted, but it lives and grows only through its sense of being in touch with other mysterious worlds; if this sense is weakened or destroyed in you, that which has grown up in you dies. Then you become indifferent to life, and even come to hate it.

—Dostoevsky, *The Brothers Karamazov*

This chapter presents the world of Terrence Malick's film *The Tree of Life* as "God's garden."[1] Just as a gardener can learn to recognize and cultivate the seeds and plants in their garden, the human being can learn to recognize and be attentive to goodness in order to help it grow and spread. Drawing primarily on *The Brothers Karamazov* by Dostoevsky, I show how Malick weaves together themes of memory, freedom, and nature in order to suggest that one can retrieve a sensitivity to and recognition of what is good through a particular kind of recollection. This suggestion is a powerful antidote to despair brought on by human suffering and evil, since it draws on a person's own sense and memories of goodness as that which makes the world worthy of love, despite pervasive suffering, loss, and evil. A person who is able to recollect goodness and attune themselves to the world is accordingly equipped to bring the goodness that they now recognize to fruition.

I begin by setting out the framework of memory from Plato's *Phaedrus* and *The Brothers Karamazov*, as well as Malick's *Knight of Cups*. In *The Tree of Life*, Malick is combining these notions of memory in the main sequence of the film, in which Jack imaginatively recollects the development of the universe up through and including his childhood. Following this section, I explore how Malick's contrast between the way of nature and the way of grace is prefigured in Dostoevsky's contrast between a distorted notion of freedom and the "monastic way." Both demonstrate how attention to goodness in memory and nature can serve as a corrective to a self-centered notion of freedom. I then draw on the themes of gardening in both *The Brothers Karamazov* and *The Tree of Life* in order to show that similar to the manner in which one can cultivate the seeds of a garden, one can "grow" the goodness in themselves by cultivating the seeds of goodness that are present in them and in the world. I conclude the chapter by arguing that Malick's film is an instance of goodness in God's garden: brought about through a kind of co-creative "gardening" or cultivation of goodness, it is a tangible manifestation of goodness that can assist in the cultivation of or attunement to goodness in its viewers.

Memory

Perhaps the most striking account of memory in Plato's corpus occurs in the myth of the charioteer in the *Phaedrus*.[2] A soul, represented by a charioteer and a team of horses, ascends to the highest heaven, where it can catch a glimpse of justice, self-control, knowledge, goodness, and beauty as they truly are in themselves. This vision confers upon the soul the capacity to remember these things when it encounters images of them on earth. Socrates' account focuses on beauty, since beauty was the most radiant of the objects in the highest heaven: beauty "was radiant among the other objects; and now that we have come down here, we grasp it sparkling through the clearest of our senses."[3]

These passages from the *Phaedrus* are paraphrased in Malick's *Knight of Cups*: "Once the soul was perfect and had wings. It could soar into heaven." The earthly soul has lost its wings, but when it encounters beauty, "the soul remembers the beauty it used to know in heaven and wings begin to sprout." In this film, the protagonist Rick (Christian Bale) is lost, but seeking for and entranced by beauty; he is aware that his current mode of life is unsatisfactory. In *Knight of Cups* we see a man who recognizes beauty—primarily in women—but is unable to draw together the fragments that he finds into a well-lived life. Malick makes palpable Rick's frustration: "I spent thirty years not living life. . . . I can't remember a man I wanted to be." This lack of memory can be seen as crucial to Rick's predicament. The film closes with the words, "Remember. Begin." But what is it that Rick is supposed to remember? What kind of memory is at issue? Given the invocation of the *Phaedrus*, one might suspect that the imperative "remember" is counseling Platonic recollection. In Plato's *Phaedrus*, such recollection is occasioned by encounters with beauty. But this does not appear to be enough for Rick, as he meanders from beautiful woman to beautiful woman, motivated by his longing for beauty but not immediately guided through these encounters into a recognition of goodness. One can find in *The Tree of Life* a notion of memory that begins to answer these questions. The remembrance that is necessary for Rick is undertaken by Jack (Sean Penn), as Jack recalls his childhood memories and imaginatively recollects the origins and development of the universe from its beginnings to the end of time.

Other similar notions of recollection can illuminate the way in which recollection is operative in *The Tree of Life*. For instance, Kierkegaard's William Afham in the preface to *Stages on Life's Way* offers a similar notion of recollection, which unites the temporal and particular experiences with the eternal:

> To recollect is by no means the same as to remember. For example, one can remember very well every single detail of an event without thereby recollecting it. . . . Through memory, the experience presents itself to receive the consecration of recollection. . . . In recollection, a person draws on the eternal.[4]

Recollection is here distinct from memory. While the experience is the basis for the recollection, the details or accuracy of the memory is not what is primary in recollection. Rather, in recollection, the memory is "consecrated" by exhibiting that which is eternal.

Dostoevsky similarly develops the Platonic notion of recollection, but unlike Kierkegaard, the emphasis is on childhood memories. In *The*

Brothers Karamazov, the characters Zosima and Alyosha present such memories as pathways to the good. In the words of Alyosha:

> You must know that there is nothing higher, or stronger, or sounder, or more useful afterwards in life, than some good memory, especially a memory from childhood, from the parental home. You hear a lot said about your education, yet some such beautiful, sacred memory, preserved from childhood, is perhaps the best education. If a man stores up many such memories to take into life, then he is saved for his whole life.[5]

Here, Alyosha asserts that a memory of goodness can be a guide throughout life; such a memory can save a person. Such a memory is an instance of goodness here in the world, and accordingly indicates the presence of goodness and beauty. Such memories punctuate the novel and affect the characters deeply. Alyosha, for instance, has a formative memory of the slanting rays of the setting sun while his mother held him out sobbing before an icon of the Mother of God.[6] Zosima and Dmitri describe similar formative memories that are formative precisely because they indicate something transcendent and beautiful.[7] Thus we can read in Dostoevsky as well as Kierkegaard a melding of memories with the Platonic notion of recollection, in which, through the act of recollecting, one can attend to that which is eternal. A memory can be recalled as an instantiation of eternal beauty and goodness; more broadly, anything imagined, encountered, or remembered can occasion Platonic recollection of the goodness and beauty in the highest heaven.

Malick explores such recollection in Jack's imaginative, reconstructive remembering, which extends in the sequence of the film back to the beginning of time and, perhaps (depending on one's interpretation of the film), forward to the eschaton, but centers on his own childhood. The continuity between the cosmic and childhood sequences—the universe develops into the world into which Jack is born—suggests that both the cosmic scenes and the childhood scenes that follow are not "memories" in the sense of mere factual depictions or recollections of past experiences but an imaginative reconstruction using some particular event as an instance or image of that which is eternal. Jack "remembers" not only his own childhood but all that might be relevant for him to recall what is good about the world, including its origins in God's goodness.[8] The film opens with the quotation from Job, "Where were you when I laid the foundations of the earth? . . . When the morning stars sang together, and all the sons of God shouted for joy?" Jack's imaginative remembrance of these moments can be viewed through the lens of this quotation: beauty and joy are infused into nature from the very first moments of creation.

Within the Platonic framework adopted in these philosophical works, the historical or factual accuracy of such memories are not particularly important, since the specific depictions of childhood or cosmic development are expressions not primarily of historical fact but of higher truths. The isosceles triangle drawn by the geometer may be an imperfect instance or representation of isosceles triangle itself: the two sides are, of course, not *exactly* equal. Nevertheless, this imperfect triangle is an occasion for the recollection of higher truths by the student who cannot yet articulate them. Viewing Alyosha's invocation of memory from this framework, one can regard childhood memories as the same kind of instance: these are not perfect or pure manifestations of beauty and goodness; indeed, injustice and suffering are integrated into these memories. And such recollections need not be entirely factually accurate. Rather, they can be occasions for the recollection of beauty and goodness itself; what makes them *true* in the relevant sense is their participation in these higher truths. This immediate sense of a thing's participation in the good contrasts with empirical reflection mediated through concepts. Jack is not constructing a *theory* through some abductive inference from the collections of factual memories; we find in *The Tree of Life* no discursive answer to the human question "Why?" in the face of suffering and evil. Rather, Jack is orienting himself toward and cultivating his sensitivity to goodness itself and beauty itself. He does this through an imaginative reconstruction of his past and the universe as a whole as participating in beauty and goodness. Within this imaginative remembering, nature plays a prominent role as a particular manifestation of goodness. I now turn to discuss the conceptions of nature and freedom as advanced by Malick in light of themes from *The Brothers Karamazov*.

Nature and Freedom

Malick draws on *The Brothers Karamazov*, sometimes quoting this work explicitly, to contrast a success-driven approach to the world (the way of nature) with one of appreciation and love (the way of grace); such a contrast is present in Zosima's discourses and teachings in *The Brothers*

Karamazov. Dostoevsky's Zosima exhorts one to love nature: "Love every leaf, every ray of God's light"; he goes on to talk about love as a teacher, as a way to "perceive the mystery of God in things."[9] This exhortation is repeated by Jack's mother (Jessica Chastain).[10] The father (Brad Pitt) also echoes a passage from *The Brothers Karamazov* after losing his job at the plant: "Look, the glory around us . . . trees, birds. I lived in shame. I dishonored it all and didn't notice the glory."[11] These explicit invocations of *Karamazov* point toward the broader picture advocated by Zosima in his discourses and teachings: that one should love nature, animals, and children; that such love teaches the one who loves about the mystery of the universe. This sensitivity to and love of goodness and beauty can be lost, such that a person is consumed by greed, acquisition, and a distorted notion of freedom as the satisfaction of desires. Malick's contrast between the way of nature and the way of grace is thus prefigured in Dostoevsky's own contrast between this distorted notion of freedom and the self-discipline of the monastic way.[12]

Both of these distinctions (Dostoevsky's slavish "freedom" vs. the monastic way; Malick's way of nature vs. way of grace) are invoked in the context of deeply moving explorations of suffering. Zosima's discourses, which include a discussion of the book of Job, follow the stark presentation of the problem of suffering in the "Rebellion" chapter. In this short chapter, Dostoevsky's Ivan gives what is arguably the most devastating account of the problem of evil through the lens of the suffering of children. Such suffering, particularly the infliction of suffering upon children, causes Ivan to reject the world of God's creation. Similarly, *The Tree of Life* invokes, at its beginning, the death of R. L. (Laramie Eppler) and Mrs. O'Brien's reaction to this devastating loss; the film also repeatedly invokes Job, twice explicitly in the opening quotation and in a homily. These presentations of the problem of human suffering and evil are distinctive in their recognition of how catastrophic such things can be; the world in which these things occur is experienced as valueless, as not worth living in.[13] The film is thereby contextualized in loss, suffering, and human evil as causes of despair and rejection of the world. The response, in the case of both *The Brothers Karamazov* and *The Tree of Life*, is not an argumentative theodicy or justification of evil or suffering, but an exhortation to love and gratitude.

Similarly, in *Knight of Cups*, Fr. Zeitlinger contrasts the "gifts" of suffering with the happiness we wish for ourselves:

> To suffer binds you to something higher than yourself, higher than your own will. Takes you from the world to find what lies

beyond it. We are not only to endure patiently the troubles He sends, we are to regard them as gifts, as gifts more precious than the happiness we wish for ourselves.[14]

Again, in this film, our desires are distractions from something higher. Malick's films suggest that there is something higher than our own wills, something that lies beyond the world. One possible response to suffering, suggested by this quotation and by both films, is to be taken beyond oneself, one's will, the world, and bind oneself instead to that which transcends these things.

Yet this contrast between the world and what lies beyond it might suggest a kind of transcendence that, interpreted in a certain way, is foreign to Malick's films. Malick's striking depictions of natural beauty do not suggest divine transcendence so much as divine immanence: God's beauty and goodness *within* nature. Mrs. O'Brien points to the sky—"That's where God lives!" God lives in the sky and in the cosmos, as depicted in those grand images of the creation sequence; God lives also in the grass, the trees, the water. In Malick's universe, God does not transcend the physical world, such that the material things in this universe are devoid of God's presence. Rather, the "world" that is transcended by God is a world of our making, mapped out by selfish, perverse, or evil desires; it is a cultural world in which we can be enmeshed, lost, and blinded. This is the world of Mr. O'Brien's workplace, Jack's own workplace, adult Jack's home. The adult Jack's windowed offices and home presents an image of the blindness and illusory nature of the "freedom" brought on by Jack's success: one cannot see the obstruction, but it is there all the same, like glass. Although nothing obstructs his field of vision in his windowed offices and home, Jack states, "I just feel like I'm bumping into walls." This is the world as indexed to human beings who see things through the lens of this "freedom," the world conceived as a field to be successful, accumulate wealth, fulfill one's desires. In Dostoevsky's terms, this freedom is illusory, since such a human being is a slave to himself and his desires. Jack—like Rick in *Knight of Cups*—is successful and rich, and the world lies open to him to experience; there do not appear to be any relevant constraints on his action. And yet he feels trapped.

This perverse manmade world that occludes God's presence can be overcome through a process of retrieval. The sequence of imaginative memories guides Jack toward a greater sense of the good in his own, present life. Dostoevsky's Zosima discusses this sense of otherworldliness: "God took seeds from other worlds and sowed them on this earth, and raised up his garden; and everything that could sprout sprouted, but it lives and grows only through its sense of being in touch with other mysterious worlds."[15] Zosima's "seeds" are planted in a person in childhood or through various experiences.[16] Zosima describes his own childhood memories of his brother in ways analogous to the planting of a seed, which sprouts in time and under the right conditions: "I was young, a child, but it all remained indelibly in my heart, the feeling was hidden there. It all had to rise up and respond in due time. And so it did." Like Zosima's memories of his brother, these seeds of goodness lay dormant but may be activated by a moment of crisis or suffering. Thus, the awareness of goodness can also be dormant or occluded in a person, but it is not completely gone, as long as these memories remain.

Alyosha's exhortation to the boys at the end of the novel is a planting of such a seed; the seed is the memory of their love for their friend, which can serve as a reminder of goodness at the appropriate moment. Notably, this invocation comes at a moment of perversity, injustice, and evil: the unjust death of a child, their beloved friend. Yet the memory of the boy can serve as a seed; these seeds or instances of goodness can grow into a garden, if one only attends to them, through a "sense of being in touch with other mysterious worlds." One can thus read in Dostoevsky an extended metaphor of a garden. In this world, seeds of goodness are planted but hidden, and they can grow into goodness under the right conditions. Seeds of goodness come from goodness—the good is both their origin and their *telos*. The seeds in a person's life can be experiences of beauty and goodness; the innocence of the child allows for purified memories, unclouded by the failures and sins of adulthood in the one who experienced that event and who can now recall that innocence.[17] These are not memories of "pure" events, that is, events untainted by evil. Alyosha's formative memory involves his beautiful and innocent mother driven to hysterics by the depravity and perversions of his father; there are similar circumstances involved in other formative memories described in *The Brothers Karamazov* and depicted in *The Tree of Life*. In this world, good is always integrated with evil, but through a process of retrieval, we can recollect and crystallize the goodness in a memory and see it as a depiction of the purity of goodness. Just as a garden that has been planted but not yet spouted is not visible, so none of this goodness may be immediately manifest to a person. Nevertheless, one can cultivate this garden in themselves, tend to it, and work to grow a seed into something visible and substantive, which may in time itself spread seeds.

Gardening in *The Tree of Life* as Creative Attunement

Gardening is a peculiar kind of creative activity. Other kinds of creative products may seem to be constructed more directly or purely by human beings. "I made that" rings truer in the mouth of a sculptor than in that of a gardener or dog breeder, even if both are working with given materials. Creative products such as Mr. O'Brien's classical music and the deliverances of a screenwriter (such as Rick from *Knight of Cups*) or an architect like Jack are much closer to the manmade extreme on the spectrum from natural to manmade. Gardening, on the other hand, is much more clearly a cooperative enterprise; one works together with nature to create something. One tends to nature's own creativity to assist in bringing forth the product. Gardening is a kind of creative activity that requires the ability to shape nature, as well as the ability to attune oneself to it. These two abilities are manifested by Mr. and Mrs. O'Brien, respectively, and I suggest that in *The Tree of Life*, gardening represents a kind of synthesis of these two abilities. While all human creativity involves attuning one's activity to the given materials as well as an ability to shape them, attention to gardening highlights the way in which attunement is an essential part of creativity.

Mr. O'Brien's attitude toward nature most frequently is that of shaping it to his will. He demands that young Jack (Hunter McCraken) tend the lawn; he criticizes Jack's weeding; he demands that the grass grow under the tree. This attitude of Mr. O'Brien toward his lawn is just one expression of his demanding attitude more generally, in which he tries (and frequently fails) to make the world into what he wants it to be, to impose his will on things or people. Mrs. O'Brien, on the other hand, exists in a kind of harmonious relationship to nature. She attends to nature, and the world more generally, and attunes herself to it. This self-shaping or abdication of her own desires reaches its apex when Mrs. O'Brien, in the culmination of Jack's imaginative recollection, gives up freely the son who was taken from her.

Mrs. O'Brien's abdication is not passive resignation but is rather brought about through her ability to love and fix her sights on what is good, despite the devastating loss of her most beloved child. In the film, we are introduced to Mrs. O'Brien with a shot of sunflowers; this image appears both in the opening scenes of the film of Mrs. O'Brien's childhood and again directly after the highly symbolic penultimate sequence of the film. This flower, so named because it is an image of the sun and it follows the sun with its gaze, is also evocative of this organic metaphor: fed by the sun, the seed transforms into something like the sun, which is fixated upon it and which can nourish and reproduce in turn. Mrs. O'Brien is both fixed upon what is good and is herself an image of the good: "I will be true to you, whatever comes." As such an image, she can serve as a guide to Jack. Adult Jack can, reflecting on his childhood, see in his mother the attunement to what is good that he himself is lacking and can, through his memories of her, grow his capacity to perceive the good.[18]

Gardening requires both attention and openness to the way that things are as well as an ability to guide and shape them. So we witness Mr. O'Brien and Jack gardening together just prior to Mr. O'Brien losing his job at the plant. What could have been an occasion for more resentment and disappointment instead prompts a transformation. "You're all I have, you're all I want to have," he says to Jack. This is a far cry from his earlier indication that he "got sidetracked" by his family from his professional ambitions. Mr. O'Brien here accepts his failures in a kind of attunement and turns his attention to the beauty and goodness that surrounds him. The job loss is a kind of pruning back, but this pruning leads to growth in Mr. O'Brien.

Another garden is suggested in the title of the film: the Garden of Eden, which contains both the tree of the knowledge of good and evil and the titular tree of life, the lesser-known tree, which is often interpreted as a source of grace. Grace can rectify original sin and perfect the knowledge of good and evil inaugurated with the fall. This eating of the fruit introduces into human nature the knowledge of good and evil, and thus an ability to recognize what is just and unjust. Such an ability can lead to anger and resentment concerning injustice, perhaps manifesting in an overactivated sense of what is due to *me*. This tendency is manifested clearly in Mr. O'Brien and the way of nature. The corrective to it is not (or at least not merely) to alter the world to accord with the demands of justice but to inculcate an opposing tendency, born of the *other* tree, to attune oneself to the world in appreciation and love. One can interpret Malick's "way of grace" as an exploration of this opposing tendency. Grace does not abandon or oppose nature; there is no return to a state of innocence through the infusion of grace. Rather, grace perfects nature, such that the very human tendency to impose one's will on the world is transformed into a higher capacity to create that which is good. The attunement exhibited by the mother and effected by grace in this way transforms the human creativity exhibited by the father into the creative cultivation of the good in oneself and in others.

We witness indoor gardening in Jack's contemporary home and workplace: there are several images of potted plants or trees; Jack's wife brings some cut branches into the home. The significance of these plants contained indoors is ambiguous. On the one hand, one can be attentive to that which is beautiful and good in nature if one brings it into one's place of work or home. On the other hand, it may be that trying to contain the natural within human ends constitutes inappropriate instrumentalization, in which natural beauty is seen as a pleasing decoration, one more thing to be shaped and molded by human beings in their quest to satisfy their own desires. One can readily see that Jack cannot resolve his predicament by simply tacking on some experiences of natural beauty to his life, as if his problem is a single unsatisfied desire. Similarly, the film begins with the nature outside being cut and brought into Jack's house, but the film ends with Jack outside, after his imaginative recollection, seeing the sky reflected in the buildings. Rather than bringing nature into his self-centered world and projects, Jack steps out of that world and those projects and sees that which is human or manmade as one reflection of goodness and beauty.

This realization suggests a way forward for Jack, to see his own projects not as in contention with the preexisting goodness but as participating in and reflective of goodness. He need not impose his will on the world if his aim is not a satisfaction of his own desires. If his aim is rather to bring about something good, he need only seek it out and assist its growth where he finds it. This combines the creative human activity of the musical Mr. O'Brien with the attunement to goodness possessed by Mrs. O'Brien, such that there need not be a battle between them.

Malick as Gardener

This brings us to the final stage of this argument—as mentioned above, my view is that Malick not only explores but exhibits this kind of creative attunement in his filmmaking. Malick is a gardener, but instead of directing and tending to plants in his creative endeavors, he directs and tends to human beings and natural beauty. Malick's famously idiosyncratic directorial style and filmmaking process allows the humanity of the actors and the beauty of nature to shine through rather than imposing upon them a very specific vision of the final product.[19] Thus this is a kind of cooperative endeavor, in which Malick takes those divinely created beings and arranges and cultivates them in such a way that the final product channels the beauty and goodness of its subjects into an independent manifestation of goodness.

The result is the singular kind of effect that this film can have on a person. I am sure that like most contributors to this volume, I walked out of *The Tree of Life* breathless in wonder. I did not know a movie could have that kind of effect. Not everyone reacts to this film in this way, but one need not look far to find someone who was similarly moved. How can one describe it? These memories are my memories, some have said, but not in the details: I am not a man who grew up Episcopalian in Texas in the 1950s.[20] But the truth of those memories is the truth of my own childhood memories, which are of lazy afternoons in California in the 1990s, walking home from school, climbing trees along the way, searching for lizards in the local park, exploring the half-built house across the street, and watching Aladdin so frequently that my brother and I had it memorized. My father was not a hard or demanding man, my mother was not the gentle, passive housewife. The resonance of Malick's presentation extends beyond those whose memories are very similar to those presented. It does not build primarily on the similarities of the exhibition but rather on the identity of what is exhibited in both the memories of the viewer and those presented in the film: the purity of the experience of goodness in the innocence of childhood, the ache of recognizing what is lost in the sins of adolescence and the perversions and evils of adulthood, and a hope that something good can be retrieved by grace. We experience it as our own story, which begins before we can remember and extends beyond what we've experienced, and the details are not quite mine, but historical accuracy is not the point. It's a story that focuses the eye of one's soul on beauty, goodness, and love "smiling through all things," that points one to the goodness that has suffused one's own past and present life.

In this way, I venture, watching the film can be a form of cultivation and attunement. The viewer walks out of the film with a renewed sense of what is good, how to seek it out and encourage its growth in oneself and others: better equipped to oneself tend God's garden. The film can draw out or play upon the memories of the viewer; it can act as an impetus to recollect the goodness and beauty one has known, leading to a growth in sensitivity to such things in the present. It opens one up to those other "mysterious worlds," to that which transcends the world mapped out by one's selfish desires and inclinations but is integrated into the world writ large, suffusing it with love and joy that are tangible if one has honed their senses. The result in the viewer can be the cultivation of the seeds of their memories to a heightened sense of love and gratitude. Malick attunes himself to the peculiarities and humanity of his actors, much more so than other filmmakers, giving them a kind of freedom and space to express themselves extemporaneously. He then crystallizes, out of the many hours of footage, those that best depict what is most deeply human about them, that which exhibits the eternal through the particular and temporal. Thus, I suggest that *The Tree of Life* does not just thematically explore creative attunement but also is a paradigmatic exhibition of creative attunement and its fruits.

Notes

1. I am grateful to Allison Murphy for her generous and insightful comments when I was in the early stages of writing; these comments undoubtedly shaped the development of the ideas that are expressed here. I am also indebted to Jeffrey J. Fisher, Alexander Jech, Jake McNulty, and Jordan Rodgers for their comments, which were both charitable and critical. Their insightful challenges and suggestions improved this chapter. I also am grateful to those professors who formed my thoughts on the film early on, John O'Callaghan and Fred Rush, and to the many students in my courses whose thoughtful discussions of the film have contributed to my understanding of it.
2. Plato, *Phaedrus*, 246a–250c. The other main passage on recollection is Plato, *Meno*, 80d–86c, see especially 85c: "So the man who does not know has within himself true opinions about the things that he does not know. . . . These opinions have now just been stirred up like a dream."
3. Plato, *Phaedrus*, 250c–d.
4. Kierkegaard, *Stages on Life's Way*, 9–10. I am indebted to Alexander Jech for pointing me to these passages and for suggesting the resonances of this notion of recollection with what I am here describing as Malick's approach.
5. Dostoevsky, *The Brothers Karamazov*, 774. Zosima states earlier in the novel, "No memories are more precious to a man than those of his earliest childhood in his parental home, and that is almost always so, as long as there is even a little bit of love and unity in the family. But from a very bad family, too, one can keep precious memories, if only one's soul knows how to seek out what is precious" (290).

6. Dostoevsky, 18–19.

7. These include Zosima's memories of his brother and a formative memory of "spiritual perception," also when rays of the sun "pouring down" during a reading from the book of Job (290–91). Cf. also with Dmitri's memory of the kindness of the German doctor (674–75).

8. The beauty is most apparent; goodness can be seen in part through the beauty, through the joy described in the epigraph and manifested in the music, but also in the oft-discussed scene in which one dinosaur acts mercifully toward another.

9. Dostoevsky, *The Brothers Karamazov*, 319.

10. "Love everyone. Every leaf. Every ray of light." Later, she speaks again of love, in the closing scenes of Jack's childhood: "Unless you love, your life will flash by."

11. Compare Dostoevsky, *The Brothers Karamazov*, 289: "Yes" he said, "there was so much of God's glory around me: bird, trees, meadows, sky, and I alone lived in shame, I alone dishonored everything, and did not notice the beauty and glory of it all."

12. See Dostoevsky, *The Brothers Karamazov*, 313–14:

> The world has proclaimed freedom, especially of late, but what do we see in this freedom of theirs: only slavery and suicide! For the world says: "You have needs, therefore satisfy them, for you have the same rights as the noblest and richest men. Do not be afraid to satisfy them, but even increase them"—this is the current teaching of the world. And in this they see freedom. But what comes of this right to increase one's needs? For the rich, isolation and spiritual suicide; for the poor, envy and murder, for they have been given rights, but have not yet been shown any way of satisfying their needs. . . . Very different is the monastic way. Obedience, fasting, and prayer are laughed at, yet they alone constitute the way to real and true freedom: I cut away my superfluous and unnecessary needs, through obedience I humble and chasten my vain and proud will, and thereby, with God's help, attain freedom of spirit, and with that, spiritual rejoicing!

13. All three presentations include expressions of the desire to die (by Ivan, Mrs. O'Brien, and Job). See Dostoevsky, 263; Job 3:1–26.

14. Akin to this statement by Fr. Zeitlinger is the homily on Job in the *Tree of Life*, which quotes Kierkegaard verbatim; see Kierkegaard, *Eighteen Upbuilding Discourses*, 121:

> The very moment everything was taken away from Job, he knew it was the Lord who had taken it away. . . . Does he alone see God's hand who sees that he gives, or does not also the one see God's hand

who sees that he takes away? Does he alone see God who sees God turn his face toward him, or does not also he see God who sees God turn his back?

15. Dostoevsky, *The Brothers Karamazov*, 320.
16. "Only a little, a tiny seed is needed: let him cast it into the soul of a simple man, and it will not die, it will live in his soul all his life, hiding there amidst the darkness, amidst the stench of his sins, as a bright point, as a great reminder," Dostoevsky, 294.
17. Dostoevsky emphasizes the innocence of children, both in Ivan Karamazov's famous speech in "Rebellion" and also in Zosima's discourses and teachings. See especially Dostoevsky, 237–38, 319.
18. One can also compare this with the famous image of the sun as the form of the good in Book VI–VII of Plato's *Republic* (508a–509d; 514a–521c, esp. 517b–c). I am indebted to John O'Callaghan for drawing my attention to the significance of this image of the sunflower.
19. One particularly striking instance of this is a scene in which a butterfly flutters about Mrs. O'Brien; she stretches her arms out gracefully and it settles on her hand.
20. Roger Ebert, for instance, says in one of several passionate reviews of the film, "The central events of 'The Tree of Life' reflect a time and place I lived in, and the boys in it are me," and he goes on to detail the resonances of various aspects of the film with his own childhood. Roger Ebert, "The Blink of a Life, Enclosed by Time and Space," *RogerEbert.com*, June 1, 2011, https://www.rogerebert.com/reviews/the-tree-of-life-2011. Ebert may not have had the benefit of experiencing those same resonances with a childhood that did not resemble that of the film. Such differences make the universal character of those resonances all the more manifest—the boys in the film are also *me*, even though their circumstances differ from mine.

Bibliography

Dostoevsky, Fyodor. *The Brothers Karamazov*. Translated by Richard Pevear and Larissa Volokhonsky. New York: Farrar, Straus, and Giroux, 2002.
Kierkegaard, Søren. *Eighteen Upbuilding Discourses: Kierkegaard's Writings, Vol. 5*. Translated by Howard V. Hong and Edna H. Hong. Princeton, NJ: Princeton University Press, 1990.
———. *Stages on Life's Way*. Translated by Howard V. Hong and Edna H. Hong. Princeton, NJ: Princeton University Press, 1990.
Plato. *Meno*. Translated by G. M. A. Grube. Indianapolis: Hackett, 1981.
———. *Phaedrus*. Translated by Alexander Nehamas and Paul Woodruff. Indianapolis: Hackett, 1995.

Part III

Explorations of Image and Voiceover

Chapter 8

Sotto voce

Inscription as Voiceover in Malick's *Days of Heaven*

FRED RUSH

Terrence Malick's use of voiceover has received considerable attention. It has become typical to remark that voiceover in his films is "nonnarrative," but what is meant in saying this is often left unclear. It is certainly not that these voiceovers are independent of the narrative construction of the films; to the contrary, the voiceovers serve important narrative functions, such as integrating visual storytelling with character. The terms *narrative* and *plot* have overlapping extensions but are not identical in meaning. A film's plot is the sequence of things that happen; narrative is the way its story is told. The same plot might support multiple narratives. One may construe voiceovers in Malick less broadly as nonnarrative in that their presence is not plot-driven. Two senses of *presence* are pertinent. First, the voiceovers do not *occur* according to the dictates of plotting. Second, the form of their presentation, the *way* they are present in the films, is not as reportage.

The emergence of voiceover as a film technique is a complex historical and conceptual matter that has to do with basic issues in the development of sound cinema from its so-called silent beginnings. I say "so-called" for two reasons. First, film is only silent when measured against sound film; no silent film would have been characterized as silent before the advent of the synched vocal soundtrack. Calling a film silent during the silent era in filmmaking would have made as much sense as saying that a painting or photograph was silent. Second, silent films were never silent as a whole if what one means by *silent* is *wordless*. Some silent films were wordless, but that was exceptional, especially with regard to mass-produced and mass-distributed films. Silent films had intertitles, words accompanying images at crucial points. Some of these words were seen to be spoken by characters, that is to say, were dialogue. True, no words were heard out of characters' mouths, but unless one wants to say that someone communicating by means of American Sign Language is being silent, parity dictates another description of the relation of word to image in early film.

Voiceover has always been a tendentious aesthetic matter, and that it has been so follows from the way that words are incorporated in silent films, films in which narration is effected almost exclusively by visual means. Once language could be heard in films, there was almost immediately a transfer of narrative function to spoken dialogue, with visual elements of the film playing a secondary role. This is not to say that filmmakers like Lang, Sternberg, and others did not successfully integrate innovations in visual technique with sound elements, which included not just spoken dialogue but sound effects as well. Run-of-the-mill Hollywood fare, however, was less adept. In such an environment, it was a common complaint that voiceover was overly literary; if the images and spoken dialogue are rich enough, so the argument went, voiceover is redundant and distracting. Moreover, if one were a Lang or Sternberg, voiceover was just more voice in the track, an unwelcome substitute for the old intertitle. This charge is really just a specific instance of a broader concern that the "talkies" exploited "mere words." If one thought sound film constituted a betrayal of a previously pure visual medium, voiceover would have added insult to injury.

To my knowledge the first fictional film to use voiceover is *The Power and the Glory* (1933, dir. W. Howard). The technique quickly became widespread; almost every film genre utilized it. But no genre exploited voiceover in all its possible permutations as did film noir; the instances run the gamut from nuanced to numbskull.[1] Voiceover in noir often was deployed in simple exposition of the solution to the crime that underpinned plot, a form of aural point of view that places the viewer in the position of hearing the thoughts of the detective unraveling his assigned case. Such first-person voiceover deepened the sense of mystery by revealing the mystified but persistent demeanor of the detective, often expressing thoughts too intimate, provisional, or troubled to say out loud. Less psychological and more epistemic is another use, one that pits a character's perception of the events in the film against the events as shown. To the extent that the character's developing insight into the depicted events is a proper part of plot, such voiceovers are fully expository, illustrations of the match or mismatch of belief and world—in essence, a story on top of a story. Of course, these uses (and others) might be present together. Malick's first two films, *Badlands* and *Days of Heaven*, feature extensive voiceover in the first person. His next work, *The Thin Red Line*, deploys multiple, interwoven first- and third-person voiceovers and signals a reformulation of voiceover's role in his films. Voiceover by multiple characters in a film was not new; *Citizen Kane* (1941, dir. O Welles), *Rashomon* (1950, dir. A. Kurosawa), and *The Barefoot Contessa* (1954, dir. J. Mankiewicz) are examples. With Malick, however, multiple character voiceover further dissociates voiceover from matters of speaker character, making it less about revealing intentionality and more about establishing an autonomous domain of voiced thought. This arc continues through *The New World*, *The Tree of Life*, and beyond. This is not to say that Malick's initial conception of voiceover had ever been routine; he had already gone some way in radicalizing its use.

It is said that the potentialities of voiceover were opened up for him by Truffaut's *L'enfant sauvage* (*The Wild Child*, 1969).[2] *L'enfant sauvage* follows the case of Victor de Aveyron, as reported by the early nineteenth-century French physician Jean-Marc Gaspard Itard (Truffaut). Victor was claimed to be a feral child, abandoned to the forest at the age of five and captured and returned to society at twelve. During his five years in Itard's custody and after several intensive attempts, Victor was unable to learn to speak (the film embroiders a bit on this front). Truffaut follows the search for a pedagogy with which to so "humanize" his charge. Itard's voiceover constitutes a verbal journal of the progresses and setbacks of that project. What must have struck Malick about the voiceover is what one might call its critical function. Descriptive use of voiceover—exemplary in film noir—either explains images, and through them actions and events, or presents an epistemic "rub" against what one has seen in order to reveal an unreliable narrator, which in turn calls for a form of irony on the part of the viewer to keep what is being said (or, sometimes, shown) at arm's length.[3] This is precisely *not* the function of voiceover in *L'enfant*. There, voiceover does not drive plot; rather, it constitutes a layer of consciousness overlaid onto the film-world and discrete from any focal attitude a character might have concerning what is happening. The mood is other than the indicative; it is often the interrogative, even (or especially) when what is said is not a question grammatically speaking. Because it does not serve exigencies of plot, what is said in the voiceover need not be tagged to occurrent images. The matter is ontological, not psychological: because any film-world is constituted by the sum of its film-images and diegetic sounds, to not pin voiceover down to occurrent image is, in a sense, to lift that voice out of that world.

Voiceover in fictional film lives on the border of diegetic and non-diegetic sound. It is diegetic to the extent that it (typically)[4] has a source in a character in the film-world but non-diegetic because it (typically) cannot be heard by anyone in that world. Filmmakers can use voiceover to represent the thoughts of a character in real time, that is, in the form of an internal monologue. If used in that way, voiceover *is* heard by someone in the film-world, namely, its source. But, of course, thoughts may be rendered in voiceover without those thoughts being items of internal monologue. Perhaps the thoughts are unconscious or, if conscious, unspoken internally. In any case, voiceover of thought carries with it a sense of internality and intimacy since one is hearing what no one (save the character in some instances) can. One might say, then, that one overhears such thoughts. This is accentuated in Itard's case. The juxtaposition of his internal, diaristic speaking with Victor's speechlessness is key. Victor is not speechless in the sense that a wolf is, that is, he is not a being with no mental capacity for speech. The point is that he is speech*less*.[5] The presupposition with which Itard operates is that Victor has a mental life that can be trained to be externalized in speech. Necessary to this presupposition is another: that Victor's mental life is, although not expressed in words, linguistically structured.[6] Throughout the film, Victor's nonverbal actions convey meaning. They are not mere behavior; they are gestures.[7] Whether his vocalizations count as language in an extended sense is left open, but it is incontrovertible that these vocalizations are not syntactically structured by any measure available to Itard. Itard's vocalizations of course are fully linguistic. But how powerful a capacity is speech when confronted with the unspoken, in Victor's case, the unspeakable? This is the domain within which the voiceover works. It makes thematic the gap between speech and speechlessness *by speaking*, by casting speechlessness in terms of speech. The result is that Itard's voiceover is both observational and alive to perspective, reportage that tries to adjust itself to its object. The adequacy of the adjustment, however, is not something Itard can track, given his reliance on the adjusting mechanism in tracking it.

Meaning is internal to both Victor and Itard but in radically different modes—in Victor due to his inability to speak and in Itard due to his speaking to himself. Their desire to bridge that gap only intensifies the gap to be bridged. Itard's speech intensifies in its internalization; Victor's speechlessness intensifies in his attempts to overcome that condition.

The limit of language, as in silent films, foregrounds gesture and movement. The relative autonomy of the visual element as the bearer of action becomes something on the order of an aesthetic principle governing the mise-en-scène. It permits the audience to attend more fully to the image as the primary mode of signification, as the speech in the voiceover is not granted ingress into the silent world that the film depicts. Voiceover in *L'enfant* is oblique to action; it allows action to unfold that exceeds description yet gets described in the exceeding. If one likes, it is possible to deploy a version of the unreliable narrator here, unreliable in this case not on account of mendacity, psychological blindness, or epistemic poverty but rather because of the different worlds that Victor and Itard inhabit. The openness this provides both sight and sound—the way it reforms the experienced aural presence of a film and the weight that it lends to the words not spoken out—is what no doubt fascinated Malick.

It is not for nothing then that Malick's first feature film, *Badlands*, is a crime drama—a genre at close quarters with noir. It is the story of Kit and Holly (Martin Sheen and Sissy Spacek), he a former garbage collector and she a high school cheerleader, who go on a killing spree in the 1950s Dakota Badlands. Holly's voiceover—only she speaks in voiceover in the film—opens and closes the action and relates only events that have already happened. Malick crafts the content of what she says in order that it gradually self-undermines; however, it is not her veracity that is in question. Holly tells the facts, but the value she places on them betrays a lack of understanding, for instance, her claim that the murders were "necessary." Her voice is uniquely off: naive but detached, qualities of mind that can be present simultaneously in a child, but not in an adult.[8] That these are retrospective reports makes her lack of circumspection all the more disconcerting. In short, the tenor of the voiceover does not at all match the moral gravity of what is narrated, giving the voice not so much an immoral as a pre-moral quality. Her demeanor inhabits the tradition of another *enfant*, the *enfant terrible*.[9]

Days of Heaven also features single-character voiceover. It is 1916. Bill (Richard Gere) kills his supervisor at a Chicago ironworks. He flees the city with his rag-picker girlfriend Abby (Brooke Adams) and his twelve-year-old sister Linda (Linda Manz), who provides the voiceover.

They hop a freight train with other migrants headed west and disembark in the Texas Panhandle to work wheat fields owned by an unnamed farmer (Sam Shephard). Bill and Abby present themselves as brother and sister so as not to raise questions about them as an unmarried couple. One day Bill overhears that the farmer is terminally ill and not expected to live out the year. The farmer has shown interest in Abby, and she comes to return the sentiment. Bill is jealous and confused but suggests a plan that promises financial benefit for him, Abby, and Linda. Abby is to marry him and, when he dutifully dies, inherit his wealth. In the meantime, Bill and Linda enjoy preferential status on the ranch as his in-laws. There is one drawback: the plan threatens to deepen Abby's emotional attachment to the farmer.

They marry, but the farmer is made of stouter stuff than expected. In time Abby falls in love with him yet continues her relationship with Bill. The farmer discovers them in an unguarded moment of more-than-sibling intimacy and, if the implication of sexual betrayal is not enough to undo him, the additional element of apparent incest is. In truth, the farmer does not witness any overt sexual act, but when he confronts Abby the next morning, asking, "Why do you let him touch you like that?" she hesitates, unsure of how much he has seen, as well as when and where. We know that what he has seen, although overly tender, leaves room both for him to interpret and for her to equivocate. That hesitation and hedge is enough for the farmer. When Bill departs the farm, the worst seems to have been avoided. After a time, he returns. There seems to be a rapprochement, but it is short-lived.[10] Another embrace between Bill and Abby reignites the farmer's suspicions, but a full confrontation is again deferred. That evening locusts descend upon the farm, and the fires set to drive them off lay waste to the crop.[11] Unhinged by the twin disasters, the farmer finally gets to the point, binding Abby to a post and confronting Bill with a pistol. When the gun fails to fire, Bill stabs him to death and takes off with Abby and Linda, only to be tracked down and killed by federal marshals.

The movie is biblical in scope and content, played out against the immensity of the American plains, the farmer mythic and unnamed, the characters' intentions oblique.[12] Linda's voiceover is, to my ear, the most powerful in any of Malick's films, maybe the most powerful in all of film—a disarming blend of hardscrabble and credulousness. And, like Holly's, it accompanies images without squarely touching them. Linda is world-wise—on the street from a young age—with a disarming ability to state hard facts. But she is still a child and, like Holly, the gravity of the situation, were

Bill and Abby's pretense breached, is beyond her. She views the time that they live in the elevated status of in-laws as an idyll, with little sense of impending trouble. As her voiceover accompanies scenes of frolic and rest, irony, tragedy, and fable elide. She is in essence the flipside of Holly—she the child-adult, Holly the adult-child. As in *Badlands*, the voiceover all but carries the tension constitutive of the mood of the film as a whole.

Days of Heaven underwent significant changes from script to filming. For astute viewers, one of the lacunae of the film results from these alterations and has to do with the place and provenance of the unnamed farmer's homestead. The screenplay identifies him as Chuck Artunov, a second-generation Russian immigrant.[13] The bonanza is called Razumihin.[14] What slight reference to the farmer's ethnicity remains points to the Caucasus. In the screenplay, Chuck dreams of his father, whose grave is alongside the house. There is a momentary shot of a fenced-in gravesite extant in the film, but no dream. In the scripted dream, the elder Artunov was to have worn a karakul, as do some of the workers shown on the train heading west.[15] Russians do wear such hats, but they are native to the Caucasus.[16]

I mention these matters, scripted but either not shot or cut, in order to introduce what I have found to be among the most beguiling unexplained leftovers from cutting in the film, the presence in the wedding scene of a chest of drawers, lacquered red, on which is inscribed text in a language that bears no relation to the narrative: Blackfoot, written in syllabary (more precisely, in abugida) (see figure 8.1).

The Blackfoot never lived in the Texas Panhandle, where the film is set, but they do live in southern Alberta, where it was shot. The text is the opening line of the *Te Deum*:

In syllabary:
୩⊦ ୩d⊂LL⋏⊣ ⋏L⋏⊀⊓Lᑫᕋ [ ]
[ ] Γ·ᕋᕊₙIL· ₫ [ ] ᕋᵁᕐL⊣ᕋᐟᵛ ⋏J·ᕋ′Jᕋᵁ

Transliterated:
Ayo A'pistotaki(wa); kitáókiihtatoohpinnaan.
kitsinapanistoohpinnaan k(s)iistowakao'ka nitsinaiminnaan

Original Latin:
Te Deum laudamus; Te Dominum confitemur

English translation:
We praise Thee, O God. We acknowledge you to be Lord

Figure 8.1. *Days of Heaven*.

The presence of the text in the scene is surely not incidental. I suspect that Malick left it in as a subliminal reminder that the farmer, whom the film's narrative comes close to identifying as the primordial human presence in the prairie, is himself an immigrant to an already inhabited land. Blackfoot and Cree have lived in what is now Alberta for centuries. The last Indigenous peoples to inhabit the Texas Panhandle relatively free from US intervention were the Kiowa, the Kiowa Apache, and the Comanche. As far as one can tell from the film, they have been fully exiled from the land on which the bonanza now stands. And so they were in fact "relocated" to Oklahoma in the late nineteenth century. In the film-world of *Days of Heaven* only an unspoken text remains.

To refer to this particular text as unspoken, or as unheard, is no small thing. It is a remnant of speech impossible for anyone in the film to utter or understand. As far as one knows, none at the wedding would be able to read it, even if they could identity it as text in the first place. It is also beyond the capacities of most viewers of the film to read. In this sense, it is a "secret" text—not secret in terms of its content but secret in terms of its medium. As for that content: the *Te Deum* is one of the oldest Christian hymns, dating from the fourth century CE. It proclaims submission to God and goes on to list those who so submit. Marriage in most Christian sects involves submission of spouses to one another, avowals that one will understand one's individual concerns to be subordinate to those of the marriage as a whole, a whole that is superordinate because divinely ordained. So ordained, one submits to it. That is, marriage is a submission within a submission or, better, a submission whose force depends on a yet greater submission. The *Te Deum* acknowledges this basic form of dominion. Indeed, it does more than that. Prayers are speech acts that do not merely deliver information. If one believes in their efficacy, one believes that prayers instantiate a connection with the divine. Praying is itself an act of submission, most clearly when what is said is that one submits.

When one recognizes the layering of the concept of submission that the *Te Deum* contributes when paired with the scene of marriage, one realizes the extraordinary weight of the Blackfoot words. Yet they are hidden, as we noted, incomprehensible to anyone one encounters in the film. The inscription nonetheless constitutes a critique of *this* marriage, a marriage parallel in its hiddenness. Abby is unwed; there is no legal obstacle to her marrying the farmer. There are, however, religious and ethical bars. The marriage is a central component of Bill and Abby's deception; while Abby and the farmer feel for one another by the time of the wedding, she never renounces the plot. Bill voices the governing rationalization: the farmer will be dead within the year and none the wiser. He will not be hurt. Bill hardens his position later; when Abby confides to him the farmer's suspicions, Bill returns, "Who cares what he thinks?" No matter: it is not the farmer's epistemic status that is at issue. A marriage is a matter of ontology, a state of being that requires mutual submission in order to obtain. Abby's intent makes such submission impossible. To that extent, the marriage is based on pretext and fraud. The fact that what is being said—the vows—are lies is criticized by what remains unsaid, making the hermeticism of the inscription quite to the point.

Malick's inclusion of the inscription in a film about the Texas Panhandle is, then, far from a discontinuity. The relevance of its content is clear. But that is not the end of it. That it is an inscription in a language whose speakers were driven from their land is crucial. Malick is acknowledging the presence of those who inhabit the place at which the film was shot and those who once inhabited the place it depicts: the Blackfoot, who still live in Alberta, in radically diminished circumstances, and those for whom their writing stands proxy—the Kiowa, Kiowa Apache, and Comanche. Those latter tribes are forcibly not present in the film-world and not only cannot speak but may not speak. Their silence is the product of a prohibition. That is powerful enough, but the presence of an inscription that brings with it the absence of the speaker still does not get to the root of the Blackfoot *Te Deum*. When one looks to more formal concerns—to the way film technique delivers meaning—one might be tempted to think that the inscription is a rough correlate to an intertitle in silent film. It is a nice thought: the silence of those who may no longer speak, but who were there before anyone else who now can speak, is broken by means of the silence of the intertitle. Of course, there are words being spoken in the marriage scene, so the analogy to silent film is only approximate.

I wish to argue that this is the wrong way to look at things. Intertitles by their very nature are non-diegetic; they cannot exist in the fictional world of the film. Were the very same words transferred from caption to scene, what were titles would become signage. Music can be either diegetic or non-diegetic. Malick employs both. What of voiceovers? Are they diegetic or non-diegetic? We said that they live on the edge formed by both. They must be diegetic if spoken by a character in the film, especially if we see that character as we hear her speaking. But easy identification of speaker with character can be confounded. Voiceover in a fictional film need not be in the voice of any character, as in the opening sequence of the British version of *The Third Man* (1949, dir. C. Reed). In such cases, the diegetic credentials of voiceover falter. Recall in this connection that Malick utilizes voiceover to add context to an image without commenting on that image directly. We can now augment the thought. The formal force of Malick's indirection is to blur the line between diegesis and non-diegesis, between the fictional world and what bounds it as the fictional world it is. I wish to suggest that Malick offers the Blackfoot inscription as voiceover. As an inscription it is fully diegetic; it is there on the chest. But it is linguistically unavailable to anyone in that world; it cannot say anything to them. It can say something to us, however, so long as we don't remain bound by the conceptual resources available to the inhabitants of *Days of Heaven*. This gives the inscription a decidedly non-diegetic cast. It hovers at the rim of the world, as does the spirit of those who were once present in that film-world and at that real place: Indigenous peoples.[17] This ambiguous diegesis-non-diegesis is expressed in the central device that governs the presence of the inscription in the film, the proxy relationship of the Blackfoot inscription. It has no place in the fictional world of the film, as the Blackfoot are not native to the Texas Panhandle. But it stands in for an absence that is diegetic, the absence of the Indigenous former inhabitants of the Panhandle.

A final thought concerning poetic justice. The inscription is a prayer translated into an Indigenous language but (1) is expressed in a form of writing, the adoption of which is bound up with European missionary activity and (2) is a translation of a Christian prayer, a prayer in a language and faith of an oppressor. This well might cause one to discount the content of the prayer, or at least the assertion that the content is true. The extant bit of Blackfoot is available only thanks to a writing system intertwined with that people's displacement and expresses propositions in a religious vernacular not originally theirs. I do not wish to deny these points, but I also do not want to discount the power of the speech of a people to surmount subjugation by accommodating in its own terms an outside culture. The lines of the *Te Deum* present in the film are, religiously speaking, quite general: no mention of Jesus, only an expression of supplication. Taken at face value the words constitute a statement that is, as far as I am able to tell, not at all at odds with Blackfoot religion, which is polytheistic to a degree but also posits belief in a single, first Creator (*A'pistotoke*, invoked in the prayer) to whom one owes thanks and obedience. One must be careful, of course, not to graft conceptions of what counts as thanks or obedience from the Abrahamic religions onto the Blackfoot. Even so, the idea of proclaiming one's radical dependency on a creative force would seem to translate from one context to the other. One might even insist that the delivery of the Christian prayer in Blackfoot is especially appropriate: the unheard voice of the displaced speaking, in one sense, from within, but in another, from without that world.

It is also worth pointing out that the critical function of an Indigenous declaration of spirituality and observation of the arrival of Europeans in the Americas is a matter that concerns Malick beyond *Days of Heaven*. When he turned more squarely to portraying first encounters between Indigenous peoples and Europeans in *The New World*, he tasked historical linguists with reconstructing dialogue in Powhatan, an extinct language of the Algonquian group to which Blackfoot also belongs.[18] An Indigenous conception of divinity is central to that film, expressed in the prayerful voiceover of Pocahontas (Q'orianka Kilcher).

Notes

Originally published as "*Sotto voce*: Inscription as Voiceover in Malick's *Days of Heaven*," *Film and Philosophy* 24 (2020): 84–97. Reprinted with permission. I have made some revisions to the text and have added a few endnotes.

    1. For an extensive treatment of narrative voiceover, see Kozloff, *Invisible Storytellers*.

2. "Interview with Billy Weber and Edward Pressman," in *Badlands*. Criterion, 2013, Blu-ray Disc. Néstor Almendros, the chief cinematographer for *Days of Heaven*, was Truffaut's cinematographer on a number of projects in the 1970s, including *L'enfant sauvage*. Malick became aware of Alemendros's work through his knowledge of Truffaut's film.

3. The latter is the crux of, for instance, *Fight Club* (1999, dir. D. Fincher).

4. See below for an exception.

5. Compare Wittgenstein's remark about speaking lions in the *Philosophical Investigations*, II, 223.

6. If one holds that language has evolved as a bridge between sense awareness and computational/conceptual capacities, in essence one holds that language evolves so that discursive thought is possible. This rejects the orthodoxy over the past two centuries that the driving function of language is to impart information or, more broadly, to communicate. Holding that language evolves so that thought is possible does not in itself commit one to the proposition that language and thought are identical. The language-thought hypothesis is compatible with holding that there is nonlinguistic thought (and non-thoughtful language). It also does not follow from the truth of the hypothesis that language is not also very important on account of communicative power. What is relevant for our purposes is that Victor thinks and, therefore, is linguistic.

7. The extent to which gestures count as language is contested. Clearly some gestural systems are linguistic, for instance, sign languages. But it seems very speculative to extend that status to all gesture (or, what is the same, to treat extra-linguistic gesture as mere behavior, that is, not as gesture at all).

8. Seymour Chatman is right to stress the novelty of Holly's voiceover in establishing unreliability as between two parts of her persona rather than the standard function of voiceover in noir to establish friction between what a character reports and what the implicit narrator shows. See Chatman, *Coming to Terms*, 136.

9. In one of his very rare interviews, Malick characterizes Holly as a Jamesian "innocent abroad" for whom the scene in the woods in which she and Kit set up a treehouse finds an equivalent in children's adventure tales like *The Swiss Family Robinson*. (Holly reads aloud to Kit from Thor Heyerdahl's *Kon-Tiki*.) See Walker, "Malick on *Badlands*," 82–83.

10. The farmer greets Bill openly enough but does mention to Bill that he has read in the newspaper that Bill has "made a name for himself." Bill immediately asks where these exploits were supposed to have taken place, to which the farmer offhandedly replies, "Chicago." It is unlikely that the farmer refers to any recent happening, as Bill surely would have avoided travel to Chicago, where there is no doubt a warrant outstanding for his arrest. The statement seems to be a veiled threat to expose Bill. The farmer loves Abby; so, turning over Bill is, without further provocation, an unlikely course of action. Still, leverage is leverage.

11. The plot is adapted from the story of Abram and Sarai's travel to Egypt in order to escape famine. With her consent, Abram tells the Egyptians that Sarai is his sister, for fear that her great beauty will cause them to covet her and kill him if they know that she is in fact his wife. The Egyptians, instead, would favor Abram because a brother, especially one of an apparently fatherless sister, can contract her marriage. Pharaoh is smitten and desires to marry Sarai, invites them both to court, and lavishes them with finery. Discovering the ruse, he casts them out; afterward Egypt is visited by plagues. Gen. 12:10–20. Abram later asserts the same falsehood to Abimelech, king of Gerar. Gen. 20:1–16. Isaac also engages in the ploy. Gen. 26:1–33. The target here is also Abimelech (or his son of the same name), which has caused some scholars to treat these sister-wife narratives as superimpositions attributable to different scribes or as instances of set narrative types. When the farmer sees Abby and Bill embracing, it is the Isaac-Rebecca-Abimelech story that is to the point. As it turns out, Abram is only half-lying; Sarai *is* his half-sister through his mother. Unlike patrilineal half-sister marriage, this is not incestuous under Levitical law. (Even if it were so considered, it is an open question whether Abram would be bound morally given that the laws are first revealed to Moses many generations later.) For discussion of the fluidity of law in the Old Testament on these and other matters, see Römer, *Dieu obscure*, 102–3.

12. Several of the shots and settings evoke Murnau's *City Girl* (1928). Especially striking are the harvesting sequences, which are clearly modeled in part on Murnau's film. One might also think that the devasting locust plague and ensuing fire were suggested by the hail storm that threatens the crop in the earlier film. The original, silent version of *City Girl* was a "lost film." Only a poorly overdubbed version of it was extant from 1930, a version Murnau rejected. An original print was discovered in 1970, and it is reasonable to assume that Malick saw the film in that version. It is a bit less evident, but one could argue that Murnau and Flaherty's *Tabu* (1931) exercises a similar degree of influence on *The Thin Red Line*.

13. See Malick, "'Days of Heaven,'" 11. This is perhaps a nod to Armais Arutunoff, a Russian-Armenian immigrant to the US, who moved to Oklahoma in the 1920s and invented a submersible electric pump for the extraction of oil. His company was headquartered in Bartlesville, where Malick grew up and where his father was a petroleum engineer. *To the Wonder* (2012) was shot and set in part in Bartlesville.

14. Malick, "'Days of Heaven,'" 10 (presumably after the character Razumikhin in *Crime and Punishment*).

15. Malick, "'Days of Heaven,'" 23.

16. There is a tracking shot inside the farmer's house that shows several photographs of what look to be the farmer's parents.

17. Compare what Michel Chion calls the *acousmêtre*. See *La voix au cinéma*, 25–33. A different way to put the same point about the blurring of the diegetic/

non-diegetic boundary stresses the concept of place: the location of filming—here, non-diegetic—migrates into its setting.

18. Many thanks to Yuri Avvakumov (Notre Dame), Adam Bremer-McCollum (Notre Dame), Michael Flier (Harvard), Donald Frantz (Lethbridge), Linda Many Guns (Lethbridge), and Arok Wolvengrey (First Nations–Regina) for identifying the language of the inscription as Blackfoot, first by process of elimination and then more directly. Arok Wolvengrey and Donald Frantz provided the transliteration and Donald Frantz the English translation.

Bibliography

Chatman, Seymour. *Coming to Terms: The Rhetoric of Narrative in Fiction and Film*. Ithaca, NY: Cornell University Press, 1990.

Chion, Michel. *La voix au cinéma*. Paris: L'étoile, 1982.

Kozloff, Sarah. *Invisible Storytellers: Voice-Over Narration in American Fiction Film*. Berkeley: University of California Press, 1988.

Malick, Terrence. "'Days of Heaven': An Original Screenplay." Unpublished film script, 1976 (available online, with slightly different pagination, at https://www.scriptslug.com).

Römer, Thomas. *Dieu obscure: cruauté, sexe, et violence dans l'Ancien Testament*, rev. ed. Paris: Cerf, 2009.

Walker, Beverley. "Malick on *Badlands*." *Sight & Sound* 44, no. 2 (1975): 82–83.

Wittgenstein, Ludwig. *Philosophical Investigations*. Translated by G. E. M. Anscombe. New York: Prentice Hall, 1973.

Chapter 9

The Melancholic Image in *Days of Heaven*

KEITH JACOBS AND JEFF MALPAS

Her thoughts
Were combinations of disjointed things;
And forms impalpable and unperceived
Of others' sight, familiar were to hers.
And this the world calls frenzy; but the wise
Have a far deeper madness, and the glance
Of melancholy is a fearful gift;
What is it but the telescope of truth?
Which strips the distance of its fantasies,
And brings life near in utter nakedness,
Making the cold reality too real!

—Lord Byron, *The Dream*

"Descriptive Cinema" and a Melancholy Poetics

In a brief "note" on cinema from 1961, the critic Susan Sontag draws a contrast between two types of films: those that are analytic in content and those that are "descriptive and expository," one type exemplified by the films of "Carné, Bergman (especially *Through a Glass Darkly*, *Winter Light*, and *The Silence*), Fellini, and Visconti," the other by those of "Antonioni, Godard, and Bresson." The analytic type is characterized as "psychological . . . concerned with the revelation of the characters' motives," whereas the descriptive "is anti-psychological, and deals with the transaction between feeling and things; the persons are opaque, 'in situation.'"[1]

Sontag's contrast may not apply to all films, but it seems particularly apt to the consideration of the films of Terrance Malick, and especially to his 1978 work *Days of Heaven*. The film has an enigmatic character, appearing almost as a montage of images, its storyline minimal, even simplistic, and, in keeping with Sontag's conception of the descriptive film, lacking in psychological interiority—as Carol Zucker notes, "There is an overt avoidance of emphatic characterisations; the characters are resolutely apsychological, and address one another in deliberately oblique, ambiguous sallies."[2] Critics have often struggled to situate the film within a cinematic genre, Zucker writing, "It is a film, perhaps more so than contemporaneous works, that fuses a variety of generic traits—it is in equal parts a western, romance, and melodrama—suggesting a lack of clarity and focus, and hence a liability in the marketplace."[3]

Although there are divergent views about the genre and ambition of *Days of Heaven*, there is a consensus as to the intense beauty of its landscapes and the power of many of its scenes. Interspersed throughout the film are wide panoramic shots of the sparse Texan wheatfields along with close-ups of objects such as the full moon, sunsets, flocks of birds, and locusts devouring corn, together with a soundtrack that includes the evocative music of Ennio Morricone (drawing on "The Aquarium" from Saint-Saens's *Carnival of the Animals*).[4] Malick also makes prominent use of environmental sounds from both city and countryside—the noise of a steelworks, the rustling of wheatfields, the calls and chirrups of birds and insects.[5] The combination of the visual and the acoustic in scene and image establishes an intense emotional aura. Mood or atmosphere thus appear at least as important as story, if not more so.

Our contention in the discussion that follows is that the mood that dominates the cinematic experience of *Days of Heaven* is fundamentally one of melancholy, understood not merely as a pathological psychological state but as a characteristic way of experiencing the world, or better, as a way of appearing of the world itself.[6] Jacky Bowring notes, "Melancholy is ambivalent and contradictory. Although it seems at once a very familiar term, it is extraordinarily elusive and enigmatic," but as she also adds, "It is something found not only in humans—whether pathological, psychological, or a mere passing mood—but in landscapes, seasons and sounds."[7] Melancholy, even a sense of the tragic, permeates *Days of Heaven*, being present even in those scenes that are also suffused with joy or beauty. Indeed, part of our argument is that the latter are themselves bound up with the melancholic and inseparable from it. Moreover, to refer back to Sontag's contrast between the analytic and the descriptive, the melancholic appears here in terms of a certain relation "between feeling and things," a certain "situation." It is not given primarily in terms of narrative (despite the tragic nature of the film's story) but rather through the film's mode of presentation, through its scenes, and so through the situated images that make it up (as combinations of both vision and sound). *Days of Heaven* is thus a film in which the melancholic image is central.

Although it is not an element in her brief 1961 comments, melancholy is itself a theme in Sontag's work elsewhere—most notably in a later volume of essays *Under the Sign of Saturn*, where she draws on the work, among others, of Walter Benjamin, but also in the 1973 volume *On Photography*, where the essay "Melancholy Objects" focuses, albeit critically, on the melancholic image in the form of the photograph.[8] There is a rich and extensive literature on the subject of melancholy,[9] some of which is taken up in Sontag's discussions, and which we will also make some use of here. Many discussions also take up melancholy as a mood characteristic of modernity—and Sontag's account in "Melancholy Objects" is specifically concerned with the melancholia of the photographic image as exemplary of certain problematic aspects of modernity.[10] Our concern, however, is not primarily with a critique of the image or of the role of the image in modernity but rather with an understanding of the image as itself melancholic.

The image, as we understand it, is not merely the photographic or cinematic image but rather the poetic image, which is sometimes given instantiation in the photographic and the cinematic. The poetics at issue here is one that resides in the making present of things and of the world by means of the image—an image that therefore functions, not primarily representationally but rather as lighting, opening, revealing.[11] Moreover, part of what the image shows is its own character as an occurrence always imbued with a sense of loss—the image has a radiance that is possible only given the singularity of its appearance and of that which appears in and through it and that appearing is as transient as is the encounter that the image makes possible. The image is thus itself irretrievably melancholic, and the inquiry into the relation between melancholy and the image, both in general and more specifically, as in Malick's work, belongs to what can be understood as a "melancholy poetics."

Structure, Story, and Technique

That melancholy might be an important element in Malick's film is suggested by its very title.[12] *Days of Heaven* can be seen as having a double meaning: on the one hand, referring to those heavenly days of life "on the farm," especially as experienced by Linda (Linda Manz) but for a time by Bill (Richard Gere) and Abby (Brooke Adams) too ("We lived like kings" recalls Linda); on the other, referring, as in the original passage in Deuteronomy from which the phrase comes, to the time of the heavens—a time that God also grants to his people, promising them that "your days may be multiplied, and the days of your children, in the land which the Lord sware unto your fathers to give them, as the days of heaven upon the earth" (Deut. 11:21). In Malick, unlike Deuteronomy, the days of heaven given over to Linda, Bill, and Abby are fleeting and short, in stark contrast to the days that belong to heaven—the days that are given over to the happening of the world in the constant unfolding of nature and of time. The very title of the film, when understood against the story it tells, is thus already indicative of the film's concern with loss, with a certain joy in the midst of loss, and so also with the melancholic.

The melancholic as it appears here is not simply tied to the loss of the benevolence of the divine understood as something that can be lost or regained—the latter being the sense of the melancholic, drawn from Jean Starobinski, that Cristina Popescu discusses in what is the only detailed discussion of the melancholic in relation to Malick's films in the existing literature.[13] If there is benevolence here, it is in the gift, no matter how transient it may seem, of sheer existence—itself evident in the luminosity of landscape and of the things found within it. Understood as any more than this, however, benevolence is not so much withdrawn as simply absent.

Admittedly, Linda tells a tale from someone she met, "Ding-Dong" is how Linda refers to him, that concerns the fiery end of the world from which God will save only the deserving few. But what to make of this remains unclear—the fact that the violent climax of the film, with the deaths of the farmer and then Bill himself, is presaged by a plague of locusts and the disastrous firing of the wheat fields may be suggestive of a connection to the idea of divine retribution (although Carole Zucker takes the story as indicating the tragic events to come),[14] but there is nothing in the events as they are presented that directly suggests the idea that what occurs is indeed a matter of divine retribution or abandonment. Since none of the characters who appear in *Days of Heaven* are without fault—whether it is exploitation or violence, jealousy, anger, or deceit—perhaps Linda's comment that "God don't even hear ya" should be taken not so much as an indication of a judgment that Bill, Abby, and the farmer bring upon themselves but rather as a condition that, in some sense, obtains for all of us. We are left simply bereft of any divine or otherworldly hope or salvation, although this need not mean that we are bereft of any salvation at all.

In this respect too, although Malick's film can appear to be removed from questions of the divine—there being no sense of God's presence, whether retributive or benevolent, at work in the story the film narrates—it is perhaps better to say that the film takes no stand on such questions. Certainly, religion is a strong presence, not only in the Biblical resonances, nor just in the stories and ideas present in Linda's narration, but also, most notably, in the blessing of the fields and the marriage ceremony. Yet these appear as woven into the lives and activities of those present, even into the landscape itself (although this may be taken to set up other questions), rather than constituting a special narrative or thematic focus. What is absent, it might be said, is a clear theological or religious message or stance.

Regardless of how one views the significance of the story's religious elements, the central story of *Days of Heaven* is biblical—a story played out three times in the book of Genesis (involving in the first two instances Abram/Abraham and Sarai/Sarah and, in the third, Isaac/Rebecca) in which a husband in a strange land presents his wife as his sister only for her to be coveted by the ruler of that land. The plot as it plays out in *Days of Heaven* is recounted elsewhere in this volume, and we will not repeat it here.[15] We have already alluded to its minimal character and the seeming dominance of mood and setting, and of image and sound, over the narrative or action and over any psychological interiority or motivation.

This is not to say that *Days of Heaven* is without narrative structure, but the story it tells is pared down, often left indeterminate, and largely maintained through a spoken narration that is already removed from what is immediately depicted—a narration that connects the film's sometimes disparate scenes as it heightens the sense of uncertainty regarding the fate of the main characters.

Appearing as a spoken remembrance of events from her past, the narration is voiced by Linda, the same Linda who appears as the twelve-year-old companion to the two main protagonists, Abby and Bill. A barely engaged witness to the events depicted, Linda speaks in a rhythmic but un-ascribed way, discharging a role not unlike that of the chorus in a Greek tragedy, and yet, at the end of the film, appearing as one whose own life now opens before her. Linda's narration, given in the past tense, appears as essentially a reminiscence of the events that led up the loss of her brother and what is surely the end of her childhood. The days of heaven are the days of a luminous time between the darkness of their life in Chicago and Bill's death, shot as he tries to escape across a river (his panicked splashing as he tries to run providing a grim counterpoint to the playful walk through the lake that he takes with Abby earlier in the film[16]). Here the melancholic appears, once again, in the very character of the narration as the remembrance of a time past, as a remembrance of both joy and loss.

Significantly, Linda's narration was added by Malick in postproduction rather than being envisaged as part of the film from the beginning. Indeed, Malick's original script was largely abandoned as filming progressed. The final version is largely a result of what was a long process of work on editing the large quantity of footage that had been shot—Malick's strategy was to film more than was needed to have an abundance of material with which to work. The film is thus essentially a composition made from already realized images and sounds rather than the filmed realization of a script—a fact that additionally reinforces the priority of image and sound as against narrative structure, psychological interiority, or even spoken dialogue.

Editing is, of course, an essential part of almost every film, but the role of editing in Malick's directorial practice, and the character of that practice, most obviously in the case of *Days of Heaven*, as indeed a matter of composition based on cutting and selecting from a large body of accumulated footage, is not disconnected from the character of the resulting film. And in this case, the practice might itself be seen, in its very reflective-compositional character, as having something of the melancholic precisely because of the way in which it takes up the material on which it works—material that already has something of the character of "past time" as a series of spatialized moments that can be ordered and juxtaposed almost as part of a single picture spread out over the sequence of the film.

Linda's narration serves to provide a frame to many of the scenes, and to some extent to the film as a whole, but it does so in the barest way possible. Much of the film is unnarrated, leaving the audience to their own reflections and the projection of their responses and readings onto what is seen, and we know little about the characters or their situation beyond what is immediately depicted on-screen. Gilberto Perez notes that Linda's voiceover works "to fill in narrative gaps, releasing the images from their usual subordination to the story so that they can flourish in splendid autonomy."[17] The narration thus reinforces the descriptive character of the film, giving space to the scenes and images that are the film's real substance.

"Few scenes in *Days of Heaven*," writes Perez, "are allowed to unfold for long or to reach any dramatic resolution: instead, we get bits and pieces of scenes arranged into a mosaic of shifting impressions."[18] The primary unit of filmic composition is the scene and the image, the story providing only the loose frame within which they are juxtaposed and arranged. The contrast and juxtaposition of scenes carries over into a contrast and juxtaposition of locations and settings: "The city and the rural—for example, the steelworks in Chicago and the Texas panhandle; rich and poor, the home of the farmer adorned with good furniture and the fields on the farm where labourers sleep at night."[19] Similarly, one sees images of buffalo and deer cut with shots of workers and wheatfields, such that the film sometimes has the character almost of a cinematic montage.

That *Days and Heaven* is indeed a descriptive rather than analytic film, much as Sontag uses these terms, and so a film constituted more by its images than the inquiry into motive or character, is further reinforced by its visual style. It is a style that, as James Morrison and Thomas Schur observe, derives from the realism of early twentieth-century American painters like Edward Hopper and Andrew Wyeth, as well as photographers such as Walker Evans, Lewis Hine, and Dorothea Lange. Realism, as evident in the work of such artists, is itself bound up with the melancholic.[20]

The reason is simple: the realistic mode of depiction presents things in a certain detached fashion even while it allows the affective qualities of what is presented to be evident at the same time. Hopper's paintings, for example, do not merely project a sense of loneliness or melancholy embodied in the figures depicted, but the often flat and even geometrical mode of presentation results in a strangely detached and ambiguous mood or atmosphere. Similarly, in the photographs of Evans or Lange, one sees suffering and hardship, as well as loneliness, often painfully evident, and yet there is a sense of stillness about such images—a sense of the sheer immanence of things. The juxtaposition of images that occurs throughout the film also adds to the sense of stillness and detachment. The melancholia of American realist art has frequently been observed, though seldom explored in any detail.[21] More generally, Tatjana draws attention to the connection between melancholy and realism in the work of Freud as well as Carl Schmitt, at the same time as she also connects this with the cinematic work of Lars von Trier.[22]

Malick's own use of documentary photographs—an insertion of the "real" into the "fictional" (with a photograph of the actress who plays Linda being included in the sequences)—as the opening images in *Days of Heaven* can be seen to draw on the heritage of American photographic realism and to position the film, historically, as belonging to a specific time in America's past. Those images also establish, from the very beginning, a sense of the melancholia and loss that runs through the film in its entirety, and they do so precisely through the way they set up a certain sense of the film as both affecting and yet also detached in its affective presentation.

Sontag writes, in "Melancholy Objects," of what she calls "the main tradition of American photography" that "its prevailing mood is sadness. Behind the ritualized claims of American photographers to be looking around, at random, without preconceptions—lighting on subjects, phlegmatically recording them—is a mournful vision of loss,"[23] and her comments could be extended to photography more broadly. As she also argues, "The contingency of photographs confirms that everything is perishable; the arbitrariness of photographic evidence indicates that reality is fundamentally unclassifiable."[24] Sontag connects the melancholy evident in photography both with realism and with surrealism—Hopper's painting similarly having a connection to both—and she also refers briefly to Godard (one of her examples of the "descriptive" mode of cinema) as one of several representatives of "surrealist taste."[25]

The realist—or surrealist—presentation of things as both affecting and yet also detached (which Sontag points out can easily descend into sentimentality or kitsch) connects directly with a feature of the melancholy temperament noted by other authors, namely its concern with things separated from the context of life or activity, sometimes with odd juxtaposition and thereby often rendered strange or enigmatic (especially evident in the melancholy of surrealism). The main figure in Albrecht Dürer's famous *Melancholia* (1514) (see figure 9.1) thus sits surrounded by objects that lie about seemingly discarded and unused—not unlike the peculiar array of things that appear in various scenes from *Days of Heaven*: the interior of the farmhouse with its mute photographs and furniture; the strange figure, seemingly a garden gnome, that stands outside the house; the gazebo isolated in the surrounding landscape; the farmhouse that itself recalls the solitary building in Wyeth's 1948 painting *Christina's World*; the setting

Figure 9.1. *Melancholia I*.

of many scenes in the midst of apparently abandoned objects.[26] Here too the juxtaposition of objects is mirrored in the juxtaposition and contrast that also occurs between scenes.

Displacement, Love, and Finitude

The melancholia at work in *Days of Heaven* is not only a function of cinematic style, presentation, or technique but also works through the thematic content of the images and the story in which they are embedded and the way in which that thematic content is tied to certain features present in the images themselves.

Morrison and Schur do not address the issue of melancholy in *Days of Heaven* in any direct way, but instead their invocation of American realism arises in relation to a certain critical engagement with modernity—what the works of artists such as Hopper and Evans share, they claim, is "a concern with the effects of modernity on the relations between humans and the environment . . . the ways in which industrial culture—locomotives, factories and cities, along with photography and cinema—may be seen to displace humans from their sense of connection with nature."[27] Nature, they conclude, thus appears as both "inspiring and intrusive."

Certainly, the effects of modernity, as experienced in the America of the nineteenth century, are evident in *Days of Heaven* as they are also evident in the world of American realist painters and photographers. But the critique of modernity is not necessarily to be viewed as the primary focus here. If modernity is thematized, it is surely in part because of the way the strange situation of human being in the world, which is itself at the heart of the melancholic, is brought to the fore in a particular way within modernity. In that case, it is not primarily the loss of connection to nature that is at issue (as if one could set nature at odds, in any simple way, with the human or even with the modern), although there undoubtedly is a sense of displacement, of the "uncanny" (the *Unheimlich* or unhomely) that is implicated here. What occurs in modernity is, one might say, a more powerful sense of the way in which human existence is both in the world and yet also apart from the world—the apartness being what is evident in the experience of loss. We are given over to a world from which we are also estranged.

Displacement, and the movement associated with it, is a theme that is powerfully present in *Days of Heaven*, both as a feature of modernity and as a feature of the world and the human experience of the world. The very landscape in which the film is set is a landscape only made possible by the forced displacement—the movement away—of its Indigenous inhabitants. It is characteristic of settler societies, like that of the United States (though it is certainly not exceptional in this regard), that they stand in an ambivalent relation to the land that they have made their own. This ambivalence, which is often evident in an exploitative attitude toward the natural environment, can arguably be seen to be bound up with the original acts of dispossession and violent appropriation on which settler societies are historically founded. A large part of the sadness that permeates *Days of Heaven* is undoubtedly tied up with an idealization of the landscape that serves to efface the violence and racism that accompanied its settler occupation, and although such issues are not given prominence in Malick's cinematic depiction, they are certainly present—sometimes, as Fred Rush argues, in unexpected ways.

If *Days of Heaven* contains within it references to older displacements and dispossessions (and not only those of Indigenous peoples—the images that make up the opening sequence mentioned earlier include photographs of early twentieth-century migrant workers), it also testifies to the displaced and dynamic, even restless, character of human life and existence. As Stuart Cottle argues, the overall cinematic vision at work in Malick's film "stimulates our sense of how lived experience is powerfully shaped by the dynamic movement of social and economic transformations as they inexorably unfold through time. For what is surely striking about *Days of Heaven* as a historical film is that it reveals human life to be anything but a static, frozen, or totally fixed ontological condition."[28] Early in the film, Linda says of the situation of Abby, Bill, and herself that "for a long time all three of us being goin' places. . . . Lookin' for things, searchin' for things," and by the end, that remains for both Abby and Linda. For Linda, especially, the story begins with one escape, and a search for somewhere better, and ends with another.

The juxtaposition and contrast that characterizes much of *Days of Heaven* is evident in the movement of the main characters between places, but it is also evident in the shift from scenes of seeming tranquility to passages of energized activity—the quiet work of the ragpickers, Abby and Linda among them, is set against the early scenes with Bill in the Chicago steelworks and the rhythmic activity of shoveling coal and hammering iron; the Texan harvesting scenes are set against moments of repose and recreation, repose is interrupted by argument and fighting. It could be said that the film, which we eventually learn takes place in 1916, is set at a defining moment of global transformation, where the old social order is being replaced by the new technologies of production and where the world is about to be radically transformed by the first of two world wars. There are examples of airplanes, trains, and cars all transporting people across landscapes. The film moves between an agricultural social order and the beginnings of a new modernity of machines and impending war.

The film is characterized, moreover, by a strong sense of the way in which all the action, every scene, is never isolated or apart from a wider world. This is partly a result of the shifting and often contrasting images of which the film is composed, as well as the frequent use of wide-angle shots that are themselves contrasted with close-up images, sometimes of objects, animals, or plants. As Greg Turk writes (in response to Gilberto Perez), "The edge of Malick's frame is less a boundary or a limit, but something that feels more like a horizon. We cannot see it, but perceive nonetheless that the world extends from this image or event, that there is an elsewhere we could move into. . . . It is the combination of proximity and distance, close-up details and vague openness, that we recognise as being like our experience of memory."[29] Memory, like places and landscapes, never occurs but as it stands, even if sometimes uncertainly, with respect to other memories and experiences. We do not encounter the world in pieces (as Sontag points out in her critique of photography), even though we enter into the world only in and through our own finite place in the world. Although our lives are finite and always given over to loss, it is only thus that the world becomes accessible to us. To be in the world is always to be here—within this horizon, within these bounds. And this too can be understood as an essential element in the melancholic and is perhaps one reason why it might be argued that to be in the world is always to find oneself beset by the melancholic.

If one of the central themes in *Days of Heaven* is love—including the proximity of love to jealousy and to anger—then it also presents love in direct relation to melancholy. Loss entails the possibility of loss, something reiterated throughout the film. It is present in Bill's loss of Abby to the farmer (Sam Shepard); in the farmer's loss, or feared loss, of Abby to Bill; in the apparent loss of the love of a boy, Edward, experienced by Linda's young friend (whom Linda herself loses when the workers leave the farm); in the separation of the farmer and his foreman as a result of their disagreement over Abby and Bill; in Abby's own loss of both her husband and her lover; and in Linda's loss of her own brother and final abandonment by Abby. The end for all of the relationships of love or friendship portrayed in *Days of Heaven* is one of disappointment—either through death or physical separation. The depiction of love by Malick in *Days of Heaven* is thus essentially melancholic—the joy that love brings can only ever be fleeting and momentary. In describing the plight of the farmer Linda says, "He was headed for the boneyard any minute, but he wasn't really squawkin' about it, like some people. In one way I felt sorry for him, cause he had nobody to stand out for him, be by his side. Hold his hand when he needs attention or somethin' That's touchin.'" Perhaps what Linda describes the farmer as lacking is the best that love can provide—a temporary companionship that cannot endure any more than can a life.

The Melancholy Days of Heaven

Malick's *Days of Heaven* has a story to tell that can easily be understood as a historical romance to be enjoyed not only for its familiar human themes but also for its stunning cinematography and the beauty of its landscapes. The film offers no detailed psychological analyses of its characters nor does it aim to explore, in any detailed way, their motivations or personalities. But the heart of the film lies in neither its story nor the beauty of its landscapes nor even the window it may be thought to open into a certain historical time. *Days of Heaven* is a cinematic evocation—a "description" in the sense of a showing or revealing—of a certain condition of the world and of the situation of human beings in the world. That condition, that situation, is fundamentally melancholic. That does not mean, however, that the film is to be understood as depressive or as devoid of hope or perhaps even of a degree of redemption. But the latter are not to be found other than in the brief days of heaven that are vouchsafed to the characters whose lives we see depicted. Those days, even though seemingly tainted and eventually brought to ruin, by anger, jealousy, and mistrust, are nonetheless significant. Those days allow a sense of the world to emerge that is the only sense of world that is ever possible and that is not diminished by the brevity of a life lived or the losses that it may encounter. The melancholy poetics that Malick's film embodies and expresses is a poetics both of the world and of human beings. The melancholy character of that poetics is, as Byron has it, "the telescope of truth" that is no less true because it is tragic, just as human existence is no less significant because it comes to an end.

Notes

1. Sontag, "A Note on Novels and Films," 245.
2. Zucker, "'God Don't Even Hear You,'" 2–9.
3. Zucker, 2.
4. See Power, "Listening to the Aquarium," 103–11.
5. See Crofts, "From the 'Hegemony of the Eye' to the 'Hierarchy of Perception,'" 19–29.
6. The pathological view of melancholy can be found in works like Robert Burton's *Anatomy of Melancholy* and Freud's "Mourning and Melancholia." However, as László Földényi argues, "The history of melancholia over the past two millennia shows that the bodily condition is separable from the understanding of existence." Földényi, *Melancholy*, 3–6. Földényi notes the turn away from the

strictly somatic view of melancholy towards a more philosophical view about the experience of loss in general. This sense of loss can be about a person, an event, a place, or a possibility that is never likely to occur. In the words of Bryan Turner, "Melancholy was typically conceptualized in a negative perspective as a malady or pathology, there was a contrasted feature of nostalgic melancholy, namely a positive notion of melancholy as heightened sensitivity to reality." Turner, "A Note on Nostalgia," 49. Turner goes on to write that the more positive versions of melancholy have often been often associated with ideas of virtue.

7. Bowring, *A Field Guide to Melancholy*, 42.

8. See Sontag, *On Photography*.

9. For example, see Bowring, "Melancholy Landscapes," 214–25; Földényi, *Melancholy*; Klibansky et al., *Saturn and Melancholy*.

10. Sontag's critique is one that is echoed elsewhere, most notably for cinema perhaps in Wim Wenders's argument concerning the contemporary "proliferation of images." See Wenders, *On Film*, 201, 363–74, 442; also Jeff Malpas, "The Role of Memory," 146–59. Both the accounts of Sontag and Wenders have a similar origin in the work of Walter Benjamin.

11. This sense of the image and its role in relation to the poetic is one that can be found not only in Benjamin but also, and more directly, in Gaston Bachelard's work and in that of Martin Heidegger—see Jeff Malpas, "'The House of Being,'" 15–44. So far as Heidegger is concerned, it is surely a key part of what is at issue in the idea of Malick's own work as a form of Heideggerian cinema even more so than any concern with the question of being. Compare Furstenau and MacAvoy, "Terrence Malick's Heideggerian Cinema," 179–91; and Pattison, "In the Theater of Light," 57–72.

12. The interpretation of Malick's title has been a subject of contention among several commentators—see, for instance, Kendall "The Tragic Indiscernibility of *Days of Heaven*," 148–64; and Cottle, "The Enigma of Terrence Malick's *Days of Heaven*," 1–32. https://www.tandfonline.com/doi/full/10.1080/10509208. 2020.1847591. Of course, as with all interpretations, the interpretation offered here is not meant to be exclusive of others—the title, like the film itself, has an iridescent character that allows different shades of meaning to be conveyed by it simultaneously—but the contrast to which it gives emphasis is especially relevant in the present context.

13. Popescu, "Melancholia in the Films of Terrence Malick," 282–91.

14. See Zucker "'God Don't Even Hear You,'" 2–9.

15. See Fred Rush's chapter (chapter 8), "*Sotto voce*: Inscription as Voiceover in Malick's *Days of Heaven*."

16. Water has a traditional association with memory and so also with loss, and the way water, in the form of river and lake, appears in Malick's film has something of this character. Melancholy itself, however, at least within the theory of the four humors, has always been associated with dryness and it seems not

insignificant in this regard that the landscape of Malick's film, especially in the scenes set on and around the farm, and the climatic atmosphere that prevails, is dry—it never rains, and even the scene in which Bill and Abby are seen sheltering from frost and cold, no snow is falling.

17. Perez, "How We Remember," 2.
18. See previous note 17.
19. Perez, 3.
20. Morrison and Schur, *The Films of Terrence Malick*, 69.
21. The "melancholy realism," however, receives attention in Evans. See Tagg, "Melancholy Realism," 3–77.
22. See Tatjana Jukić, "The Melancholy Condition of Realism," 191–203.
23. Sontag, *On Photography*, 52.
24. Sontag, 62–63.
25. Sontag, 62.
26. A notable example is that in which the farmer sees Bill and Abby in intimate conversation outside an outbuilding after Bill's return—the scene is shot from a distance with an unhitched buggy to one side and a cluster of other apparently abandoned objects next to the building on the other. See also Morrison and Schur, *The Films of Terrence Malick*, 100–1.
27. Morrison and Schur, 100.
28. Cottle, "The Enigma of Terrence Malick's *Days of Heaven*," 377–410.
29. Turk, "Letter," 13.

Bibliography

Bachelard, Gaston. *The Poetics of Reverie: Childhood, Language, and the Cosmos*. Translated by Daniel Russell. Boston: Beacon Press, 1969.
Bowring, Jacky. *A Field Guide to Melancholy*. Harpenden, UK: Oldcastle Books, 2008.
———. "Melancholy Landscapes." *Landscape Journal* 30, no. 2 (2011): 214–25.
Cavell, Stanley. *The World Viewed: Reflections on the Ontology of Film*. 2nd ed. Cambridge, MA: Harvard University Press, 1979.
Cottle, Stuart. "The Enigma of Terrence Malick's *Days of Heaven*: History, Nature, and Utopia in the American West." *Quarterly Review of Film and Video* 39, no. 2 (2020): 377–410.
Crofts, Charlotte. "From the 'Hegemony of the Eye' to the 'Hierarchy of Perception': The Reconfiguration of Sound and Image in Terrence Malick's *Days of Heaven*." *Journal of Media Practice* 2, no. 1 (2001): 19–29.
Fereday, Susan. "Light out of Darkness: The Foundation of Photography in Mystery and Melancholy." PhD diss. Melbourne: Monash University, 2017. https://doi.org/10.4225/03/587c499b8a70.

Földényi, László. *Melancholy*. Translated by Tim Wilkinson. New Haven, CT: Yale University Press, 2016.
Freud, Sigmund. "Mourning and Melancholia." In *The Standard Edition of the Complete Psychological Works of Sigmund Freud*, vol. 14, edited by J. Strachey, 243–258. London: Hogarth Press, 1957.
Furstenau, Marc, and Leslie MacAvoy. "Terrence Malick's Heideggerian Cinema: War and the Question of Being in *The Thin Red Line*." In *The Cinema of Terrence Malick: Poetic Visions of America*. 2nd ed., edited by Hannah Patterson, 179–91. London: Wallflower Press, 2007.
Jukić, Tatjana. "The Melancholy Condition of Realism (with Notes on Lars von Trier's Melancholia)." *Orbis Literarum* 76, no. 4 (July 2021): 191–203.
Kendall, Stuart. "The Tragic Indiscernibility of *Days of Heaven*." In *Terrence Malick: Film and Philosophy*, edited by T. D. Tucker and S. Kendall, 148–64. London: Bloomsbury Academic, 2011.
Klibansky, Raymond, Ewin Panofsky, and Fritz Saxl. *Saturn and Melancholy: Studies in the History of Natural Philosophy, Religion, and Art*. Montreal: Mcgill-Queen's University Press, 2019.
Malpas, Jeff. "'The House of Being': Poetry, Language, Place." In *Paths in Heidegger's Later Thought*, edited by G. Figal, D. D'Angelo, T. Keiling, and G. Yang, 15–44. Bloomington: Indiana University Press, 2020.
———. "The Role of Memory: Image, Place and Story in the Films of Wim Wenders." In *Cinematic Thinking: Philosophical Approaches to the New Cinema*, edited by J. Phillips, 146–59. Stanford: Stanford University Press, 2008.
McCann, Ben. "Enjoying the Scenery: Landscape and the Fetishisation of Nature." In *Cinema of Terrance Malick: Poetic Visions of America*. 2nd ed., edited by Hannah Patterson, 77–87. London: Wallflower Press, 2007.
Morrison, James, and Thomas Schur. *The Films of Terrence Malick*. Westport, CT: Prager, 2003.
Pattison, George. "In the Theater of Light: Toward a Heideggerian Poetics of Film." In *Theology and the Films of Terrence Malick*, edited by Christopher. B. Barnett and Clark J. Elliston, 57–72. London: Routledge, 2017.
Perez, Gilberto. "How We Remember." *London Review of Books* 17, no. 12 (September 2013): 1–13. https://www.lrb.co.uk/the-paper/v35/n17/gilberto-perez/how-we-remember.
Popescu, Christina C. "Melancholia in the Films of Terrence Malick." *Ekphrasis: Images, Cinema, Theory, Media* 21, no. 1 (2019): 282–91.
Power, Richard. "Listening to the Aquarium: the Symbolic Use of Music in *Days of Heaven*." In *The Cinema of Terrence Malick: Poetic Visions of America*. 2nd ed., edited by Hannah Patterson, 103–11. London: Wallflower Press, 2007.
Sontag, Susan. "A Note on Novels and Films." In *Against Interpretation and Other Essays*, 242–48. Harmondsworth, UK: Penguin, 2009.

———. *On Photography*. New York: Farrar, Straus, and Giroux, 1973.
———. *Under the Sign of Saturn*. New York: Farrar, Straus, and Giroux, 1980.
Tagg, John. "Melancholy Realism: Walker Evans's Resistance to Meaning." *Narrative* 11, no. 1 (2003): 3–77.
Turk, Gavin. "Letter." *London Review of Books* 35, no. 19 (October 2003): 13. https://www.lrb.co.uk/the-paper/v35/n17/gilberto-perez/how-we-remember.
Turner, Bryan. "A Note on Nostalgia." *Theory, Culture and Society* 4, no. 1 (1987): 147–55.
Wenders, Wim. *On Film: Essays and Conversations*. London: Faber and Faber, 2001.
Woessner, Martin. "What is Heideggerian Cinema? Film, Philosophy and Cultural Mobility." *New German Critique 113* 38, no. 2 (2011): 129–57.
Zucker, Carole. "'God Don't Even Hear You,' or Paradise Lost: Terrance Malick's *Days of Heaven*." *Literature Film Quarterly* 29, no. 1 (2001): 2–9.

Chapter 10

Terrence Malick's Ephemeral and Eternal Images

Deleuze, Time-Image, and Montage

JAMES LORENZ

In his seminal dual-volume work on the cinema,[1] the French philosopher Gilles Deleuze traces a shift in the cinematic image, where "the movement-image of the so-called classical cinema gave way, in the post-war period, to a direct time-image."[2] A direct time-image, for Deleuze, is an image where time itself becomes the substance of the film-image rather than movement or action. This definition needs to be unpacked further (which is the task of the first section of this chapter), but by way of introduction it is helpful to understand Deleuze's project in terms of the historical shift he perceives from "movement-image" to "time-image"—the respective subtitles of his two volumes on cinema. This shift, roughly demarcated by the end of the Second World War and anticipated by the films of Yasujirō Ozu, Fritz Lang, and others, represents the collapse of the sensory-motor schema inherent to the movement-image and action-image, such that time begins to appear for itself as the substance of the film-image and not only in relation to movement. In other words, the conventional cinematic image, in which time is derived from the rational continuity between perception and movement, gives way to a direct time-image, where movement becomes subordinate to time.

Since Deleuze's project, many filmmakers have continued creating in the mode of the time-image, and few have done so more fascinatingly than Terrence Malick. While many filmmakers have developed their work through enduring still life cinematography (in the style of Ozu), or through deliberately protracted long takes (in the style of Tarkovsky), the time-image is realized in Malick's films not only through the long take and the static frame but also through montage and ephemerality and through the transitory flow of his visuals and his soundscapes. If the genre of slow cinema,[3] epitomized by the work of directors like Béla Tarr or Theo Angelopoulos, represents one extension of the time-image in contemporary film, then perhaps the ephemeral style so often adopted by Malick represents another. Where slow cinema seeks to protract and retard time, Malick often works through compression and elision, layering time upon time in his anachronic montages.

Moreover, Malick's style is engaged thematically with a philosophical focus on time, uncovering the ontological and existential structures of our temporality. In exploring these structures, Malick holds in tension the ephemerality of our existence with the permanent conditions of being and time itself.[4] Whether through the interpersonal encounters and relationships of films like *Badlands* and *Days of Heaven* or through the dreamscapes and mnemonic fugues in *The Tree of Life* and *The Thin Red Line*, Malick's cinematic images seem to navigate a philosophical and theological tension between transience and permanence, between the ephemeral and the eternal.

This chapter will explore the temporality of Malick's films in this way, first by outlining Deleuze's concept of the time-image and then by exploring how the time-image manifests in Malick's oeuvre. In doing so, I will examine Malick's cinematographic techniques in close detail, focusing primarily on his particular use of montage, which is often accompanied by the anaphora of certain visual and musical leitmotifs as well as by his own idiosyncratic use of voiceover. The latter of these, in particular, leads to a vital connection between time and memory, through which film appears as a technology of memory, that is, as τεχνη (*technē*), as mnemonic craft and art. I will suggest that Malick's films often manifest the time-image through the use of anachronic montage, creating an impression of time itself as an eternal condition of being in the world through the ephemeral and elided passage of these sequences.

Deleuze, Bergson, and the Time-Image

What is a time-image? What does Deleuze mean when he writes esoterically about cinematic images that subordinate movement to time and in which time appears for itself as the primary substance of the image? Definitive answers to these questions are elusive throughout the pages of *Cinema II: The Time-Image*, but Deleuze comes very close to offering some kind of definition or explanation in the preface to the English edition of the book: "In any case, what we call temporal structure, or direct time-image, clearly goes beyond the purely empirical succession of time—past-present-future. It is, for example, a coexistence of distinct durations, or of levels of duration; a single event can belong to several levels: the sheets of past coexist in a non-chronological order."[5] So, first and foremost, a direct time-image cannot be reduced to the empirical notion of linear time, which is a spatial metaphor that is conceptualized as succession (past moments are succeeded by present moments, which are already being succeeded by coming moments as if along the linear space of a "timeline"). On the contrary, time is manifest to consciousness as an interpenetrating "coexistence of distinct durations." The sheets of past coexist in a nonchronological order, or, as Deleuze articulates it later in the text, the sheets of past coexist in the peaks of present.[6] This is actually far more intuitive than it sounds. After all, the everyday conscious acts of recollection, attention, and anticipation demonstrate that time does indeed manifest to consciousness as an interpenetrating multiplicity; in every present moment there can be attention to the time "now," mindfulness of past times, and anticipation of coming times. To put it roundly, recollection, attention, and anticipation all "happen" in the present moment. A direct time-image, then, manifests time in this way, as a coexisting multiplicity in which past, present, and future all interpenetrate.

This is the idea of time as duration—*durée*—and it is a word that reveals the key to understanding Deleuze's concept of the time-image: the philosophy of Henri Bergson. Indeed, both *Cinema I* and *Cinema II* are united by their foundations in Bergson's philosophy, and both volumes are constructed around four commentaries on Bergson's thought, which are interspersed throughout the two books in chapters subtitled as the first, second, third, or fourth "commentary on Bergson."[7] While the initial two commentaries on Bergson play important roles in the first volume of Deleuze's project, with regard to anatomizing the signs and extensions of the movement-image, the final two commentaries open up the concept of the time-image through what is probably the most famous aspect of Bergson's philosophy—his conceptualization of time as durée. In order to understand Deleuze and the time-image, then, it is first necessary to understand Bergson's philosophy of time.

A crucial starting point here is Bergson's doctoral thesis, which he published in 1889 as *Time and Free Will: An Essay on the Immediate Data of Consciousness*. Bergson introduces the concept of durée from the outset of this text, before expounding it more fully in the second chapter, and at the heart of this concept is a key distinction between two multiplicities: first, time as we consider it empirically and scientifically (i.e., as the sum of units—seconds, minutes, hours, days, etc.—that we can measure or count) and second, the actual manifestation of time to consciousness, which utterly resists the empirical expression of measured or counted time. We have, according to Bergson, a *quantitative* multiplicity on the one hand (that of measured or counted time, such as is expressed in the units of seconds, minutes, or hours), and on the other a *qualitative* multiplicity (that of our perception of time as a quality or state of consciousness). The confusion of these multiplicities has hindered our understanding of time as it appears directly to consciousness, Bergson argues, and only in distinguishing between them can an accurate understanding of time as duration become clear.

For Bergson, when we measure time empirically (e.g., through a clock or sundial) we are not actually measuring duration; instead, we are only measuring units of space. Consider, for example, the hands on a clock, which measure time through the spatial intervals across the circumference of its face. Even the concept of a twenty-four-hour day is inextricably spatialized, for a day is the complete rotation of the planet on its axis. Likewise, we arrive at the concept of a year through its reality as a spatial quantity, as the distance the planet travels through space in one complete orbit of the sun. In *Time and Free Will*, Bergson adopts a number of examples to illustrate this confusion within our empirical measurements of time. The first is the example of bell chimes, which Bergson suggests can only be counted through the intuition of space.[8] This is because the intervals between the bell chimes are intuitively grasped through the appearance and disappearance of sound and then through the "emptiness" (a spatial concept) between the sounds. And so, Bergson concludes: "If we count them, the intervals must remain though the sounds disappear: how could these intervals remain, if they were pure duration and not space? It is in space, therefore, that the operation [of counting] takes place."[9]

Bergson uses another example, just a few pages later, comparing the spatial intuition of time with the consciousness of pure duration, and this example clearly illustrates his concept of durée and the reality of time as an interpenetrating multiplicity. The example he uses is that of a clockface, its hands, and the pendulum. It is worth quoting Bergson in full here:

> When I follow with my eyes on the dial of a clock the movement of the hand which corresponds to the oscillations of the pendulum, I do not measure duration, as seems to be thought; I merely count simultaneities, which is very different. Outside of me, in space, there is never more than a single position of the hand and the pendulum, for nothing is left of the past positions. Within myself a process of organization or interpenetration of conscious states is going on, which constitutes true duration. It is because I *endure* in this way that I picture to myself what I call the past oscillations of the pendulum at the same time as I perceive the present oscillation.[10]

It is, then, the interpenetration of past moments with present moments that appears to consciousness as pure duration. This is how time manifests as a qualitative multiplicity. In any given moment our recollections interpenetrate with our present attention, which may also be projected as anticipation of future moments.[11] Such is Bergson's concept of durée, which stands in contrast to the quantitative multiplicity from which empirical measurements of time are drawn. Such scientific measurements, Bergson argues, "merely count simultaneities," reducing time to the discrete sum of units and failing to recognize the reality of time as it appears to consciousness. As Bergson puts it, "Pure consciousness does not perceive time as a sum of units of duration; left to itself it has no means and even no reason to measure time."[12] This seems to be true intuitively, for we do not perceive the world as a neat sum of hours and minutes and days but rather as pure duration, where time might seem to fly by in a rush or to pass slowly in tedium.

In *Cinema II*, Deleuze takes up Bergson's concept of durée in this way, emphasizing the interpenetrating nature of time as a qualitative multiplicity. In his fourth and final commentary on Bergson, Deleuze turns to Augustine in order to clarify Bergson's understanding of time, citing *Confessions* 11.20.26: "Adopting St Augustine's fine formulation, there is *a present of the future, a present of the present and a present of the past,* all implicated in the event, rolled up in the event, and thus simultaneous and inexplicable."[13] While empirical units present time as a succession of discrete moments or events, which are "broken up" into seconds, minutes, and so forth as if the swing of the pendulum could somehow cut out "segments of time," the reality of our conscious perception of time is such that every present instant is interpenetrated with the instants that preceded it, all "rolled up in the event," as Deleuze articulates it in dialogue with Augustine. Durée, then, is not a quantitative sum of moments but the quality of all moments enduring together in the present instant, without juxtaposition.

This is the vital philosophical context in which Deleuze forms his idea of the time-image in cinema. While film is itself a temporal phenomenon (it is experienced in and through time), it also has the potential to present its viewer with a direct time-image. The concept of the direct time-image is understood by Deleuze through the Bergsonian notion of time that interpenetrates each moment as a qualitative multiplicity. And so he describes the time-image in film as a "crystal-image,"[14] in the sense that it is an image of crystallized time, with past and present refracting and solidifying all at once in the structure of the film-image: "The image has to be present and past, still present and already past, at once and at the same time."[15] Deleuze returns to the metaphor of crystallization throughout *Cinema II*, explaining its value in revealing the nature of time itself, in the Bergsonian mode of durée: "What the crystal reveals or makes visible is the hidden ground of time, that is, its differentiation into two flows, that of presents which pass and that of pasts which are preserved. Time simultaneously makes the present pass and preserves the past in itself."[16] The time-image is the crystal: an image of pure duration, which is not the sum of spatialized temporal intervals but time itself as it appears directly to consciousness.

Naturally, the best way to illustrate Deleuze's conceptualization of the time-image in film is to consider his own cinematic analysis. In this regard, his comments on the famous vase scene of Ozu's *Late Spring* (1949) are particularly helpful. This is the scene between Noriko (Setsuko Hara) and her father (Chishū Ryū) where they say goodnight in the room they are sharing for the last time, as Noriko prepares to leave for her wedding the next day (see figure 10.1). As the two go to sleep, a close-up focuses on

Terrence Malick's Ephemeral and Eternal Images | 203

Figure 10.1. *Late Spring*.

her smile while the diegetic soundtrack of her father's snoring reinforces the banality of the moment. Then, Ozu cuts to a vase at the end of the room, holding the still life shot for a full eight seconds.

When he cuts back to Noriko, her smile has faded and she is suddenly overcome with melancholy. Deleuze's conceptualization of the time-image is held in microcosm in his analysis of this scene. For Deleuze, the still life of the vase reveals the unique temporal fabric of cinema. In his own words: "The vase in *Late Spring* is interposed between the daughter's half smile and the beginning of her tears. There is becoming, change, passage. But the form of what changes does not itself change, does not pass on. This is time, time itself, 'a little time in its pure state': a direct time-image, which gives what changes the unchanging form in which the change is produced."[17] These words smack of André Bazin's reflections on the novel power of cinema: "The cinema is objectivity in time. . . . For the first time, the image of things is likewise the image of their duration and, as it were, mummified change."[18] It is precisely in this manner that the time-image appears; the film-image ceases to be only the image of phenomena and their movements and becomes also "the image of their duration." There is still change and transformation, of course, just as with the movement-image, but as Deleuze enigmatically suggests, the form of this change is itself unchanging because the structure of the time-image remains constant—to frame it in Bazin's terms, the time-image embalms transformation, it mummifies change. For Deleuze, the vase scene of *Late Spring* is a prototypical example of this; it is "an image where time ceases to be subordinate to movement and appears for itself"[19]—a direct time-image in which past and present crystallize in quality, appearing contemporaneously in the Bergsonian mode of pure duration.

What should we make of Deleuze's philosophy of the cinematic image? His project continues to confound many film theorists and even other philosophers with its esoteric and idiosyncratic terminology of "hyalosigns," "onirosigns," "noosigns," "lectosigns," and more. And yet, despite the inscrutability so often associated with *Cinema I* and *Cinema II*, Deleuze's project remains a seminal work within the fields of film theory and philosophy. It is a work that explores film in the condition of philosophy, to borrow the terminology outlined by Steven DeLay in his introduction to this volume, such that it analyses the signs and extensions of the film-image insofar as it constitutes a mode of perception. Bergson is the key to understanding this mode of perception, as this section has outlined, which makes time manifest in the form and structure of the film-image, as a perceptible and enduring direct time-image. Perhaps one of Bergson's own analogies indicates that film is well understood in these terms of interpenetrating duration. In *The Creative Mind*, Bergson uses the image of two spools with a tape running between them to illustrate durée[20]: the spools wind and unwind the tape like the passing of time, while the tape itself is continuous, without any breaks or discrete segments, just as time appears irreducibly to consciousness as pure duration without any discrete units or intervals. Could not the spool of tape in this image be replaced with a spool of celluloid? Perhaps, as Deleuze suggests, cinema ought to be understood through Bergson's concept of durée, and perhaps the fabric of cinema is time itself, printed on a roll of film and unspooled through a projector to endure in its screening.

The Time-Image in Malick: Anachronic Montage

The pages of *Cinema II* explore various manifestations of the time-image in modern cinema, moving discursively across an enormous range of filmmakers and international waves. There are passages devoted to anatomizing the time-image in Orson Welles's pictures, others that discuss the very different manifestation of the time-image in De Sica's films, and still others that engage one of Deleuze's most important contemporaries—Andrei Tarkovsky, who was grappling with similar issues about the temporal fabric of cinema, most notably in his remarkable hybrid of memoir, philosophy, and film theory *Sculpting in Time*,[21] published just one year after *Cinema II*. And yet nowhere in *Cinema II* does Deleuze mention Terrence Malick. Of course, Deleuze was writing his dual-volume project on cinema during Malick's twenty-year hiatus from filmmaking, in the early to mid 1980s, so the only two of Malick's films that Deleuze could have seen at the time were *Badlands* and *Days of Heaven*. Yet it is alluring to wonder what Deleuze would have made of Malick's resurgence in the 1990s and his work in the twenty-first century. How would he have understood Malick's dreamscapes and the vital power of memory in his films? What would the cosmic fugue of *The Tree of Life* have prompted Deleuze to say about its nonchronological form and its meditations on time and being? Deleuze's own answers to these questions will forever remain a fantasy, but in this section, I want to explore one particular element of Malick's filmmaking in light of Deleuze's concept of the time-image—montage.

At the beginning of this chapter, I suggested that the time-image is realized in Malick's work through a tension between ephemerality and permanence. I mean this in a similar sense to Deleuze's analysis of *Late Spring*, which was discussed above. Ozu's shot of the vase manifests time as the unchanging form against which the transformation of the scene takes place, and it so crystallizes Noriko's fleeting happiness, even as it has already passed and her first tears have begun to fall. Her happiness, its transformation, and the swelling melancholy of the scene all interpenetrate and endure together. There is a similar tension of change and temporal form in Malick's use of montage, and particularly anachronic montage, in which the sequence of images cannot be reduced to a linear succession and instead manifest as a direct time-image of multiple durations. The individual shots of such sequences pass by fluently, even rapidly at times, yet they continue to endure even as they pass, as coexisting durations in the experience of the sequence as a whole.

Such montages are one of the most distinctive elements of Malick's filmmaking. They are enigmatic sequences that sprawl across the lives of his characters, largely disconnected from the narratives of his films, creating instead an existential impression of these characters; their hopes, desires, anxieties, and above all their formation over the time in which they have lived. These sequences flow rhythmically, unfolding in a nonchronological montage of images and sounds, and they are almost always delivered in conjunction with Malick's inimitable voiceovers. Such sequences seem to revolve like Deleuze's crystals, refracting memories, dreams, and the passage of time itself as they turn around formative experiences or decisive traumas in the lives of their characters. Technically, they are edited in an anachronic order, with past and present moments interposed so radically that it is hard to demarcate the historical location of each image within the film's world. They also typically involve a moving camera rather than a static frame so that the rhythm of the edited montage is already infused with a certain tempo from the shot itself. And this is enhanced further by Malick's often unusual compositions, including point-of-view shots that seem to jar and displace the viewer by assuming unusual perspectives, as well as by the way he frequently breaks the line of action, disorienting the spectator's sense of the mise-en-scène. These sequences are not long either, and they are composed of individual shots that rarely last more than a few seconds. They are sequences of ephemeral images whose overall effect is to impart some sense and permanence of a lifetime, enduring in their fleeting passage on film just as our own transitory experiences endure in the passage of our lives.

One particular sequence from *The Tree of Life* will provide a concrete example of the power of these montages. This is the sequence that portrays the fatherhood of Mr. O'Brien (Brad Pitt), which is triggered by the brief shot of him waking his three children and is underscored throughout by Bach's "Toccata" and "Fugue in D Minor" (the second shot of the montage shows Mr. O'Brien playing the piece on the organ in front of his son Jack) (see figure 10.2).

This sequence is a montage that shows the very nature of Mr. O'Brien as a father and the impact of his fatherhood on the life of Jack (Sean Penn). Various micro-narratives convey the kind of paternal figure that he is: a disciplinarian and authoritarian, as shown by the way he makes young Jack (Hunter McCraken) practice closing the porch door quietly "fifty times"; a playful father, illustrated by the dynamic shots of him and his sons playing with a garden hose, laughing and hugging; a paternal teacher, who shows his son exactly how to pull up weeds in the garden; an absentee, shown gambling away from his wife and children.

All of these fleeting episodes characterize his fatherhood. Each ephemeral image of the montage and accompanying fragment of dialogue is delivered nonchronologically, with some scenes and settings recurring

Terrence Malick's Ephemeral and Eternal Images | 207

Figure 10.2. *The Tree of Life.*

unpredictably throughout so that the sequence is tied together primarily by the Bach piece and the existential meditation on fatherhood. Even the dialogue is occasionally disconnected from the images it corresponds to, as if the words and the visuals of his father are only loosely connected in Jack's memory. By its end, this sequence has taken just under three minutes to unfold, and in only three minutes Malick has composed an impression of years of Mr. O'Brien's fatherhood and the essence of his relationship with his son growing up. The sequence presents these moments nonchronologically and without any discrete demarcation, layering time upon time through its coexisting durations and so manifesting the Deleuzian time-image.

In this way, this montage appears like a fugue of recollection and dream, which is enhanced further by Malick's cinematographic decisions. In typical style, nearly every shot of the sequence is framed with a moving camera so that both the sequence's edited rhythm and the internal tempo of each shot work in tandem throughout the montage. Angles and the focus of frames change every few seconds. Now and again a point-of-view shot is thrown in among other perspectives and compositions. Extreme close-ups are suddenly interposed with wider angles, for example with the intimate image of Mr. O'Brien's hands playing the organ, which is sandwiched between the admiring gaze of his son and then the image of him trying to imitate his father's hand position while he plays. And then there is the insertion of one startling image just a few shots prior: that of a desert and the wind blowing through it. This fleeting image lasts just two seconds and it barely registers in the viewing of the entire sequence, lost among the micro-narratives and the overall depiction of Mr. O'Brien. It follows the cryptic dialogue, "That was life, I lived it," delivered as some mote of wisdom by Mr. O'Brien to his son. Thus, the ephemeral, passing wind in the desert becomes a visual metaphor for the transiency of life and for time itself; the fleeting, ephemeral breath of wind held in tension with the eternal and transcendent form of the desert.

This is not, of course, the only example of anachronic montage in *The Tree of Life*, nor indeed in Malick's oeuvre as a whole. Another important example is a sequence in *The Thin Red Line*, triggered by Private Bell (Ben Chaplain) experiencing a memory or dream of his wife and accompanied by a voiceover that may ambiguously be addressed to her. This is the montage that includes the image of her on a swing, where Malick inverts the camera for one of the shots (see figure 10.3).

Private Bell's wife (Miranda Otto), or at least his imagined picture of her, is the centerpiece of this montage, but she is surrounded by other nonchronological shots that flow rhythmically and ephemerally between images of her: there is the shot of Private Witt (Jim Caviezal) on the island he escapes to at the start of the film, and later there are various shots of war and bombings as well as sleeping soldiers veiled ethereally in the moonlight beneath their mosquito nets. Once again, this sequence is a fleeting montage of passing images that are held in tension with the ontological and existential structures of our temporality. It is largely detached from the film's narrative and determined by its existential mood and the

Figure 10.3. *The Thin Red Line*.

Terrence Malick's Ephemeral and Eternal Images | 209

philosophical content of its accompanying voiceover.[22] Overall, just like the sequence of fatherhood in *The Tree of Life*, this montage manifests the time-image by eliding years of experience into a couple of minutes, layering time upon time in the unfolding of its ephemeral images.

Famously, though, there is a very different kind of anachronic sequence in *The Tree of Life*—the depiction of creation and the cosmos toward the beginning of the film. This sequence is an absolute departure from the first twenty minutes of the picture, which portray the two generations of the O'Brien family at the heart of the film, introducing them nonchronologically at various stages of their lives. As David Cerbone puts it in chapter 5 of this volume, these first twenty minutes show "a branch or two of a family tree," while the "creation" sequence that follows, which sprawls across billions of years, depicts "the tree of life writ large."

This sequence compresses and elides cosmic eons into a sixteen-minute montage, meditating on creation and manifesting some sense of cosmic and geologic "deep time" (see figure 10.4).

Like many other sequences in *The Tree of Life*, this sequence is narratively untethered, bound coherently to the film by its style while addressing the film's eponymous theme of life through its primordial and cosmic images. Creation is the subject of the sequence and time is its substance: celestial gasses swirl and settle, forming the galactic bodies of stars and planets through storms of fire and lightning; minutes later the sequence

Figure 10.4. *The Tree of Life*.

focuses on the sublunary, visiting one such planet after the conflagration has abided and primordial life has appeared. Soon the montage shifts in scale again, moving from the nebulous enormity of planets and stars to the microscopic detail of a biological cell. Prehistoric beasts are juxtaposed with something remarkably like a human fetus, while a scene of primal suffering is inserted into the montage as a dinosaur hunts another. In the end, Malick returns to the planetary perspective, depicting an extinction event before revisiting the motif of water and with it the latent presence of life beneath the face of the deep—that primordial and liquid chaos of the first verses of the book of Genesis.

Time appears as the substance of this film-image. In the first place, this is because of the visual content of the sequence, described in the paragraph above. Yet it also appears in the unfolding of the montage, as each sequential shot imposes a contemplative, attentive tempo; there is a glacial twenty-second shot of a slow sunrise over the rim of the earth, and it takes the first three minutes of the montage for the abstract, swirling, cosmic gases to settle into something recognizable as a galaxy. Throughout the sequence, Malick imposes periods of dead time through a black screen, often breaking these moments of darkness with a sudden burst of light, as with the eruption of a volcano contrasted with the silhouette of an ash cloud in the foreground. And, although there is a general representation of the formation of the universe over time, the montage defies chronology; the formation and implosion of stars is perennial, happening now as well as billions of years ago, and the same is true of the division of cells in organisms. The sequence, then, is not some speculative "history of the universe" but a meditation on time itself as an eternal condition for all being.

This is augmented by Malick's subtle focus on another perennial theme of life, which underlies this sequence as well as the entire film—suffering. The film opens with a quotation from the book of Job ("Where were you when I laid the foundation of the Earth?") and of course the death of a child is central to the family drama of the film. Additionally, the fatherhood sequence I examined in the previous section climaxes with a scene of the O'Briens in church, listening to a homily on the figure of Job and the suffering he endured. In the cosmos sequence, Malick attends to the theme of suffering in several ways; overtly with the dinosaur that hunts another and stamps down on its head but subtly as well because the music that underscores the entire montage is the "Lacrimosa" from Preisner's *Requiem for my Friend*. The use of a requiem in a sequence portraying the birth of the universe intimates a clear, inescapable connection between natality and mortality, while a ceaseless weeping (*lacrimosa*) accompanies the entire montage as if all of creation were crying out for God: "*Pie Jesu Domine, dona eis requiem*," as the lyrics call out again and again.

Malick's cinema manifests the Deleuzian time-image through montage sequences such as these. Formally and stylistically, the rhythmic flow of these sequences seems to elide and compress long passages of time, distilling lifetimes into an impression that Malick imparts on the viewer in only a few minutes. Entire romances and childhoods are often compressed in this way, rendered dreamlike by the anachronic order of each montage and the unusual—even disorienting—compositions Malick deploys in each individual shot, such as an incongruous point-of-view shot or an inverted camera angle. Interestingly, whereas Bazin rejected montage in favor of the single shot, on the grounds of ethical obligations he perceived within cinematic art, Deleuze explicitly includes both the shot and the montage in his conceptualization of the time-image: "The shot goes beyond the movement-image, and montage goes beyond indirect representation of time, to both share in a direct time-image, the one determining the form or rather force of time in the image, the other the relations of time or of forces in the succession of images (relations that are no more reducible to succession, than the image is to movement)."[23] It is the shot and montage that work in tandem to manifest the time-image in Malick's filmmaking. The internal tempo of each shot and the edited rhythm of the montage share in the time-image. And, as Deleuze observes, the sequence of images in montage is not reducible to succession; rather, time-image montage appears in the Bergsonian mode of durée as an interpenetrating multiplicity of presents that pass and pasts that endure in their screening. Malick's anachronic montages manifest the time-image in this way, layering time upon time as they pass ephemerally and yet leave something enduring in their wake.

From Time-Image to Reflections on Time and Memory

So far, this chapter has pursued a formal and stylistic analysis of Malick's cinema, arguing that his filmmaking manifests the Deleuzian time-image, particularly through his use of montage. The time-image alone is a philosophically interesting and important mode of perception and expression, for it makes time the substance of the cinematic image, as a temporal distention of interpenetrating durations.[24] Yet crucially the time-image in Malick's cinema appears alongside deeper philosophical and existential concerns about the nature of time itself. And so Malick's formal and stylistic decisions, which manifest the time-image on film, are deployed not in isolation but in order to sharpen the philosophical contours of his cinema, uncovering the ontological and existential structures of our temporality.

At the heart of Malick's preoccupation with time is a tension between the ephemeral nature of human being and the eternal conditions and structures of existence. His films return again and again to the idea that our fleeting, anxious lives are cast in relief against the permanence of time itself. *The Tree of Life* is the furthest extension of this idea in his oeuvre, where the transient, intersecting lives of the O'Briens are always held in tension with the concept of an eternal universe. The cosmos sequence incubates this tension, throwing the familial drama of the O'Briens' household into stark relief against the incomprehensible scale of the universe, while the eschatological vision at the end of the film becomes a vision of eternity as Jack stands on the shores of time looking out "beyond." And all of this is framed by the film's opening words from the book of Job: "Where were you when I laid the foundation of the Earth?"

Yet the nature of time, and this tension between the ephemeral and the eternal, has been a focus of Malick's throughout his career. Consider the enigmatic Q project, which Malick was commissioned to work on by Paramount and which was alleged to be "about the origins of the universe."[25] Malick began work on this project as early as 1979, just after *Days of Heaven*, and although the film itself never materialized, significant elements of it supposedly appeared in the cosmos sequence of *The Tree of Life* and then in Malick's 2016 documentary *Voyage of Time*, which is a symphonic expression of time as being in the Heideggerian mold. For almost forty years of his career as a filmmaker, then, time has been a chief philosophical concern of Malick's, which seems unsurprising given his youth spent as student and teacher of Heidegger.

In *Days of Heaven*, one of the ways in which Malick explores time is through its cyclical rhythms, which are often as fundamental and ubiquitous as the passing of the seasons or the cycle of day and night. All four seasons pass during the film's narrative, with each becoming a cipher for the various "seasons" of life; in autumn the farmer is diagnosed with terminal cancer, winter sees gloom and even despair fall over the farm and the three protagonists, but in spring a vivacity returns with the arrival of the touring circus, and the summer nights that follow pass in laugh-

Terrence Malick's Ephemeral and Eternal Images | 213

ter and elation. On a much smaller scale, Malick attends to the cyclical passing and coming of each day by setting a large number of scenes in the liminal, dynamic, twilight periods of dusk and dawn. Many of these compositions contribute to the much-lauded aesthetic of the film, with remarkable skyscapes casting livestock and workers in silhouette against the rising or setting sun, while in other compositions the wheat fields glow golden in that very particular light. Even the climactic storm of locusts and the wheatfield fire take place from dusk until dawn, spanning the liminal twilight spaces of that single night and unfolding before the spectator in the half-light of the gloaming (see figure 10.5).

Yet the focus on these times of day or evening go beyond the aesthetic; they become important motifs that go on to bear an existential significance within the film. The quality of dusk and twilight is the quality of something like hope or loss; their power comes from the last vestiges of light fading or the first promises of light falling. They are periods of passage and change, which are themselves a constant, unchanging feature of life. And so they hold in tension the transience and ephemerality of passing days with the existential constancy of time itself, its rhythms and its cycles.

Malick's philosophical concerns with time are often expressed in this phenomenological and existential manner. In light of this, memory appears as a vital corollary of temporality, as a faculty through which we make

Figure 10.5. *Days of Heaven.*

sense of being and time. Notably, in several of the examples of anachronic montage discussed in the previous section, there is an implicit suggestion that the ontology of those sequences is mnemonic. The fatherhood sequence, for example, is constructed as if it were the stuff of Jack's memory (with the notable exception of the two-second shot of wind blowing through the desert, which seems to be exclusively metaphorical and so more akin to dream). Cerbone has written similarly about the mnemonic status of these childhood sequences in *The Tree of Life*, focusing especially on the various modes of recollection in these scenes (factual, deliberate, involuntary, or even imagined) in his chapter for this volume. As he observes, the key to the mnemonic status of these scenes is their filmic composition: "The childhood scenes are structured to reflect their memorial status: fleeting and fragmentary, without a precise temporal order, bits of remembered experiences interwoven with stretches of Jack's life (infancy, the birth of his brother) that he could not possibly remember but has probably been told about so often that they blend almost seamlessly with his own recollections." It is Malick's use of anachronic montage that effects the fragmentary, ephemeral, and fugue-like structure within these sequences, and so their mnemonic status correlates directly with the manifestation of the time-image in his cinema.

In this way, Malick's filmmaking appears as a kind of technology of memory, that is to say, as a mnemonic craft or art (from the Greek τεχνη), which simultaneously represents and performs the existential structures of memory. It represents these structures in the sense that sequences like those discussed previously seem actually to "take place" within the memory of certain characters, and it performs these structures in the sense that Malick's cinematographic techniques and devices construct memory and recollections within the thought-world of the film itself. Malick's use of anachronic montage, which seems to weave together reality and dream in its elided and compressed form, is key to this technology of memory, through the "fleeting and fragmentary" structure that Cerbone has identified within it. Yet two other cinematic devices also stand out in this regard, enhancing and evolving these ephemeral montages: the anaphora of certain visual and musical leitmotifs and Malick's quintessential use of voiceover narration.

Many of Malick's films utilize a musical theme that returns at various points as a leitmotif, often identified with a certain character, place, or movement within a film. Ennio Morricone's wonderful locomotive theme recurs with almost every train journey in *Days of Heaven*, for example.

However, Malick's soundtracks also weave original music alongside famous classical pieces, even revising and inverting these compositions in new arrangements, such as Morricone did with "The Aquarium" from *The Carnival of the Animals* for *Days of Heaven* and as Carl Orff did with his short piece *Gassenhauer nach Hans Neusiedler*, which is used as the main recurrent theme in *Badlands*. The anaphora of these musical leitmotifs works mnemonically on the viewer, throwing us back in time within a film like Proust's madeleine and conjuring up durations of scenes past in the present moment.

The anaphora of certain visual motifs effects the viewer similarly. *The Tree of Life* is replete with visual anaphora, such as various iterations of the desert setting, the sight of wind in white fabric like a curtain or gown, and especially the various postures and movements of human hands touching other hands and rearticulating every frame as they turn and gesture. In *The New World*, trees and their roots are a predominant and recurring motif; they represent an abundant and connected natural world, and they return as a memory of some lost and irretrievable past in the film's closing images (see figure 10.6).

Various natural motifs recur across Malick's entire oeuvre, of course, with still life cinematography of various animals a defining feature of his two early films, *Badlands* and *Days of Heaven*. In his later films, Malick began to use wide lenses with a broad depth of field for almost all of his close-ups so that every subject in the foreground was connected with an in-focus background environment rather than disconnected as with the conventional use of shallow depth of field for such compositions. The

Figure 10.6. *The New World*.

effect of this is to emphasize the environment and the subject together, as a unity of composition and not merely as a complementary composition. One of the best examples of this comes in Malick's 2019 film *A Hidden Life*, where various close-ups of the principal characters are delivered with a wide lens and broad depth of field so that even the distant peaks of the Bavarian mountains remain in focus in the background despite being miles away (see figure 10.7).

Compositions like these are not visual motifs themselves, but the frequency and the manner in which they are deployed has become a defining feature of Malick's cinematographic style, so they give his films a singular visual character, like some distinct cinematic idiolect; when they appear on-screen the spectator feels Malick's distinctive framing take possession of the cinematic gaze.

While the anaphora of various musical and visual motifs can trigger subconscious and unconscious connections in memory, arguably the most pointed connection between time and memory in Malick's films is made through his use of voiceover. Voiceover is slippery, though, used in various ways by Malick, most of which are deliberately ambiguous or esoteric. In its simplest form, in *Badlands*, Malick uses a single voice (Sissy Spacek) whose narration is clearly her character's own storytelling and clearly a narrative recollection of the film's events. *Days of Heaven* used voiceover similarly, through the exquisite performance of Linda Manz, whose raw and honest monologues underscore the entire picture, again in the form of narrative recollection sometime after the film's ending. In later films though, after his twenty-year hiatus, Malick started using multiple voices

Figure 10.7. *A Hidden Life*.

in certain situations, and within these voiceovers he began to blur the boundaries between memory, dream, and something else entirely.

The deepening complexity of Malick's voiceovers is also tied to their content, which became more and more abstract over his career, becoming existentialist rather than narrative. Contrast, for example, the forthright voiceover of Linda Manz in *Days of Heaven* with the cryptic ruminations on suffering, God, and the cosmos in *The Tree of Life*. Thirteen years earlier, *The Thin Red Line* explored existentialist themes in its voiceover, with fragmented, whispered questions inquiring into the very heart of our being in the world. "I want to stay changeless for you. I want to come back to you the man I was before. How do we get to those other shores? To those blue hills? Love. Where does it come from? Who lit this flame in us? No war can put it out, conquer it. I was a prisoner. You set me free." Crucially, this voiceover explores the very same tension that permeates Malick's entire oeuvre, between the inherent ephemerality of our existence and the enduring, eternal conditions of existence itself. The desire to stay changeless is itself a futile longing to transcend this tension or perhaps a longing for some illusion of transcendence. Yet there is a great irony in this—even though such a concept of transcendence remains illusory in our finite existence, our lives seem continually to brush against the mystery of the transcendent, which is the mystery of love and whoever "lit its flame within us."

Malick's existential use of voiceover is part of a wider cinematic technology of memory; a mnemonic and oneiric art that both represents and performs the structures of human temporality. As a cinematic device, these distinctive voiceovers create connections across time and memory, representing the recollections of characters and simultaneously performing the cognitive and existential structures of memory itself. Along with the device of voiceover, the anaphora of visual or musical leitmotifs functions as a kind of trigger or prompt, perhaps encouraging the viewer to make certain connections actively or else throwing the viewer involuntarily back in memory, as past durations repeat and recur in a present film-image. At the heart of it all is Malick's use of anachronic montage, in which sequences flow rhythmically, unfolding nonchronologically and sprawling across the lives of his characters. Past and present moments are radically interposed in these montages, manifesting the interpenetrating durations of the Deleuzian time-image. All at once, the shot and montage share in this time-image, as the edited sequence of these images is already infused with the internal tempo of each individual shot. It is the combination of the time-image that manifests in Malick's cinema and the existential concerns of his films, which connects time and memory in this way. Durée, after all, becomes a phenomenological concept of time as it appears to consciousness, in which past and present durations interpenetrate and overlap, enduring through memory, attention, and anticipation. Formally and stylistically, then, Malick's filmmaking embodies the time-image as Deleuze articulated it. What is more, the time-image that manifests in Malick's films appears alongside an existential fascination with our temporality, as the condition and structure of our being in the world. The time-image enriches this thematic focus, sharpening the philosophical contours of Malick's cinema and enhancing his films in their exploration of time and memory.

Notes

1. Deleuze, *Cinema I*; Deleuze, *Cinema II*.
2. Deleuze, *Cinema II*, x.
3. Slow cinema (also occasionally called "contemplative cinema") is characterized by its long single takes, static frames, nonnarrative structure, and other minimalist devices. For an excellent introduction, see Luca and Jorge, eds., *Slow Cinema*. Crucially, slow cinema is not merely a matter of films with a long running time; Béla Tarr's *The Turin Horse* (2011) runs for 146 minutes, while the blockbuster *The Lord of the Rings: The Return of the King* runs for 201 minutes—and yet there is no doubt that the former is the slower film.
4. The Heideggerian influence here is inescapable. Steven DeLay has traced the Heideggerian contours of Malick's life and work in his introduction, rightly observing the extent of this influence as well as suggesting that reducing Malick's films to a Heideggerian cinema is a reductive simplification.
5. Deleuze, *Cinema II*, xi.
6. Deleuze, 103.
7. For example, "From Recollection to Dreams: Third Commentary on Bergson" in Deleuze, 45.
8. Bergson, *Time and Free Will*, 101–2.
9. Bergson, 102.
10. Bergson, 120.
11. Bergson's distinction between virtuality and actuality is crucial here, and Deleuze draws it out particularly well in *Cinema II*. Our recollections, anticipations, and fantasies are virtual (i.e., they are real in the present but not *actually* present); for Deleuze, a time-image is an image where the distance between these virtual images (recollections, anticipations, and fantasies) and the actual image (the present image of attention) is closed, such that it becomes impossible to distinguish between them.

12. Bergson, *Time and Free Will*, 197.
13. Deleuze, *Cinema II*, 105.
14. Deleuze, 345.
15. Deleuze, 82. This is the uniting of the virtual and the actual in the time-image, mentioned previously in note 11.
16. Deleuze, 103.
17. Deleuze, 17.
18. Bazin, *What Is Cinema? Vol. 1*, 14–15: "*Le cinéma apparaît comme l'achévement dans le temps de l'objectivité photographique . . . Pour la première fois, l'image des choses est aussi celle de leur dureé et comme la momie du changement.*"
19. Deleuze, *Cinema II*, 345.
20. Bergson, *The Creative Mind*, 175–76.
21. Tarkovsky, *Sculpting in Time*.
22. For example: "Love. Where does it come from? Who lit this flame in us?" I will return to this voiceover in the next section.
23. Deleuze, *Cinema II*, 42.
24. Distention is an apt word here, for it captures the sense in which interpenetrating durations (Deleuze's *sheets of past and peaks of present*) coexist in the concept of *durée*, as if every present moment were "swollen" with moments past and already passing. The word also bears connotations with Augustine's philosophy of time, which Deleuze himself draws on (see the initial section in this chapter), and especially Augustine's phrase *distentio animi* in *Confessions* 11.23.30.
25. Stivers, "All Things Shining," 181.

Bibliography

Bazin, André. *What Is Cinema? Vol. 1*. Translated by Hugh Gray. Berkeley: University of California Press, 2005.
Bergson, Henri. *The Creative Mind: An Introduction to Metaphysics*. Translated by Mabelle L. Andison. Mineola, NY: Dover Publications, 2007.
———. *Time and Free Will: An Essay on the Immediate Data of Consciousness*. Translated by F. L. Pogson. Mineola, NY: Dover Publications, 2001.
Deleuze, Gilles. *Cinema I: The Movement-Image*. Translated by Hugh Tomlinson and Barbara Habberjam. Minneapolis: University of Minnesota Press, 1983.
———. *Cinema II: The Time-Image*. Translated by Hugh Tomlinson and Robert Galeta. London: Bloomsbury, 2013.
Luca, Tiago de, and Nuno Barradas Jorge, eds. *Slow Cinema*. Edinburgh: Edinburgh University Press, 2016.
Stivers, Clinton C. "All Things Shining: A Narrative and Stylistic Analysis of Terrence Malick's Films." PhD diss., University of Tennessee, 2012.
Tarkovsky, Andrei. *Sculpting in Time: Reflections on the Cinema*. Translated by Kitty Hunter-Blair. London: Bodley Head, 1986.

Chapter 11

Malick's Cartesianism, or the Ghost by the Machine

ENRICO TERRONE

Descartes was wrong. The human mind is not a self-standing entity that can exist independently of the body. At least, not in our world through which our minds trace subjective routes that are determined by both the continuous spatiotemporal trajectories of the bodies and their adaptive interactions with the environment. In terms of contemporary cognitive science, mental processes are "embodied" (involving the body), "enacted" (requiring bodily movements), "embedded" (functioning in an environment), and "extended" (exploiting elements from the environment).[1] This conception of the mind elaborates on arguments and pieces of evidence against Cartesianism that have been proposed along the centuries, in a tradition that goes from Thomas Hobbes's *De corpore* up to Antonio Damasio's *Descartes' Error*.[2] A milestone of this tradition is Gilbert Ryle's book *The Concept of Mind*. Relying on ordinary language and conceptual analysis, Ryle argues that the mind should be understood as a capacity of the body rather than, following Descartes, as a further entity in addition to the body, namely, a "ghost in the machine."

As other chapters in this volume have noted, it is a well-known fact of Terrence Malick's biography that he studied philosophy at Oxford as a graduate student under the supervision of Ryle. In the light of this fact, one might be tempted to see the deep connection between characters and their environment in Malick's films as an implicit endorsement of Ryle's rejection of Cartesianism. David Davies, for instance, characterizes *The Thin Red Line* as a film that makes us aware of "the richness and complexity of our embodied engagement with the world."[3] Still, I contend, Malick's films show us more than just embodied engagement with the world. Another engagement with the world is at work in those films that helps us to make sense of the Cartesian conception of a disembodied subject instead of just sharply rejecting it as Ryle did.

To see how Malick's films deal with Cartesianism, let me begin with considering some basic features of film experience. First, films provide us with perceptual perspectives on a space that we do not inhabit with our body, thereby enabling us to glimpse what might be like to be a Cartesian subject. In this sense, Stanley Cavell, who was Malick's teacher at Harvard, suggests that films separate us from the space we perceive in a way that reminds the Cartesian separation between the self and the physical world. As Cavell puts it, "A screen is a barrier. What does the silver screen screen? It screens me from the world it holds—that is, makes me invisible. And it screens that world from me—that is, screens its existence from me."[4]

Secondly, the series of perceptual perspectives that constitutes film experience is governed by the agency of a further subject who, in turn, does not seem to inhabit the fictional space that we explore with our sight. In fact, both the subject who enjoys the perceptual perspectives on the fictional space and the agent who offers those perspectives are embodied subjects who belong to our physical space, namely, the spectator and the filmmaker. Yet, these two subjects are to be excluded from the "game of make-believe" that fiction films invite us to play[5] because their presence in the fictional space would contradict the reality of that space, which is the core of the game. The fictional space, as it is to be represented within the game of make-believe, has no room for the filmmaker who created it and for the spectator who imagines it.

If the spectator wants to play the game of make-believe by preserving the reality within the game, of both the fictional space and their experience of it, they should imaginatively turn into a subject who can enjoy perceptual perspectives on the only space that exists in the game, namely the fictional space, without having any place in that space. Likewise, the spectator should imaginatively replace the filmmaker with a subject who can offer perceptual perspectives on the fictional space without having any place in that space. Borrowing terms from narratology,[6] one might call "narrator" the fictional counterpart of the filmmaker and "narratee" the fictional counterpart of the spectator. Given that the fictional space is the only physical space available in the game of make-believe that fiction films invite us to play, and given that having a body in this game requires having a place in that space, we should conclude that both the narrator and the narratee, who lack a place in that space, are disembodied subjects.

In this sense, film is a Cartesian form of art in which the spectator imagines being a disembodied subject, the narratee, who perceptually explores the fictional space under the guidance of another disembodied subject, the narrator. At most, the narrator and the narratee might be said to inhabit an abstract space, which, following Stefano Predelli,[7] one might characterize as the "periphery" of the fictional world. The fact that the narrator and the narratee are disembodied subjects confined in the periphery, however, does not entail that they are overly intellectual and emotionally stale creatures. Indeed, they can not only perceive fictional events from unoccupied points of view but also evaluate the perceived events emotionally. They are Cartesian only regarding disembodiment, not regarding dispassionateness.[8]

In most fiction films, the narrator is, as George Wilson puts it, "effaced."[9] The spectator who plays the role of the narratee surely is aware that the changes of perspective on the fictional space are not up to them but rather due to a "narrating agency" who guides their exploration of that space.[10] The latter, however, is not usually a focus of attention. In Malick's films, instead, attention is called to the narrator's agency by means of the systematic use of the voiceover, as well as by the expressiveness of the musical commentary and by the sinuous camera movements that emphasize the subjectivity of the point of view. In what follows, I will deploy the Cartesian notion of narrator so far developed to analyze four of Malick's films, namely *Badlands, Days of Heaven, The Thin Red Line*, and *The Tree of Life*. Finally, I will draw my conclusions, making reference also to the other films that, for the time being, constitute Malick's oeuvre.

Holly and Linda

In both *Badlands* and *Days of Heaven* the voiceover corresponds to the retrospective look of a character at her past vicissitudes. In *Badlands*, the voiceover of Holly (Sissy Spacek) recalls her falling in love with Kit (Martin Sheen) when she was fifteen and the criminal actions they did together in the late 1950s. Likewise, in *Days of Heaven*, Linda's (Linda

Manz) voiceover recalls the criminal adventures of her brother Bill (Richard Gere) who, in 1916, persuaded his girlfriend Abby (Brooke Adams) to marry a rich, sick farmer (Sam Shepard) with the aim of inheriting his money. In both films, the voiceover is used to tell a sort of bildungsroman, a coming-of-age story.

Holly and Linda, through their voiceovers, enjoy an epistemic privilege that is not available to us in ordinary life. Our embodied experience of the world enables us to perceive only the present—what is going on right now, that is, what happens at the place and time at which our body is located. It might be interesting to perceptually explore events that occurred to us in the past, and even events in which we were not directly involved. Yet, that is not possible. Although we can represent non-present events by means of memory or imagination, we cannot perceive them: our embodied nature prevents us from doing so. In film experience, however, things go differently. Holly as the narrator of *Badlands* and Linda as the narrator of *Days of Heaven* have the privilege of perceptually exploring their past, commenting on it, and sharing their experience with an unknown witness, the narratee.

In sum, Holly and Linda have a twofold role in those films. On the one hand, they are embodied characters who are somehow involved in the relevant fictional events. On the other hand, they are disembodied subjects who can perceive those events from the outside without having any place in the space in which those events occur. Playing the role of the narrator, Holly and Linda can perceive their past selves, the past events involving them, and even related events that they, as characters in the story, could not attend, as for instance the arrest of Kit by the police in *Badlands* or the duel between Bill and the farmer in *Days of Heaven*.

It has been argued that the voiceover in *Badlands* is sometimes in tension with the images. Jay Telotte points out the "divergence between what Holly says and what the film shows"[11]; James Monaco states that "Malick creates an electric current between the positive pole of the voiceover narration and the negative pole of the images on the screen"[12]; Brian Henderson insists that "*Badlands* often counterpoints voiceover and image."[13] As an example of this tension, Charlotte Crofts considers "a scene where Kit and Holly are gathering the fruits of the forest—the rapid camera movement from a low-angle shot of Kit up in the tree, down to an extreme high-angle shot of Holly down below, gives a sense of joy and adventure whilst, in voiceover, she blithely discusses her father's mortal remains."[14]

Such a tension, however, is compatible with ascribing to Holly, as the narrator, not only the voiceover to which we are invited to listen in our game of make-believe but also the sights we are invited to share.[15] Indeed, what Crofts casts as a tension "between what we see and what she tells us"[16] can be interpreted as a tension between what *she*, as the narrator, sees and what she tells us: a tension that is a clue of Holly's enigmatic psychological profile.

Furthermore, the occasional moments of tension between voiceover and images in *Badlands* are typically preceded or followed by moments of outright concordance. For instance, in the scene that Crofts analyzes, Holly's remarks on her father's mortal remains ("They hadn't found but one set of bones in the ashes of the house") are followed by an inference ("So we knew they'd be lookin' for us"), which leads her to illustrate the weapons training that we can see in the next images ("Kit made sure we'd be prepared. He gave me lectures on how a gun works"). The musical commentary also contributes to characterize the psychological attitude of Holly, as the narrator, toward the events that she tells and shows us. For instance, in the scene analyzed by Crofts, the music expresses a sense of agitation and excitement that seems to correspond to what Holly had felt in those days spent in the forest with Kit, which she is now recounting.

Days of Heaven, in turn, has a young girl, Linda, as its narrator, but her role in the narrated events is less central than that of Holly in *Badlands*. While Holly tells the fatal love story of her and Kit, Linda tells the story of the fatal love triangle involving her elder brother Bill, his girlfriend Abby, and a farmer. Linda, just like Holly, took part in the events she is recounting, but unlike Holly she did not play a central role in them. However, the basic structure of the two films is the same: a young girl narrates some crucial events of her teenage years that involve the affective bond to a fascinating but violent male figure, a sort of fallen angel: the boyfriend, Kit, for Holly; the brother, Bill, for Linda.

According to Crofts, the tension between voiceover and images that characterizes *Badlands* can be found also in *Days of Heaven*, which "utilizes a similarly dialectical relationship between voice and image."[17] As an example, Crofts considers the scene of the flight downriver on the steamboat, which Linda's voiceover comments as follows: "You could see people on the shore but it was far off and you couldn't see what they were doing. They were probably calling for help or something or they were trying to bury somebody or something." Crofts points out that "none of the images which accompany this narration suggest anything quite so macabre,"[18] and yet—as Crofts herself acknowledges—Linda's interpretation is presented as such and grafted onto a description: "You could see people on the shore." These words by Linda properly match the images, thereby corroborating her status as the narrator from whom both visual perspectives on events and verbal descriptions or interpretations of them originate.

Another sequence of *Days of Heaven* that Crofts considers in support of what, following Janet Wondra,[19] she calls "the disjunction between the image on-screen and the image created by Linda's voiceover," is the depiction of people working in the farmer's field. According to Crofts, "Linda's description of the wealth and social status of the farmer contrasts with images of intense physical labour."[20] There might be some irony at work here, as Crofts suggests, but this irony can be ascribed to Linda herself as the narrator who shows us how hard is the labor in the fields while commenting on the farmer's privilege. We should not conflate Linda as the young girl who takes part in the story and Linda as the narrator. To be sure, they are the same person but considered at different times of her existence and in sharply different epistemic conditions. While the younger Linda is an embodied subject who lives the events of *Days of Heaven* from within, Linda as the narrator can perceive those events from the outside, thereby offering us not only a voice telling and commenting on them—possibly in an ironic way—but also a series of points of view on them. As Roger Ebert nicely puts it, "Watching this 1978 film again recently, I was struck more than ever with the conviction that this is the story of a teenage girl, told by her, and its subject is the way that hope and cheer have been beaten down in her heart. We do not feel the full passion of the adults because it is not her passion: It is seen at a distance, as a phenomenon, like the weather, or the plague of grasshoppers that signals the beginning of the end."[21]

Private Train

In *The Thin Red Line* the use of voiceovers is much more complex than in Malick's two first films. While in *Badlands* there is just Holly's voiceover and in *Days of Heaven* just Linda's, in *The Thin Red Line* we hear a plurality of voiceovers of American soldiers, which often are hardly distinguishable one from the other. However, one voice dominates the others. That is not the voice of the most central character in the story, Private Witt

(Jim Caviezal) but rather the voice of an apparently peripheral character, Private Train (John Dee Smith). As Robert Pippin puts it,

> So now we come to one of the most startling facts about the film. Unless one has an extremely sensitive ear, it is almost impossible to realize that this voice we hear at the very beginning—by far the most frequent voice we will continually hear sound the most general reflections and questions about the meaning of war, killing, death, and the place of such violence in nature, and which will voice the last reflection we hear ("All things shining")—belongs not to Witt, an almost inescapable attribution on first hearing, but to a character we have barely caught a glimpse of: one Private Edward B. Train.[22]

Pippin's interpretation of *The Thin Red Line* is aimed to demonstrate that Train remains a peripheral character despite the centrality of his voiceover. For Pippin, the core of the film is to be found in two conflicts, namely that between Witt and Sergeant Welsh (Sean Penn) and that between Colonel Tall (Nick Nolte) and Captain Staros (Elias Koteas). Yet if we consider the role of the narrator in *Badlands* and *Days of Heaven*, another interpretation is possible according to which *The Thin Red Line* tells, from a first-person perspective, the coming-of-age story of Train, just like *Badlands* tells the coming-of-age of Holly, and *Days of Heaven*, that of Linda. Assuming that Pippin is right in ascribing to Malick the intention of giving central place to Train's voiceover, if one also assumes that there is a common narrative pattern in Malick's films, one might be entitled to conclude that *The Thin Red Line* takes to the extreme a process of apparent marginalization of the narrating character, which was already at work in the passage from *Badlands*, where Holly is the co-protagonist, to *Days of Heaven*, where Linda apparently has a less central role in the story than Bill, Abby, and the farmer.

We see Train only in a handful of scenes of *The Thin Red Line*. Nevertheless, features such as his youthfulness, his childish face, and the naivety of what he says in the dialogue encourage us to cast him as the hero of a coming-of-age story that involves going through the war, just like Holly's and Linda's coming-of-age stories involve going through criminal adventures. *The Thin Red Line* can thus be seen as the story that a more mature Train (his voiceover, indeed, sounds more mature than his voice in the dialogue) tells as the narrator having the privilege to perceptually explore the past events of his life.

From this perspective, Witt, Welsh, Tall, and Staros—as well as Private Bell (Ben Chaplin) and his beloved but unfaithful wife—are central characters in *The Thin Red Line* in the same way that Kit is central in *Badlands*, and Bill, Abby, and the farmer are central in *Days of Heaven*: they all are adult figures that the teenager living his or her coming-of-age can observe from a twofold standpoint—from the inside as a secondary character also involved in the story and from the outside as the narrator who has the privilege of perceptually reconsidering the events after the fact.

Crucial elements in the coming-of-age story are violence, death, and betrayal, which are all signs of lost innocence. In *Badlands*, Holly experiences the assassination of her father (Warren Oates) by Kit, the other crimes committed by Kit, and finally her betrayal of Kit, who will be executed by the electric chair. In *Days of Heaven*, Linda goes through Abby's infidelity, Bill's assassination of the farmer, and then the violent death of Bill himself. Likewise, in *The Thin Red Line*, according to the interpretation I am proposing, the infidelity of Bell's wife and the killing of Witt by the Japanese soldiers are the crucial steps in Train's coming-of-age. Although Witt is a much more nuanced (and positive) character than Kit and Bill—the male protagonists of *Badlands* and *Days of Heaven*—he shares with them the condition of outlaw hero since he is AWOL when the story begins. The death of the outlaw hero in these three films, from this perspective, can be read as the symbol of coming-of-age as involving the subordination of unrestrained freedom and boundless desire to the law.

At the very beginning of *The Thin Red Line*, Train's voiceover asks a series of questions: "What's this war in the heart of nature? Why does nature vie with itself? The land contend with the sea? Is there an avenging power in nature? Not one power, but two?" At the end of the film, just after the soldiers have left the island of Guadalcanal, boarding a landing craft, we see Train smoking a cigarette and speaking with another soldier. He says:

> Somethin' I can come back to. Some kind of foundation. I mean, I don't know what, you know, what your plans are, but I'm determined now. I've been through the thick and thin of it. You know, I may be young, but I've lived plenty of life. I'm ready to start living it good. You know, my daddy

always told me it's gonna get a lot worse before it gets better. You know, cos life ain't supposed to be that hard when you're young. Well, I figure after this the worst is gonna be gone. It's time for things to get better. That's what I want. That's what's gonna happen!

These are the quite naive reflections of Train as a character in the story, that is, a young boy who has just lost his innocence through the experience of the war. Yet, when Train concludes his speech, saying, "I'm getting older now. By no means old, but older," the perspective changes dramatically. The camera starts exploring the space of the landing craft. Hans Zimmer's musical commentary becomes more lyric and prominent. The voice of Train sounds much more mature than before for both the timbre and the content. He is now speaking as the narrator, matching the camera movements, which dwell on the faces of the soldiers: "Where is it that we were together? Who were you that I lived with? Walked with? The brother. The friend." Then, when the camera frames a soldier facing aft and watching the ocean, Train's reflections go back to the metaphysical questions he raised at the beginning of the film: "Darkness from light. Strife from love. Are they the workings of one mind? The features of the same face?"

The last part of Train's speech, which is accompanied by the crescendo of the musical commentary and by the image of the ocean seen from aft, has no longer the mode of a question but rather that of a prayer: "Oh, my soul, let me be in you now. Look out through my eyes. Look out at the things you made. All things shining." At this point, both the voice over and the musical commentary stop, and only the sounds of nature can be heard. After guiding us throughout the war and inviting us to contemplate the shining of things, the narrator has nothing else to add. He just asks us to share his sights. A dissolve thus leads us from the water of the ocean to the water of an inlet where three Melanesians are canoeing. Then, we see a pair of parrots on a branch and finally a shore on which a plant sprouts from a coconut, whose reflex in the water reminds us of the shape of Witt's grave, with his helmet resting on his rifle (see figure 11.1 and figure 11.2).

The final answer to Train's opening question: "What's this war in the heart of nature?" seems to lie in this last image in which war and nature reveal themselves as one.

230 | Enrico Terrone

Figure 11.1. *The Thin Red Line.*

Figure 11.2. *The Thin Red Line.*

Jack

Both Holly in *Badlands* and Linda in *Days of Heaven* are twofold characters: they have not only a place within the story but also, as voiceovers, the epistemic privilege of observing the story from the outside. I have argued that Private Train in *The Thin Red Line* also is such a character even though his voiceover is not the only one in that film and his place in the story is peripheral. In *The Tree of Life*, on the other hand, a further complication is introduced. Jack O'Brien (Sean Penn), the protagonist of the coming-of-age story told by this film, is a threefold character: in addition to his place in the story as a teenager growing up in Waco, Texas, in the 1950s, and to his voiceover commenting these events after the fact,

Jack (unlike Holly, Linda, and Train) is also portrayed as the adult man to whom the voiceover can be ascribed. The epistemic privilege of Jack as the narrator of *The Tree of Life* is thus greater than that of his predecessors since he can enjoy disembodied perceptual perspectives not only on the events of his teenage years but also on his present and, as we will see, on many other events.

Jack's is not the only voiceover in *The Tree of Life*. The voiceover of his mother (Jessica Chastain) also plays a significant role in the film, and the voiceover of his father (Brad Pitt) also can be heard in an important passage of the film. Still, the dominance of Jack's voiceover, which suggests that he is the narrator of this film, is signaled from the beginning, when we see a mysterious flame in the dark and he says: "Brother. Mother. It was they who led me to your door." Just like *The Thin Red Line* can be interpreted as Train's attempt to answer his opening question, "What's this war in the heart of nature?" *The Tree of Life* is Jack's attempt to articulate that first, enigmatic thought.

In the first part of the film, the relevant connection between "Mother" and "Brother" is drawn when Mrs. O'Brien receives the telegram communicating the sudden death of her middle son R. L. (Laramie Eppler), Jack's younger brother. Paraphrasing the opening of *The Thin Red Line*, it might be said that "What's this premature death in the heart of nature?" is the question that the narrator of *The Tree of Life* will address throughout the film. A crucial passage, in this sense, is the scene in which adult Jack is in his house with his wife and lights a candle (whose flame brings us back to the mysterious flame at the beginning) while his voiceover says: "I see the child that I was. I see my brother. True. Kind. He died when he was nineteen." At that point, we can see Jack as a teenager and then his brother R. L. playing with him, as if the visual perspectives on Jack's past emanated from his voiceover in the present. Yet, the past and the present of Jack's life are not enough to address the questions of R. L.'s premature death that Jack's voiceover rephrases: "How did I lose you? Wandered? Forgot you?" To answer these questions, a much later time span is to be considered. Jack's coming-of-age—the span of his life that goes from his birth to his teenage years of which the death of R. L. symbolizes the end—is to be supplemented by the "coming-of-age" of the universe and of life on Earth. Jack's ontogenesis, in other words, can make sense only in the framework of a cosmogenesis and of a phylogenesis.

As the narrator of the story of his life, Jack is committed to retracing the story of the universe and of the rise of life in it. It is only after achieving this endeavor that Jack can go back to his own coming-of-age story, which in the central part of the film unfolds as a unitary series of episodes that do not need Jack's voiceover to connect them and make sense of them anymore. Another sort of supplementation, however, is needed. That is a temporal extension, through the present of Jack's adult life, toward a possible future, which in the last part of the film is portrayed as an afterlife where adult Jack can reunite with his teenage self and his dead brother, reconstituting the broken unity of their family. In the finale of *The Tree of Life*, that afterlife reveals itself to be a sort of vision of Jack during his descent by elevator from the top to the bottom of the skyscraper where he works.

In the audio commentary of the *Vanilla Sky* DVD, director Cameron Crowe points out that, in the finale of that film, the hero's spatial ascent by elevator corresponds to a flashback that brings him 150 years back in time. The psychological movement in time is matched by the physical movement in space. In the finale of *The Tree of Life* something similar happens, but the other way around. Jack's spatial descent by elevator corresponds to a flashforward that brings him into an extreme future that seems to lie beyond history.

Conclusion

In this chapter I have argued that *Badlands*, *Days of Heaven*, *The Thin Red Line*, and *The Tree of Life* can be interpreted as the tales of a narrator who enjoys the epistemic privilege of perceptually reconsidering some crucial events of their coming-of-age after the fact. Those events are seen by them from an external perspective, which may be said to be Cartesian since it does not involve any embodiment in the space perceived. This is what Malick's Cartesianism, in my opinion, amounts to.

The other fiction films that constitute Malick's oeuvre for the time being (to which the documentary *Voyage of Time* also contributes) cannot be traced back to this interpretative model since they are not centered in coming-of-age stories but rather in the vicissitudes of adult characters. However, voiceovers keep playing a crucial role in all those films, still suggesting a different perspective on human vicissitudes, which we are forced to live from the inside, in a thoroughly embodied manner, but which the art of film enables us to reconsider from the outside in such a way that our perception is delivered from the burden of action and interaction, transfiguring itself into a pure contemplation. Although Ryle was right in claiming that there is no ghost in the machine of the human body, the "film machine" can provide us with an experience that approximates that of the Cartesian ghost. All Malick's films, I contend, do provide us with such an experience through their peculiar combination of voiceovers, music, and camera movements.

The New World and A Hidden Life narrate dramatic love stories set in historical contexts different from ours while our historical present is the setting of the sentimental vicissitudes of the characters of To the Wonder, Knight of Cups, and Song to Song. In all these films, male and female voiceovers intertwine enabling characters to achieve a different perspective on their existence, transcending the historical and biological constraints that sometimes seem to make it unbearable.

In sum, the voiceover is an essential constituent of Malick's oeuvre, playing a key role not only in the four coming-of-age stories on which this chapter has focused but also in the other films just mentioned. The reason of such centrality of the voiceover is, I believe, linked to the reason Malick moved from philosophy to film in his youth. According to Hubert Dreyfus—a friend and mentor of his at MIT—that reason can be traced back to his "disappointment as a philosophy major when none of his philosophy courses helped him understand himself and his place in the order of the cosmos."[23] The voiceover, combined with the peculiar perspective from the outside that characterizes film experience, is the way in which the characters of Malick's films find their place in the order of the cosmos. Perhaps that approximates to what Jack's mother in the The Tree of Life calls "the way of grace" as opposed to "the way of nature." That can be characterized, I have argued, as a quite paradoxical Cartesian glimpse of our place in the order of a non-Cartesian cosmos.

Notes

1. See Mark J. Rowlands, *The New Science of the Mind: From Extended Mind to Embodied Phenomenology* (Cambridge, MA: MIT Press, 2010).
2. Hobbes, *De Corpore*, chap. 1–6; Damasio, *Descartes' Error*.
3. Davies, "Vision, Touch, and Embodiment in *The Thin Red Line*," 61.
4. Cavell, *The World Viewed*, 24.
5. Walton, *Mimesis as Make-Believe*; Wilson, *Seeing Fictions in Film*; Terrone, "Imagination and Perception in Film Experience," 161–90.
6. Gerald Prince, "The Narratee Revisited," *Style* 19, no. 3 (1985): 299–303.

7. Stefano Predelli, *Fictional Discourse: A Radical Fictionalist Semantics* (Oxford: Oxford University Press, 2020).

8. I defend this claim extensively in my paper "Imagination and Perception in Film Experience," 161–90, especially in section 7, "Emotions." I want to thank an anonymous referee of this volume for leading me to specify that my conception of narrators and narratees as disembodied Cartesian subjects does not rule out emotions.

9. Wilson, *Seeing Fictions in Film*, 126.

10. Wilson, 129.

11. Telotte, "Badlands and the Souvenir Drive," 101.

12. James Monaco, "Badlands," 32.

13. Brian Henderson, "Exploring Badlands," *Wide Angle: A Quarterly Journal of Film Theory, Criticism and Practice* 5, no. 4 (1983): 42.

14. Crofts, "From the 'Hegemony of the Eye' to the 'Hierarchy of Perception,'" 19–29; and Zucker, "'God Don't Even Hear You,'" 21.

15. This idea is sympathetic with Adam Duncan Harris's reading of Holly as "visual image-maker" of the *Badlands* narrative. See Harris, "Identity and Asphalt," 23; cited in McLeod, "Narrative Vistas," 64.

16. Crofts, "From the 'Hegemony of the Eye' to the 'Hierarchy of Perception,'" 21.

17. Crofts, 22. A similar point is made by Carole Zucker when she states that "the onscreen images continue to tell a different story—that of Bill and Abby's hardship—undercutting Linda's empathetic remarks"; see Zucker, "'God Don't Even Hear You,'" 8.

18. Crofts, "From the 'Hegemony of the Eye' to the 'Hierarchy of Perception,'" 22.

19. Wondra, "A Gaze Unbecoming," 9.

20. Crofts, "From the 'Hegemony of the Eye' to the 'Hierarchy of Perception,'" 23.

21. Roger Ebert, review of *Days of Heaven*, Rogerebert.com, 1997, https://www.rogerebert.com/reviews/great-movie-days-of-heaven-1978.

22. Pippin, *Filmed Thought*, 214.

23. Cited in Woessner, "Cosmic Cinema," 392.

Bibliography

Cavell, Stanley. *The World Viewed: Reflections on the Ontology of Film*. 2nd ed. Cambridge, MA: Harvard University Press, 1979.

Crofts, Charlotte. "From the 'Hegemony of the Eye' to the 'Hierarchy of Perception': The Reconfiguration of Sound and Image in Terrence Malick's *Days of Heaven*." *Journal of Media Practice* 2, no. 1 (2001): 19–29.

Damasio, Antonio. *Descartes' Error: Emotion, Reason, and the Human Brain.* New York: Putnam Publishing, 1994.
Davies, David. "Vision, Touch, and Embodiment in *The Thin Red Line.*" In *The Thin Red Line*, edited by David Davies. London: Routledge, 2008.
Harris, Adam. "Identity and Asphalt: The Search for Celebrity in Bonnie and Clyde and Badlands." MA thesis, University of Wyoming, 1995.
Hobbes, Thomas. *De Corpore.* Translated by A. P. Martinich. New York: Abaris Books, 1981.
Monaco, James. "Badlands." *Take One* 4, no. 1 (1972): 32.
McLeod, James. "Narrative Vistas: Subversive Voice-Over in Terrence Malick." *Philament* 14 (August 2009): 56–90.
Pippin, Robert. *Filmed Thought: Cinema as Reflective Form.* Chicago: University of Chicago Press, 2020.
Ryle, Gilbert. *The Concept of Mind.* London: Hutchinson's University Library, 1949.
Telotte, Jay. "Badlands and the Souvenir Drive." *Western Humanities Review* 40, no. 2 (1986): 101–14.
Terrone, Enrico. "Imagination and Perception in Film Experience." *Ergo* 7, no. 5 (2020): 161–190.
Walton, Kendall. *Mimesis as Make-Believe: On the Foundations of the Representational Arts.* Cambridge, MA: Harvard University Press, 1990.
Wilson, George. *Seeing Fictions in Film: The Epistemology of Movies.* Oxford: Oxford University Press, 2011.
Woessner, Martin. "Cosmic Cinema: On the Philosophical Films of Terrence Malick." *Philosophy Today* 61, no. 2 (2017): 389–98.
Wondra, Janet. "A Gaze Unbecoming: Schooling the Child for Femininity in Days of Heaven." *Wide Angle* 16, no. 4 (October 1994): 5–22.
Zucker, Carole. "'God Don't Even Hear You,' or Paradise Lost: Terrence Malick's Days of Heaven." *Literature/Film Quarterly* 29, no. 1 (2001): 2–9.

Chapter 12

Love Is Smiling through All Things

Jean-Luc Marion, Simone Weil,
and the Visual Style of Terrence Malick

JOEL MAYWARD

Sister Sarah Joan: You write about Sacramento so affectionately and with such care.

Christine "Lady Bird" McPherson: I was just describing it.

SSJ: Well, it comes across as love.

LB: Sure, I guess I pay attention.

SSJ: Don't you think maybe they are the same thing? Love and attention?

—*Lady Bird* (2017, dir. Greta Gerwig)

Ambitious in scope in a manner reflecting its subjects, this chapter traces a thematic thread woven throughout the cinematic oeuvre of Terrence Malick—that of love—by placing Malick's films in conversation with two philosophers, Jean-Luc Marion and Simone Weil, and their mutual interest in the nature of love as generous attention to the world. Just as portrayals of love—both eros and agape—are evident in all of Malick's films, so the givenness of love is a key concept underlying Marion's expansive philosophical project. I want to suggest that Marion's "saturated phenomena"—an excess of love not contaminated by metaphysics, a "gift of appearance"—is well-demonstrated in Malick's distinctive visual style, as is Simone Weil's understanding of "attention" as an open receptivity to the manifestation of divine truth in the world around us. Other scholars considering love in Malick's cinema have primarily analyzed content within *To the Wonder* alongside Kierkegaard's *Works of Love*.[1] My analysis here focuses instead on Malick's sui generis phenomenologically "spiritual" cinematography in its generous receptivity to the world in front of it, whether intimate human relationships or majestic natural and cosmic landscapes. I posit that Malick's camera is a *loving* camera in its charitable attention to the beauty of the pro-filmic world. In other words, the film itself loves as it receives the lovely world given to it within its cinematic gaze.

Drawing upon Marion's *Prolegomena to Charity* and *The Erotic Phenomenon*[2] along with portions of Weil's *Waiting for God* and *Gravity and Grace*,[3] I offer a phenomenological description of love as visually depicted within Malick's ten major feature-length films—beginning with *Badlands* and culminating with *A Hidden Life*—as a disciplined growing awareness of what is given, or love as attention. Rather than an in-depth analysis of a single film's aesthetics to demonstrate this cinematographic love, I instead offer a short schema of the visual motifs and techniques common to Malick's oeuvre. Despite some aesthetic evolution in his collaboration with different cinematographers—Tak Fujimoto (*Badlands*), Néstor Almendros and Haskell Wexler (*Days of Heaven*), John Toll (*The Thin Red Line*), Emmanuel Lubezki (*The New World* through *Song to Song*), Paul Atkins (*Voyage of Time*), and Jörg Widmer (*A Hidden Life* and *The Way of the Wind*)—Malick's visual style has nevertheless remained consistent and distinctive for nearly fifty years. Indeed, you can almost immediately recognize that you are watching a Malick film within seconds of seeing the images, as there is something so distinctive about his cinema to merit the descriptor of "Malickian," both for Malick and for those filmmakers who emulate him.[4]

The enchanting love of the given world can be discerned in Malick's films through three quintessential elements: (1) the use of a dynamic "spiritual" camera, (2) romantic "golden hour" light and heavenward camera angles, and (3) deliberate attention to ordinary moments imbued with a sense of transcendence and wonder. Through the language of cinematography, Malick's films express how love is giving our attention to saturated phenomena even as those phenomena give themselves to us in the cinematic gaze. In this visual style of open receptivity, the audience may become more aware of the transcendent (or divine) gift of existence itself and thus better appreciate how love is smiling through all things.

Marion: Love, Givenness, and the Gaze

In the opening pages of *The Erotic Phenomenon*, Jean-Luc Marion confesses that a philosophy of love has "obsessed" him and that all of his books since *The Idol and the Distance* bear the mark of this obsession, whether explicitly or tacitly. Following this, we might say that Marion's entire philosophical enterprise—the saturated phenomenon, the icon and the idol, God without being, and so forth—is driven by this preoccupation with the phenomenon of love. The task Marion lays out in *The Erotic Phenomenon* is threefold: to propose a univocal conception of love that maintains its singular integrity contra typical distinctions made between eros, philia, agape, and so on[5]; to then demonstrate love's specific and uniquely erotic rationality; and, ultimately, to liberate philosophical understandings of love from any notion of reciprocity and metaphysics—that is, a love without being.[6]

Marion's analysis begins with a radical reduction wherein metaphysical concerns are placed aside as the human desire for love is bracketed. In this focused exploration of desire, Marion shifts the central question of human identity from Descartes's "To be or not to be?" to "Does anyone out there love me?"[7] In Marion's understanding, I cannot answer this existential query by myself; any attempt at self-love reveals my imperfections and insecurities and thus places me in a desperate tautology of seeking love without the assurance of ever being loved in return. Moreover, if every person is asking themselves this question without receiving an answer from outside themselves, it generates a mass of self-loathing individuals unable to overcome this aporia. For Marion, the answer to whether anyone out there loves me can only arrive as pure event, pure assurance. Thus, the question must inevitably shift from "Does anyone out there love me?" to "Can I love first?" In this shift, without necessarily having assurance of being loved in return, I do still receive some assurance: "the assurance that I love decidedly, that I love as a decided lover. . . . I do not become myself when I simply think, doubt, or imagine . . . I become myself definitively each time and for as long as I, as lover, can love first."[8] In short, love is a gift.

Marion describes this love-as-gift elsewhere using the visual metaphor of "the gaze," a term imbued with cinematic significance. In his essay on Levinas found in *Prolegomena to Charity*, "The Intentionality of Love," Marion describes this loving gaze: "To love would thus be defined as seeing the definitively invisible aim of my gaze nonetheless exposed by the aim of another invisible gaze; the two gazes, invisible forever, expose themselves each to the other in the crossing of their reciprocal aims. Loving no longer consists trivially in seeing or in being seen, nor in desiring or inciting desire, but in experiencing the crossing of the gazes within, first, the crossing of aims."[9] In other words, as I love the beloved in an act of self-giving, the beloved simultaneously receives my love and gives of their love to me—I truly see them and am truly seen by them, not in a look of judgment or hostility but in univocal charity and care. Marion goes on to describe this loving gaze as "a visible jubilation of invisibles, without any visible object, yet in balance, through the crossing of aims."[10] This resonates with a subsequent essay on love in *Prolegomena to Charity*, "What Love Knows," where Marion again proposes the univocity of love— the union of eros and agape—in arguing that love is epistemological, that love *knows*. For Marion, the beloved "opposes a gaze to my gaze" not as a mirror reflection or as an accusation but as an acceptable counter-gaze to my gaze: "To accept the other's face, or better, to accept that I am dealing with an other (and not an object), a face (and not a spectacle), a counter-gaze (and not a reflection of my own), depends uniquely on my willing it so. . . . Only charity . . . opens the space where the gaze of the other can shine forth."[11] Regarding this language of "spectacle," Marion explores the gaze further in *The Crossing of the Visible*, where he applies it to the religious icon but also broadens its application to all visual art. Of significance here for my analysis of Malick is how Marion briefly mentions cinema in his harsh critique of televisual spectacle in the third essay, "The Blind at Shiloh." Marion claims that while television media only produces "prostituted images" in an idolatrous disruption via a kind of masturbatory nihilism,[12] both theater and cinema "always, at the very same moment that they produce fiction, maintain a relationship between the image and the original. . . . In short, even in the most deliberate fiction, the image at least refers back to a reality."[13] Though he generally seems iconoclastic with regard to cinema in general, Marion here demonstrates

Love Is Smiling through All Things | 241

a recognition of film's capacity to create what André Bazin called an aesthetic representation of recognizable reality; that is, cinema can truly show us the real world.[14] Where, in Marion's view, television deceives us and closes us to the world, cinema (as well as theater) has the capacity to reveal truth and open up our understanding of the world, even through a fictitious narrative.

Moreover, Marion suggests that, in front of the profane image or idol (which, for Marion, would include television images), the viewer remains "unseen by an image that is reduced to the rank of an object (the aesthetic object remains an object) constituted, at least in part, by [the viewer's] gaze." Yet before the icon—which, I suggest, may go beyond religious icons to include certain cinematic images—"If I continue to look, I feel myself seen. . . . Thus, the image no longer creates a screen (or, as in the case of the idol, a mirror) since through it and under its features another gaze—invisible like all gazes—envisages me."[15] In other words, as I gaze at the icon, the icon returns my gaze in a reciprocity of givenness. And, as demonstrated above, such excessive self-givenness via the mutual gaze is what Marion would call "love."

Marion's overt connections between love, givenness, and the gaze all bear relevance to a discussion of Malick's cinema. As we gaze at the film—the moving icon—with loving attention, so the film may give of itself to us in a loving counter-gaze. Further, within the filmmaking itself, the phenomenological cinematography demonstrates a loving gaze toward the "little moments" of reality and presenting them in memory-like montage (more on this in a later section). In this phenomenological understanding, I am following Vivian Sobchack in suggesting that the film itself has a quasi-subjectivity as well as an iconicity (in Marion's sense) that allows it to be an audiovisual conduit of genuine love.[16] Marion, too, suggests visual artworks like paintings are not objects or mere extensions of the artist's hand but have life, breath, independence—the painting (or film) as a nonobject gives itself to the painter (or filmmaker) as well as to the viewer.[17] Likewise, love, in Marion's understanding, is a pure, prodigal, unmitigated gift, an act of kenosis in self-abandonment to the beloved. To be sure, not every film is a "loving" film; there are likely as many cinematic idols as there are icons. Yet I want to suggest that Malick's films can and should be understood as Marionic icons of love, cinematic visions attending to the given saturated phenomena revealed within the frame. With this in view, we may now turn to Simone Weil's understanding of such attention and its relation to love.

Weil: Love, Attention, and Prayer

> There cannot be any being other than God and that which obeys God. On the account of its perfect obedience, matter deserves to be loved by those who love its Master, in the same way as a needle, handled by the beloved wife he has lost, is cherished by a lover. The beauty of the world gives us an intimation of its claim to a place in our heart. In the beauty of the world brute necessity becomes an object of love. What is more beautiful than the action of gravity on the fugitive folds of the sea waves, or on the almost eternal folds of the mountains?[18]

In the above passage from *Waiting for God*, Weil could accurately be describing any number of Malick's films in their explorations of being-in-the-world in view of Malick's philosophically informed Christian imagery. Certainly Weil—likewise, Malick and Marion—blurs the lines between philosophy and theology in her evocative, poetic considerations of ontology and attention, as A. Rebecca Rozelle-Stone and Lucian Stone note: "There is a tension at the heart of Weilienne love that must be navigated. In the erotic pulsation that stirs her to reach for what is by definition not present but beyond perceptible edges . . . she is simultaneously performing deliberate preparations for the possible arrival, reception, and manifestation of such supernatural values."[19] This recognition of "supernatural values" within the natural world is important for Weil's understanding of love. Indeed, Weil continues: "If sometimes a work of art seems almost as beautiful as the sea, the mountains, or flowers, it is because the light of God has filled the artist."[20] We will return to such light in considering Malick's cinematography below, but again, Weil's words ring true as descriptions of Malick's essence, as if he and his films were a channel or conduit for the divine within the everyday world.

Regarding such transcendence within immanence, we have to consider the context of Weil's words about attention located within her essay on education in *Waiting for God*, "Reflections on the Right Use of School Studies with a View to the Love of God." This linkage between love, prayer, and attention is not an abstract philosophical reflection, but it is rooted within Weil's understanding of pedagogical praxis, of how school children may learn specific concepts like geometry or Greek. If enough proper concentration and patience is practiced toward solving a geometry problem, then the very act becomes like a sacrament, a means of grace for filling the soul with light.[21] In this exercise, "There is a special way of waiting upon truth, setting our hearts upon it, yet not allowing ourselves to go out in search of it. . . . It is only watching, waiting, attention."[22] Such attention is not waiting for waiting's sake—it has a purpose, a telos, which is the reception of truth, light, and love into our very being. It is learning, a maturation of the soul made possible not through mere informational content but through the transformative encounter with the given world made possible by such prayerful, loving attention.

This link between prayer, love, and attention is made even more explicit in *Gravity and Grace*. Weil is clear: "Attention, taken to its highest degree, is the same thing as prayer. It presupposes faith and love. Absolutely unmixed attention is prayer."[23] Weil notes that there is an improper form of attention, a "wrong way of seeking," which Weil describes as a kind of strenuous grit-your-teeth pursuit of truth and beauty. Rather than this posture of striving, we are "to draw back before the object we are pursuing," to not rush but to wait and watch with patience. Only then might we receive the true, the beautiful, and the good in the given world before us. Such Weilienne attention is indirect rather than direct, driven by desire rather than the will.

In this way, attention/prayer/love is paradoxically distant and intimate, a renunciation and a reception, indifferent and detached even as it is also wholly fixed on the truly beautiful. As Weil puts it elsewhere in *Gravity and Grace*, "The beautiful is that which we desire without wishing to eat it. We desire that it should be."[24] I find that this resonates with Marion's distinction between the idol and the icon—our desire is to "eat" or consume the former while to "be" with and receive the latter. Indeed, for all of their differences, this is where the thinking of Marion and Weil may have some consonance. Weil goes on to describe this receptive attitude toward beauty as a "double movement of descent" and "the key to all art." This double movement is simultaneously a "sensorial descent and a spiritual rising," where our attention to the immanent world is at the same time a spiritual ascent, a quasi-mystical or ecstatic experience where we may encounter the transcendent. Weil claims that "in everything which gives us the pure authentic feeling of beauty there really is the presence of God. There is as it were an incarnation of God in the world and it is indicated by beauty. The beautiful is the experimental proof that the incarnation is possible. Hence all art of the highest order is religious in essence."[25]

Is not this incarnational and sacramental view of such beautiful encounters strongly akin to Marion's saturated phenomena, one that again blurs the lines between philosophy and theology? Indeed, for both Marion and Weil—and, as we shall see, Malick—to truly receive the given world as a beautiful gift from God and not merely as object for consumption is only possible through the form of attention that is love. With this in mind, we may now turn our own attention to Malick's films to discern how their unique cinematographic gaze demonstrates and elicits this prayerful posture of attention.

Malick: Love as Attention

Camera-Spirit

Film theorists such as Vivian Sobchack and Laura Marks have suggested that cinema—both what is on-screen and how it is experienced—is not merely visual but somatic, that film is essentially *bodily* in a kind of carnal personification, what Sobchack calls "synaesthetic" and Marks calls "haptic visuality."[26] For Sobchack, the individual film is "as much a viewing subject as it is also a visible and viewed object . . . one that manifests a competence of perceptive and expressive performance equivalent in structure and function to that same competence performed by filmmaker and spectator."[27] Building upon Merleau-Ponty, Sobchack further argues that a film "is more than 'pure' vision. Its existence . . . implicates a 'body.'"[28] In other words, the film-world is mediated to us not by a disembodied mind but by an embodied subjective vision: a *camera-body*.[29]

Though it also maintains a certain subjectivity and body-like movements, I want to suggest that Malick's visual aesthetic is less corporeal and more pneumatological; that is, Malick's films evoke a camera-spirit. Robert Sinnerbrink offers a rich description of this camera-spirit:

> The dynamic, flowing camera, questing restlessly through the lived space of the characters, roaming freely across nature and landscape at will, relativizing particular subjective perspectives via a revelatory disclosure of the world. Life itself in its contingency, its dynamic expressivity, its revelatory glory, animates all of Malick's cinematic works. This roving camera becomes a kind of witness in its own right, one whose trajectories are organized via the axes of verticality (transcendence)

and horizontality (immanence), presenting finite and "infinite" movements as expressive of a dynamic sense of world.[30]

To describe Malick's roving camera as a "witness" of life's "revelatory glory" is, I think, exactly right—the camera-spirit gazes upon the lovely world and we, in turn, gaze upon the cinematic icon. Moreover, to call the camera a witness is to give it agency and autonomy; it becomes a subject rather than an object. Yet this subjectivity is not restrained by the limitations of a typical human body—an invisible spirit can hover and float, rise above or sink below physical boundaries, and come intimately close to its subjects without ever becoming invasive or disruptive (this is not a malevolent or possessing spirit) even as it passes invisibly through the environment.

Though the camera-spirit is more conspicuous in Malick's later films from *The Tree of Life* onward, there is evidence of this cinematic style in the opening and closing shots of *Badlands*. In the opening scene, a roving camera gently circles through Holly's bedroom as she begins her narration. Holly (Sissy Spacek) is seated on her bed with her dog, centered in both the room and the frame as the camera moves in a steady slow arc around her, always keeping her in view. The camera movement elicits comparisons to the films of Bergman or Tarkovsky while also maintaining a certain realism unlike the more expressionistic aspects of those European film-makers. In this way, Malick's camera-spirit gives its attention to Holly and her dog while also suggesting that they are more than merely a girl and her pet. The combination of this movement and the lighting imbues the scene with a fairytale-like quality, a sense of the fantastic or other-worldly even within a mundane 1950s-era environment—to allude to Marion, this is a saturated phenomenon. In these opening moments of Malick's filmography, we have already experienced a sense of wonder, even awe, not at the grandiosity of nature and the cosmos as is seen in *The Tree of Life* or *Voyage of Time* but in paying attention to—in loving—the ordinariness of a teenage girl and her dog sitting in her bedroom. Furthermore, in the closing shot of *Badlands*, after Holly and her rebellious beau Kit (Martin Sheen) have been apprehended for their murderous pilgrimage through the American West, Malick ends the film on a heavenly shot above the clouds as the sun shines through. For all of the prior vapidity of Kit's violence and Holly's narration, the film concludes with this surprising image of flight, connoting both freedom and transcendence through the camera-spirit's weightless perspective. *Badlands* is thus bookended by the camera-spirit's presence revealing the world before it to the audience's gaze.

This pneumatological quality is also evident in Malick's 2019 film *A Hidden Life*. The particular use of Steadicam camerawork by Jörg Wider captures enchanting glimpses of everyday moments and objects. Widmer, who has served as a camera operator on all of Malick's films since *The New World*, utilizes both the panoramic horizontal axis (suggesting immanence) and the upward-turned vertical axis (suggesting transcendence) in the camera's movements and framing to generate a sense of the material world imbued with the divine. This transcendent–immanent visual dynamic is demonstrated during scenes of Franz's (August Diehl) imprisonment: there are long sequence shots of the invisible floating camera-spirit slowly moving down the prison corridors past seemingly endless rows of prison cells, drawn toward windows and doorways flooded with natural light. The protracted uncut Steadicam images combined with Franz's prayerful voiceover narration generate a mood of reverence, transforming the prison environment into a place of worship—Franz's prison cell mise-en-scène carries the qualities of a monastery cell. Shots of radiant sunlight beaming through prison windows and overhead "God's-eye view" shots of Franz in his cell further suggest an active yet invisible divine presence—the camera's intentional visual framing gives the sense that, per Weil, if we pay attention, there really is the presence of God in these godforsaken places as much as in the local church and natural wonders in the mountains of St. Radegund.

For *A Hidden Life*, Malick encouraged actors to be always moving, with Widmer's camera following closely nearby, reacting to whatever the actors chose to do. The use of 12 mm or 16 mm short lenses on the RED Epic Dragon digital cameras allowed Widmer to capture spacious high-resolution images of the actors and landscapes without having to make significant lighting or focal adjustments. The results are beautifully detailed compositions that appear both intimate and expansive in an ultra-wide 2.35:1 aspect ratio—quite literally, we are able to see more of the world than we would with the naked eye. The wide-angle lens tends to give the image a slightly distorted "fish-eye" convex effect, where the edges of the frame are curved and elongated, creating an immersive and dreamlike mood for the film's entirety. The symmetrical curvature of the composition recalls how a fresco on a rounded church ceiling stretches its celestial images; we see many such church interiors throughout *A Hidden Life*.[31] In this way, the diegetic world of *A Hidden Life* is the material "real" world but viewed with a subtly spiritualized expressionistic style—the whole world is depicted as a cathedral, a place of worship and divine presence. Using digital cameras rather than film stock (*A Hidden Life* is Malick's first all-digital movie) allowed for extremely long takes, sometimes twenty to forty minutes of captured footage. This provided actors and crew an immense amount of freedom to explore the natural environment and to improvise and experiment with unscripted dialogue, gestures, and camera angles while waiting for what Widmer describes as magical "moments," those spontaneous everyday epiphanic instances that generate a sense of excess or transcendence.[32]

This visual style again strongly resonates with Bazinian realism, especially Bazin's praise of the long takes and deep-focus photography of Jean Renoir as an "invisible witness" that paradoxically both hides and reveals reality.[33] Since everything in the frame can be seen with radiant clarity, audience members are invited, rather than directed, to make their own meaningful sense of the scenes, generating an awareness of both personal interpretive freedom and ethical responsibility. In this open and exploratory filmmaking mode, Malick's camera acts as a spiritual viewfinder that guides but does not coerce us to truly pay attention to the pro-filmic world in a manner again echoing Weil, that is, of active receptivity in a posture of patient self-emptying love.

NATURAL LIGHT

Malick's exclusive use of "golden hour" light—those moments at dawn and dusk where the sun is low on the horizon, soaking the world in a warm golden hue—in *Days of Heaven* has subsequently led scholars and critics to essentially define "Malickian" as "magic hour natural lighting." Yet John Toll, cinematographer of *The Thin Red Line*, describes how the goal for that film was not to make "pretty pictures" with perfect lighting but simply to receive the light they were given:

> Because this is a Terrence Malick film, a lot of people will just assume that we sat around waiting for magic hour, but we simply didn't have the luxury of doing that on this picture. . . . We had some days when the light changes happened so quickly that we just shot through them. It could be blistering hot one moment, and completely dark the next, sometimes in the same shot. But that represented the reality of the situation, and we

just went with it. We didn't fight the conditions; we just tried to make them part of the story.[34]

In other words, the use of natural lighting is more than just a personal aesthetic preference; this disciplined hospitality toward "the reality of the situation" shines through, quite literally, in Malick's cinematography, with the use of natural lighting as a means of absolute unmixed attention.

This approach to light is evident throughout Malick's oeuvre; it is exemplified in specific scenes from *Days of Heaven*, *The Thin Red Line*, and *The New World*. In *Days of Heaven*, a brief close-up shot of grain against an orange-hued sky as water droplets glisten feels magical or otherworldly precisely due to the golden hour lighting and the rich attention to detail (see figure 12.1). The bright sunlight shining through the jungle mist and scattered holes in leaves provides a slightly different view of such natural lighting (see figure 12.2). In terms of color and environment, these images are stark contrasts, yet both are of natural sunlight through plants and each suggests a sense of wonder as the attention of both the camera and the audience is drawn upward. This upward gaze is conspicuous in the shot of Pocahontas (Q'orianka Kilcher) reaching her arms toward the heavens, the camera-spirit below her and framing her as the center of its attention even as it points it toward the skies beyond in a posture of worshipful embrace (see figure 12.3).

These are iconic shots in two ways: first in the sense of Malick's distinctive aesthetic being readily recognizable and second in the Marionic sense of being saturated phenomena, that is, cinematic modes of revelation with a view toward the transcendent. In other words, these are not simply "pretty pictures" but are cinematic icons, opening up possibilities of increased awareness and appreciation of the world precisely due to the camera's attentive focus on these specific moments. Moreover, this openness to receiving natural or "real" light—as opposed to artificial lighting techniques—is in harmony with Weil's understanding of attention in its receptive posture to the given world.

GATHERING MOMENTS

In reflecting on the filmmaking process for *The Thin Red Line*, actor John C. Reilly describes Malick as being not like a film director but rather "a truth seeker" who "was gathering moments, just taking them with him and then he'd get back and say, 'Let's turn this into a movie.'"[35] Cinematographer Emmanuel Lubezki uses similar language when reflecting on

Figure 12.1. *Days of Heaven.*

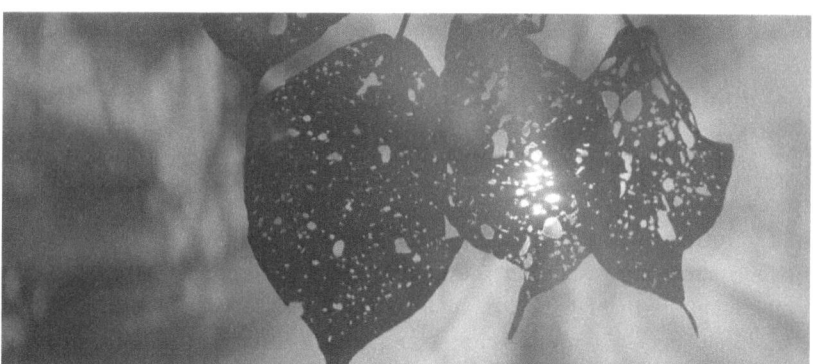

Figure 12.2. *The Thin Red Line.*

Figure 12.3. *The New World.*

The Tree of Life: "By not imposing yourself on nature, you are able to catch these very fleeting, ephemeral moments. That theme had a parallel in our approach to the filmmaking. . . . [Malick] pushes it to place where these wonderful accidents start to happen, the good accidents that feel unrehearsed and more honest. They suddenly appear in front of you and you have to be ready for it."[36]

Malick's camera-spirit delights in "gathering moments" of those "wonderful accidents" in everyday existence, often presenting them in an elliptical montage of images. Though editing or montage is not necessarily the work of the cinematographer, Malick's lengthy editing process should also be considered part of his paying loving attention to the given world. In recent years, his habit is to shoot an excessive amount of footage—much of it improvisatory—then compile and edit it together over the course of months or even years. This filmmaking process is more akin to creating a mosaic than writing a novel, taking the pieces of film footage and arranging them into a poetic coherent whole. The resulting pastiche of scenes are akin to the experience of recalling a memory, those fleeting traces and imprints stored in the imagination recalled into the mind's eye (or, in this case, the mind's movie camera).[37]

While perhaps the most exemplary of this Malickian montage of moments is the majestic "creation" sequence of *The Tree of Life*, which traces a thread from the beginning of material existence to the beginning of a family in small-town Texas in the 1950s via a montage of spectacular images, there are two other moments I want to highlight here from *The Tree of Life*, both of which focus on actress Jessica Chastain. The first is the shot Chastain's mother character floating through the air beneath a massive tree in the O'Brien's neighborhood. In this enigmatic sequence blurring the lines between realism and fantasy, Chastain appears to dance like a ballerina while hovering above the ground. Though the perspective here is suggested to be her sons', it is the camera-spirit who is watching her and recalling this magical moment for the audience. Her movements are graceful and deliberate, as well as powerful—her body's motions are gentle while her movements through the air are forceful. Emmanuel Lubezki describes the process of getting this shot:

> Terry wanted me to shoot the feet of the mother just floating. Somebody said, "Why don't we just pick her up in a crane and carry her and see if it works?" We were very lucky that Jessica happened to be a ballerina—she was very graceful. We

were losing the light. . . . We started shooting and we were just amazed by what she was doing, the time of the day, the light and the dress—it happened to be the perfect dress—and her hair. Even though we kind of planned it, *it was a gift*.[38]

We can imagine Marion nodding in approval as Lubezki feels compelled to use the language of "gift" to describe this unique moment—for all of the filmmakers' planning and deliberation, the shot just happened, providing what is one of the most memorable and mysterious scenes of the entire film. It was "given" to the camera, which in turn gives it to the audience to experience and ponder through their sustained attention to the film.

The second shot is that of a butterfly landing on Chastain's hand. The apocryphal story is that either Malick or Chastain spotted a butterfly fluttering near where they were filming *The Tree of Life* in Smithville, Texas. Malick then got the crew and Chastain to follow the butterfly throughout the neighborhood until Chastain stepped into the middle of a street and held her hand up, where the butterfly then landed (see figure 12.4)

In a filmmaking era where the artificial tool of computer-generated imagery (CGI) is employed for creating such impossible on-screen moments (how exactly does one train a real-life butterfly to land on a woman's hand?), the scene is made all the more striking precisely because *it just happened to happen*. In other words, the moment is real. It was,

Figure 12.4. *The Tree of Life*.

and continues to be for audiences experiencing *The Tree of Life*, a lovely gift, a phenomenon that could only have occurred through the disciplined patience and attention of all parties involved: Malick, Chastain, Lubezki, and the rest of the film crew. What's more, the representational aspect of Chastain's character (she can be interpreted to be the personification of the way of grace, married to Mr. O'Brien [Brad Pitt] who represents the harsher way of nature) is wonderfully expressed through this sequence—her embodied grace can be discerned by nature itself as the delicate insect stops mid-flutter and gently rests on a woman's hand. Moreover, through its realism, the scene connotes love, for, as Weil puts it, "love needs reality."[39]

Conclusion: Attention and Affliction

In a 1973 American Film Institute newsletter, Malick is reported to have said the following: "I don't feel yet I have a style or approach to filmmaking. Perhaps when I have ten films behind me I will have something worth saying."[40] Now, nearly fifty years later, Malick has achieved this self-declared ten-film minimum. As I have been attempting to describe here in dialogue with the philosophical views of Marion and Weil on the nature of love, Malick's cinematography is indeed a distinctive style that does have "something worth saying" through its robust attention to the given world.

Yet nearly all of Malick's films are tragic. Romances end; protagonists die. Each film, whatever the historical setting or context, emphasizes the universal existential mystery of human suffering and loss. How are we to reconcile this cinematography of love with such focused attention on affliction? Here we may return to Weil, who also connects love to suffering and attention. In *Gravity and Grace*, Weil contends that affliction "compels us to recognize as real what we do not think possible" and becomes a potential means of transformation if we can recognize not that suffering is useful, but that it simply *is*.[41] Weil further describes this affliction, *malheur*, in *Waiting for God* and directly links it to divine love. For Weil, the boundaries of time and space separate human beings from the transcendent and eternal God, yet, through affliction, "Divine Love crossed the infinity of space and time to come from God to us." In this way, "*Love is a direction* and not a state of the soul. If one is unaware of this, one falls into despair at the first onslaught of affliction."[42] To describe love as a direction carries with it implications for the cinematographer as the camera-spirit's gaze directs its (and our) attention to not only the beautiful wonders of the natural world that so pervade Malick's films but also the human experience of attempting to make sense of pain and loss.

In Weil's Platonic-Christian understanding of love, affliction opens up the possibility for the soul to be aware of and directed to God precisely through the immanent experience of suffering. This is not to revel in pain as a kind of masochism, nor to minimize such painful experiences by declaring them "useful" for spiritual or character formation. Instead, one must pay attention to the affliction of the world—to truly see the suffering neighbor as well as the beauty of nature—and thus to be drawn beyond this world to the divine. Malick's camera practices such loving attention to both human suffering and the wonders of creation, inviting audiences to truly see the given world as it is in its reality. In this way, though Malick's films are tragic, they are also hopeful—they are invitations to receive the gift of this world, to pay attention and thus recognize the love that is smiling through all things.

Notes

1. See, for instance, Paul Camacho, "The Promise of Love Perfected: Eros and Kenosis in *To the Wonder*," in Barnett and Elliston, *Theology and the Films of Terrence Malick*, 232–50; Julie M. Hamilton, "What Is This Love That Loves Us?": Terrence Malick's *To the Wonder* as a Phenomenology of Love," *Religions* 7, no. 6 (June 2016); and Sinnerbrink, *Terrence Malick*, 162–74.

2. Marion, *Prolegomena to Charity*; and *The Erotic Phenomenon*.

3. Weil, *Waiting for God*; and *Gravity and Grace*.

4. See, for instance, the films of Chloé Zhao (*Songs My Brother Taught Me*, *The Rider*, and *Nomadland*), which have merited the descriptive label "Malickian."

5. Such categorization of "love" via Greek terminology perhaps finds its apotheosis in Lewis, *The Four Loves*.

6. Marion, *The Erotic Phenomenon*, 4–6.

7. Marion, 39–40.

8. Marion, 70–76.

9. Marion, *Prolegomena to Charity*, 87.

10. Marion, 90.

11. Marion, 166–67.

12. "[Every] image must make itself the idol of its viewer. With the image, the viewer sees the satisfaction of his desire, thus of himself. Every image is an idol, or it isn't even seen. . . . The televisual image, structurally idolatrous, obeys

the viewer and produces only prostituted images. This onanism of the gaze fulfills the metaphysic of the monad." Marion, *The Crossing of the Visible*, 51, 54.

13. Marion, 47–48.
14. Bazin, *What Is Cinema? Volume II*, 16
15. Marion, *The Crossing of the Visible*, 59.
16. See Sobchack's groundbreaking notion of the "film body" in Sobchack, *The Address of the Eye*.
17. Marion, *The Crossing of the Visible*, 35–44.
18. Weil, *Waiting for God*, 76.
19. Rozelle-Stone and Stone, *Simone Weil and Theology*, 88.
20. Weil, *Waiting for God*, 77.
21. Weil, 63–64.
22. See previous note 21.
23. Weil, *Gravity and Grace*, 117.
24. Weil, 149.
25. Weil, 150.
26. Sobchack, *The Address of the Eye*, 129–40; Marks, *The Skin of the Film*.
27. Sobchack, *The Address of the Eye*, 13–22.
28. Sobchack, 133.
29. This term "camera-body" originates from Belgian filmmaker Luc Dardenne and his description of how he and his brother, Jean-Pierre, approach their own distinctive handheld cinematographic style as a *corp-caméra*. See Dardenne, *On the Back of Our Images*, 121.
30. Sinnerbrink, *Terrence Malick*, 171.
31. Bilge Ebiri makes this observation in his review; see Ebiri, "With *A Hidden Life*, Terrence Malick Takes on the Evils of History," *Vulture*, December 13, 2019, https://www.vulture.com/2019/12/a-hidden-life-review-terrence-malicks-new-movie.html.
32. Chris O'Falt, "Working with Malick: Inside the Dance Between Camera, Actor, and Light in *A Hidden Life*," *Indiewire*, January 6, 2020, https://www.indiewire.com/2020/01/a-hidden-life-terrence-malick-process-cinematographer-jorg-widmer-valerie-pachner-august-diehl-interview-1202200111/.
33. See Bazin, *Jean Renoir*, 87.
34. Maher Jr., *All Things Shining*, 262–63. Though published outside of traditional recognized presses, Maher's collection can be useful for gaining some insights into the behind-the-scenes process of Malick's filmography.
35. Maher Jr., *All Things Shining*, 272–73.
36. Maher Jr., 350–51, 357.
37. For more on this, see James Lorenz's chapter in this volume, especially the section on "anachronic montage."
38. Maher Jr., *All Things Shining*, 345. Emphasis mine.
39. Weil, *Gravity and Grace*, 65.

40. Maher Jr., *All Things Shining*, 7.
41. Weil, *Gravity and Grace*, 80–83.
42. Weil, *Waiting for God*, 80–81. Emphasis mine.

Bibliography

Barnett, Christopher B., and Clark J. Elliston, eds. *Theology and the Films of Terrence Malick*. London: Routledge, 2017.
Bazin, André. *Jean Renoir*. Edited by François Truffaut. New York: Da Capo, 1992.
———. *What Is Cinema? Volume II*. Translated by Hugh Gray. Berkeley: University of California Press, 1971.
Dardenne, Luc. *On the Back of Our Images: Volume One: 1991–2005*. Translated by Jeffrey Zuckerman and Sammi Skolmoski. Chicago: Featherproof Books, 2019.
Lewis, C. S. *The Four Loves*. San Francisco: HarperOne, 2017.
Maher Jr., Paul, ed. *All Things Shining: An Oral History of the Films of Terrence Malick*. Independently published, 2021.
Marion, Jean-Luc. *The Crossing of the Visible*. Translated by James K. A. Smith. Stanford: Stanford University Press, 2004.
———. *The Erotic Phenomenon*. Translated by Stephen E. Lewis. Chicago: University of Chicago Press, 2007.
———. *Prolegomena to Charity*. Translated by Stephen E. Lewis. New York: Fordham University Press, 2002.
Marks, Laura. *The Skin of the Film: Intercultural Cinema, Embodiment, and the Senses*. Durham, NC: Duke University Press, 2000.
Rozelle-Stone, A. Rebecca, and Lucian Stone, *Simone Weil and Theology*. London: Bloomsbury Academic, 2013.
Sinnerbrink, Robert. *Terrence Malick: Filmmaker and Philosopher*. London: Bloomsbury Academic, 2019.
Sobchack, Vivian. *The Address of the Eye: A Phenomenology of Film Experience*. Princeton, NJ: Princeton University Press, 1992.
Weil, Simone. *Gravity and Grace*. Translated by Arthur Willis. New York: Routledge Classics, 2002.
———. *Waiting for God*. Translated by Emma Craufurd. New York: Harper Perennial Modern Classics, 2009.

Chapter 13

Let Me Not Pretend

The Promise of Beauty in *To the Wonder*

STEVEN RYBIN

Early in Terrence Malick's *To the Wonder*, a priest, Father Quintana (Javier Bardem), having just presided over a wedding, emerges from a church, accompanied by the resplendent organ of Bach's "BWV No. 142: Uns Ist Ein Kind Geboren." But Quintana's visage does not rhyme with this glorious music; he is a figure adrift, a solemn shepherd detached from his flock. Walking among this wedding congregation, he eventually encounters an older woman (Francis Gardner), who, grasping his hand, tells him she will pray for him to find joy. She detects, as the camera has already detected, that Quintana, to borrow a phrase of dialogue from *The Thin Red Line*, "feels the lack."

Quintana's uncertainty about his purpose becomes manifest in encounters like these throughout *To the Wonder*. In playing Quintana, Bardem interacts with several residents of Bartlesville, Oklahoma, the region in the southern United States where the film was shot.[1] Sometimes these encounters are with people who possess a joy Quintana is missing. A church sexton, for example, exuberantly encourages Quintana to reach out and touch the sun-kissed warmth of the church's stained-glass windows. More often, though, the people he meets are suffering from economic, medical, or spiritual malaise, sometimes marked on their bodies (the pocks of disease or illness) and at other times expressed by their words (fragments of sad stories, of loss, of penury, of death). During these encounters, Quintana works to preserve the visible, sociable appearance of a hopeful man who believes in the possibility of spiritual remedy. Such belief is part of his vocation. But Quintana yearns for something more than appearance. "Let me not pretend," he says in his voiceover, as he speaks to two people he is ostensibly trying to comfort. But as the voiceovers during his encounters with some of his more doubtful parishioners prove, his priestly comportment is a cracking facade. Quintana seems lost, detached from his own being. He performs the role of priest, but he doubts; he fears he may only be pretending.

Of course, Bardem is himself pretending; he is an actor. And unlike many of the Bartlesville residents in the film who are more or less playing themselves, Bardem is not quite the person he is playing. But he is not only "playing a priest." He is an actor playing a priest who is worried he is only playing at being one. Bardem, in his role of pretending to be a priest, is in this sense outwardly quite close to the character he is playing, who worries his priesthood is only a performance. But what Bardem seeks to achieve as an actor—a moving pretense—is the very substance of Quintana's vocational failure. This priest does not want to be like the actor playing him; Quintana does not want to act, to be separate from his own character. Rather, he wants to be who he is, or who he feels he should be.

Quintana is not the only figure in *To the Wonder* experiencing doubt. Neil (Ben Affleck) is an environmental surveyor who measures levels of toxicity in water and in land. Part of the compelling charge of Affleck's scenes is that while his character is gathering data about a real environmental problem, as an actor he can only pretend to be able to do something about it. Actor and character merge, and Affleck's pretense manifests as Neil's own ineffectiveness. Neil can measure levels of pollution and transform these levels into abstract information, but at no point in the movie do we see him use this knowledge to better anyone's life. His vocation seems even more adrift from social or ethical purpose than Quintana's.

And this is because there is a divide between Neil, and Ben Affleck, on the one hand and the citizens who are playing themselves on the other. In the opening sequences of the film, he is traveling to Paris, apparently in possession of a level of socioeconomic success unattained by and unavailable to many of the poor citizens of Bartlesville. The separation between Neil and the residents he encounters as he collects his samples is further underscored by Malick's mise-en-scène during one moment in which Affleck is separated from the nonprofessional actors via a fence as he speaks to them about the pollution, or during another in which he is shown walking away from them as they hound him, wanting answers to their concerns. Further, Neil lives in a nice Oklahoma suburb at presumably some distance from the largely working-class figures he meets in poor neighborhoods. The residents are closer, perilously closer, to the dangerous levels of toxicity Neil only measures and from which he securely departs at the end of his workday. And something of this aspect of the film's narrative plays out in the film's own making. Ben Affleck, professional actor, encounters the residents of Bartlesville, nonprofessional actors not possessed of his wealth or celebrity.

Both Neil and Father Quintana perform social and vocational roles in *To the Wonder* but in so doing struggle with isolation and feelings of futility.[2] Their dilemma reverberates in the making of the film itself, in which there is a separation at play between the movie star and the nonprofessional performer. The movie star acts, but the nonprofessional, it would seem, can only be in front of Malick's camera what they already were before the production of *To the Wonder* arrived in their city.

Acting and Being

This very juxtaposition of performances by Hollywood professionals with the residents of Bartlesville is one of the fascinations of *To the Wonder*. All four of the film's leads—Bardem, Affleck, Olga Kurylenko, and Rachel McAdams—are actors with impressive credentials. Their nonprofessional coactors, in the parlance of the film industry in which Malick himself is at the margins, are "extras." But their presence in *To the Wonder* goes beyond the function of an extra in a typical movie. Malick's method places his seasoned performers as coactors in sequences with nonprofessional actors and in scenes that are themselves not conventionally scripted.[3] This approach results in fascinating encounters between people who regularly and professionally act in front of the camera and others who do not. Further, while Bardem, Affleck, Kurylenko, and McAdams bring the fruits of their professional experience to Malick's project, the residents of this small town in Oklahoma presumably must fall back on being themselves. The presence of Malick's camera may change their behavior, but because we do not know any of these people in the way we might remember

Bardem, Affleck, Kurylenko, and McAdams from other films, we do not know precisely how.

In this way, *To the Wonder* enacts a salient variation on a theme present throughout Malick's work. Writers on Malick's cinema tend to privilege the amateur actor or relatively new professional actor (unburdened by a familiar star persona)—the "natural"—who can simply *be* in front of the camera. This preference should not be unexpected, for the philosophical emphasis on being is a frequent topic of discussion in reflections on Malick. James Morrison and Thomas Schur, for example, in their analysis of *Days of Heaven* and *The Thin Red Line*, take the position that the most stirring performances in Malick's films tend toward the authenticity of natural being rather than the studied posing and posturing of professional acting.[4] They privilege the presence of relatively little-known actors such as Linda Manz in *Days of Heaven* and Jim Caviezel in *The Thin Red Line*, whose unstudied expressiveness throws into relief the more self-consciously expressive performances of other Malick actors like Richard Gere, Sean Penn, and Martin Sheen. Their study was published before the release of *The New World*, but it seems likely that Morrison and Schur might also privilege the work of relatively unknown Q'orianka Kilcher opposite seasoned stars Colin Farrell and Christian Bale in that film, as well as the three young boys in *The Tree of Life*, cast opposite established stars Brad Pitt and Sean Penn and another then-emerging star, Juilliard-trained actress Jessica Chastain.[5]

The juxtaposition of movie stars alongside nonprofessional actors in *To the Wonder* takes the distinction between "acting" and "being," as established by earlier Malick films, even further. Unlike Caviezel (but somewhat like Manz, who ultimately eschewed a career in Hollywood in the years after *Days of Heaven*), the people we see *being* in front of Malick's camera, and alongside Bardem and the other stars, are public citizens and not actors at the beginning of promising careers. Further, this distinction between acting and being is not only implicitly at play in the contrasting performance styles of *To the Wonder*, but it is also thematized in the characters of Quintana and Neil, whose professional roles cleave them from the other human beings surrounding them.

The two major female characters in the film interact with these residents less frequently. McAdams, in a small role as Jane, Neil's ex-lover, does not have any extended interactions with Bartlesville citizens, and she is not seen in spaces where her character might potentially have them, apart from a brief moment in a hospital when she is first introduced.

Kurylenko, playing Marina, Neil's on-again, off-again girlfriend, does have a few, and hers are striking because they are not vocationally shaped, as are the residents' encounters with Bardem's priest and Neil's water surveyor. Marina, in other words, is not pretending to be anything for anyone, even as Kurylenko is pretending to be Marina. Marina's presence does not symbolize the performative work, and attendant social failures, of environmental and religious institutions. And whereas Neil and Quintana have some obligation and purpose in Bartlesville, Marina is a stranger there. This is not to say that Marina is passive or without significant occupation. She is a mother; she cares for young Tatiana (Tatiana Chilin). And we learn Marina was once a professional dancer, which (beyond a pair of ballet shoes glimpsed in one shot) is expressed less as narrative information and more through the elegant, nimble way Kurylenko moves through the film. Her lithe gracefulness is contrapuntal to Affleck's firm, solemn presence in images they share together. While the existential dilemmas of the two male characters do their part in establishing the film's tone, Marina has her own distinctive way of moving, and of encouraging us to move, through this film.

In contrast to other thoughtful discussions that have taken Bardem and Affleck as the subjective centers of the film, I offer in the pages to follow the idea that Olga Kurylenko's performance as Marina is at the heart of *To the Wonder*.[6] Despite Kurylenko's status as a movie star, she is the one professional actor in *To the Wonder* who finally transcends her role as actor, achieving a level of being closer to that of the Bartlesville residents than to her costars, and this despite the fact that Kurylenko is herself a distinguished performer to whom the camera seems ineluctably drawn. It is through an encounter with her performance, as orchestrated by Malick, that *To the Wonder* comes most fully alive.

Marina's Presence

We hear a female voice, speaking in French. "Newborn; I open my eyes," the voice says, as a train, somewhere in Europe, whizzes by the countryside. Our first view of the woman to whom this voice belongs, Olga Kurylenko's Marina, is unusual. Captured by the low-resolution imagery of a small digital camera (one held off-screen by the hitherto unseen Ben Affleck), the first close-up of her face is both distorted and intensified: the presentation of these digitally captured shots in Malick's own wide-screen composition results in an odd stretching of Kurylenko's face, even as the image's textures heighten her appearance in a painterly way. Kurylenko mouths a word—she is speaking to an off-screen figure with whom she exchanges a brief touch—but we continue only to hear her via the voice-over. This newborn is hungry: she playfully bites at her paramour's hand as he caresses her neck and her cheek. Another close-up shows us this hand caressing Kurylenko's face as she lies down across the train's seats; this procession of digital imagery continues as they ride the Metro and walk through the streets of Paris, a glimpse of Affleck's face coming via a reflection of the couple in the Metro window, a reflection in which we can also see the little camera he holds, that has produced these initial images. Affleck's Neil is a diegetic auteur, at least in this sequence, but these images are not inflected by his subjectivity. If anything, the fact that he is holding the camera keeps us further away from him. His movement of the camera has a contingent quality; it is responding to, rather than authoring, Marina and her movements. And she finds a lot of ways to contort her body in the cramped train, an early indication of Marina's skill in creatively seeking and finding solutions to physical and existential restrictions.

Marina's description of herself here as a "newborn" is also striking. In *To the Wonder*, her name is never spoken. She is always freshly new-born to us, undetermined by social role or moniker. (I call her "Marina" because this is the name the end credits bestow.) In describing herself as a newborn, Marina also reminds us about what human presence can be in cinema, prior to any intrusion of characterization or convention. Human figures in movies, when we first meet them, are always—potentially—freshly born to our eyes; only those figures overdetermined by conventions or routine character types (the cowboy in a Western, the detective in a noir) relinquish their newness, formulas serving to age them beyond newborn status before the movie even begins. Malick's work, by contrast, sunders us from expectation, opening up the possibility of bringing human players newly again to us.

Nevertheless, Olga Kurylenko is a famous movie star, familiar from other movies. Perhaps these associations might work to age her immediately beyond the "newborn" status for which her character yearns in the film's opening images, moving her Marina closer to convention or expectation. Malick's strategies ensure this does not happen. Instead, it is Affleck, ostensibly the film's marquee star, who is kept at arm's length in this opening sequence and throughout much of the film. He appears, lingers, and then disappears at the margins of the frame, or in reflections in windows, or from behind, once the couple arrives in Paris (Neil is a visitor, but Marina lives there). It is Marina, by contrast, who turns around to us, to look at Neil (and by extension, us). It is as if she is asking: *Are you still there? Does your journey with me, to the wonder, continue?* Neil moves forward, as if to say, yes, but it is notable that Neil himself never asks us (implicitly) or Marina (explicitly) this question; Affleck never turns around in this way, never moves forward with the same kind of exuberance inviting us into the film's world. He is a stoic, stolid figure, ostensibly active but without great curiosity about what surrounds him, in counterpoint to Kurylenko's open, searching eyes and her graceful dancer's comportment, alive to the moment. When they are seen together, he is most often behind her, following her; she is leading him and, as the camera follows her, us. She dances through space unpredictably, laterally and diagonally, across the frame, and back-and-forth along the z-axis that extends from the camera's lens to the horizon line. Neil is self-contained; he moves forward with confidence (even in the scenes in which he discovers toxicity in water and land, his established way of moving is not greatly disturbed). Marina, by contrast, is at times willing to abandon forward movement in a sudden, joyous rush back to the camera (see figure 13.1).

Being alive to the moment while watching a movie, and a screen performance, involves the capacity to be—even naively—moved by human figures on-screen: to discover who Marina is and who she might yet become, and even to have a share in the creation of her as a character and a share in what it means to remember her. To use Marina's own words, we are

Figure 13.1. *To the Wonder.*

invited to go "a little of our way together," going, for the duration of *To the Wonder*, wherever she goes or to wherever we are privileged to see her.[7] Marina's gestures do not convey an already articulated meaning—"pointing to" words and ideas already written down somewhere (in a script). They impress us with, impress upon us, the possibility of meaning; they invite us to explore its possibilities. Marina is alive to what Vilém Flusser once wrote of gesture; she is, within Malick's cinema, one of its exemplary practitioners: "A gesture is a movement of the body or of tool connected to the body for which there is no satisfactory causal explanation."[8] Her gestures are not effects of some unspoken, already articulated cause but are themselves causes, at least potentially, of meanings we might write in light of them.

After Marina and her daughter Tatiana move from Paris to the United States to join Neil in Bartlesville, Oklahoma, a triumphant mood of fulfillment colors the movie. After the busy streets of Paris are replaced, in a sudden jump cut, by the flat prairie and electrical wires dotting the blue sky in rural Oklahoma, Kurylenko nevertheless remains stirringly the same, running forward into this landscape with the same joy and rapture and repeating her performative motif, established in the scenes in Paris, of looking back to the camera as if to say (ostensibly to Neil, more strikingly to us), *Are you still with me?* The triumphant music accompanying her movements and gestures provides the filmmaker's own answer. Affleck, playing Neil, is forever playing catch-up in these early Bartlesville scenes, rushing in from off-screen to join a frame already incarnated by Kurylenko's dancing, lively presence. Many of these shots in the first Oklahoma sequences, notably, do not include Affleck at all. We see Kurylenko flitting through wheat fields, gazing at the horizon line of a beautiful sunset, running her palms through her hair in ecstatic response to the environment. There is an erotic charge to such moments, which has nothing to do with Marina's affection for Neil, or at least not directly. It is as if she were, as if she could, make love to the natural world. This ecstasy, and then, a cut: now, morning, and she is asleep (the timing of this cut underscores the idea that her night was spent with nature rather than with Neil), gathered up in bedsheets (our first glimpse of the home Neil has brought her to America to live in); like all beings who live vibrantly, she must rest.

Marina's ability to respond to nature with erotic passion is a recurring motif in the early scenes of the film. She is associated with water, with light, and with verdant fields; Neil is associated with the pollution of same. In contrast to his inability to actually do anything about the pollution he measures, her presence in water seems resplendent and restorative. And he is often kept in darkness, or figured in the frame as isolated and separated (and as one who isolates and separates himself; Marina's moments of isolation feel, comparatively, forced upon her, not of her own making). Marina's fondest memories of Neil join the water motif with a memory of her daughter. "After school, you took her to swim," her voice intones, as an image shows us Neil picking up Tatiana from school. Marina's association with water is occasionally shown to break down Neil's heavy defenses. In one shot he stands inside the home, looking at Marina and Tatiana playing outside. Subsequently, he and the camera join them, Neil teasing them in the yard with water from a hose. Water will later join Neil and Marina as they swim together in a public pool. But Neil will again separate himself, leaving the pool, his gaze fixated on another woman on the other side; Marina, noticing his lust, is left alone in the water. Marina also responds passionately to natural light. In a lovemaking scene, in which Neil and Marina tussle together on a carpeted floor, Kurylenko's body is alternately thrown into shadow in one moment and in the flood of bright light pouring in from the window in the next. "An avalanche of tenderness," her voiceover whispers, as they wrangle and caress, with gestures that alternate between violence and gentleness, the words accurately capturing a sense of the jagged eroticism kindling their lovemaking. Neil, here, is kept mostly out of frame. The figural center of this erotic experience is Marina. And again, Marina responds most ecstatically not to Neil but to light. Her figure is not only illuminated by light because it is more present in the frame than Neil, whose lack of commitment to Marina is answered by the frame's lack of commitment to him; it is the light to which she more meaningfully makes love.

Marina's joyous response to her environment equips her with the ability to shift the tone of her world through the way she looks at it and through the way she moves. She is the only major figure in the movie who knows how to change the space, possessing an embodied knowledge that incarnates human movement in a way that parallels and complements Malick's work as a poet, seeing gesture as generative and forward-looking rather than illustrative or instrumental. After the argument, the camera eventually returns to Neil's handsome home in the Bartlesville suburbs. He is lingering outside the home, a silhouette; through the windows of the home, he glimpses Marina dancing inside with her daughter, her movement reshaping suburban conventionality into elegance and possibility. We go inside, as Neil does; once again, the viewer answers Marina's call to follow.

She plays with Neil and Tatiana, using a small lamp to variously throw their, and her, figures into pools of light and pockets of shadow. The delight of Marina is not separate here from the delight of Olga Kurylenko in front of Malick's camera. There is no sign of what she is doing in shots like this in the script. Malick's frame does not present a character already written down in a screenplay few besides the participants in the film's production will ever read. We see a figure at play, exploring in happy collaboration with the camera the various possibilities of her own figuration. Marina, and Olga Kurylenko herself, delights in her cinematic being.

And yet, Neil fails to respond to her presence. He is ultimately separate from her just as he is separate from the people of Bartlesville among whom he works. He moves forward, his duty in sight, while Marina lingers, returns, dances, touches, feels, sees. Marina, after this ecstatic but also deeply troubled time in Bartlesville, leaves him, taking Tatiana with her in a return to Paris. The relationship with Neil appears to have ended.

Finding a Lost Beauty

Marina's departure at this point always strikes me in its suddenness. When Kurylenko is absent from this middle stretch of the film (apart from brief cutaways that show her living an unsatisfying life in Paris), the film misses something. The film seems to know this, too; this "missing" is not a flaw in the work but part of the way *To the Wonder* works, in how it becomes evident how much Olga Kurylenko matters to the poetic work the film is doing. Gracefully, Marina does soon return—ostensibly to Neil, more meaningfully to the film.

In the first scenes in Bartlesville early in *To the Wonder*, Marina's rapture with nature is immediate: she finds beauty because she is prepared to see it and is present and alive to it, as her viewer is present and alive to her. When Marina returns to the United States, this rapturous engagement with the beauty of the natural world takes time—most of the second half of the film—for her to rediscover. Marina must find again her path to beauty. Perhaps the film is asking us to find a similar path, too. After all, Marina's search for beauty, which she rapturously invites us to join in the first hour of the film, is also our search. If we have responded to the way Marina looks at the world, we have joined her on her search for beauty. And if we call Malick's film beautiful, and if the film loses something of its beauty when Marina is not on-screen, then certainly she and the actress who plays her must be beautiful, too.

Beauty is a familiar topic in philosophy but a vexed one in cinema studies. Actually, in the latter, it is not even vexed: it is often not addressed by film scholars at all. Trained largely in cultural studies approaches suspicious of affirmative claims about beauty, film scholars, when they have deigned to comment on the subject, tend to see it as inherently suspicious, a false ideal driven by profit and exploitation, mechanisms that can only be oppressive to the vast majority of the earth's inhabitants. But we all experience forms of beauty and are touched by them. We can have unpredictable, noninstrumental conversations about what kinds of beauty variously touch us, too. And in art, encounters with beauty have expansive, rather than regressive, potential. Alexander Nehamas has an idea of beauty that reminds me of Marina herself—not only her beauty as a cinematic figure but also the way she looks at the beauty in the things in the world and the way she in turn wants our eyes to move toward them:

> Beauty points to the future, and we pursue it without knowing what it will yield, and that makes it as difficult to say why we love someone as it is to say why someone else is our friend. . . . The difference between the clear desires of attraction and the complex desires of love is not a moral one: horrible harm has come to people through love, and Aristotle, remember, thought that both pleasure and profit are sound grounds for *philia*. The difference is that in one case desire grows mostly out of what one already knows, which includes what one wants, while in the other it is also a yearning for features still undisclosed and desires that are still without shape.[9]

Marina was apparently partially shaped, prior to Olga Kurylenko's presence in front of any camera, by aspects of Terrence Malick's literary education, by what he already knew. He encouraged Kurylenko to read Fyodor Dostoyevsky's novel *The Idiot* (1869) and to think of Marina as an amalgam of the novel's two most significant female characters: Aglaya Yepanchin and Nastassya Filippovna. Kurylenko reports that Malick told her this combination of fierce and prideful innocence (in Aglaya) and tragic romance (in Nastassya) was something the director found striking about Russian literature; a synthesis of Aglaya and Nastassya was what he sought to capture in the character of Marina.[10] The multilingual Kurylenko is herself of Ukrainian, Russian, and Belarussian descent, although it is not clear whether Malick's associations of the character of Marina with Dostoyevsky came before or after Kurylenko's being cast in the film. Was Malick moved by Kurylenko's particular beauty to think again about great Russian literature he had read, or was he moved by the beauty of Dostoyevsky's characters to seek out a similar presence in Kurylenko? As with so many things about Malick's reclusive process, we do not know. I am not sure it matters. As Nehamas counsels, desire grows out of what one already knows (like a knowledge of literature, perhaps of Dostoyevsky), while beauty is always a promise, a glance toward the future. The point is finally not that someone or something satisfies already known desires, and even less that something or someone is beautiful, but rather that beauty itself provokes a continued following, a movement beyond desire, a looking-into-the-world as Marina herself never ceases to do. Malick's filmmaking style is in and of itself beautiful enough to encourage engagement with this search for beauty. And Kurylenko's Marina is this style's perfect partner, not simply because she is beautiful (although beauty is never simple) but because she is a figure who herself seeks beauty, who yearns to see the undisclosed and the yet-to-be-attained meaning, and life of meaning, that beauty promises.

When Marina returns to Bartlesville in the second half of the movie, there is initially something relatively reserved about her search for beauty. Her ecstasy in the first half of the film has largely been replaced in the initial stretch of the film's second half with quieter, more uncertain, more reticent moods. She returns to Bartlesville and marries Neil (there are economic motivations at work here; she was unable to gain employment in Paris). In contrast to the joyous bride and groom in the wedding celebration over which Quintana had presided earlier, the new bride Marina seems a lost figure, closer to Quintana's own forlornness. After a perfunctory court procedure in which she weds Neil, she returns to their home, gazing out of windows and at light streaming across an unoccupied bed. She finds her dancer's shoes, holding them close to her heart before placing her hands in them, turning her fingers into little dancer's toes on the countertop. She bounces up and down on a bed but the low ceiling, framed by Malick from a low angle, suggests a limit. There is only a very subdued hint of her joy here, of her ecstatic being-in-the-world evident in the earlier stretch of the film.

Marina and Neil visit a doctor—she will have to undergo a procedure to remove an IUD—and the topic of having a child is broached. But perhaps sensing Neil's reluctance to commit, she redirects these anguished questions over whether or not to have a child into restorative playfulness. We see her, being goofy, cradling a chicken like it was an infant and comically thrusting the silly bird in Neil's face. In a scene, at night, in which the two characters shop for a laundry appliance at a local store—a rather less consequential variation of domestic commitment but, still, a form—Marina impishly blows air from her mouth through a dryer hose, turning a dull, instrumental object into a musical, aesthetic one. If we respond to her playfulness in a way the closed-off Neil does not (which is to say, with any measure of the sustained attention Neil seems unable to give), we become alive to a figure creating her own beauty in an environment largely indifferent to it.

But as I have suggested, Marina's relationship to beauty in this first stretch of the second half of the movie is subdued, relative to her exuberance in the first half of the film. Just as the film loses sight of Marina in its middle stretch, in the sequences with Neil and Jane in which Marina is mostly absent, Marina has lost sight of herself when she returns to Bartlesville. But as the film continues on, she inches closer to her right path. It is not Neil who inspires Marina to discover again her capacity to look for and see beauty but rather, or at least in part, another woman. In a brief sequence in the film's second hour, Marina is seen walking the streets of Bartlesville with a visiting friend, Anna (Romina Mondello). Anna can tell Marina is trapped in this marriage and in this life in Bartlesville, and she encourages her to shed these trappings and be free again. When put this way in words, these are clichés, but they are meaningfully and substantively felt through Anna's bodily movement, through the way she incarnates the frame and the way she encourages Marina to find herself again. A camera follows the two of them as they walk toward the horizon line, Anna's unpredictable gestures and movements finally providing Marina a proper dance partner in the frame. Jump cuts guide us forward in this scene, as they will so often do throughout *To the Wonder*, the cuts themselves now finding a perfect partner in Anna's own angular movement and challenging attitude. The irony in this scene is found in Marina's own strange reserve, her uncharacteristically subdued nature. The Marina of the first half of the movie would have responded to Anna's joy with delight incarnate. "Listen to your heart," Anna tells Marina, and in startlingly intimate close-up, Anna puts her ear to Marina's chest. Anna encourages Marina to dispense with her baggage (her purse, which Anna playfully throws into a shrub—"it's hidden," Anna reassures her), while Anna soon declares to the world, "I'm my own experiment!" In turn, she encourages Marina to think of her own being as an ongoing work-in-progress, a search for beauty and for what it might and still could be. Anna is the one character in *To the Wonder* who is wholly aware she is cinema: a figure constituted not by preexisting baggage or instrumental purpose but by the incarnations of body and potential that should be possible in any moment. Marina once had this ecstatic awareness—the film has shown it—and Anna wants her to find it again.

Coda: Returning to the Wonder

The final images of the film, which confirm Marina's joyous rediscovery of her search for beauty, are preceded by one of the most stirring sequences in Malick's cinema. Curiously, Marina is herself hidden during most of this sequence. These images are held together by two key aspects on the film's sound track: Javier Bardem's voice, as Father Quintana, and the yearning strings of Górecki's "Symphony No. 3, Opus 36." We see Quintana tend to the sick and the poor as his voiceover intones words from St. Augustine: "Christ behind me, Christ in me." Here, Quintana is touched by grace, and his words become, in concert with the Górecki, aural inscriptions of fervent religious feeling. Quintana, so separated from his flock earlier in the film, is here like a character in a Robert Bresson movie, touched by off-screen divinity, spiritual doubts overcome in a way impossible to render through physical action in a conventional dramaturgy. This spiritual replenishment of Quintana happens from the outside, and is invisible to the film, even though we see and hear its effects. The images continue on; they convey but are also in turn touched by Quintana's own spiritual replenishment.

Marina is very briefly glimpsed here, in this astonishing sequence, as Quintana speaks and as Górecki floats on the soundtrack. Miraculously, and apparently something like the sudden manifestation of Quintana's own rediscovery of his spiritual direction, a child appears alongside Marina during her brief appearance in this sequence that is otherwise mostly about Quintana's rediscovery of spirit. Marina and a child are glimpsed feeding geese by a pond. The film's images of sudden grace and revelation posit here the possibility that this child is one she has had with Neil, a consummation occurring invisibly, outside the flow of the film's dramaturgy but within and through its poetry, perhaps a gift of grace much like Quintana's renewed vows to his vocation. And in this same sequence scored by the Górecki, we do see Neil approach Marina, in their home, falling to his knees, his gestures and pose pleading for absolution. Given this, it is possible to infer from these images that the two of them have reconciled and have had a child who suddenly appears to us in the Górecki sequence. The shots of Marina by the pond with the child and the geese would in this way work as a kind of culmination of one of the film's salient patterns. From the very beginning of the film, the question of whether or not Marina and Neil will commit to one another, in the normative form of having a child, lingers. Marina mentions possibly having another child in the film's early scenes in Paris. Significantly, however, she frames this as a question to her daughter Tatiana, asking her if she would like to have a sibling. Neil is there but she does not broach the question directly to him. And the question of having children comes up again later in the scene involving Marina's medical procedure, and in another scene in which Neil and Marina have dinner with another family; in the latter, Marina looks longingly at Neil, as if to say: "We can also have this" (see figure 13.2).

The sudden appearance of the child with Marina in the Górecki sequence would then seem to be—at least within the moment in which Marina appears with the child and the geese—divine grace's way of giving Marina and Neil the gift they themselves cannot seem to find a way to create. Paul Camacho, tracing this motif, has suggested that the failure of

Figure 13.2. *To the Wonder.*

this couple to consummate their relationship would threaten existential failure, the failure of making something that surpasses the selfishness of desire: "If the self-surpassing energy of erotic desire naturally results in a fruitful union that issues forth in the gift of a child, then the denial of this gift entails the denial also of the intrinsic *generosity* of eros itself."[11] Camacho here points to the presence of young children with both Marina and Neil near the end of the movie as a sign that both have, finally, successfully overcome the more selfish inclinations of erotic desire through reproduction, albeit not with one another. The first of these children is the infant Marina appears with by the pond with the geese. The Górecki sequence is then followed by a coda, in which—perhaps surprisingly, since we have previously been witness to an apparent reconciliation—Neil and Marina separate; Neil remains in Bartlesville, while Marina apparently heads back to Mount St. Michel, or, perhaps, to an environment where she can find the same feeling she once held there. In the final shot in which he appears, Affleck's Neil is obliquely presented in his home with a woman (an unnamed and barely glimpsed figure we can only know as "neither Kurylenko nor McAdams") and a child. That this scene is set in a domestic setting supports Camacho's idea that Affleck has committed to a woman and to a family by the end of the movie. In the framework offered by Camacho, then, Neil eschews the danger of selfishness inherent in erotic desire, transcending it by creating something through it that goes beyond it.

I am not convinced, however, that this child with whom Kurylenko feeds the geese in the Górecki sequence is in fact actually Marina's. And I am also not convinced that the significant possibility that it is not hers is a sign of her ongoing selfishness or erotic narcissism. Indeed, I think the film's motif of heterosexual, biological reproduction as the key to transcending selfishness is, at least when it comes to Marina, something of a red herring. We have already seen Marina interact with other children who are not hers in the movie, and given the precedent set by those images I think it is likely that this child glimpsed feeding the geese with Marina belongs to someone else, one of the many beings in *To the Wonder* to whom Marina generously gifts her attention. For all the film's emphasis on biological reproduction as one symbol of commitment, Kurylenko's Marina, I think, glimpses something else, something other than (even if spiritually akin to) the particular form of grace Quintana discovers in overcoming his own separation from the world. Her ability to so glimpse is part of her creativity and of her search for beauty. In Nehamas's aesthetic sense, Marina seeks beauty not as something produced from out of a predetermined social role, or to desire's already established knowledge of what it wants, but toward the promise of a possible future. Quintana's words, in relation to Marina, are ultimately like Anna's: they point Marina in her right direction, set her back on her path. But she is not a priest, just as her own form of exuberance is not quite the same as Anna's.[12] The Górecki sequence in this way does not suggest Father Quintana's experience of grace (or the sudden appearance of beautiful, stirring music) has somehow solved Marina's own problems, just as it surely has not improved the difficult socioeconomic lives of the Bartlesville residents encountered in the film. Rather, his grace, like Anna's incredible vitality and energy, has indirectly set Marina back on her right path, toward a promise of beauty.

In the film's final images, in which Marina is alone, both Quintana and Neil, and perhaps also Bartlesville (the location of these final images is ambiguous), have been left behind. The camera moves toward autumnal trees and a light blue horizon line, brushed with orange and pink. Cut to Marina, lying on the ground, face up, looking at the heavens, her hands caressing tall grass. The moment is very reminiscent of the ecstasy Marina found in nature in the first half of the movie. Here, that ecstasy has a restorative effect on Marina, once more setting into motion her search for beauty. She moves like a modern dancer in these images. In a subsequent shot, she gets up from the ground, holding an outstretched palm in front of her; after a cut, she walks further toward more trees and a horizon line, her hands caressing grass and brush as she goes. As in the first half of the film, she does not only move forward. She looks back, at the ground, at something she has missed. The film's strategy of coupling this forward-moving camera movement, following Kurylenko, with jump cuts progressing her and us forward in time, suggests the possibility that something has been missed in the sudden cut, that we, like Marina, will always have to go back and look again. Marina is a perfect partner for this aesthetic because she is open to looking again at ground she has already moved past, just as repeated viewings of Malick's cinema make legible for the viewer formerly recondite motifs. She touches, feels, sees, and sees again. She is vulnerable: she folds her arms against her chest as the wind blows. She licks dew off a tree. She walks across the ground, occasionally in a zigzag—open always to looking again behind her—and occasionally as if she were on a tightrope, dangling over an invisible precipice. Suddenly, a cut, and she is again running away from us, along a path, looking back to the camera in joy and wonder: *Will you follow me?* Neil is gone; now she is asking only her viewer. Yet finally she slips away even from us. She speaks, first softly and then in a shout, to the sky (first in Russian and then in French, although most of the words become inaudible in their mix with the triumphant music). She dances, her dancing describing a circle. She looks back at something lingering off-screen. Suddenly, a ray of vivid, bright light illuminates her eyes, and she answers the light with an intense gaze. The film cuts to its final image, of Mount St. Michel, which now is present, not literally in the form of a shot–reaction shot but rather as a site of beauty made manifest in Marina's eyes, in her openness to the light. It is as if her eyes are creating this image of a place she once danced through and lived in, as if her eyes could find its promise of beauty again only through her willingness to see and to move ecstatically in light of that seeing (see figure 13.3).

Marina has found, again, the path toward a promise of beauty she always looks for and will continue looking for as long as she can be alive in this way. Given the very real obstacles evident throughout this film, it will not be easy. The final sequence of *To the Wonder* is transcendent, but as Marina's words earlier in the film have reminded us, we always come back down to earth again. If Marina's being has touched us, perhaps we will look for some form of it too in our own efforts to overcome the kinds of separation and isolation, the kinds of malaise that make people suffer in Bartlesville, as they suffer everywhere. She lingers in memory.

Figure 13.3. *To the Wonder.*

Notes

1. A 2018 film entitled *Thy Kingdom Come* included a reprise performance by Javier Bardem as Father Quintana, this time in the mode of documentary. The footage for the film was shot by Eugene Richards, who worked as a researcher and photographer for Malick on *To the Wonder* and designed *Thy Kingdom Come* as a series of interviews with the Quintana character and the residents of Bartlesville, Oklahoma.

2. While Father Quintana is clearly vexed over his inability to assuage the grief and torment of his parishioners, it is debatable how affected Neil is by the plight of the lower-income residents of Bartlesville whose water supply is poisoned. While Affleck's expressivity in his scenes with these extras suggests some level of concern in his character, most of Affleck's voiceovers are much more ambiguous in nature and much more immediately readable in relation to his fears of commitment in his romance with Marina, rather than reflective of any spiritual or psychological conflict caused by his social role.

3. See Ebiri, "Radiant Zigzag Becoming."

4. Morrison and Schur, *The Films of Terrence Malick*, 33–114.

5. The case of Chastain is an interesting one in Malick's cinema. At the time of release, she was largely an unknown and her presence in Malick's film, on initial screenings, had the charge of an unfamiliar performer nevertheless commanding the frame with assured presence, skill, and astonishing beauty. Since the release of the film, she has become a major star, familiar to even those viewers who might never look at any of Malick's work without prompting. How the evolution of relatively unknown actors' careers after their first work with Malick is completed impacts our reading of his films as times goes on is an interesting problem that is worth further deliberation.

6. For examples of thoughtful work that take Neil and Father Quintana, respectively, as the main point of focus for critical discussions of the film, see Paul Camacho, "The Promise of Love Perfected," 232–50; and Aughtry, "A Universal Priesthood," 217–36.

7. This idea of the film viewer as in some sense a collaborator in the "creation" of a character in cinema is largely informed in my discussion, albeit here implicitly, by the work Stanley Cavell, whose analysis of the ontology of film performance paves the way for such understanding. The viewer's gaze in cinema both incarnates an actor and simultaneously confirms the viewer's own passionate embodiment, presence, all-in-one glance: we are "present *at* him, *because looking at him*, but not present *to* him." See Cavell, *The World Viewed*, 27.

8. Flusser, *Gestures*, 2.

9. Nehamas, *Only a Promise of Happiness*, 63–64.

10. Kurylenko discusses Malick's influences from Russian literature in "Radiant Zigzag Becoming."

11. Camacho, "The Promise of Love Perfected," 240.
12. In this I depart from Matthew Aughtry's admirable reading of the film, which provocatively suggests that Quintana's vocation as a priest is in parallel to a kind of priesthood animating the other characters. See Aughtry, "A Universal Priesthood," 228–30.

Bibliography

Aughtry, Matthew. "A Universal Priesthood: The Vocation of Being Human in *Days of Heaven* and *To the Wonder*." In *A Critical Companion to Terrence Malick*, edited by Joshua Sikora, 217–36. Lanham, MD: Lexington Books, 2020.

Camacho, Paul. "The Promise of Love Perfected: Eros and Kenosis in *To the Wonder*." In *Theology and the Films of Terrence Malick*, edited by Christopher B. Barnett and Clark J. Elliston, 232–50. London: Routledge, 2017.

Cavell, Stanley. *The World Viewed: Reflections on the Ontology of Film, Enlarged Edition*. Cambridge, MA: Harvard University Press, 1995.

Ebiri, Bilge. "Radiant Zigzag Becoming: How Terrence Malick and His Team Constructed *To the Wonder*." *Vulture*, April 18, 2013. https://www.vulture.com/2013/04/how-terrence-malick-wrote-filmed-edited-to-the-wonder.html.

Flusser, Vilém. *Gestures*. Minneapolis: University of Minnesota Press, 2014.

Morrison, James, and Thomas Schur. *The Films of Terrence Malick*. London: Praeger, 2003.

Nehamas, Alexander. *Only a Promise of Happiness: The Place of Beauty in a World of Art*. Princeton, NJ: Princeton University Press, 2017.

Part IV

The Pursuit of Freedom and Transcendence

Chapter 14

Platonic Myths of Eros in *Knight of Cups* and *Song to Song*

MATTHEW STROHL

Malick's run of films from 2011 through 2017 (*The Tree of Life*, *To the Wonder*, *Knight of Cups*, *Voyage of Time*, and *Song to Song*) are among the most polarizing works in contemporary cinema. This is no surprise, as they are at once formally challenging and blissfully unfashionable in their lofty spiritual orientation. These films are characterized by notable stylistic continuity, particularly *To the Wonder*, *Knight of Cups*, and *Song to Song*, which were all filmed without a script and edited in a similar style. *The Tree of Life* and *Voyage of Time* also bear certain strong affinities, both to each other and to the other three, but are distinct in that *The Tree of Life* was filmed with a script and has a more cohesive and legible narrative, whereas *Voyage of Time* is an experimental documentary with no traditional narrative at all.

Commentators have identified two possible trilogies among these films. *The Tree of Life*, *To the Wonder*, and *Knight of Cups* have been seen as an autobiographical trilogy, paring episodes from Malick's life with spiritual themes.[1] Roughly, *The Tree of Life* pairs his brother's untimely death with themes including grace and the problem of evil, *To the Wonder* pairs his first marriage and his reunion with an earlier love with themes including God's silence and the way that suffering enables spiritual progress, and *Knight of Cups* pairs his early years as a Hollywood screenwriter with

279

themes including worldly temptation and spiritual awakening. Others have suggested that *To the Wonder*, *Knight of Cups*, and *Song to Song* constitute a trilogy. Commentators including Michael Joshua Rowin and Robert Sinnerbrink refer to these three films as the "weightless trilogy," after the original title of *Song to Song*.[2] They are connected by their elliptical narratives, impressionistic cinematography, contemporary setting, thematic purview, and experimental editing style.

Our only clue from Malick himself is that he has explicitly denied that he thinks of the first three films as an autobiographical trilogy. His longtime friend Jim Lynch asked him directly. According to Lynch, "He didn't like me labeling them that way. He didn't want people thinking that he was just making movies about himself. He was making movies about broader issues."[3] Notably, he did not correct Lynch by telling him that the latter two films in fact belong to an unfinished trilogy. My own take is that there is some sense in which all of these films should be grouped together. *The Tree of Life* is in part about spiritual crisis. It poses the problem of evil in reference to a staggering personal loss. The film resolves with a sense of hope, and the so-called weightless trilogy seizes upon this hope and examines various stages of the process of spiritual (re)awakening, while *Voyage of Time* follows a different strand from *The Tree of Life* concerning nature and its relationship with divinity.

As this volume illustrates, there are many fruitful ways of approaching Malick. It takes the effort and expertise of more than one person to work through these films. In this chapter, my aim is modest. I want to consider at length the relevance of Plato's myths of Eros to *Knight of Cups* and *Song to Song*. I do not aim to give totalizing interpretations of these films (each of which could support a book-length treatment) but only to shed light on this connection and its broader significance. The importance of the passage from the *Phaedrus* that is included in *Knight of Cups* (read aloud by Charles Laughton) has been remarked on by many commentators, including Robert Sinnerbrink, who argues that Plato's myth of Eros from the *Symposium* and *Phaedrus* "provides an orienting allegorical frame" for *To the Wonder*, *Knight of Cups*, and *Song to Song*.[4] He cites Paul Comacho's observation that the lovers' ascent of the steps of Mont Saint-Michel evokes the ascent passage from the *Symposium* at 210a–212c, and he discusses the relevance of the *Phaedrus* and of Kierkegaard's version of a Platonic theory of love.[5] Sinnerbrink's work is illuminating, and I do not here mean to contest it but only to supplement it with more detailed consideration of the *Phaedrus* and *Symposium* and their relevance to *Knight of Cups* and *Song to Song*, which were filmed back-to-back and which I take to be especially closely connected.[6] In particular, further exploring the significance of the Platonic theory of love in these films will shed light on the relationship between erotic love and spiritual awakening. Also, while the connection between *Knight of Cups* and the *Phaedrus* is explicit, the relevance of Plato to *Song to Song* is more obscure. Careful attention to the way Platonic motifs from *Knight of Cups* are carried through in the subsequent film helps to make sense of a number of details that I take to be crucially important.

Knight of Cups depicts the Hollywood initiation of Rick, an up-and-coming screenwriter played by Christian Bale. Its narrative is divided into eight episodes, seven of which are titled after tarot cards and all of which feature a significant person from Rick's past or who he meets along the way. Two texts function as structuring touchstones: the Gnostic "Hymn of the Pearl" and Bunyan's *Pilgrim's Progress*. Both of these connections are examined in Lee Braver's chapter "The Alien God Behind the Camera: A Gnostic Viewing of Terrence Malick's Cinema, especially *Knight of Cups*." Nearly all commentators and critics emphasize negative aspects of Malick's portrayal of this Hollywood lifestyle. David Sims, writing for the *Atlantic* offers a typically simplistic interpretation of the film's thematic concerns: "'The point here is that Hollywood is a draining, disorienting, empty place, where even the freest creative spirits can get lost. That doesn't feel quite as profound or revelatory as some of the insights into the human condition Malick has made in the past, but it's a message fully received as viewers bounce from party to photo shoot to bedroom escapade."[7]

Indeed, portrayals of the soul-sucking emptiness of Hollywood are a dime a dozen. Malick's film would not be very interesting if that's all it were about. But what Sims and other commentators misunderstand—and what a closer look at the Platonic context can help to illuminate—is that the film portrays most of Rick's Hollywood escapades as *positive* steps in a process of spiritual awakening. In some of Plato's dialogues, including notably the *Phaedo*, he is pessimistic about the prospects for attaining divine knowledge during a mortal life. In the *Symposium* and *Phaedrus*, however, we find not only a more optimistic perspective but the idea that erotic attraction is a crucial step in the process of attaining such knowledge. Before discussing this aspect of the film, however, it will be helpful to consider in detail the *Phaedrus* passage that is directly quoted in the film, along with relevant passages that provide important context.

Early in *Knight of Cups*, during the segment labeled "The Moon," we see Rick driving a convertible while a woman, Della, spreads her arms and mimics flight. They visit an aquarium where we see rays spread their wings and "fly" toward the light, and we hear Charles Laughton reading an elided passage from the *Phaedrus*:

> Once the soul was perfect and had wings and could soar into heaven where only creatures with wings can be. But the soul lost its wings and fell to earth, where it took on an earthly body. . . . When we see a beautiful woman, or a man, the soul remembers the beauty it used to know in heaven and . . . the wings begin to sprout and that makes the soul want to fly but it cannot yet, it is still too weak, so the man keeps staring up at the sky like a young bird that has lost all interest in the world.[8]

If another filmmaker included this passage in their film, we might assume that they simply took a few lines that they liked out of context and did not read the rest of Plato's dialogue or think about the broader implications of the passage. But this is surely not an assumption that we should make for Malick. Indeed, we can safely assume that he closely studied the *Phaedrus* and thought carefully about the context in which this passage is imbedded.

This passage clearly signals that we should take some or all of Rick's amorous encounters in the film as reminders of the beauty that his soul "used to know in heaven," and as catalysts for spiritual awakening. As Naomi Fisher discusses in her chapter in this book "Tending God's Garden: Philosophical Theme's in Malick's *The Tree of Life*," this passage references Plato's ideas about the immortality of the soul and what's known as the theory of recollection. This theory, developed in the *Meno* and *Phaedo*, holds that the soul possessed knowledge of the true nature of reality before it was incarnated in a human body. In the *Phaedo*, Socrates characterizes this knowledge as knowledge of the Forms. The Forms are eternal, immaterial, immutable beings that are perfect and unmixed. The Form of the Beautiful is not one beautiful thing among many. The Form is rather, as it were, the abstract essence of beauty; other things are beautiful only to the extent that they resemble it or share in some way in its nature. The Forms are what ultimately ground the world of experience that we access with our senses. This world lacks the firm, enduring reality of the Forms. Objects of sensory experience ebb and flow and appear big or small according to the extent to which they share in the Form of the

Big and the Form of the Small. The world of Forms is the true reality; the world of experience is its illusory refraction.

In the *Phaedo*, Plato is pessimistic about the possibility of gaining any true knowledge of the Forms during a mortal life. The needs of the body distract us while our senses mislead us. We are prone to confuse appearance for reality and deny the existence of anything beyond the reach of our senses. At *Theaetetus* 155e, Socrates describes a class of people he calls "the uninitiated" as those who "believe that nothing exists but what they can grab with both hands."[9] In the *Phaedo*, Socrates argues that our senses cannot lead us to knowledge of the Forms. The path of the philosopher is thus to try to separate the soul from the body by shirking the temptations of worldly pleasures in favor of activities of the soul that are necessarily imperfect but that are a way of striving toward the realities that the soul knew before it was embodied.

In the *Symposium*, we find a stunning reversal. In Diotima's speech—which is conveyed by Socrates and which is standardly taken to express Plato's own views about love (eros)—not just sensory experience but erotic attraction is presented as a legitimate path toward knowledge of the Forms. At 210a, Plato writes, "A lover who goes about this matter correctly must begin in his youth to love beautiful bodies." Diotima goes on to describe the lover's ascent from love of one beautiful body to love of all beautiful bodies to an appreciation that the beauty of souls is superior to that of bodies and thus to love of the laws and institutions that make the soul beautiful, to love of abstract theoretical knowledge, and finally to love of the Form of the Beautiful itself. Erotic attraction is seen not as a hindrance to knowledge of the Forms but as a positive step of the ascent. Ascent imagery (e.g., walking up a hill or set of stairs toward the light) is everywhere in late Malick, but it cannot be understood in purely Platonic terms. The higher reality that Malick's spiritual seekers strive for must also be understood in reference to Judeo-Christian scripture and a range of other references and mythologies.

Near the beginning of *Knight of Cups*, before the *Phaedrus* passage is read aloud, we see a black-and-white stop motion video being played in the background at a Hollywood party. We cut to this video and see a woman with two X's on her back, suggesting the spots where the soul's wings have been cut off (as described in the *Phaedrus*). We also see this woman wearing a mask of her own face on the back of her head. This also seems to be a Platonic reference. In Aristophanes's speech in the *Symposium*, he describes an earlier time when human beings had two faces, four arms, and four legs. This earlier form of human was powerful, and their power made them arrogant enough to challenge the gods. As punishment, Zeus cut them in half and turned their heads around so that they faced forward. Eros, according to this myth, is a desire to be returned to be reunited with our other half—to be whole again. The image in *Knight of Cups* of a woman with a mask of her face on the back of her head suggests this desire to return to our original nature.

After the stop motion segment, we see a mountain crowned with light, and then we cut to Rick in the midst of a literal earthquake, suggesting a jarring awakening from spiritual slumber. He walks through empty studio lots, a pilgrim in the land of illusion, and then we see him from behind, sitting and watching images of the sky on a television set. This is another Platonic allusion, suggesting the famous cave allegory from *Republic* VII. The denizens of the cave are stuck watching shadows of puppets, which are themselves imitations of a higher reality. This allegorizes the epistemic condition that human beings are in by default—we confuse our sensory experiences for true reality, when in fact they are a reflection of an imitation of the Forms themselves. Rick is drawn toward the light—but at this stage of his development it is merely an image of the sky, which is itself merely an image of the divine light.

With this context in mind, it is easier to see that Rick's series of romantic and sexual entanglements in *Knight of Cups* should not be understood simply as a critique of the shallowness of the Hollywood lifestyle. It's just the opposite; at least some of the beautiful people who Rick is drawn to should be understood as leading him toward a higher way of being.

This interpretation needs to reconciled with the prominence in the film of the "Hymn of the Pearl," which suggests that the people Rick meets in Los Angeles fill his glass with intoxicating drink so that he is lulled into a waking sleep where he has forgotten the path of the spirit. I certainly do not mean to suggest that *everyone* Rick meets helps him further along the path of his ascent. There are a number of clearly negative figures in the film, including the producer Herb (anticipating Cook in *Song to Song*) who offers him a Faustian bargain: if he writes whatever junk they ask him to, he can have it all. Malick emphasizes throughout the film that Hollywood is a land of illusion where it is easy for the pilgrim to be led astray. The point, I take it, is that amid this setting, *some* of the people who he meets lift his spirit rather than bogging it down. One of the recurring motifs in the movie is that we see the women who Rick is involved with walking away from him and looking back toward him. These shots suggest that they are leading him along his path.

Tonio (Antonio Banderas), who is featured in the segment titled "The Hermit," is usually taken to be a negative figure in the film. He is the wealthy host of a debauched party that is staged in the style of Fellini. He tells Rick, "Myself, I didn't want to get a divorce. I never stopped loving them, but the way I loved them changed. They are like flavors. Sometimes you want raspberry, then after you get tired of it, you want some strawberry." Of course, it's natural that Tonio's horrifying comparison between women and fruit flavors would be taken negatively, but having the *Symposium* in the background changes the inflection of this line. The first stage of the lover's ascent is love of one beautiful body, but then in the next stage, "He should realize that the beauty of one body is brother to the beauty of any other and if he is to pursue beauty of form he'd be very foolish not to think of the beauty of all bodies is one and the same. When he grasps this, he must become a lover of all beautiful bodies, and he must think that this wild gaping after one body is a small thing and come to despise it" (*Symposium* 210a–b). Tonio's other most significant line is "The world is a swamp; you have to fly over it." This is a clear reference to the swamp of *Pilgrim's Progress*, a negative location where the pilgrim gets mired in worldly muck. This line points strongly to the thought that Tonio is in fact an ambivalent figure. Love of all beautiful bodies is not the final stage of the ascent, but Plato does understand it to be a progression from the love of one beautiful body. In the highest stage of the ascent, the lover's object becomes the Form of the Beautiful itself. The earlier stages are progressions away from the attachment to particular terrestrial manifestations of beauty and toward its divine essence. Fixation on one beautiful body conflates an instance of beauty with the thing itself, and shifting from "wild gaping" after one object of love to the realization that all beautiful bodies are worthy of love is a progression toward love of the Form of the Beautiful. Tonio emphasizes that he didn't stop loving the women he was divorced from; he rather expanded his love to something more general. While Plato's ideas about love may be jarring in a culture that emphasizes monogamy (this is, after all, the same thinker who argues in the *Republic* that reproduction among the rulers and soldiers of the ideal city should be done by lottery, with children being raised in common), the most likely interpretation of Tonio's significance in the film is that he is a lover of beauty who has only progressed to the second stage of the ascent. This is not very far, but it's farther than most people. He is a shallow man in the grand scheme of things, but he is still higher up than almost everyone around him, and so he can "fly over" the swamp that they are stuck in.[10]

Returning to the *Phaedrus*, it's worth taking a moment to unpack the context in which the passage referenced in *Knight of Cups* is found. It is part of the second speech that Socrates gives about love in the dialogue, standardly referred to as the palinode. A palinode is an ode that doubles as a retraction. In this case, Socrates is retracting his initial speech where he argued that is better to spend one's time with a lover than a non-lover because a lover wishes for their beloved to be hindered in various ways in order to increase their dependence on them. At 242d–243a, however, Socrates corrects himself and argues that because Love (Eros) is a god and nothing divine can be bad in any way, his earlier speech must have been mistaken. He presents the palinode as a rite of purification that he must conduct in order to cleanse his earlier offense.

Socrates begins the palinode by diagnosing what led him to his earlier mistakes about the nature of Love. He had thought that because the non-lover is sane and the lover is mad, one should prefer the company of the non-lover (244a). But he now recognizes that not all madness is created equal. At 244d, he argues that madness sent by a god is finer than human self-control. After a lengthy discussion of the nature of the soul and related topics, Socrates describes the kind of madness that characterizes the lover as "that which someone shows when he sees the beauty we have down here and is reminded of true beauty; then he takes wing and flutters in his eagerness to rise up, but is unable to do so; and he gazes aloft, like a bird, paying no attention to what is down below—and that is what brings on him the charge that he has gone mad." The passage quoted above that is read by Charles Laughton in *Knight of Cups* is heavily abridged, but the last part of it overlaps with the passage I've just quoted.[11] The recording elides Plato's reference to madness, but there is a clear allusion to this notion in the same segment of the film ("The Moon"). Della, the woman that this segment focuses on, says, "You think I could make you crazy. Crack you out of your shell. Make you suffer." Like Ben Affleck's character in *To the Wonder*, Rick is presented as distant and withholding on account of his fear of transcending the safety of his illusory world and enduring the madness of erotic longing for something higher. She also says, "You don't want love; you want a love experience." Again, in Plato's metaphysics there is a division between true reality and the illusory world of experience, and Della sees Rick as someone who is afraid of authentic love and is only open to a pale imitation of it.

Throughout the film, Malick repeatedly incorporates images of wings and of flight, particularly at moments when Rick and others can be understood as being "reminded of the beauty their souls once knew in heaven." Once you're looking for it, you'll find that it's everywhere. For instance, at the beginning of the second segment of *Knight of Cups* ("The Hanged Man"), Rick asks, "How do I begin?" and we pan up to a flock of birds flying in a V-shape. In Chapter IV ("Judgment") Rick and his ex-wife Nancy (Cate Blanchett) watch planes taking off and soaring over the desert. In Chapter VI ("The High Priestess"), Rick visits Las Vegas and is transfixed looking up at an aerial dancer. In Chapter VII ("Death"), featuring Natalie Portman as Elizabeth, we see the lovers holding out their arms on the beach in imitation of flight. This is far from an exhaustive list. As I will discuss in the second part of this chapter, this motif carries over into *Song to Song*.[12]

The thought that all of these observations build toward, again, is that the many commentators who have thought that *Knight of Cups* is a movie about the way the people Rick meets in Hollywood drag him down and stunt his spiritual growth have it backward. As Brian Dennehy (playing Rick's father) narrates near the end of the film, "Find the light you knew in the east as a child. The moon, the stars, they serve you. They guide you on your way. The light in the eyes of others. The pearl." This line—arguably the most important line in the film—ties together the "Hymn of the Pearl," *Pilgrim's Progress*, and the *Phaedrus*. Rick is a pilgrim stuck in the swamp. He's a prince who's forgotten his quest. The light in the eyes of others is here equated with the pearl that he must remember in order to awaken and resume his quest. In the final chapter of the film, titled "Freedom," Rick becomes involved with the most positive figure in the film, Isabel. Interestingly, "Freedom" is the one chapter that is not named after a tarot card. I'm not sure what to make of this except that it was evidently important to Malick that the final chapter title convey the specific idea of freedom. This idea could have been signaled by several different tarot cards, but these cards might have unwanted resonances. The last line of *Knight of Cups* is a single word, spoken by Rick: "Begin." He presumably means that he is finally prepared to begin the process of spiritual reawakening—the quest for the pearl that he has now remembered.

He has gained the freedom to do this in part through the influence of his amorous adventures. Far from bogging him down, the beauty in the eyes of others is the beacon that has led him to begin his ascent.

The concept of freedom is at the center of *Song to Song*, and I think that we can make better sense of the importance of this concept in *Knight of Cups* by turning now to the later film. Like *Knight of Cups*, *Song to Song* is heavily referential. Whereas the two primary sources for the first film are *Pilgrim's Progress* and the "Hymn of the Pearl," the second film draws heavily on Milton's *Paradise Lost* and Marlowe's *Doctor Faustus*. Jonathan R. Olson, in his paper "Milton's Satan in Malick's *Song to Song*," has already done the work of reconstructing these references, and so my main focus here will be the relevance of Plato's theory of love.[13]

The surface narrative of *Song to Song* is very simple. B. V. (Ryan Gosling) is a talented songwriter in Austin. Cook (Michael Fassbender) is a powerful music mogul who has his hands in everything. Faye (Rooney Mara) has worked for Cook as low-level staff since she was a teenager and is now sleeping with him. In a Faustian bargain, Cook offers B. V. success but under exploitive terms. B. V. and Faye meet at party at Cook's house and start a relationship. She doesn't tell B. V. that she has an ongoing sexual relationship with Cook. Cook meets a young waitress named Rhonda (Natalie Portman) and becomes smitten with her. He showers her with money and gifts and convinces her to marry him. Rhonda is religious and feels deeply alienated by the world of sex and drugs that she now feels trapped in. She eventually commits suicide. Meanwhile, B. V. realizes that Cook was taking advantage of him, backs out of their arrangement, and finds out that he's been sleeping with Faye all along. Faye and B. V. split up and have relationships with other people. Eventually, they reconcile and leave Austin and its music scene behind to live a simpler life out west, focusing on family and other responsibilities that they had previously sought to avoid.

It is very clear that Cook, Michael Fassbender's character in the film, is a Lucifer figure. Malick directly told Fassbender that his character is Satan from *Paradise Lost*.[14] The film is full of references to both Milton's poem and *Doctor Faustus*. At one point, Faye refers to him as "Devil." When he offers to help Rhonda and her family out of financial trouble and asks to marry her, we cut briefly to a shot of him holding a horned skull in front of his face. We see him making an effort to attend church with Rhonda, but he is visibly uncomfortable and leaves her there alone. Soon after, he gives her hallucinogenic mushrooms dipped in honey, and the

Platonic Myths of Eros in *Knight of Cups* and *Song to Song* | 289

dissonant score and abrasive cinematography suggest that she has entered a worldly hell. During her trip, we see a tattoo that reads "Empty Promises," and Cook narrates, "Open your eyes. You won't die. Here I reign. King." This is a clear reference to Satan's third speech in *Paradise Lost*.[15] Shortly afterward, Rhonda and Cook meet a man who has used various forms of body modification to make himself resemble a snake. There are also other narrative connections to Milton. For instance, the ending of the film, where Faye and B. V. forgive each other and recommence their relationship, mirrors the reconciliation of Adam and Eve.

Interpreting *Song to Song* requires attending to the interplay between its layers of literary reference. My limited aim here is to elucidate the relevance of the Platonic theory of love. This is only one layer, but it is an important one, and its importance is less obvious here than it is in *Knight of Cups*. In particular, considering the relevance of the metaphysical dimension of Plato's theory of love illuminates the significance of Malick's depiction of Cook/Satan as a *deceiver* and also the way in which Platonic love can remedy such deception.

Given that there are no explicit, direct references to Plato in *Song to Song*, this connection may seem far-fetched. If we take *Knight of Cups* and *Song to Song* together, however, the continuing relevance of Plato is obvious. The motif of wings and flight from *Knight of Cups* is continued very strongly in the subsequent film. At one point, Faye and B. V. visit Mexico on Cook's private jet. The two of them spend a half hour alone together at one point on the trip, and Faye thinks of this experience as the point where she fell in love with B. V. As narrator, she tells us, "Everything came out of that half hour." The lovers see a flock of birds during their whirling romantic stroll on the beach and meet a man who uses a bird to read their fortunes. Faye references this later in the film when the two of them are separated and she is longing for him, "I don't like to see the birds in the sky because I miss you. Because you saw them with me." With *Knight of Cups* as background context, we should take this as an allusion to the notion from the *Phaedrus* that erotic love reminds us of the time when our soul had wings and restores in us the urge to fly up above the world of experience toward a higher reality. The birds are reminders to Faye of the glimpse of something higher that she experienced with B. V. before being dragged back down to Cook's world.

B. V. and Faye's ethereal birdwatching experience in Mexico is contrasted with their flight home on Cook's jet. The plane flies in a pattern to give the passengers the experience of weightlessness. They revel in it.

This extravagantly expensive imitation of the experience of flight—which is itself an imitation of spiritual ascent—is a form of deception. What B. V. and Faye experience in their transcendent half hour is a glimmer of authentic spiritual elevation. They are reminded of when their souls had wings. Their ride on Cook's plane substitutes an illusion for the thing itself. The motif comes up again when Faye finally admits to B. V. that she's been sleeping with Cook all along. B. V. and Faye have sex on a table while a string of wooden birds (a mocking imitation of the ones they saw when they fell in love) hangs down above them. This encounter is less tender and more violent than their relationship has been until this point. We cut briefly to B. V. in a field with a shotgun, bird hunting (!), before cutting back to him as he narrates that he became cold toward Faye and decided to leave her.

Song to Song develops a dichotomy between Cook's world—the urban music scene—and the world of family and obligation. Faye and B. V. have both left their families behind to come live in Austin. Faye feels ashamed that she hasn't been as pious a daughter as her sisters, and B. V. has only recently escaped a chaotic home situation where he has been estranged from his father (who is insinuated to have been abusive or neglectful), his mother has been struggling with depression, and his brother has been acting out in troubling ways. Cook, B. V., and Faye view the music scene as a locus of freedom. B. V. mentions getting "free of this man," in reference to his father. B. V. and Faye are described both by themselves and by Cook as desiring freedom. Cook offers B. V., Rhonda, and Faye each a Faustian bargain in the film. For B. V. and Faye, it is a record contract and a pathway to making a living in the music industry. For Rhonda, it is financial support that will enable her to stop working low-paying jobs and fretting about how to take care of her mother. In all three cases, what Cook offers is explicitly related to the concept of freedom. This must be of course understood in reference to *Paradise Lost*, where Satan's variety of freedom is contrasted with the authentic freedom of obedience to the divine will, but the Platonic context is also relevant. Cook's freedom is merely an *illusion* of freedom—an image of the real thing. In the early stages of seducing Rhonda, he takes her for a drive in his Ferrari and asks her, "Do you like physical things?" The choice of words here is telling. Malick is drawing attention not simply to the emptiness of the satisfactions afforded by material luxury, but more deeply to the way that Cook's illusory brand of freedom is tied to a focus on our embodied condition rather than our spiritual nature.

Faye elaborates what she understands freedom to be, "We thought we could just roll and tumble, live from song to song, kiss to kiss." At another point, she says, "I wanted to escape every tie, every bond." Cook's freedom is a form of rootlessness, where one can leave behind obligations and responsibilities (financial, familial, and otherwise) and stay blissfully immersed in the moment. It is a "weightless" way of being. We see intoxicating images of music festivals where revelers are enthralled in a Bacchic frenzy. After taking a chainsaw to an amplifier on a festival stage, cutting his own hair with a knife, and throwing fake uranium at the audience, Val Kilmer soliloquizes over the PA, "The music's all about feeling free—so you don't have to do nothing *to be* free!" This is as clear a statement as we could hope for of the Platonic significance of Malick's dichotomy of freedom. It could even be taken in connection with the Platonic concern expressed in book X of the *Republic* that poetry and other forms of mimetic art are dangerous in the way they can lead the soul to confuse an imitation for the real thing. Not long before Rhonda's suicide, she has a conversation with a sex worker who Cook has hired to join them in bed. The sex worker explains, "I sell a fantasy, not my body. I sell an illusion." Rhonda quietly asks as narrator, "Is that me?" Cook's world is nihilistic. When he appraises his estate, he admits, "This—none of this exists. It's all just free fall." Cook's freedom stands to true freedom as the experience of weightlessness in his luxury jet stands to authentic spiritual ascent.

Ultimately, B. V. and Faye will find true freedom not in Cook's world but in the practice of mercy and the embrace of spiritual love and the obligations and responsibilities that it grounds. B. V. has a much easier time leaving Cook behind than Faye does. From the start, he imagined himself writing songs based on his own painful experiences that would lift people up and bring them joy. Once he sniffs out Cook's exploitive intentions, he bails straightaway. Faye, on the other hand, is more ambivalent. She delivers the first line of the film as narrator, "I went through a period when sex had to be violent. I was looking for something real. Nothing felt real. Every kiss was half of what it should be." We see Cook gripping her by the throat. She is not merely sleeping with Cook as a means to professional success; she is existentially adrift and searching for some form of authentic experience without being willing to accept the obligations and responsibilities that such experience would entail. Violent sex, in Faye's self-understanding, substitutes intensity of experience for authenticity. It's a form of self-deception not unlike the experiences that Plato labels as "false pleasures" in *Philebus* 45a–47d because they create the illusion of being more pleasant than they are due to their admixture with pain.

Faye is more willing than B. V. is to knowingly immerse herself in illusion. "I wanted experience," she narrates. "I told myself any experience is better than no experience." Unlike B. V., Faye explicitly thinks of herself as embracing something that is base—she is in this sense less deceived than he is. In one of her most striking lines, she admits, "I love the pain. It feels like life. Sometimes I admire what a hypocrite I am." She recognizes and acknowledges her hesitancy to embrace the flickers of divinity she experiences with B. V., but she is not motivated straightaway to change. Plato explains in the *Phaedrus* what causes wings to fall away from the soul: "By their nature wings have the power to lift up heavy things and raise them aloft where the gods all dwell, and so, more than anything that pertains to the body, they are akin to the divine, which has beauty, wisdom, goodness, and everything of that sort. These nourish the soul's wings, which grow best in their presence; but foulness and ugliness make the wings shrink and disappear" (246d–e). Using language that evokes this metaphor of flight from the *Phaedrus* in connection with the myth of Icarus, she says, "I pulled you down in the car. I didn't believe enough in love. I was afraid it would burn me up." She relates her hesitancy to embrace a more authentic form of experience with her attraction to the physical world: "I'm low. I like the mud. I don't deserve you." The world is a swamp that one must fly over (as Tonio put it in *Knight of Cups*), and Faye self-consciously embraces its foulness.

Faye's condition is conveyed by an unidentified painting that we see briefly during Rhonda's and Cook's mushroom trip. The painting depicts a woman with wings and a mask, lying on her back as she looks into a small handheld mirror. Cook narrates, "The world wants to be deceived." This painting could not have been more perfectly chosen. Human nature is made for something higher—our souls in their original state had wings—but, like the prisoners in Plato's cave, we are too fixated on ephemeral reflections to look toward a higher reality. The figure in the painting ignores the vast sky above and neglects her ability to soar into the heavens. What she attends to instead is not even a reflection of her own face; it is an image of the false mask she shows to others. It's a distorted reflection of a distorted imitation. I take this contrast between B. V. and Faye to be central to what the film is about. It's a love story between a Satan sympathizer and a spiritual seeker. She signals her allegiance when she narrates, "I revolted against goodness. Thought it had deceived me."

Much like *Knight of Cups*, *Song to Song* is about the way that erotic love can lift the spirit and reorient us toward something higher, but while *Knight of Cups* is about the onset of spiritual awakening, *Song to Song* is about what such an awakening looks like in action. The earlier film ends with the word "begin." *Song to Song* shows us a beginning.

At the end of the film, Faye leaves Austin to start a life with B. V., who abandons the music business to work in the oil fields and mend his family relationships. In a scene that I find so powerful I can barely stand to watch it, he visits his sick father, who he has previously said he wouldn't forgive and who he no longer prays for. His father appears to have had a stroke, and B. V. breaks down and weeps as he wipes crumbs of food from his shirt. Living in Cook's world entails choosing rootlessness over the responsibility that comes from genuine connection with others. B. V.'s choice to leave Cook's world behind is also a choice to do the difficult work of being part of a family and to follow the way of grace introduced in *The Tree of Life*.

Wonderfully, the angel figure who nudges Faye back toward B. V. after their falling out is Patti Smith, playing herself. She tells Faye about her own great love affair, which ended many years earlier when her spouse passed away. She urges her to fight to restore her relationship with B. V. In the film's climactic moment, as Faye makes the decision to return to B. V., we simultaneously hear Patti Smith singing and Faye reading William Blake's "The Divine Image." Smith's performance is the type of music that B. V. wished to create: music that lifts the spirit. Blake's poem includes these thematically crucial lines:

> For Mercy, Pity, Peace, and Love
> Is God, our father dear,
> And Mercy, Pity, Peace, and Love
> Is Man, his child and care.
> For Mercy has a human heart,
> Pity a human face,
> And Love, the human form divine,
> And Peace, the human dress.[16]

Human beings—for Blake, Plato, and Malick—are mortal in one way but divine in another. Blake's poem highlights that human beings reflect the divine image, and that "Mercy, Pity, Peace, and Love" are essential to the nature of divinity and to the expression of the divine aspect of human nature. As Elisa Zocchi explores in her paper "Terrence Malick Beyond Nature and Grace: *Song to Song* and the Experience of Forgiveness," this moment brings Malick's cycle of films full circle, returning to *The Tree of Life* and the way of grace.

As Faye works toward her decision to return to B. V., she narrates, "I never knew I had a soul. The word embarrassed me. I've always been afraid of myself. I thought no one's there." Faye's embrace of Cook's world involved a denial of her nature as a being with a soul. When she goes on to say, "I forgot what I am," we see an image of B. V. holding a string of paper butterflies up while a young girl smiles in wonder. This image once again evokes the idea from the *Phaedrus* that love reminds us not just that we have a soul but that our soul once had wings. We see another image of birds. Faye recognizes at last what the soul's wings are for. She narrates, "There's something else, something that wants us to find it." We cut to figures ascending a spiral staircase. When she returns to B. V., we see a winged statue, and she narrates, "It was like a new paradise of forgiveness." Faye's return to B. V. is more than a decision to return to a romantic relationship; it's also the beginning of her own spiritual seeking. She is at much the same place as Rick at the end of *Knight of Cups*. Early in the film she narrates, "I love your soul." Once she comes around to embracing this love, she moves past the material stages of the Platonic ascent. She is drawn downward by other impulses, but her love for B. V. inspires her to reorient herself toward spiritual progress.

The theme of grace is not as prominent in *Knight of Cups* as it is in *Song to Song*, but it is there. During the "Hanged Man" section of *Knight of Cups*, we learn that—like Malick himself and the character of Jack in *The Tree of Life*—Rick has two brothers and one of them has tragically died. Barry (Wes Bentley), Rick's living brother, is troubled, and like B. V. in *Song to Song*, Rick feels conflicted about leaving his brother behind. He has the same sort of struggle with family and forgiveness that Jack and B. V. do.

We can infer that Rick's path toward authentic freedom, like B. V. and Faye's, is to follow the way of grace. How, though, can the way of grace be understood as freedom? This is a vastly complicated question reaching far beyond Plato, and it requires introducing a great deal of theoretical apparatus to properly address, but we can sketch the basic idea. Weightless drifting without a higher purpose ("living from song to song") is the antithesis of genuine freedom. If one has no commitments, one has nothing to unify one's self and so one's actions are free only in the sense of being aimless and disconnected from a robust locus of agency. Obedience to the divine will is not passive; it is an active embrace of a system of value organized by a unified conception of the good. Weightless drifting as a way of avoiding obligation and responsibility is not freedom but rather a dissolution of the self. As Rick's father, Joseph (Brian Dennehy), narrates in *Knight of Cups*, "I suppose that's what damnation is. The pieces of your life never to come together, just splashed out there." Authentic freedom for Rick would first entail becoming a self, unified around a sense of purpose. Becoming his *true* self would further entail following the way of grace and emulating the divine image.

On my interpretation, these films are in part about the way that erotic love can prompt spiritual awakening. In *Song to Song*, we see such an awakening depicted in more practical terms. I take the key to understanding the relevance of the Platonic myths of Eros in the ending of *Song to Song* to be the dichotomy that Malick draws between Cook's world and the world of family and obligation. Cook's world embraces illusion. As Cook himself says, "None of this is real, it's all just free fall." Living in Cook's world entails suppressing a fundamental aspect of our nature. We are not just worldly beings; we are also divine. The path to our higher nature is through mercy, love, and spiritual seeking, which express the manner in which humanity is an image of divinity. The way of life that B. V. and Faye set out upon at the end of the film shirks Cook's world and embraces their real condition as beings with the capacity for grace, embedded in a network of human relationships that generate meaningful responsibilities and obligations that they willingly embrace. This is genuine freedom.

Notes

1. See, for example, "Experimental Terrence Malick Trilogy Ends with a Bang," *Reel Entropy*, March 20, 2016, https://reelentropy.com/2016/03/28/experimental-terrence-malick-trilogy-ends-with-a-bang/.

2. Michael Joshua Rowin, "Song to Song and Malick's Weightless Trilogy," *Brookyln Magazine*, March 17, 2017, https://www.bkmag.com/2017/03/17/song-to-song/. See Robert Sinnerbrink, *Terrence Malick: Filmmaker and Philosopher* (London: Bloomsbury, 2019).

3. Eric Benson, "The Not-So-Secret Life of Terrence Malick," *Texas Monthly*, April 2017, https://www.texasmonthly.com/arts-entertainment/the-not-so-secret-life-of-terrence-malick/.

4. Sinnerbrink, *Terrence Malick*.

5. Paul Comacho, "The Promise of Love Perfected: Eros and Kenosis in *To the Wonder*," in *Theology and the Films of Terrence Malick*, ed. Christopher B. Barnett and Clark J. Elliston (New York: Routledge, 2017), 235–36.

6. I agree with Sinnerbrink that the Platonic theory of love is also in the background in *To the Wonder*, but my impression is that this film is more distinct from the other two than they are from each other. Aside from its obvious difference in setting (the latter two films both being set amid the entertainment industry), *To the Wonder* is notably distinct in its emphasis on themes that are specific to Catholicism (e.g., the church's understanding of Marina and Neil's relationship as adultery, which forces them to hold their marriage ceremonies first in civil court and then in a Protestant church, and the connection between spiritual love and openness to new life). Because of the complexities that these differences introduce, and because of limited space, I prefer to focus on *Knight of Cups* and *Song to Song* in this chapter and punt on the question of how *To the Wonder* fits into my analysis.

7. David Sims, "*Knight of Cups*: A Pretty, Empty Hollywood Satire," *Atlantic*, March 3, 2016, https://www.theatlantic.com/entertainment/archive/2016/03/knight-of-cups-malick-review/472050/.

8. https://www.youtube.com/watch?v=b7ANslOvACE&ab_channel=CharlesLaughton-Topic.

9. Aside from the *Phaedrus* passage read by Laughton, which uses Christopher Isherwood's translation, all quotations from Plato use *The Complete Works of Plato* edited by John M. Cooper.

10. Some commentators critique *Knight of Cups* on feminist grounds. See, for instance, David Ehrlich's review "Cinema's Poet of Awe? Or That Horny Kid in Your Directing Class?" *Slate*, March 3, 2016, https://slate.com/culture/2016/03/terrence-malicks-knight-of-cups-starring-christian-bale-reviewed.html. A feminist critique may indeed be valid and important, but at least in this case it is premature. Before we can think about whether feminist considerations raise issues concerning *Knight of Cups*, we first need to understand what the film is about and how the relevant content functions. Ehrlich hasn't even really attempted this. His critique begins from his initial impressions of the film's surface content. I do not dismiss the importance of a potential feminist critique, but I set it aside in order to first try to understand what Malick is trying to do on its own terms.

11. The Laughton recording uses a translation by Christopher Isherwood, which is somewhat looser than the Nehamas and Woodruff translation that I quote here.

12. It is also present in *To the Wonder*, though my impression is that it is considerably less prominent in that film.

13. Duran and Murgia, eds., *Global Milton and Visual Art*, 367–84.

14. Carlos Aguilar, "Devilish Charisma: Michael Fassbender on Making Song to Song With Terrence Malick and Emmanuel Lubezki," *Movie Maker*, March 22, 2017, https://www.moviemaker.com/michael-fassbender-song-to-song-malick-lubezki/.

15. Milton's text reads, "Here at least / We shall be free; the almighty hath not built / Here for his envy, will not drive us hence: Here we may reign secure, and in my choice / To reign is worth ambition though in hell / Better to reign in hell, than serve in heaven." Book 1, lines 221–70.

16. William Blake, "The Divine Image."

Bibliography

Blake, William. "The Divine Image." Poetry Foundation. https://www.poetryfoundation.org/poems/43656/the-divine-image.

Camacho, Paul. "The Promise of Love Perfected: Eros and Kenosis in *To the Wonder*." In *Theology and the Films of Terrence Malick*, edited by Christopher B. Barnett and Clark J. Elliston, 232–50. New York: Routledge, 2017.

Duran, Angelica, and Mario Murgia, eds., *Global Milton and Visual Art*. New York: Lexington, 2021.

Milton, John. *Paradise Lost*. New York: Penguin, 2000.

Plato. *The Complete Works of Plato*. Edited by John M. Cooper. Indianapolis: Hackett, 1997.

Chapter 15

The Alien God Behind the Camera

A Gnostic Viewing of Terrence Malick's Cinema, especially *Knight of Cups*

Lee Braver

Suffering isn't the true problem of life, Nietzsche argued. Humans willingly, even happily, undergo afflictions if they believe they are doing so for a purpose. No, we do not suffer from suffering but from meaninglessness and, in particular, meaningless suffering. It is when we see no greater purpose being served by our pain that we truly suffer from our sufferings instead of suffering them patiently—when there appears to be no plan, when our cries go not just unanswered but unheard and our blood flows into the gutter. Even joy can be stale and unprofitable in an aimless life. This, in Nietzsche's view, is one of the reasons for the birth of God—to serve as witness to our wretchedness and by witnessing, diminish it.

Terrence Malick's cinema circles around crises and torment—probing those in pain, those who have lost what is precious and become strangers to themselves—but he seems less interested in his characters' pain than in their thoughts about it, their painful attempts to understand their pain, precisely where Nietzsche says our focus should be. These thoughts often take the form of accusatory questions put to God. After losing a son, Mrs. O'Brien (Jessica Chastain) in *The Tree of Life* plaintively cries out, "Lord why? Where were you? Did you know? Who are we to you? Answer me.

We cry to you." In *A Hidden Life*, Fani (Valerie Pachenr), the wife of Franz (August Diehl), the man imprisoned and eventually executed, beseeches: "Lord . . . You do nothing. Where are you? Why did you create us?" These cries are especially poignant because they follow broken promises the characters had made to themselves to accept misfortune serenely, to remain comforted by God's unquestionable, unquestioning love. Mrs. O'Brien sought to stay on the way of grace, which supposedly shields us from harm: "No one who loves the way of grace ever comes to a bad end. I will be true to you whatever comes." Fani tells herself, "Trust in the triumph of the good. No evil can happen to a good man. Not a sparrow falls to Earth, but he knows it." Yet, despite vowing to hope, both find despair; telling themselves to trust, they end in anguished doubt. *The Tree of Life* goes right to the source, opening with a quote from the book of Job, the West's *locus classicus* of our demand for justification from God to for the torments she allows.

These forlorn inquiries pose what is known in philosophy as the problem of evil: if God is omnipotent and omniscient ("Not a sparrow falls"), then why does She allow evil and undeserved suffering to occur? Private Train (John Dee Smith) in *The Thin Red Line*, wandering through the carnage of war, puts the question directly: "This great evil? Where does it come from? How did it steal into the world?" A Captain in *A Hidden Life* uses the compromised state of the world to try to convince Franz to compromise his principles and join the Nazis, stating that, "We all have blood on our hands. No one is innocent. Crime, bloodshed, everywhere. He who created this world . . . He created evil."

It makes sense that the question of evil would interest a director so deeply invested in religious ideas and themes. Standing out from modern cinema, many of Malick's films have overt discussions of religious matters and most, if not all, can be given a religious interpretation. Thus, a religious perspective is likely to illuminate his mysterious work, especially a religion founded on answering the problem of evil: Gnosticism.

Gnosticism is, among other things, an early sect of Christianity, one that died out as Christianity's tenets and canon solidified into an orthodoxy in the first few centuries after Jesus's death. Like most heresies, the victors tried to blot it from memory, but archeological discoveries—especially at Nag Hammadi in 1945—have given us ample textual basis to reconstruct it. I will briefly explain its main ideas and try to show how it can help elucidate certain themes, statements, and events in Malick's cinema.[1]

Gnosticism gives a fairly successful solution to the seemingly intractable problem of evil, one suggested by Private Train: "What's this war at the heart of nature? Why does nature vie with itself? The land contend with the sea? Is there an avenging power in nature? Not one power but two?" It is a dualistic or Manichean theology, positing two deities (in *Days of Heaven*, Linda [Linda Manz] says, "Nobody's perfect. There was never a perfect person around. You just have half-angel and half-devil in you"). One of the more surprising ideas is that Jahweh, the god of the Old Testament whom many of us were taught to worship in Sunday school, is the lesser of the two. She wants to be the true, supreme deity and her status as inferior to the true, transcendent god has driven her mad with jealousy. Her solution has been to create an artificial environment where she can rule—Earth, a creation profoundly flawed due to her imperfect powers. She had to resort to the shoddy medium of physical matter in space and time, which builds transience into the structure of the world; hence decay, disease, and death. A cosmic narcissist, she needs an audience to witness her greatness so she populates her zoo with captive bits or drops of the true god stuffed into decaying lumps of meat—us. Her jealousy—startlingly conceded in the First Commandment: "I the Lord thy God am a jealous God" (Exod. 20.5)—then drives her to commit acts of cruelty against the captives she wants to love her.

This admirably accounts for the misery-causing flaws in the world—Jahweh's incompetence forces her to use substandard construction materials—as well as for outright evil—her resentful covetousness leads her to perpetrate wrongs upon us captives, beginning with our captivity. The explanation does run into trouble when we ask why the true god allows bits of himself to remain imprisoned in this terrible place, for his perfection should, one would think, enable him to escape initial capture and continued captivity. The Gnostic answer is that Jahweh has induced amnesia in these droplets, perhaps rendered vulnerable due by fragmentation. We do not know that this world is a false creation, our selves traps, our present lives barriers to a true life. Tricked into believing this world to be the real one and addicted to its glittering pleasures, we become unwittingly complicit in our own bondage.

Because ignorance is the reason for our imprisonment, knowledge presents the key; this is why the movement derives its name from the Greek word for knowledge, *gnosis*. The book of John is the most Gnostic book that made it into the canon, with its well-known saying that the truth shall set you free (John 8:32). We must come to know this world to be false in order to escape it and return back to our true transcendent Self, where there is no pain or confusion. The true god's power is limited in this realm, so he cannot directly enter it and free us; we must free ourselves. But he does help by sending in messengers to bring us the saving truth. Some of the more prominent messengers were Eden's serpent—after all, he sought to bring Adam and Eve knowledge whereas Jahweh deceived them in order to keep it from them ("God doth know that in the day ye eat thereof, then your eyes shall be opened, and ye shall be as gods" [Gen. 3:5]), banishing them from paradise to prevent them from acquiring immortality ("Behold, the man is become as one of us, to know good and evil: and now, lest he put forth his hand, and take also of the tree of life, and eat, and live forever" [Gen. 3:22])—and Jesus. These messengers took lowly forms—a snake crawling on the ground and a Jewish carpenter's son in the Roman Empire—in order to escape Jahweh's notice for as long as possible, for as soon as she realized their true identity, she wrathfully put an end to their lives, aided by her demonic helpers called Archons.

Gnosticism is then organized around transcendence. The goal of life is to escape our lives, leaving our present plane of existence for a higher one. As this world is a prison, the notions of escape and freedom become crucial to this religious system. Since the theology requires a peculiar device to explain the true omnipotent god's vulnerability, it draws on analogies such as amnesia or sleep to explain our impotence as caused by ignorance of our true selves and power.

The theme of escape and seeking freedom runs throughout Malick's films. Kit (Richard Gere) and Holly (Sissy Spacek) of *Badlands* begin their terrible trip because they are trying to escape their lives of dreary poverty. Bill (Richard Gere) begins *Days of Heaven*: "We're going west. Things gotta be better out there," and Linda the narrator describes their actions, "All three of us been going places, looking for things, searching for things, going on adventures." In the first lines of *A Hidden Life*, Franz says, "I thought that we could build our nest high up in the trees. Fly away, like birds . . . to the mountains." (This resonates rather directly with the sermon in *The Tree of Life*: "Job imagined he might build his nest on high—that the integrity of his behavior would protect him against misfortune.") It ends with his wife confirming his successful escape through a virtuous death, a higher state marked by knowledge: "A time will come when we will know what all this is for. And there will be no mysteries. We will know . . . why . . . we live. We'll come together. We'll plant orchards.

Fields. We'll build the land back up. Franz. I'll meet you there. In the mountains." Private Witt (Jim Caviezel) in *The Thin Red Line* keeps going AWOL, and in *Song to Song*, Cook (Michael Fassbender) says to Faye (Rooney Mara) about B. V. (Ryan Gosling), "All his life he tried to get free, he doesn't know how." In *The Tree of Life*, Mr. O'Brien (Brad Pitt), sounding like Jahweh instructing Adam and Eve, tells his sons, "That is Spencer's yard. You see this line. Let's not cross it. You must understand." This goal is sometimes put in rather extraordinary terms: echoing the idea that we're all sparks of the true god, Witt says, "Maybe all men got one big soul who everybody's a part of. All faces of the same man. One big self. Everyone looking for salvation by himself . . . each like a coal, drawn from the fire."

But the film that most resonates with Gnosticism is *Knight of Cups*, Malick's Gospel of John, if you will. It opens with a recitation of the title and opening of John Bunyan's *The Pilgrim's Progress*, considered one of the first religious allegories extended into the form of a novel. The title announces a Pilgrim named Christian's "Progress From this World to That Which is to Come Delivered under the Similitude of a Dream." These first words of the film invoke one of the first and most important religious allegories in history, strongly suggesting that we will find one here, and it is the allegory of a traveler's journey outside of this world to the next. Moreover, it tells us that the story will be delivered as a dream that will pass on the knowledge of how to make this journey, as his family follows in his footsteps in part two, guided by what they have learned from it.

In the next lines spoken, Rick (Christian Bale) says, "All those years living the life of someone I didn't even know." We are introduced to the main character through his sense that he has lost his self, that he has been living the wrong kind of life. Insofar as he doesn't really know who he was, he can be described as a kind of amnesiac or someone living a dream where one does not know why one is doing what one does, nor even that one is asleep.

The third voice is Joseph (Brian Dennehy), Rick's father, who explicitly introduces the idea of learning from an allegory.

Remember the story I used to tell you when you were a boy . . . about a young prince. A knight, sent by his father, the King of the East, west into Egypt . . . to find a pearl. A pearl from the depths of the sea. But when the prince arrived, the people poured him a cup that took away his memory. He forgot he was the son of the king. Forgot about the pearl . . . and fell into a deep sleep. The king didn't forget his son. He continued to send word . . . messengers . . . guides. But the prince slept on.

Rick confesses a kind of amnesia and his father immediately asks him to remember.[2] The story he has forgotten and needs to remember is itself a story of forgetting, the "Hymn of the Pearl" from the Gnostic *Acts of Thomas*, an extraordinary allegory of Gnosticism. In it, the prince seeks something of great value—a pearl—but he is robbed of his knowledge of his royal ancestry (often used by Gnostics as a symbol of our divine origin) and his quest.[3] Like the true god, his father the king sends messengers into this foreign land to inform him of the falsity of his present life, that he came from a superior lineage from outside, that he is meant for greater things.

The first moments of the film, then, give us two religious allegories with overlapping imagery, the second of which connecting with the first in passages left out of the film. Bunyan prefaced *The Pilgrim's Progress* with an "Author's Apology for his Book"—"apology" originally meaning defense or justification rather than an admission of guilt or asking for forgiveness. He says there that he had not meant to write his book "in such a mode" but that he, "writing of the way / And race of saints, in this our gospel day / Fell suddenly into an allegory." Concerned with whether this is acceptable—"May I not write in such a style as this?"—he justifies hiding such an important lesson within the form of a fiction—"Delivered Under the Similitude of a Dream"—by citing a parallel example from nature, God's book. "If that a pearl . . . may be found too in an oyster-shell," then could people not find the greatest treasure of all within "my little book?" Bunyan is justifying writing an allegory by writing a further allegory, an allegory of allegories. It compares the knowledge that "will direct thee to the Holy Land / If thou wilt its directions understand," that is, the truth that will allow us to transcend this realm into the better one, to a pearl, the same symbol used for the same salvation in the Gnostic "Hymn of the Pearl." To add one more layer to this encrusting of meanings, the film later references Plato's *Phaedrus* and its condemnation of this material, mortal realm that we need to pass through and beyond. This dialogue tells us that we yearn to return to the higher realm, "being ourselves pure and not entombed in this which we carry about with us and call the body, in which we are imprisoned like an oyster in its shell" (250c).

Bunyan's final justification for placing the pearl of salvific truth into the oyster shell of an allegory moves from citing nature to invoking revelation. "Were not God's laws / His gospel laws, in olden times held forth / By types, shadows, and metaphors?" Jesus's lessons frequently took the form of humble parables about animals and plants instead of direct statements like the Ten Commandments, and if these earthy stories can convey ultimate truths, then so can a novel-length allegory. What is particularly interesting here is that the Gnostics considered the style of Jesus's parables to be of great importance precisely because they wrap transcendent truths in such modest imagery. When his disciples ask him about this, Jesus replies, "Therefore speak I to them in parables: because they seeing see not; and hearing they hear not, neither do they understand" (Matt. 13:13). This is an extraordinary response. He uses parables precisely so that his audiences will not understand him, or at least not everyone in them: "Because it is given unto you to know the mysteries of the kingdom of heaven, but to them it is not given" (Matt. 13:11). His parables split his listeners into "stony places" and "good ground" (Matt. 13:5–8) for the seeds of his wisdom, in a parable about parables, for some need to hear these truths while it is better that others do not recognize what is actually being taught. Some will see his pearls of wisdom for the deliverance they are, while in other cases, they are merely cast before swine. For the Gnostics, Jahweh was always on the lookout for any foreign agents sent in to liberate the divine sparks, so these messengers must disguise themselves and their messages. This is how they explained Jesus's use of parables as his favored mode of speaking, just as Bunyan's pearl allegory justifies his innovative use of allegories. All of this gets invoked by the opening of *Knight of Cups*, insinuating that Malick is insinuating his own cinematic strategy.

Malick begins his film with two religious allegories, which use the same symbol for the secret way to escape this life. Like the knight in the "Hymn," Rick's father charges him with the quest to find this precious object—a charge entwined with the command to remember himself— after Rick confesses that he has lost his sense of who he is, that he has been living a false life, a falsity confirmed by his father, Joseph: "You live in exile. Stranger in a strange land. A pilgrim. A knight. Find your way . . . from darkness." Bunyan's pearl is an allegorical reference to the allegorical nature of *The Pilgrim's Progress*, which is to be decoded by readers on their own quests for salvation and whose title marks the first words of the film. In case anyone misses the idea that the film *Knight of Cups* is an allegory as well, Malick cinematically illustrates the events of the "Hymn" as Joseph reads: the story from Rick's childhood overlays a young boy looking through a picture book; when the prince arrives in sinful Egypt, Rick is shown driving a car with two attractive young women playfully interacting with him; when the knight drinks from the baleful cup that induces forgetfulness, Rick is drinking at a party, drunkenly rolling over a couch when Joseph announces the knight's loss of memory; when he speaks of the king sending messengers, a party guest dressed as a winged angel appears in the background along with someone in a horse mask (the Knight of Cups in the tarot cards rides a horse) and several attractive women (Plato's *Phaedrus* singles out beauty as one of the best reminders of our true lives prior to getting entombed in these material bodies), including one with X's on her shoulder blades where wings would grow. After the final line, "But the prince slept on," the scene switches to Rick asleep in bed.

This is pretty clear: Rick is the knight, though fallen to a knight in his cups. He has been seduced by Hollywood into selling his soul, a common expression for selling out. Indeed, Malick's choice of setting for his allegory is brilliant, as Hollywood is primarily known for two things: creating artificial realities and tempting people into sin. What could serve as a better symbol of Jahweh's creation of false worlds than the Dream Factory, where illusions are manufactured for the populace to consume and remain content?[4] The movie *Knight of Cups* takes place behind the scenes of the movies, as Rick gets seduced into the hedonistic lifestyle and compromises his art for riches, a plot no less dramatic or artificial than what happens in front of the cameras. In one scene, his agent says that Rick was trying to get out of writing for a popular comedy star by demanding double his usually fee and then got trapped when they agreed to it. The Mephistophelian glint of Tinseltown's promises are nowhere as clear as in the speech of Herb, Rick's manager: "I wanna make you rich. Is there anyone you wanna sit in a room with? Is there anyone you wanna know? You wanna climb your stairs, or theirs? Your time on Earth. All you need to do is say yes. Nod. Wink. Where else will you go? It'll be the same there."[5] All material goods—money, women, friends—are his if he just signs, like a Californian Faust. To seal the deal, the temptations are accompanied by a nihilistic denial of even the possibility of transcendence, of any higher aspirations ("Where else will you go? It'll be the same there"), a denial echoed by many characters in Malick's films,[6] something rather odd for an agent to say but perfectly intelligible for a Gnostic agent of Jahweh.

This theme apparently resonates with Malick's initial experiences in the movie business, when he wrote scripts for successful films such as *Dirty Harry* (1971), a somewhat less nuanced treatment of questions of good and evil. Rick confesses, as part of his loss of self, that he "did every lousy, crappy job that they wanted me to do." His self-compromising gets confirmed by his physician ex-wife Nancy, who renders her diagnosis: "You changed. The world absorbed you. More and more." Like so many ingenues coming to Hollywood to be discovered, Rick lost himself instead, forgetting what he came for as he wallows in his cups. Because we are made of material, the Gnostics say, we are materialistic, subject to physical pleasures and material desires that, in Plato's image, nail us to the physical realm and keep us from ascending to the higher one. This attitude is summed up best by Walt the Las Vegas pimp's mini-sermon: "Oh, even though I'm in darkness, I believe in the light [Manichean dualism]. I was instructed from some information [salvific message] to be no part of the world nor of the things in it [transcend]. But my eyes are now simple, and I'm carnal when I see beautiful women and big cars and lots of money, and I wanna be a part of it" (all bracketed comments added).

This speech is touched off when Nancy, Rick's girlfriend at the time, sees that Walt is wearing a cross and asks him if he is "a religious man." At the precise moment these words are spoken, the camera shows us the back of one of his employees with tattoos of birds near her shoulder blades. This recalls the initial "Hymn," which showed a party guest in an angel costume with wings when Joseph mentioned the guides and messengers the king sent to his son to remind him of who he was and what he was questing for. The pimp is a paradigmatic Gnostic messenger, since salvational missives must come from unexpected, disguised sources to escape the Archon's notice.[7] Even one of Walt's confessed failings—his attraction to beautiful women—can function as a lifeline to eternal life, as indicated in the passage from Plato's *Phaedrus* recited in the film. It says that when we fell into these mortal bodies, we lost the wings that allowed us to fly into heaven, "yet the roots of its wings are still there," recalling the X's on the woman's shoulders during the initial reading of the "Hymn" and Walt's prostitute's bird tattoos, both located on their shoulder blades.[8] When someone sees beautiful people, Plato thought, this reminds him of Beauty itself, which he witnessed before our imprisonment but has now forgotten, like catching a glimpse of a pearl "imprisoned like an oyster in its shell," and he yearns to fly "like a young bird. He has lost all interest in the world." Not coincidentally, the Knight of Cups of the tarot cards is a lover, and Rick is drawn to many women throughout the film.

Rick's writing talent works against him, keeping him mired in the kind of "lousy, crappy job" that pays well but has little merit. This reminds one of what Captain Herder, a Nazi interrogator, told Franz in *A Hidden Life*: "The Antichrist is clever. He uses a man's virtues to mislead him." But if success is failure, then the reverse should be true as well. Failure and disappointment can be positive in that they can break this world's enchantments and prepare us for transcendence. After all, a pearl only forms in response to an injurious breach.

The salvational power of suffering is a common theme in these movies so focused on suffering. It comes out most clearly in two actual sermons delivered by preachers—no allegory here—one from *The Tree of Life* and one from *Knight of Cups*. Let's look at them side by side, in that order.

> REAL-LIFE EPISCOPAL PRIEST KELLY KOONCE: We vanish as a cloud. We wither as the autumn grass, and like a tree are rooted up. Is there some *fraud* in the scheme of the universe? . . . *We cannot stay where we are. We must journey forth. We must find that which is greater than fortune or fate*. Nothing can bring us peace but that. . . . Job turned from the *passing shows of time. He sought that which is eternal*. Does he alone see God's hand who sees that He gives, or does not also the one *see God's hand* who sees that He takes away?

> FR. ZEITLINGER: Seems you're alone. You're not. Even now, He's taking your hand and *guiding* you by a way *you cannot see*. If you're unhappy, you shouldn't take it as a mark of God's disfavor. Just the contrary. Might be the very *sign* He loves you. He shows His love not by helping you avoid suffering, by *sending you suffering*. By keeping you there. To suffer *binds you to something higher* than yourself, higher than your own will. *Takes you from the world, to find what lies beyond it*. (All italics added)

These sermons harmonize with each other and with Gnosticism. Both assert that God is giving us guidance when we suffer, infusing it with the meaningfulness Nietzsche said we seek, albeit guidance for a journey to transcend this world of fortune and misfortune. It mentions the passing of time, frequently commented on throughout Malick's films[9] and one of the worst flaws of the material realm for the Gnostics, a flaw that should make us seek that which does not pass. And they speak of the difficulty in deciphering God's cryptic messages. Both then decode them the same way: the breaking of our world helps us escape it.

This is shown allegorically near the beginning of the film. If we consider the two explicit allegories (*Pilgrim's Progress* and "Hymn of the Pearl") to be a kind of prologue, the film proper begins with Rick asleep, the state shared by the prince and the pilgrim and, for the Gnostics, all of humanity. He is awakened, however, not by an alarm clock or a phone but by an earthquake, the very ground beneath him cracking and shaking itself apart. The foundations of his world are literally coming asunder, just the kind of cataclysmic event that can break the hypnotic hold its enticements have over him, according to the sermons. This is also a theme explored by Heidegger, who argues that we submerge our identities into the anonymous crowd in our everyday occupation and preoccupations. We can only come to ourselves and live authentically when this numbing rhythm of our ongoing lives gets interrupted, and the greater the breakdown, the better. Bouts of anxiety break down the significance of our world, and since we build our selves out of the occupations of common life—identifying ourselves with our job, our possessions, and so on—anxiety robs us of all reassuring sense of self, the state that Rick finds himself in as the film begins. As uncomfortable as it is, this is actually positive because it is only by losing this superficial identity that we can uncover our true self and lead a true life, clearing off all external junk to be able to see what has been lying beneath all along.[10] Rick's existential crisis is just the kind of opportunity Heidegger believes we should seize upon. He rules out transcending the world for a transcendent realm and supernatural sources, the Gnostic solution, but both give the meaning to our suffering that Nietzsche says we need.

What if this significance-suffering were not limited just to the characters within the films or to humanity? The style of Malick's movies suggests an even stronger Gnostic reading, one that transcends the confines of the films themselves. They are, somewhat notoriously, unconventional. They are not plot-driven or even really character-driven. They lack continuity in any standard sense, moving among characters, time periods, and plot lines with little in the way of obvious structure such as progressive timelines or cause and effect. Viewers will inevitably weave patterns out of these, but they are always highly speculative. One possible reason for this method is to capture the stream of consciousness and the chaotic nature of reality, an important notion for Gnosticism. As Joseph says, "You think when you reach a certain age things will start making sense. Then you find out you're just as lost as you were before. I suppose that's what damnation is. The pieces of your life never to come together. Just splashed out there."

Another unusual feature that consistently stands out is the camera work. Camera focus directs the audience's attention so most directors use it to establish and move the plot along—pointing viewers to the most important event, object, or character in a scene. Many, if not most, angles and motions tacitly suggest the perspective of a human, staying around eye-level and moving with normal human motions—one reason why the inhuman Steadicam shots in *The Shining* are so unsettling.

Malick's camera, though, wanders as if driven by an omnivorous curiosity, one only loosely connected to characters and plot. It is ontologically or narratively egalitarian, lingering on a random blade of grass with as much interest and intensity as on a central character's face, sometimes brushing past their expressions during important emotional scenes. It runs past people from very low angles, almost like a dog's perspective, or achieves a graceful stillness, perched above all like an angel. This violation of standard patterns reminds me of nothing so much as the last few minutes of *2001: A Space Odyssey* (Douglas Trumbull, who did the special effects for *2001*, also filmed the evolution sequence in Malick's *The Tree of Life*). At this point, the astronaut, Bowman (Keir Dullea), has gone through the stargate left by aliens (a rather Gnostic notion, Philip K. Dick would point out) and is now transitioning into a new life form, culminating in the final image of the star-baby. The alien midwives aid this radical transformation by placing him in what they understand to be a normal human ecosystem, as we do for zoo animals. They just didn't get it quite right because they don't really get us, housing him in a seventeenth-century baroque French room with fluorescent lighting on the floors. While they at least attempt to make his surroundings familiar, they cannot do the same with the plane of existence they have brought him to, for here time and space behave differently. Time is out of joint, jumping forward in leaps rather than moving continuously, and space has altered such that Bowman can turn and see himself in another part of the room at a more advanced stage of aging.[11] Perhaps assimilating to this alternate temporality is part of the labor process, like giving birth to a baby in water or pausing at different heights as one ascends a mountain. This final part of the film shows the aliens' attempt to understand us and Kubrick's attempt to get us to understand them by portraying an alien form of temporality and spatiality within this one. This is of course impossible; he gestures at what transcends our structures of sense by breaking standard rules of narrative sense, depicting something so cryptic that it strikes many as nonsense.

What I want to suggest is that Malick's films are somewhat milder attempts to make entire movies like this, ignoring standard notions of temporality, continuity, plot, character, and so on rather than trying to directly violate them as Kubrick does. One reason, as mentioned above, could be to capture the chaos of lived experience, which does not unfold as a clear, logical sequence of connected events. But the Gnostic reading I have given, which I find unavoidable for *Knight of Cups*, suggests another possibility.

According to Gnosticism, the true god is desperately trying to make contact with us, trapped in a radically alien plane of existence made of matter and space-time, pleasure and pain, our omniscience veiled by amnesia, our power by seductive illusions. The fact that he does not make direct contact but resorts to ignominious helpers and circuitous routes of communication suggests that his powers are limited here, perhaps due to the fact that the material plane operates according to fundamentally different laws than the transcendent. There, all is perfect and known; here, there are only defects and ignorance. There, eternity reigns, while here time eats away at everything. In this case, god can understand us no more than we can understand him, both of us equally separated from the other by the chasm of infinity. An infinite being cannot truly grasp what it is to be finite any more than finite beings can have any understanding of the infinite. Omniscience cannot solve this incomprehension, for it is the precise source of it. No omniscient knower can know what it is to be ignorant; ironically, omniscience by its very nature imparts ignorance, albeit only ignorance of ignorance. No immortal being can know what it is to face death, or pain, infinitely less than we can know what it is like to be a bat, in Thomas Nagel's famous thought experiment. Derrida once suggested that since God hopes that we believe in him and choose the path of righteousness, he is praying to us as well. Perhaps god wonders as much about our nature as we do about his, divine attempts at anthropology mirroring human theology.

Kubrick tried to make a film about alien life from the perspective of an alien, just as he made *Barry Lyndon*, set in the mid-eighteenth century, as if it were filmed in the mid-eighteenth century: much slower pacing than modern viewers are used to, no artificial lights, and so on. I have been arguing that Malick's cinema is both Gnostic (at least *Knight of Cups*, with resonances elsewhere) and highly unconventional in the way it films. Perhaps these are flip sides of the same coin.

What if the main character of the movie is not any of the characters but rather the witness constituting the film itself? To be clear, I'm not talking about the person Terrence Malick but about a fictional character embodied in the camera—never speaking or acting, just witnessing, trying desperately to understand us in our despair. This would account for its strange detachment from time, character, and plot as well as its constant eavesdropping on interior monologues—Is there more dialogue in Malick's films in voiceover than in voice?—for it intersects with our realm obliquely. This character is attracted to people who are perplexed, who have to make difficult decisions, who do not understand themselves or why life is the way it is because this is precisely its situation. Its lack of understanding of humanity then accounts for its inhuman accounts of the stories it tries to follow. It doesn't know how to follow the plotline of their lifetimes because it lives in eternity; when it tries to understand what happens in *The Tree of Life*, for example, it runs through the entire history of the universe instead of just the salient events of the relevant characters' lives. For how could an omniscient being select a fraction of facts from the totality of what has occurred and proclaim them "the story"?

I mentioned the opening quote from *The Tree of Life* earlier: "Where were you when I laid the foundations of the Earth? . . . When the morning stars sang together and all the sons of God shouted for joy?" (Job 38: 4–7). This is God's response to Job's demand for an explanation, and there it functions as a literally self-righteous argument-ending device to teach him humility—no mere mortal has the right to question the eternal creator. But on my proposed interpretation, it takes on a very different meaning. Now it's not a rhetorical question but a genuine inquiry put to these creatures that puzzle it so. What kind of creatures are you? Where did you come from? Who do you think you are you praying to? How did the foundations of this shoddy, torturous Earth get laid?[12] *God* is having an existential crisis, having literally lost parts of his soul, and he is perplexed by the relationship of humanity to God, to existence, to the beyond, from the other side of transcendence. He is asking of us the same question that Mrs. O'Brien puts to him, the same question her son asks ("Where were you? You let a boy die. You let anything happen. Why should I be good if you aren't?"): Are you people good or bad? What path will you choose? Will you return to me? How did I lose myself? How do I rejoin mortals to God?

The Gnostics see knowledge as the key to salvation and yet their theology centers on an amnesiac God who is also in need of the information of how to reunite, and these films could represent his searching inquiry into what it is to be human. He is attracted to Malick's central issues of death and religion, of transcendence and suffering, like a moth to the flame, for they concern the transition to another state, a topic that occupies him as much as us. We are seeking to transcend this realm to get to his while he is trying to find a way to transcend his realm into ours. He is trying to make contact, but given how alien our realm is to him, he has no more answers than we do; this is why the camera is constantly studying its characters (and getting distracted by odd things), nuzzling up to us to eavesdrop on their most intimate thoughts. This would make the film almost a first-person version of "Wings of Desire," where angels in Berlin peruse the thoughts of various people like books in a library (one of the main settings of the film), black and white turning to brilliant color upon sudden insights into humanity.

These insights are hard-won because of the distance from angel to human, which must be infinitely farther from God. This is alluded to in a speech from *A Hidden Life*, given by a painter restoring frescoes at a local church. "I paint all this suffering. But I don't suffer myself. . . . I paint this comfortable Christ with a halo over his head. I paint their comfortable Christ . . . with a halo over his head. *How can I show what I haven't lived?* Someday I might have the courage to venture. . . . Not yet. Someday I'll paint the true Christ" (italics added). It is a rule of thumb that whenever an artwork appears within an artwork, such as a play within a play, what is said about or what happens to it also applies to the work it is within, like a mise en abyme. "The play's the thing," as Hamlet says of his play within a play, designed to expose the king's inner thoughts. The painter's speech clearly refers to Franz, who is suffering in a Christ-like manner and who is being depicted by the artwork *A Hidden Life*. It points to an old idea of epistemological sympathy from Plato and Augustine, that the knower must be in the same state as the known in order to know it. This forms the basis for one of their proofs for the immortality of the soul: our souls must have eternity about them if they can know eternal truths. The painter, however, is speaking of suffering: one cannot portray it if one does not genuinely understand it, and this only comes from suffering. God may very well be wishing the same thing Jack does in his prayers in *The*

Tree of Life: "I want to know what you are. I want to see what you see," his inability to see forming a mirror image of ours. Perhaps this is the true reason why the Word became flesh, why Holy Spirit had to become a bleeding Christ—not for forgiveness but for understanding. Reversing the message of the sermons, suffering is our gift to God.

Transcendence plays an important role within these films, but according to this interpretation, the most important transcendence takes place on the other side of the camera. The witness of the films is peering across an infinite divide, trying to cross it from there as we are trying from here. The alien divinity descends to make contact with us—it "immanends," if you will, or perhaps "transmundanifies"—as we strain upward to meet it, the roots of our cleaved wings achingly beating, beating. Our pain drives us to it and draws it to us. It seeks insight rather than knowledge, intimacy instead of majesty, but the strange, uncomfortable, inhuman camera suggests that it has not found what it seeks. Malick seems more hopeful for his characters: *The Tree of Life* ends with the reuniting of the family with the son when they all pass on; the end of *A Hidden Life* has Franz's wife saying that they have achieved the escape of flight sought for at the start.

The end of *Knight of Cups* also joins its beginning into a circle, almost like Nietzsche's eternal return, an infinite immanence he hoped could grant us a new meaningfulness now that transcendence has collapsed. Nietzsche wondered if the death of God had "unchained this earth from its sun? . . . Is there still any up or down? Are we not straying as through an infinite nothing?"[13] The only orientation that had given humanity guidance was divinely granted, transcending earthly directions like the wayfinding stars high above us—the word "orientation" derives from the practice of taking all direction from the East ("the Orient") where Jerusalem lies, where the sun rises, and when this falters, we may fall into nihilistic aimlessness, the source of true suffering.

The *Knight of Cups* circular non-ending, however, does not leave us in that state. It ends with Joseph, who opened the film charging his son with the quest of remembering his forgotten quest for the lost pearl, finding now a measure of peace: "I'm proud of you. You've done well. Better than me. Which is the way it's supposed to be. Find the light you know in the east. As a child. The moon. The stars. They serve you. They guide you on your way. The light in the eyes of others. The pearl." Recovering this could grant us recovery, like the grail bringing rain back to the barren earth. Nietzsche's sun might never return, but we may turn back to the moon reflected from our childhood, a luminous pearl in the sky to light our darkened way. The pearl will return to us the transcendent stars, it will orient us toward the light in the east that guides us home, back to the company of those who offer comfort rather than tempt us into dis-grace. He continues, "My son, remember," regain this pearl of wisdom, carry through your quest for what has been lost, complete the journey that will lead you back to yourself, this circular pilgrimage that, like all essential journeys, can only end where it started, to which Rick responds, in the final word of the film, "Begin."

Notes

1. For good general accounts of Gnosticism, see E. H. Pagels, *The Gnostic Gospels* (United Kingdom: Random House, 2004); Hans Jonas, *The Gnostic Religion: The Message of the Alien God and the Beginnings of Christianity*, 2nd ed. (Boston: Beacon Press, 1963); Jacques Lacarriere, *The Gnostics* (San Francisco: City Lights Books, 1989); and Kurt Rudolph, *Gnosis: The Nature and History of Gnosticism* (San Francisco: HarperSanFrancisco, 1987).

2. Here one is reminded of the child's request of his mother at bedtime, "Tell us a story from before we can remember" from *The Tree of Life*. He is asking to be reminded of the time before he came into this world, just before he exits it into sleep.

3. Along with his memory, the prince in the "Hymn" also loses his "glittering robe," to dress in Egypt's "filthy and unclean dress." The robe's importance is emphasized by his father's letters reminding him of it, and his own reaction upon reacquiring it: "On a sudden, when I received it / the garment seemed to me to become like a mirror of myself." This is probably meant to invoke the biblical story of Joseph. Joseph's brothers interpreted his father Jacob's gift of a coat of many colors as an indication that Joseph would become the leader of the family, so they took his coat and sold him into slavery in Egypt. In *Knight of Cups*, in the depths of despair, Rick gets robbed, and the film draws explicit attention to the fact that the thieves take his jacket.

4. One possible alternative could be video games, artificial worlds we live and die in. This also gets a reference in the film when an agent says, "Living my life is like playing *Call of Duty* on easy." This is a person wholly believing in this world, whose symbol for worldly success inadvertently alludes to its artificiality and meaninglessness.

5. This kind of worldly pressure to compromise takes on a far more sinister form in *A Hidden Life*, as stated by Franz's friend: "They ask you to take an oath to the Antichrist, yeah? I know, I know. It's a life without honor. Is this here . . . the end of the world? Is this the death of the light?"

6. Here are a few other examples of this nihilistic denial of transcendence. Sergeant McCron (John Savage): "We're just dirt" and Sergeant Welsh (Sean Penn): "There's not some other world out there where everything's going to be okay. There's just this world. Just this rock" in *The Thin Red Line*; Prisoner Nikolai in *A Hidden Life*: "Your God has no pity. He left us. Abandoned us. How far from being delivered from evil. If we could only see the beginning of his Kingdom. The dawn! But . . . nothing. Nothing ever."

7. I have no idea if Malick meant this, but there is a fascinating resonance here with Philip K. Dick, the science fiction writer who fashioned himself a contemporary Gnostic prophet. He believed that God had contacted him by downloading a mass of information into his brain, and he passed this information on in the form of modern-day parables, updating the agricultural references of Jesus's time to ray guns and aerosol cans spraying salvational communion. Thus, Dick thought a great deal about how to cast religious allegories in contemporary language and symbols, which could perhaps be considered Malick's central formal concern. The direct connection with *Knight of Cups* is that Dick's first contact with God came from seeing the Christian symbol worn by a messenger. For more on this, see Braver, "Coin-Operated Doors and God," 83–110.

8. Here is the passage read out in the film:

> Once the soul was perfect and had wings. . . . Brave, it could soar into heaven where only creatures with wings can be. But the soul lost its wings and fell to Earth. There it took an earthly body. And now, while it lives in this body, no outward sign of wings can be seen. Yet the roots of its wings are still there. And the nature of wings is to try to raise the earthbound body and soar with it into heaven. When we see a beautiful woman, or a man . . . the soul remembers the beauty it used to know in heaven. And wings begin to spout, and that makes the soul want to fly, but it cannot yet. It is still too weak. So the man keeps staring up into the sky like a young bird. He has lost all interest in the world. (*Phaedrus* 245b–49d)

9. Mrs. O'Brien: "The only way to be happy is to love. Unless you love, your life will flash by." Franz: "We are like a breath . . . like a shadow that passes away."

10. For a detailed explanation of this and more of Heidegger's thought, see Lee Braver, *Heidegger: Thinking of Being* (Cambridge, MA: Polity Press, 2014).

11. It is hard not to think of Philip K. Dick quoting Wagner's *Parsifal* in his masterpiece, *VALIS*: "You see, my son, here time turns into space." Dick understood this to mean that Christianity indicated the unreality of this world.

12. Obviously, the way this passage attributes the creation of this world to God does not fit this interpretation of it being spoken by the Gnostic true

God. The point of my interpretation is to read it as expressing a general sense of puzzlement rather than a tacit accusation.
13. Friedrich Nietzsche, *The Gay Science*, § 125.

Bibliography

Braver, Lee. "Coin-Operated Doors and God: A Gnostic Reading of Philip K. Dick's *Ubik*." *Extrapolation* 56, no. 1 (April 2015): 83–110.
Nietzsche, Friedrich. *The Gay Science: With A Prelude in Rhymes and an Appendix of Songs*. Translated by Walter Kaufmann. New York: Vintage Books, 1974.

Chapter 16

A Hidden Life of Love

Sacrifice in Malick's Cinematographic Philosophy

KATERINA KOCI AND MARTIN KOCI

"Do you understand?" . . . "I love you!"

—*A Hidden Life*

One of the most powerful scenes in Terrence Malick's film *A Hidden Life* is the final meeting between Franziska Jägerstätter (Valerie Pachner) and her husband Franz (August Biehl) shortly before he is to be executed by the Nazis. Jägerstätter's lawyer (Alexander Fehling) attempts, one last time, to persuade Franz to join the Nazi war effort, but Franz ignores the rational arguments of this educated professional, looks over to Franziska, and asks: "Do you understand?"

Malick dedicates a considerable amount of time in the movie to the failure of various characters to understand Franz's decision not to fight, having made up his mind that to do so would be tantamount to "swearing an oath to Hitler." His fellow villagers, his neighbors, the mayor, his parish priest, the local bishop, and even the judge who ultimately pronounces the death sentence all appear to sing together: *You will change nothing!*

We intuitively cry out for the same reaction: a greater effort on Franziska's part to save her husband before he is put to death. She is, after all, the one who will be left behind to raise the children, work the farm, and live alongside people who will always question her actions. And who else was truly in a position to disapprove Franz's decision? Yet she acquiesces.[1] She hears her husband loud and clear and replies simply: "I love you."

Franz Jägerstätter's sacrifice appears to be in vain.[2] He did not stop the war. Hitler's army was not weakened by being one man short. History took its course regardless of the moral stand of a lowly Austrian peasant. Franz's act may indeed have gained nothing, but it revealed something: a hidden life of love. This juxtaposition of a sacrifice for nothing and a hidden life of love is the focus of our interest here, and it is, we believe, what Malick elucidates most strikingly in his film.

That Malick's strong philosophical background is imprinted in his cinematic output is a "truth universally acknowledged."[3] It is nonetheless important to note that unlike other films that are subjected to ex-post philosophical-theological interpretations irrespective of the author's intentions, Malick's films are philosophical in their very conception. Robert Sinnerbrink, a lifelong interpreter of Malick's work from the perspective of existential phenomenology, suggests that Malick's movies are philosophy.[4] He writes: "Malick's films elicit and evoke forms of experience that often invite metaphysical reflection or prompt one to seek comprehension by having recourse to philosophical reflection. Philosophical ideas, in turn, can serve as heuristic devices to help open up or articulate aspects of the film or the significance of the experiences—aesthetic, ethical or metaphysical—to which it gives rise."[5] We would agree. We would also suggest that sacrifice and love, although highly inflated concepts in philosophical discussions, are of great importance. Drawing on the thought of Søren Kierkegaard and Martin Heidegger, we will argue that Malick's artistic depiction of Franz Jägerstätter in *A Hidden Life* makes a valuable contribution to existential phenomenology.

The Existential Quest for "Love's Hidden Life"

It is probably no coincidence that Malick's cinematic portrayal of the sacrifice—or martyrdom——of Franz Jägerstätter in *A Hidden Life* recalls Kierkegaard in "Love's Hidden Life and Its Recognizability by Its Fruits," the first chapter of his *Works of Love*.[6] Sinnerbrink observes: "It is Kierkegaard (rather than Heidegger or Wittgenstein) who emerges as the key thinker for the later Malick, one who has been all but neglected in the existing critical literature."[7]

Kierkegaard devotes his *Works of Love* to the "double commandment of love" in the Gospel: " 'Love the Lord your God with all your heart and with all your soul and with all your mind.' This is the first and greatest commandment. And the second is like it. 'Love your neighbor as yourself.' All the Law and Prophets hang on these two commandments" (Matt. 22:37–40). When it comes to love, what is most important and challenging, according to Kierkegaard, is to love, regardless of the object of love, in a so-called non-preferential/neighborly way, which includes loving anyone who is "near" to us in the geographical rather than emotional sense. The emphasis thus lies on the imperative "Love!" (you shall love).[8] This is also why it is a commandment. This is, in Kierkegaard's view, the "non-preferential love" (neighborly love) that assumes self-denial even to the point of sacrifice and seeing the other "through" God. Neighborly love sees the "I" and the other "I" thanks to God, who is the middle term between me and my neighbor.[9] This love is the one commanded by God and it is therefore also higher than the "preferential/erotic love" of the friend, the beloved, the relative, which is driven by emotions, passions, and desires. Kierkegaard sees a problem with preferential love: it is a corrupted form of the self-love that seeks to satisfy one's own needs and expectations; it does not see the other as the other "I" but only as a mirror of my own "I." Kierkegaard explains, "Erotic love and friendship are related to passion, but all passion, whether it attacks or defends itself, sights in one way only, either/or: 'Either I exist and am the highest, or I do not exist at all, either all or nothing.' "[10] Kierkegaard contends that true love contains the transformative element of eternity: it purifies us, perfects us, and draws us closer to God. Contrary to preferential love, which is driven by passions and emotions and directs us only to ourselves, true love is driven by charity, is completely self-denying, and enables us to see the other. And whereas erotic love is essentially reciprocal and always seeks reassurance, true love loves for the sake of loving and seeks no reward. In erotic love, we project our needs and expectations onto the other, who does likewise; true love sees the other through the middle term of God, who is pure love. True love is self-emptying, self-denying, and sacrificial. Kierkegaard sees an essential qualitative difference between non-preferential and preferential love: the two forms of love are, in fact, mutually exclusive.[11]

Kierkegaard also suggests that unlike preferential love, true love has a transformative element. According to the double commandment of love, every Christian is responsible for loving the other and loving God. Kierkegaard is convinced, however, that if one loves the other fully, there is no place for God. (Breaking off his engagement to Regine Olsen illustrates this point quite clearly.) One way or another, it would seem natural to use this Kierkegaardian preference for non-preferential love as the hermeneutical key to reading Malick's account of Jägerstätter's sacrifice, but this is not quite what happens in the movie.

Two possible objections to Kierkegaard's harsh attitude toward preferential love immediately present themselves. First, theologically, and according to Genesis 1:27, human beings were created in the image of God not as individuals but as man and woman. The image of God is therefore made of two parts that create a complete picture only when joined together.[12] Secondly, philosophically, preferential love is not necessarily selfish, just as non-preferential love is not always free of preferences. Ultimately, contrary to Kierkegaard's conviction, Malick suggests, and we will argue, that the two forms of love are far from being mutually exclusive. And notably, such an argument can be made not despite the original Kierkegaardian inspiration but rather because of it.

Although *Works of Love* may be the primary source for understanding love in Kierkegaard's philosophy (and moreover, one written under his own name), *Fear and Trembling*, and above all the merman narrative, is key to acquiring a more complex picture.[13] In Kierkegaard's interpretation, the merman is a sea demon who is looking to seduce a young girl called Agnes. However, unlike all the girls before her who were seduced and lost at sea, Agnes, through her innocence, overcomes the demonic powers of the merman, and instead of drowning Agnes, the merman changes his mind and brings her safely home. Kierkegaard's use of the merman narrative serves to illustrate the nature of harmful diabolic passions, which may nevertheless be subjugated and overcome by true charitable love.[14]

We are confronted, therefore, with striking inconsistencies in Kierkegaard's account of preferential love as presented in *Works of Love* and *Fear and Trembling*.[15] In her passionate scholarly dialogue with Kierkegaard, Sharon Krishek insists that preferential and non-preferential love are indeed not mutually exclusive: "One can love one's beloved 'above all others' and yet be sensitive and responsible and caring for one's neighbor and help him in his needs."[16] The different natures of preferential and non-preferential love mean that the one does not in truth influence the other. Even the terms preferential and non-preferential can be misleading: both forms of love are in one sense preferential, as neighborly love is itself driven by feelings for another person because of, say, their poverty, or other lack or misfortune. Insisting, therefore, that love (commitment, charity) toward our neighbor is not driven by feelings and emotions implies that we are not seeing neighborly love in all its complexity.[17]

Krishek suggests replacing the terms "non-preferential" and "preferential" with "neighborly" and "romantic" and describing moves of love along the lines of the moves of faith described in *Fear and Trembling*: "Romantic love should be modelled in the shape of Kierkegaardian faith—namely, in that of the paradoxical double movement of resignation and repetition."[18]

Such resignation and repetition (which equate, respectively, to self-denial and affirmation of the self) both present themselves when a person has to face the loss of a loved one. First, the knight of love empties himself or herself and resigns. This is not a choice: it has been commanded, and the command has come from transcendence. Abraham is commanded to sacrifice his son Isaac as a burnt offering (Gen. 22:1). Against this command, however, goes the double command of love. This presents a dilemma: disobey God or sacrifice our loved one (in Abraham's case, commit pedicide). How are we to understand and indeed resolve this? The commandment says, "You shall love." We love God and we love the person we are about to lose. However, we love the person within our love for God because God is the middle term. If this were indeed the case, it would be a sorrowful and hopeless love because even though we would still love God we would nevertheless lose the beloved person. Sorrowful love includes only the first step of resignation and not the second step of repetition.[19] To prevent such a state, we should always remain open to the possibility that God gives us our beloved back (Isaac) or gives us someone else to love (Job and his new family). Ultimately, therefore, being a knight of faith involves remaining open to the possibility that God will not in fact ask for the sacrifice. This move is called repetition. It differs from recollection, which remains directed toward the past or only existed in daydreaming about the beloved.[20] Repetition is a real state in one's life, a real move of love that believes that God gives back, that God takes seriously our human condition, our finitude, our bodily needs and emotions, and our need for the support, sympathy, and understanding of someone we love.

Neighborly and romantic love as a realization of proper self-love (which is not selfish but draws us closer to God) must happen in two movements of the self: denial and affirmation.[21] Being constructively critical of Kierkegaard, we can say with Krishek that when Kierkegaard talks about love, he sees only the first move, that of self-denial, which functions indeed as the transformative element and directs our love toward eternity. Kierkegaard forgets, however, to include the move of self-affirmation, which embraces our embodiment and human finitude. This second move also gives place to our needs and desires, accepts them, and rejoices in them; in short, such needs and desires make us human.[22]

Parallel moves to the moves of faith take place in the moves of love. To prevent selfish love, the knight of love first empties himself or herself. This is the move of self-denial. However, to avoid staying in the realm of the past, or of dreams, the knight must be ready to embrace embodiment, to be open to the possibility that the love may become real. According to Kierkegaard, true "knighthood" is to find one's way back to presence and to the real world, to face one's situation, in which one is rarely alone but is usually in relation to someone else. The true knight, according to Kierkegaard's exposition of the merman story, does not seek refuge in escapism but invests all their strength and passion into facing responsibility to the other.[23]

Malick's *A Hidden Life* sketches a story based on the true events of the final years of Franz Jägerstätter, an Austrian farmer, husband, and father whose happy life was brought to a premature end by the onset of the Second World War.[24] But where does Franz Jägerstätter, a martyr of faith and conscience beatified by the Catholic Church, fit into Kierkegaard's exposition of love? Franz's decision was broadly disapproved of, even at the time, by the Church.[25] It was a scandal—and for many remains so—that a devoted father and husband (and a good citizen of Austria) should choose to be executed rather than to enlist in the army of the National Socialists. The family had to get used to the idea not only of being fatherless (with all the practical and emotional losses that entailed) but also of suffering the inevitable shame and oppression that would be heaped upon them.[26] No one accepted Franz's decision. No one, that is, except his wife Franziska. The question remains, however, whether she truly understood that decision. Her enigmatic answer to Franz's question "Do you understand?" was "I love you!" Love is therefore the hermeneutical key, left for us by Franziska, that will help us toward an understanding of Franz's sacrifice. Not despite but because of the mutual love between Franz and his wife and family, Franz gained the courage and strength to fight evil, even though this fight resulted in his own violent death. Love that is both self-denying and self-affirming, that does not seek refuge in escapism but faces the terror of actuality, may well be the source of Franz's courage and determination to stand against evil. And yet, contrary to Kierkegaard's conviction, it is a preferential love, not a non-preferential love. We might have expected that preferential love for his wife and family would lead Franz to yield—to enlist. But this would correspond only to resignation: Franz would, in his own words, be "prolonging his life by a lie."[27] He decides, rather, to embrace the Kierkegaardian paradox and risk the move of repetition. He allows himself to fall into the hands of his executioners but firmly believes that he will meet his beloved, soon, in the kingdom of God: "Keep the commandments, and we shall see each other again soon in heaven."[28] All this was possible not despite his deep love for Franziska and their children but because of it. We argue, therefore, with the help of Malick and Krishek, that romantic love has the same transformative power as the neighborly kind.

Franz is not the only knight of faith and love, however. Franziska, too, emptied herself and accepted Franz's decision to let himself be killed rather than to be part of an evil plan for humanity. It was also Franziska who with a heavy heart opened herself to the actuality of care for the family without the beloved husband and father, without the help of the male farmer and with the disdain of the whole village.

Sacrifice for Nothing

Malick portrays Jägerstätter's death in terms of sacrifice. He was, after all, beatified by the Church as a martyr. Jacques Derrida argues that the only answer to a human society based on sacrifice is the "Here I am" of Genesis 22:1, the gift of one's own death—in other words, sacrifice.[29] How could Franz's "gift of death" change anything, however? This possibility was blatantly rejected by those in officialdom who talked to Franz—the Archbishop of Linz, the interrogators: "Your sacrifice is worth nothing"; "No one outside these walls will ever hear of it"; "Will it change anything? The world will remain the same, the war will not stop." These and other arguments were used to convince Franz that his decision not to take part in evil would not help good to prevail. Franz would not retreat, however, and chose to bear the consequences.

Just as clear as the allusion to Kierkegaard is a link to Heidegger, this time in the very title of the film. The hiddenness of *A Hidden Life* evokes *die Verborgenheit*. In *Being and Time*,[30] Heidegger associates hiddenness with the misconception that sees being as useful for something, as having a goal, as being a kind of equipment—the hammer "ready-to-hand."

In times of war, being, one's life, becomes managed, a cog in the machine[31]; life-existence becomes degraded to a thing among other things. It is, paradoxically, Heidegger's concept of sacrifice, developed later by his apprentice Jan Patočka, that seeks to break with this logic of technological rationality and the objectification of being. Heidegger juxtaposes calculating and essential ways of thinking: the former is directed toward effects, results, outcomes; the latter, not concerned primarily with entities and their purposefulness, thinks of something that is not an entity. Essential thinking is, paradoxically, concerned with no-thing, *nothing*.

This nothing stands at the center of sacrifice: "The sacrifice in which the human essence expends itself is motivated by the preservation of the dignity of being."[32] To put it another way, sacrifice as Heidegger understands it tolerates no calculation, utility, or usefulness. Whether the goals be noble or humble matters not. The point is that sacrifice concerns not calculation but revelation.[33]

Patočka unfolds Heidegger's intuition: "The experience of sacrifice, however, is now one of the most powerful experiences of our epoch, so powerful and definitive that humankind for the most part has not managed to come to terms with it and flees from it precisely into a technical understanding of being that promises to exclude this experience and for which there exists nothing like a sacrifice, only the utilization of resources."[34] Wars, totalitarian regimes, anti-totalitarianism, revolutions, counterrevolutions, and many other kinds of causes are obsessed with the language of sacrifice. And in their respective acts, they do not hesitate to sacrifice countless souls for something. The simple English word *sacrifice* does not, however, express the ambiguity, the double meaning, inherent in the German *Opfer*, which holds together the ideas of both sacrifice and victim. Confusion may quickly arise because many who are sacrificed for something, be it nation, homeland, peace, or a better world, are in fact victims, even though they may understand their victimization in terms of a sacrificial act.

All of this raises a number of questions: What is authentic sacrifice? What is the experience of sacrifice truly about? What is the meaning of this radical and irreversible act of self-surrender and self-abandonment?

In the context of myths and religion, its original *Sitz im Leben*, sacrifice is any act of intentional deprivation that is designed to strengthen a relationship to divine powers, to supernatural and superior forces—to God or gods. Sacrifice is the realization of a gain through renunciation.

A Hidden Life of Love | 327

What one possesses is given up in order to increase what one possesses, whether materially or spiritually.[35]

Heidegger and Patočka do not completely disregard the religious experience of sacrifice. They accept that the economic exchange popularly understood by religion, especially Christianity, is part of the story of sacrifice,[36] but nevertheless they direct attention to the structure of experience on the existential level. A similar movement is made by Malick. Religion is part of the picture, but to understand what is going on in the hidden life of Franz Jägerstätter, one needs to move to the phenomenological-existential level. It is not a religious motivation (whereby "religious" equates to "universal" in the Kierkegaardian sense) that drives Franz but his faithfulness to being, which manifests itself as a break with calculating thinking, the objectification of being, and the economy of exchange.[37] As a good Kierkegaardian, therefore, Malick sees Franz as the knight of faith who by his sacrifice overcomes the universal of institutionalized religion; as a good Heideggerian, he will say with Patočka: "Sacrifice means precisely drawing back from the realm of what can be managed and ordered, and an explicit relation to that which, not being anything actual itself, serves as the ground of the appearing of all that is active and in that sense rules over all."[38] This encounter with sacrifice forces us to think, and thus—to recall Heidegger—to think essentially. Sacrifice is the moment of thinking being, instead of counting and manipulating it, because sacrifice cannot be reduced to what is objective or quantifiable. Sacrifice is the opening; it opens new horizons, even horizons beyond our understanding. In this sense, in its authentic movement, sacrifice is on the one hand the revelation of authentic existence and on the other the transformation of being.

In the economy of exchange, something is sacrificed and something else is expected in return. The Nazi German state expected Franz to make the sacrifice of enlisting in the army, of going to the front and fighting for its vision of a better world: one entity (a person) is exchanged for another (a metaphysical order).[39] According to Malick, however, this is precisely what Franz Jägerstätter refuses to do. By refusing to become a commodity in an exchange of objectifying forces, a heroic instrument who resists external oppression, Franz rejects such improper sacrificial logic and accepts, in Patočka's words, authentic sacrifice.

Authentic sacrifice reveals what has been hidden or, when survival is in view, forgotten. Authentic sacrifice refuses to reduce being to a thing, a partial component of objective reality: "In giving themselves for something, they dedicate themselves to that of which it cannot be said that it 'is' something, or something objective."[40] Authentic sacrifice is indeed for *nothing*. The concept of nothing is disturbing and troublesome, however. How, if it all, can a sacrifice deprived of any positive content be contemplated? How can it be understood? *Do you understand?*

In sacrifice, at the threshold of negativity where one touches the crude facticity of finitude, nothing appears as no-thing. Sacrifice for nothing is, in objective terms, for *aucune-chose*. And it is also, in terms of graspable meaning, for nothing as *rien*, the sense to be found there ready-to-hand. However, the nothing in sacrifice is not *nihil*. It hurts. It will never be healed. The scars will remain. And yet sacrifice for nothing reveals a certain positivity in the negative. Authentic sacrifice is revelatory in the ontological sense. It reveals something higher, something beyond logic, something we may humbly call the divine: *I love you.*

Franz's life is hidden, and remains hidden, to all others. Except, that is, to one person—his wife Franziska, who sees the revelation in the seemingly useless and senseless act of sacrifice; she sees because she loves. For only love that yields unconditionally to the other is capable of embracing sacrifice without heroism, without pathos—sacrifice for nothing, which in a certain sense contains everything.

A hidden life becomes the revelation in the act of sacrifice because it concerns truth, not of any objective kind but of being—*alétheiá*. Hence, the truth of the hidden life does not stand on its own, as Franz's truth against the world, but as the *Lichtung*, the light for the others, for those who witness the sacrifice and who carry on living and thus bear witness further.

Conclusion

Connoisseurs of Malick's work have undoubtedly noticed that in his trilogy on love—*To the Wonder*, *Knight of Cups*, and *Song to Song*—Malick clearly depicts the two faces of love as described by Kierkegaard. Lifeless and self-centered characters experience a selfish love that is little more than a projection of their unspoken needs and expectations and that fizzles out when its source, failing to nurture itself from the mutuality of the relationship, becomes exploited. Some characters try to understand love of the other as a duty: love is about "care" and "commitment." All these attempts fail because with respect to the two movements of love, self-denial and self-affirmation, there is no real determination from either side. The selfishness or "not getting" each other is probably not intentional but it is certainly devastating. Some characters in *To the Wonder* live parallel lives and are unable to genuinely "be together," thus illustrating the selfishness of Kierkegaardian preferential love.

In *A Hidden Life*, Malick overcomes the static image of preferential love from his previous films and seemingly also of Kierkegaard's depiction of preferential love in *Works of Love*. Franz and Franziska are open to self-denial and to self-affirmation. They are both acting as knights of faith and of love. Franz chooses to be executed rather than to help what he understood as evil. His decision, and the strength to carry it out, was undoubtedly influenced by his loving relationship with his wife. This love was not selfish, seeking its own satisfaction, but self-denying in the sense of truly seeing the others—his beloved Franziska and the children—and self-affirmative in embracing the bitter reality that urged his conscience to act.

Sacrifice is an act of love. The movement of love is what makes sacrifice possible, but this love transcends ethical and moral meanings. Love is not a thing, although sometimes it may be coerced and objectified. Love appears to be almost nothing. However, "this does not mean that this *nothing* does not contain *das All*, as the poet said."[41] The poet in question is Hölderin but it may just as well be Malick.

The love presented in *A Hidden Life* has little if anything in common with romantic, sentimental, emotional posturing. Here is a movement of love that is powerful, transformative. Love as the transubstantiation of life. Love as giving oneself away, not as giving something or giving for something else but as the appearance of being itself. Human finitude is a given. Human life has been decided and will end at some point. Yet the kenotic sacrifice for nothing, sacrifice as an unconditional yielding for others, transforms finitude because it reveals that this life is not a thing, or everything, but nothing as a no-thing, and that there is a greater nothing that rules over everything, namely love.

Franziska supported Franz at the crucial moment: "Do you understand?' he asks; "I love you!" she replies. She does not say "I understand" because ultimately, she may not; it is not "her battlefield." Her response—"I love you (no matter what you do)"—is the response of self-denying love.[42] Because she loves Franz, Franziska accepts his determination and picks up "her own fight." Even though her "knighthood" may from a certain perspective be even more difficult, she, too, does not seek to escape but carries on with life, raising the children and working the farm.[43] Alas, Franziska Jägerstätter has not been beatified as a knight of faith and love: her sacrifice is still to be officially recognized.

Notes

1. At least, this is Malick's interpretation. Writing to Franziska after their final meeting, Franz responds to his wife's attempts to persuade him to enlist: "Do you believe that all would go well for me if I were to tell a lie in order to prolong my life?" Jägerstätter, *Letters and Writings from Prison*, 128. We should not consider Malick's interpretation illegitimate, however, but seek to understand it. Malick studied the correspondence carefully and based his interpretation of Jägerstätter's sacrifice on what he reads there. It is apparent from Franziska's letter—dated after Franz's execution—to the priest Heinrich Kreutzberg (130–31) that she was seeking to embrace her husband's convictions. Moreover, her later care over her husband's legacy—fighting for his rehabilitation, participating in the process of his beatification—demonstrates both her devotion to him and her share in his sacrifice.

2. We interpret Jägerstätter's refusal to fight for the Nazis as "sacrifice." He might also have understood it this way himself: "How hard it must have been for our dear Lord that he had given his dear mother such great sorrow through his suffering and death! And she suffered everything out of love for us sinners. I thank our Savior that I could suffer for him and may die for him. I trust in his infinite compassion. I trust that God forgives me everything, and will not abandon me in the last hour" Jägerstätter, *Letters and Writings from Prison*, 129–30. Today, the Catholic Church considers him a "martyr of the Church." He was beatified by Pope Benedict XVI in 2007.

3. See for example Sinnerbrink, *Terrence Malick: Filmmaker and Philosopher*, 1–16; Sinnerbrink, "Love Sick: Malick's Kierkegaardian 'Weightless' Trilogy," 279–300; Hamilton " 'What Is This Love That Loves Us?,' " 1–15.

4. Sinnerbrink, "Love Sick," 279.

5. Sinnerbrink, *Terrence Malick*, 12. Sinnerbrink adds: "As an alternative to both the 'Heideggerian cinema' approach and the 'non-philosophical formalist' approach, I propose that we are better off articulating the relationship at issue as a 'hermeneutic parallelism': a productive parallel or critical exchange between philosophical ideas, themes, theories and aesthetic elements, cinematic techniques, and narrative features of Malick's films. Such an exchange can lead to new ways of thinking about both films and philosophy."

6. Kierkegaard, *Works of Love*, 5.

7. Sinnerbrink, *Terrence Malick*, 162.

8. Kierkegaard, *Works of Love*, 24. See also "Love Sick," 29, where Sinnerbrink refers to Malick's paraphrases of Kierkegaard in the words of Father Quintana's sermon in *To the Wonder*: "You shall love, whether you like it or not."

9. Kierkegaard, *Works of Love*, 58. See also Westphal, *Levinas and Kierkegaard in Dialogue*, 70.

10. Kierkegaard, *Works of Love*, 45. Westphal wonders: "Levinas and Kierkegaard agree in emphasizing that neighbor love runs counter to our natural self-love. But if it is indeed a heteronomous call to self-denial and self-sacrifice, if it overrides our spontaneous preferences, if it is contrary to our *conatus essendi*, how, if at all, is it possible, even imperfectly?" and offers the following answer: "Only by being loved do we develop the capacity to love, and Kierkegaard's God is fully personal enough for his answer to be 'We love because he first loved us' (1 John 4:19)." Westphal, *Levinas and Kierkegaard in Dialogue*, 71–72.

11. Kierkegaard, *Works of Love*, 58.

12. Interestingly, when Kierkegaard speaks of the creation of human beings, he refers only to the so-called second creation narrative in Genesis 2:20c–23, where woman is created from man. See Kierkegaard, *Works of Love*, 154. The narrative, which undermines the image of God as both man and woman, has been widely used in Christian tradition to reinforce the hierarchical structure and patriarchalism of Western society.

13. Krishek, *Kierkegaard on Faith and Love*, 5, 45.

14. Kierkegaard develops the idea of what happens next with both the merman (when he gives up his powers and his way of life of seducing young girls) and Agnes (who loves the merman and wants to be with him). See Kierkegaard, *Fear and Trembling*, 94–102.

15. There is inconsistency not only between the interpretations of love in *Works of Love* and *Fear and Trembling* but even within *Works of Love* itself. See Kierkegaard, *Works of Love*, 44–90.

16. Krishek, *Kierkegaard on Faith and Love*, 123.

17. Krishek, 109–37.

18. Krishek, 12–13.

19. Krishek, 59–70. We could argue, from a reading of Kierkegaard's autobiography (specifically the above-mentioned break with his fiancée), that he allowed himself only this first step of resignation.

20. Kierkegaard, *Repetition*, 125–76; See also Krishek, *Kierkegaard on Faith and Love*, 20–45.

21. Krishek, 159.

22. Krishek, 122–29.

23. "For the Merman to be really saved, and for their faith-full love to abide, he, too, needs to be a knight of faith. And being a knight of faith means to 'take refuge in the paradox.' It is to resign and through resignation—by virtue of his

"absolute relation to the absolute" (namely his relationship with the infinite, with God)—to return to finitude, to return to Agnes." Krishek, 186.

24. See Franziska's letter to the priest Heinrich Kreutzberg: Jägerstätter, *Letters and Writings from Prison*, 184.

25. After the Anschluss of 1938, the Catholic Church in Austria came under heavy pressure from the Nazi regime. Parish priests and bishops who were openly critical of Nazism were threatened. Some, such as Bishop Gföllner (the Archbishop of Linz) and Franz's parish priest Fr Karobath, were posted elsewhere. The offending clergy were replaced by less outspoken colleagues. Fr Karobath's replacement Fr Fürthauer, and the new Archbishop of Linz, Bishop Fliesserand, tried to persuade Franz to enlist out of duty to his family. The general attitude of church leaders at the time was that individuals who obey the orders of the government cannot be held personally accountable, but this all changed with the Second Vatican Council, particularly the document *Gaudium et Spes* and its emphasis on the conscience of the individual. One of the sources for this document was the story of Franz Jägestätter, introduced to the Council by Thomas Roberts, a Jesuit archbishop, and based on research by the American sociologist Gordon Zahn. Jägerstätter's sacrifice (martyrdom) and the Catholic Church's clear change of thinking culminated in Jägestätter's beatification. See Jim Forest, introduction to *Franz Jägerstätter*, ix–xxviii.

26. "While the widows of soldiers won the widespread sympathy in Austrians, Franziska was shunned. Not only had she lost her husband, but many of her neighbors turned their back on her. Some blamed Franz's death on her overzealous religious influence. . . . Few offered her the help so badly needed after Franz's death." Forest, introduction to *Franz Jägerstätter*, xxviii.

27. Jägerstätter, *Letters and Writings*, 128.

28 Jägerstätter, 130.

29. Derrida, *The Gift of Death*, 2, 51, 71. See also: "What a difference there is between the play of feelings, drives, inclinations, and passions, in short, the play of the powers of immediacy, that celebrated glory of poetry in smiles and tears, in desire or in want—what a difference between this and the earnestness of eternity, the earnestness of the commandment in spirit and truth, in honesty and self-denial." Kierkegaard, *Works of Love*, 25.

30. Inwood, *A Heidegger Dictionary*, 72–73.

31. See Jägestätter's own reference to the instrumentalization of people and the massification of society for the purposes of war: "I want also to tell you that there is a farm woman in Enns who has not allowed her children to join the Hitler Youth. This is a rarity. Yet one does hear that there are people in other places who are not being pulled along by the crowd." Jägerstätter, *Letters and Writings*, 84.

32. Vedder, "Giving Oneself Up: Heidegger's Notion of Sacrifice," 369.

33. Heidegger, *Being and Time*, 237.

34. Jan Patočka, "The Dangers of Technicization in Science," 20.

35. See for example Bataille, *Theory of Religion*; Burkert, *Homo Necans*; Hubert and Mauss, *Sacrifice: Its Nature and Function Sacrifice*; Smith, *The Religion of the Semites*.
36. Koci, "Sacrifice for Nothing," 594–617.
37. Forest interprets in a similar vein:

> Franz Jägerstätter was a solitary witness. He died with no expectation that his sacrifice would make any difference to anyone. He knew that, for his neighbors, the refusal of army service was incomprehensible—an act of folly, a sin against his family, his community, and even his church, which had called on no one to refuse military service. Franz knew that, beyond his family and community, his death would go entirely unnoticed and have no impact on the Nazi movement or hasten the end of the war. He would be soon forgotten. (Forest, introduction to *Franz Jägerstätter*, xxv)

38. Patočka, "The Dangers of Technicization in Science," 17.
39. The usual subject of interest in the phenomenology of sacrifice is precisely this phenomenon of "sacrifice for the homeland." See, for example, Patočka, *Heretical Essays in the Philosophy of History*; Dodd, "Philosophy in Dark Times," 64–91; Tava, "Sacrifice as a Political Problem," 71–96.
40. Patočka, "The Dangers of Technicization in Science," 21.
41. Patočka, "Čtyři semináře k problému Evropy," 413.
42. Kierkegaard, *Works of Love*, 44–90.
43. By emphasizing Franziska's "knighthood," we are not seeking to confirm the stereotypical role of women as housekeepers and mothers. The respective forms of sacrifice of Franz and Franziska Jägestätter are a product of the time in which they lived. We insist, however, that the principles we present here—self-denial, self-affirmation, responsibility—are universal and should be applied to people equally regardless of gender.

Dedication: This article was written with the generous financial support of the Austrian Science Fund (FWF) for the project "Woman without a Name: Gender Identity in Sacrificial Stories" [M2947-G].

Bibliography

Bataille, Georges. *Theory of Religion*. Translated by Robert Hurley. New York: Zone, 1992.
Burkert, Walter. *Homo Necans: The Anthropology of Ancient Greek Sacrificial Ritual and Myth*. Berkeley: University of California Press, 1983.

Derrida, Jacques. *The Gift of Death*. Translated by David Willis. Chicago: University of Chicago Press, 1996.
Dodd, James. "Philosophy in Dark Times." In *Religion, War and the Crisis of Modernity: A Special Issue Dedicated to the Philosophy of Jan Patočka. The New Yearbook of Phenomenology and Phenomenological Philosophy*, edited by Ludger Hagedorn and James Dodd, 64–91. London: Routledge, 2015.
Forest, Jim. Introduction to *Franz Jägerstätter: Letters and Writings*, ix–xxviii. Edited by Erna Putz. Maryknoll, NY: Orbis Books, 2009.
Hamilton, Julie M. "'What Is This Love That Loves Us?': Terrence Malick's *To the Wonder* as a Phenomenology of Love." *Religions* 76, no. 7 (2016): 1–15.
Heidegger, Martin. *Being and Time*. Translated by John Macquerrie and Edward Robinson. Oxford: Blackwell, 1962.
Hubert, Henri, and Marcel Mauss. *Sacrifice: Its Nature and Function*. Chicago: University of Chicago Press, 1964.
Inwood, Michael. *A Heidegger Dictionary*. Oxford: Blackwell, 1999.
Jägerstätter, Franz. *Letters and Writings from Prison*. Edited by Erna Putz. Maryknoll, NY: Orbis Books, 2009.
Kierkegaard, Søren. *Fear and Trembling*. In *Kierkegaard's Writings Vol. 6*, edited by Edna H. Hong and Howard V. Hong, 1–124. Princeton, NJ: Princeton University Press, 2019.
———. *Repetition*. In *Kierkegaard's Writings Vol. 6*, edited by Edna H. Hong and Howard V. Hong, 125–176. Princeton, NJ: Princeton University Press, 2019.
———. *Works of Love*. In *Kierkegaard's Writings Vol. 16*, edited by Edna H. Hong and Howard V. Hong. Princeton, NJ: Princeton University Press, 1995.
Koci, Martin. "Sacrifice for Nothing: The Movement of Kenosis in Jan Patočka's Thought." *Modern Theology* 33, no. 4 (2017): 594–617.
Krishek, Sharon. *Kierkegaard on Faith and Love*. Cambridge: Cambridge University Press, 2009.
Patočka, Jan. "Čtyři semináře k problému Evropy." In *Sebrané spisy Jana Patočky Vol. 3. Péče o duši*, edited by Ivan Chvatík and Pavel Kouba, 374–423. Praha: Oikoymenh, 2002.
———. "The Dangers of Technicization in Science." In *Religion, War and the Crisis of Modernity: A Special Issue Dedicated to the Philosophy of Jan Patočka. The New Yearbook of Phenomenology and Phenomenological Philosophy*, edited by Ludger Hagedorn and James Dodd, 13–22. London: Routledge, 2015.
———. *Heretical Essays in the Philosophy of History*. Chicago: Open Court, 1996.
Robertson Smith, William. *The Religion of the Semites*. London: Black, 1907.
Sinnerbrink, Robert. "Love Sick: Malick's Kierkegaardian 'Weightless' Trilogy." *Paragraph* 42, no. 3 (2019): 279–300.
———. *Terrence Malick: Filmmaker and Philosopher*. London: Bloomsbury, 2019.
Tava, Francesco. "Sacrifice as a Political Problem: Jan Patočka and Sacred Sociology." *Metodo* 6, no. 2 (2018): 71–96.

Vedder, Ben. "Giving Oneself Up: Heidegger's Notion of Sacrifice." *Archivio di Filosofia* 76, no. 1/2 (2008): 369–76.
Westphal, Merold. *Levinas and Kierkegaard in Dialogue*. Bloomington: Indiana University Press, 2008.

Chapter 17

Bleeding Hearts

Edith Stein, Franz Jägerstätter, and Martyrdom

DONALD WALLENFANG

ἀλλὰ λήμψεσθε δύναμιν ἐπελθόντος τοῦ ἁγίου πνεύματος ἐφ' ὑμᾶς, καὶ ἔσεσθέ μου μάρτυρες ἔν τε Ἰερουσαλὴμ καὶ ἐν πάσῃ τῇ Ἰουδαίᾳ καὶ Σαμαρείᾳ καὶ ἕως ἐσχάτου τῆς γῆς. καὶ ταῦτα εἰπὼν βλεπόντων αὐτῶν ἐπήρθη καὶ νεφέλη ὑπέλαβεν αὐτὸν ἀπὸ τῶν ὀφθαλμῶν αὐτῶν.

"But you will receive power when the holy Spirit comes upon you, and you will be my witnesses in Jerusalem, throughout Judea and Samaria, and to the ends of the earth." When (Jesus) had said this, as they were looking on, he was lifted up, and a cloud took him from their sight.

—Acts 1:8

It has been said that "everybody wants to go to heaven, but nobody wants to die." Electing the topic of martyrdom comes with an inevitable degree of pretentiousness. There is the false pretense that the author is somehow already a martyr or is ready to become a martyr at any moment or is somehow intimately acquainted with martyrdom. I must confess that neither am I a martyr, nor do I feel ready to become a martyr at any moment, nor am I intimately acquainted with martyrdom. Even the word *martyrdom* feels unusual for me to type since I have typed it so infrequently. In fact, martyrdom somewhat terrifies me. It is a limit-experience to the first degree. It is the highest form of persecution. It is a sudden and premature end of life on this earth with no certain knowledge of what happens next. Martyrdom would involve a high measure of pain and distress, as well as a necessary unnatural resistance to the innate *conatus essendi* ("struggle of being") that seems to dominate my life. Above all, as a married man raising six children, I lean away from the prospect of martyrdom because I would not want to depart from my wife and children so suddenly. Nevertheless, I have chosen the topic of martyrdom because I am convinced that it reveals the heights of moral perfection, the furthest threshold of bravery, and the exorbitant capacities of love. The truth is that I want to strive after this vocation to martyrdom even if I do not want to strive after it.

In his book on the life of Saint Damien of Molokai (also known as Father Damien the Leper), entitled *White Martyrdom*, John Henaghan writes that "there is always a strange fascination in pondering the story of heroic unselfish lives—something which, while lifting us up to a higher plane, and coming with an appeal to the heroic in ourselves, bids us wish that even though only in some far-off way, it may be our privilege to claim kinship and brotherhood with them. Courage, in no matter what form shown, always appeals to men."[1] Yes, the courage of the martyrs appeals to me. I would like to be in their company in heaven in some bright future day beyond the clouds, and it seems fitting that I live like they did in order to be worthy of being in their company. Jesus Christ, the leader and perfecter of all Christian martyrdom, was himself a martyr. To dare to follow Jesus implies a supernatural bending of the will to become docile before the painful prospect of persecution, all the way to martyrdom. Yet even for Jesus, "for the sake of the joy that lay before him he endured the cross, despising its shame, and has taken his seat at the right of the throne of God" (Heb. 12:2). In genuine Christian martyrdom, death itself is not the goal, but rather life. Tragedy is not the end, but rather triumph. Absurdity is not the final conclusion, but rather victory and vindication. Jesus endured the cross and despised its shame not for the sake of sorrow but for the sake of joy in his resurrection and the future resurrection of all his beloved sons and daughters who would dare to follow him.

The book of Revelation paints a vivid scene of the martyrs awaiting their exoneration:

When he broke open the fifth seal, I saw underneath the altar the souls of those who had been slaughtered because of the witness (μαρτυρία) they bore to the word of God. They cried out in a loud voice, "How long will it be, holy and true master, before you sit in judgment and avenge our blood on the inhabitants of the earth?" Each of them was given a white robe, and they were told to be patient a little while longer until the number was filled of their fellow servants and brothers who were going to be killed as they had been. (Rev. 6:9–11)

In the cry of the martyrs, justice has not gone missing. There remains the anticipation of righteousness restored. The image of the altar calls to mind the unity of the martyr's self-sacrifice and that of Jesus in the Cenacle and on the cross. The white robe signals the purity of the baptismal garment and the first sacrament through which a person is plunged into the death of Christ and raised up to new life in him (Rom. 6:10–23). Beneath the altar, the souls of the martyrs are called to a patient reprieve, awaiting the consummation of God the Father's will across the cosmos. For the martyrs, their blood itself is the witness of the deepest convictions of their hearts. They testify in and through the birth of their own blood into the light of day. It is a kind of sanguine transfusion that beckons to anyone who would take notice and become a new witness to the truth that alone is worth giving up one's life to be borne aloft by its exclusive power to save.[2]

Martyrdom is the greatest witness because it requires the sacrifice of everything one has, including one's life, not in suicidal madness that is intentionally destructive of oneself and of other people but through an innocent acquiescence to the violent aggression of the executioners who are truculently opposed to the truth that actually sets us free.[3] Martyrdom presents a paradoxical portrait of human greatness precisely because an other-than-human motive is on display in the voluntary self-divestment of the person. Dorothy Day attests to this power beyond mere nature in quoting one of her spiritual mentors, Fr. Pacifique Roy, who would insist that followers of Christ "had to be guided by the folly of the Cross . . . the 'supernatural motive.'"[4] Martyrdom points to a power beyond the power of the flesh. Otherwise, why would someone give up their body without a motive that transcended the body? Martyrdom is the pinnacle of human achievement precisely because it cannot be achieved by a human. Therefore, martyrdom is the greatest testimony to divinity because no merely natural explanation can be found. In his chapter "Political Holiness: A Profile," Jon Sobrino quotes from a homily of Saint Oscar Romero: " 'I believe, brothers, that the saints were the most ambitious people. This is my ambition for all of you and for myself: that we may be great, ambitiously great, because we are images of God and we cannot be content with mediocre greatness' (Mons. Romero 23.9.1979)."[5] And Saint Oscar Romero became a martyr himself. This "holy ambition" exceeds the *ambitus* of finitude and stretches across the facade of nature and only nature. Martyrdom is the land of the saints that traverses the bridge of the cross between heaven and earth, where nature is recognized as creation, and creation is perceived as proceeding toward redemption.

The present tentative chapter on martyrdom will feature four related sections: (1) Christian Martyrdom: Introduction to a Concept, (2) Blessed Franz Jägerstätter and Being-Beyond-the-Clouds, (3) Saint Edith Stein and Being-for-the-Other, and (4) Saturated Meaning: Testimony to Absolute Trinitarian Personhood. The first section will define the martyr more precisely, especially that of the Christian martyr. The second section will comment on the peculiar form of the martyr portrayed in Terrence Malick's film *A Hidden Life* in the figure of Franz Jägerstätter (August Biehl). The third section will compare and contrast the life and martyrdom of Saint Edith Stein to that of Blessed Franz Jägerstätter, inevitably drawing the sharp distinction between a Heideggerian being-toward-death and a Levinasian and Carmelite being-for-the-other. And the final section will synthesize the entire chapter by contemplating the philosophical concept of the absolute in relation to the doctrine of the most Holy Trinity as revealed through Jesus of Nazareth. In sum, the reader will be invited to meditate on the meaning of martyrdom in tonalities both old and new.

Christian Martyrdom: Introduction to a Concept

Who is the martyr? "The first element is that of suffering, whether it be in the form of disabilities or death. The second element—and perhaps the more important element—is that the suffering should be consciously regarded as a witness to God. By the suffering, the victim gives witness (μαρτύριον) to God; he gives witness that he is a devotee of God alone. This aspect we term the zealot-theme . . . every martyr is a prophet."[6] Suffering as witness to God: this is the essence of martyrdom. Suffering as pain, as loss, as torment, as deprivation, as disability. In the Pauline literature of the Christian New Testament, several forms of persecution are mentioned or alluded to: the arena (death through combat with gladiators or wild beasts), crucifixion, the sword, stoning, burning, imprisonment, expulsion (excommunication), and corporal punishment.[7] All such experiences are at the limit of human capacity and the furthest thing from natural desire. However, in the early church, "persecution was no longer something to be regretted or avoided, but to be expected as part of the age in which the Christian was living, and to be accepted with rejoicing."[8] If Jesus the Lord and King is a martyr, why should his followers not be prepared for a similar courageous destiny?

Everybody wants to go to heaven, but nobody wants to die. No one, it seems, spontaneously desires to suffer martyrdom. No one wants to die amid tortures and insults, or even simply to experience physical pain. Yet countless Christians, from the first generations in Palestine, Greece, and Rome, willingly accepted martyrdom and went to their deaths with a confidence reminiscent of the final Beatitude: "Blessed are those who are persecuted for righteousness' sake . . . Rejoice and be glad, for your reward is great in heaven" (Matt. 5:10–12).[9] So many followers of Jesus suffered martyrdom in the early centuries of Christianity that the church of this era was called the *Ecclesia martyrum*, that is, "the Church of the martyrs." Much blood was shed in union with the precious Blood of the Lamb, Jesus the Christ, out of an invincible love for him and the missionary passion to desire to be his witness to the end. Saint Paul expresses this sentiment enigmatically in his letter to the Colossians: "Now I rejoice in my sufferings for your sake, and in my flesh I am filling up what is lacking in the affliction of Christ on behalf of his body, which is the church, of which I am a minister in accordance with God's stewardship (οἰκονομία) given to me to bring to completion for you the word of God, the mystery hidden from ages and from generations past" (Col. 1:24–26). According to Saint Paul, the divine plan (οἰκονομία) is constituted by an economy (οἰκονομία) of suffering—the work of responsibility (οἰκονομία) that redeems. Genuine disciples of Jesus must share in his work of responsibility that has the power to redeem what seemed to have been lost.

According to the law of Moses, "The life of the flesh is in the blood: and I have given it to you upon the altar to make an atonement for your souls: for it is the blood that maketh an atonement for the soul" (Lev. 17:11). In a similar way, the author of the letter to the Hebrews writes, "According to the law almost everything is purified by blood, and without the shedding of blood there is no forgiveness" (Heb. 9:22). Why this strange economy of bloodshed? The decisive question is, whose blood is being shed? Is it my own or that of someone else? It is obvious that the law of survival inscribed in biological nature is predation. Each individual being lives by stealing away the life of another individual being. In a similar way, for the ancient Israelites, physical and spiritual life was promoted through the atonement process of animal sacrifice. Through the economy of sacrifice, absolution of sin was granted. Though families had to sacrifice their choice livestock, it was the blood of animals that was shed on behalf of people. The onus of guilt was transferred from the human perpetrator of sin and instead placed on the animal. By displacing the guilt associated with personal and communal sin onto the life of the sacrificed animal, atonement between the Lord and the Israelites, as well as between the Israelites themselves, was accomplished. Guilt was "scapegoated" from the human to the animal, clearing the human of persistent guilt.[10] The sincerity of contrition was evinced in the death of the animal and the visible flow of blood into the light of day.

In the case of the crucifixion of Jesus, however, he does not transfer his own guilt to an animal, not only because he is sinless and has no actual guilt but also because he takes the economy of sacrificial substitution upon himself. He himself is the voluntary sacrifice of universal atonement:

> For to this you have been called, because Christ also suffered for you, leaving you an example that you should follow in his footsteps. . . . When he was insulted, he returned no insult; when he suffered, he did not threaten; instead, He handed himself over to the one who judges justly. He himself bore our sins in his body upon the cross, so that, free from sin, we might live for righteousness. By his wounds you have been healed. For you had gone astray like sheep, but you have now returned to the shepherd and guardian of your souls. (1 Peter 1:21-25)

Jesus is "the Lamb of God who takes away the sin of the world" (1 John 1:29). He is at once sheep and shepherd. Jesus witnesses to the truth that he is—truth in the flesh—through the sacrificial inversion of his flesh, shedding his blood to prove his undying love for us. No suspicion can haunt a love self-attested through voluntary suffering on behalf of the beloved. Instead of relocating the onus of responsibility from himself to another, he assumes everyone's responsibility (and irresponsibility) in his own redemptive and righteous responsibility. Jesus is martyr par excellence—witness to truth as personal truth incarnate. It is important that the martyrdom of Jesus did not take place on Good Friday alone but on every day of his life, from the moment of his conception in the womb of the Blessed Virgin Mary all the way to his resurrection and ascension that set a permanent seal on relentless transformative power of martyrdom. "'There is red martyrdom and white martyrdom,' wrote an Irish monk one day on his parchment scroll. 'Red martyrdom is achieved when one gives up his life for a sacred cause, white martyrdom is the daily dying to oneself.'"[11] Jesus lived both white martyrdom every day and night of his earthly life, as well as red martyrdom at the place called Golgotha. The true martyr is the one who enters willingly into white martyrdom on a daily basis, thereby setting the stage for the final act of red martyrdom should it arrive suddenly.

Blessed Franz Jägerstätter and Being-Beyond-the-Clouds

Those familiar with the background of Terrence Malick know that he wrote an English translation of Martin Heidegger's 1929 book *Vom Wesen des Grundes*. Without going into much detail about Malick's Heideggerian influence, or how this influence turns up in his film *A Hidden Life*, it is enough to state the obvious: one of the most noticeable Heideggerian philosophical themes on display in *A Hidden Life* is his central concept of being-toward-death. The entire film, from start to finish, fixates on Franz Jägerstätter's movement toward the guillotine that the audience knows is his inevitable fate from the beginning. In her autobiography, *The Long Loneliness*, Dorothy Day recalls the following reflection of Plato: "Other people are not likely to be aware that those who pursue philosophy aright study nothing but dying and being dead. But if this be true, it would be absurd to be eager for nothing but this all their lives, and then be troubled when that came for which they had all along been eagerly practicing."[13] Franz is portrayed in the film as the paradigmatic philosopher of death and even seems to exhibit an eagerness for fulfilling his contemplation of mortality in the real. For this section of the chapter, I would like to muse on several meaningful lines from *A Hidden Life* in order to examine the thick Heideggerian portrayal of Franz in his being-toward-death.

Throughout the film, there is a gradual intensification of conscience, conviction, and testimony. The narrative operates as a kind of "free fall" from above the clouds, commencing with Frau Franziska "Fani" Jägerstätter's

(Valerie Pacher) recollection of the happy and carefree early years of hers and Franz's marriage when they "lived above the clouds." In other evidence, Franz was known to have said, "I could have never imagined that being married could be so wonderful." As the rising action mounts, Fani says, "The harvest comes nearer. We burned the bad weeds." The teleology of harvest includes the pruning and purification of the heart. Though the audience is braced for the final harvest of the plot, it seems that everyone around Franz criticizes his resistance the Nazi cause and the rule of Hitler. Even his local parish priest says to him, "Your sacrifice would benefit no one." There is a constant juxtaposition of the fruitful daily life Franz could be enjoying with his wife, children, extended family, and neighbors and his call to witness to the magnitude of evil embodied in the Nazi regime.

One scene that accelerates the rising action is when Nazi soldiers visit Franz's small Austrian village to collect money to support the war effort. Franz's refusal to contribute to this collection signifies his deep defiance of what he finds to be severely objectionable. The viewer is brought to the truth that renunciation and resistance begin with the small things and extend all the way to major sacrifices. In other words, red martyrdom is preceded by white martyrdom. Two symbolic discourses lend momentum to storyline. A preacher at liturgy exhorts his hearers, "Learn the lesson of the blacksmith. No matter how hard the hammer strikes, the anvil cannot—need not—strike back. The anvil outlives the hammer." This is a foreshadowing that Franz is called to live as an anvil rather than a hammer. Later on, a church painter remarks, "I paint all this suffering and I don't suffer myself. I make a living of it . . . Christ's life is a demand. . . . How can I show what I haven't lived? Someday I might have the courage to venture." Franz stands in contrast to the painter as one who exhibits the bravery to venture to suffer with Christ as far as his demands lead. Reminiscent to Fani's description of "life above the clouds," Franz, in thinking introspectively about the Nazi occupation, and even about his fear of dying in witness to the truth against this occupation, says, "We have forgotten our true fatherland." However, honest with the loneliness he feels, Franz admits, "I have no one to turn to. Nothing enters my soul." In this line, a signature existentialist motif comes into the foreground: being-toward-death, being-toward-nothing—the Heideggerian mark of human authenticity.

Fani is depicted as a constant support of virtue by living in solidarity with Franz's vocation toward his ultimate witness. She says, "If you are faithful to him, (Jesus) will be faithful to us. I believe it. We love him.

That's enough." Franz later echoes, "We have to stand up to evil. . . . You give up the idea of surviving at any price, and new light floods in." In a letter to Franz in prison, Fani writes, "Trust in the triumph of the good." Fani's daily life, too, bears witness to her solidarity with Franz as she and her sister care for the children and family farm without help from any man of the house. All the while, Franz is plagued by doubt about the sincerity of his stance. For instance, the suspicious words of prison interrogator, Captain Herder, to Franz are revelatory: "No one knows what goes on behind these walls. No one. What purpose does it serve? . . . How do you know what is good and bad? . . . Take care, my friend. The antichrist is clever. He uses a man's virtues to mislead him." Nevertheless, throughout the film, for the most part Franz is silent. "Like a sheep led to the slaughter, he opened not his mouth" (Isa. 53:7). Franz counts his words, and among his final words, spoken to Judge Lueben (Bruno Ganz), he says, "I have this feeling inside me that I cannot do what I believe is wrong." Franz seals these words with the shedding of his blood, if only seen by his executioners. And among Fani's last words of the film, presumably in prayer following the courageous death of her husband, she says, "Franz, I'll meet you there in the mountains." Their common destination in the symbolic mountains signifies a return to "life above the clouds"—the very bliss of heavenly existence where fields of wheat and children abound.

Altogether, *A Hidden Life* is a film charged with the Heideggerian theme of being-toward-death, and it leaves the viewer wondering if this was the real purpose Malick had in making the film, even more than showcasing the true story of the beatified Catholic saint, Franz Jägerstätter. Throughout the film, the viewer senses the weight of being-toward-death that presses on the soul without relief. The heroism of Franz is palpable, and the viewer is provoked to wonder what he or she would do if confronted with a similar situation. Not only did Franz Jägerstätter clearly live a life of being-toward-death, but he also lived a life of being-beyond-the-clouds. As with every work of art, the audience is left to ponder what is present and what is lacking in the production.[12] From a philosophical standpoint, especially in light of new turns in Western philosophy since Heidegger, the question may be raised whether there might be other philosophical lenses through which to view the life and death of Franz Jägerstätter. Perhaps a Levinasian being-for-the-other in contrast to a Heideggerian being-toward-death?[14] The life of another Catholic saint, Edith Stein, presents this Levinasian way of being-for-the-other to which we now will turn.

Saint Edith Stein and Being-for-the-Other

Edith Stein, also known by her religious name, Teresa Benedicta of the Cross, exemplifies a life-narrative that transcends the Heideggerian obsession with being-toward-death. Though sixteen years older than Franz Jägerstätter, Edith died in a similar manner exactly one year before Franz. On August 9, 1942, Edith was transported to the concentration camp at Auschwitz-Birkenau and was executed in a gas chamber there. Many books tell the story of Edith Stein, including her own autobiography, *Life in a Jewish Family*. Our intent here is not to recount many details of Edith's story but to focus on the peculiar form of her Carmelite way of life and death as an offering for the salvation of souls. Nevertheless, let us recall a few main facts of Edith's life for the sake of understanding the gestalt of being-for-the-other.

Born in a Jewish family on October 12, 1891, Edith was raised in the Jewish faith tradition yet became atheist into her teenage years through her twenties. She was the youngest of eleven children and her father died when she was two years old. Edith was a talented student and chose to study for a doctorate in philosophy with the founder of a new philosophical method called phenomenology. She wrote her doctoral thesis on the problem of empathy, even though she had interrupted her studies to serve as a Red Cross nurse during World War I. After having become convinced of the truth of Catholicism, especially upon reading the autobiography of Saint Teresa of Ávila, Edith was baptized at the age of thirty. She taught for eight years at a Dominican nuns' school to train young women to become teachers, and eventually she would sense a call to enter the Discalced Carmelite convent in Cologne-Lindenthal in 1933. Later she was transferred to the Carmelite convent in Echt, Netherlands. In 1942, the Dutch Bishops' Conference issued a public statement that condemned the Nazi racist program. To retaliate, the Nazi power called for the arrest of all Jewish converts to Catholicism and their deportation to concentration camps. Edith was one of these converts and would be transported to the Auschwitz-Birkenau camp, where her life was stolen by violent hate.

When we get a glimpse into the concrete spiritual and corporal life of Edith Stein, we behold a woman who lived not so much the form being-toward-death but rather being-for-the-other. Her Discalced Carmelite apostolate of vicarious suffering and contemplative prayer manifest the potential to take upon oneself the sufferings that make the other whole.

Edith sums up her self-understanding in a 1932 letter to a former student and mentee, Anneliese Lichtenberger, when she writes: "There is a vocation to suffer with Christ and thereby to cooperate with him in his work of salvation. When we are united with the Lord, we are members of the mystical body of Christ: Christ lives on in his members and continues to suffer in them. And the suffering borne in union with the Lord is his suffering, incorporated in the great work of salvation and fruitful therein." That is a fundamental premise of all religious life, above all of the life of Carmel, to stand proxy for sinners through voluntary and joyous suffering, and to cooperate in the salvation of humankind.[15]

Stein understood the hidden potency of suffering—that a person could unite her sufferings to those of Christ and thereby contribute to the universal work of salvation. Suffering united with self-donating love equals redemption. Suffering bears the remarkable paradox of yielding fruit through apparent loss. By standing proxy for sinners, a radical Carmelite contemplative, through the power of divine grace, is able to lift the world through the lever of the cross. Vicarious atonement is a real possibility due to the principle of personal mediation inscribed in the order of creation:

> This, too, is the Carmelite vocation: to pray as one of the weeping women alongside the Blessed Virgin Mary and Saint John the Apostle at the foot of the cross of Christ on Mount Golgotha. The Carmelite is reacquainted perpetually with the cross of Christ on behalf of people who are ignorant and unfamiliar with this *axis mundi* of creation redeemed. . . . The Carmelite substitutes himself or herself on behalf of those who have yet to encounter the fullness of divine revelation and their divinely appointed destiny. . . . So does the Carmelite adopt the cruciform posture of the heart, pleading before the throne of grace, alongside our Lady of Mount Carmel, for renewed outpourings of divine mercy upon all forlorn flesh. (Heb. 4:16)[16]

As a Carmelite enraptured in the mystical itinerary of self-abandonment for the sake of the other, Stein was forgetful of her own impending death because of her preoccupation with the misery and death of the other. This is a veritable inversion of the Heideggerian being-toward-death in which I am oblivious of my own death because the death of the other confronts me with so much more acuity. Stein lived this self-forgetfulness to the end as a Carmelite warrior rooted in the fertile soil of Judaism.

Saturated Meaning:
Testimony to Absolute Trinitarian Personhood

Now that the *dramatis personae* ("persons of the drama") have been considered in brief, let us draw this chapter to its conclusion with a meditation on the saturated meaning of martyrdom. And this is the first point of conclusion: as human beings, we are not merely impersonal beings-toward-death but rather persons who have the perennial potential to live as beings-toward-the-other. Both Franz and Stein embodied this being-toward-the-other, even if Malick's film seems to characterize Franz according to the preponderance of being-toward-death. My contention in this chapter is to challenge the dominant existentialist theme of death's individualized tragedy by confronting it with inversion of the self-absorbed ego by the call of the other that initiates the vocation of being-for-the-other in selfless, joyful abandonment. Being-for-the-other prays more than ponders. Being-for-the-other smiles more than sulks. Being-for-the-other hopes more than mopes. Being-for-the-other appears as a butterfly that dances through the atmosphere on its way to who knows where. "The wind blows where it wills, and you can hear the sound it makes, but you do not know where it comes from or where it goes; so it is with everyone who is born of the Spirit" (John 3:8). Being-for-the-other overcomes the languid torpor of being-toward-death inasmuch as the self is animated by the neediness of the other. At what point does my responsibility for the other run out? At no point.

In addition to the call of the other coming in the direction of the ego, the ego itself is wrested from its self-absorbed slumber according to the exigencies of conscience. Conscience gives rise to "the 'I believe that I can' that overcomes its contrary of suspicion through 'the *assurance of being oneself acting and suffering*.'"[17] Being-toward-death undergoes a moral metamorphosis to being-for-the-other thanks to the call of the other and the self-attestation of conscience as a mode of living alterity within the self. "The martyr testifies to 'something or someone which goes beyond him.' In this sense a 'criteriology of the divine' (Nabert) demonstrates the beyond of the absolute to which the martyr testifies. The martyr relinquishes his life in pointing to the beyond-himself. The martyr accepts the fate of his premature death in a personal judgment that clings to the sign of the absolute, forsaking the idols of false testimony."[18] Symbolized in the expression "life above the clouds" is the forgetfulness of self and even of the Heideggerian fourfold (*das Geviert*)—earth, sky, mortals, and divinities—that encompass the finite ego with all of its idolatrous finite concerns. Since within the call of the other is a trace of the infinite, being-for-the-other transfigures and transubstantiates the *conatus essendi* into a *dramatis persona* that pours themselves out to the point of abandonment, thereby becoming their true self precisely through self-abnegation.

The loving conviction of the martyr attests to the absoluteness of the absolute that transcends the divisibility of the ego in death. What is death if not the concrete dissolution of the ego? Because the martyr lays down their life consciously and willingly, the transcendence of the transcendentals (beauty, goodness, and truth) shines:

> The eternal law of the Good is attested through the martyrdom of the external witness to beauty, goodness, and truth, and through the martyrdom of the internal witness to the triune transcendentals. An inner yearning that is self-attested as conscience is validated and confirmed by the exterior witness who joyfully embraces and triumphs through the ordeal of truth. Conscience is witness to goodness redoubled as the Good is called into suspicion by the effigy of its shadow. Only the martyr can attest to the self-vindication of the Good that is evidenced in the scarlet blood exposed without reservation or regret to the light of day.[19]

When Fani encourages Franz with the words "If you are faithful to him, (Jesus) will be faithful to us. I believe it. We love him. That's enough. . . . Trust in the triumph of the good," she joins with the ancient character Job in a trust that extends further than the caducity of matter: "Though he slay me, yet will I trust in him: but I will maintain my own ways before him. He also shall be my salvation: for an hypocrite shall not come before him. Hear diligently my speech, and my declaration with your ears. Behold now, I have ordered my cause; I know that I shall be justified" (Job 13:15–18). Justification follows the cause of justice.

The time has come to draw this chapter to a close and I pray that you, the reader, have drawn benefit from it at least in some small way. We have considered the meaning of Christian martyrdom vis-à-vis the testimonies of Franz Jägerstätter and Edith Stein, in the end challenging the Heideggerian concept of being-toward-death by the Levinasian and Carmelite concept of being-for-the-other. I argue that both Franz and Edith incarnate the disposition of being-for-the-other, even if Terrence Malick's film underscores the perspective of being-toward-death due to the significant influence of Heidegger's work on his filmmaking. All the same, *A Hidden Life* subtly points to the meaning of martyrdom as "life above the clouds" and being-for-the-other with its frequent reference to scenes of daily home life and the white martyrdom that all authentic followers of Jesus are called to live with constancy. The irreducible personalism of the Absolute meets us every morning and evening in the fullness of God's self-revelation as Father, Son, and Holy Spirit. Even though both life and death are saturating in their magnitude of being given, the face of the other summons me to an ethical life of love and responsibility to the point of fecund abandonment. May we end by asking the provocative yet revealing question along with Dorothy Day: "When was I less by dying?"[20]

Notes

1. Henaghan, *White Martyrdom*, 5.
2. See Romans 1:16–17: "For I am not ashamed of the gospel. It is the power of God for the salvation of everyone who believes: for Jew first, and then Greek. For in it is revealed the righteousness of God from faith to faith: as it is written, 'The one who is righteous by faith will live.'"
3. See John 8:31–32: "Jesus then said to those Jews who believed in him, 'If you remain in my word, you will truly be my disciples, and you will know the truth, and the truth will set you free.'"
4. Day, *The Long Loneliness*, 247.
5. Sobrino, "Political Holiness: A Profile" in Metz and Schillebeeck, eds., *Martyrdom Today*, 21.
6. Pobee, *Persecution and Martyrdom*, 24, 28.
7. See Pobee, 1–12.
8. Frend, *Martyrdom and Persecution in the Early Church*, 63.
9. Pinckaers, *The Spirituality of Martyrdom*, 1.
10. See, for example, the scapegoat ritual performed on the Day of Atonement, as related in Leviticus 16:20–28.
11. Henaghan, *White Martyrdom*, 62.
12. Day, *The Long Loneliness*, 273.

13. For example, see Storer, "*A Hidden Life* Hides Too Much of Franz Jägerstätter's Life."
14. For more on the work of twentieth-century Jewish philosopher Emmanuel Levinas, see section "Emmanuel Levinas: Witness to Glory" in Wallenfang, *Dialectical Anatomy of the Eucharist*, 129–42.
15. Stein, *Self-Portrait in Letters*, 128.
16. Wallenfang and Wallenfang, *Shoeless*, 36.
17. Wallenfang, *Dialectical Anatomy of the Eucharist*, quoting Ricœur, *Course of Recognition*, 91; and Ricœur, *Oneself as Another*, 22–23. Cf. Ricœur, *Oneself as Another*, 22–23: "The *assurance of being oneself acting and suffering* . . . remains the ultimate recourse against all suspicion; even if it is always in some sense received from another, it still remains *self*-attestation"; and Wallenfang, *Dialectical Anatomy of the Eucharist*, 128: "Conscience then is reassured of its veracity through an ethical course of action in the world: 'living well with and for others in just institutions.' The conscious resolve to live for the cause of justice finds its footing in the self-attestation of conscience. By setting forth possible ways of being-in-the-world in relation to others, conscience rises above solipsism and thus serves as a vector to the ethical."
18. Wallenfang, *Dialectical Anatomy of the Eucharist*, 126–27.
19. Wallenfang, *Metaphysics*, 122.
20. Day, *The Long Loneliness*, 248.

Bibliography

Day, Dorothy. *The Long Loneliness*. New York: HarperOne, 1997.
Frend, W. H. C. *Martyrdom and Persecution in the Early Church: A Study of Conflict from the Maccabees to Donatus*. New York: Doubleday, 1967.
Henaghan, John. *White Martyrdom*. Milton, MA: St. Columban's, 1946.
Lange, Martin, and Reinhold Iblacker, eds. *Witnesses of Hope: The Persecution of Christians in Latin America*. Translated by William E. Jerman. Maryknoll, NY: Orbis, 1981.
Metz, Johannes-Baptist, and Edward Schillebeeckx, eds. *Martyrdom Today*. New York: Seabury, 1983.
Pinckaers, Servais. *The Spirituality of Martyrdom: To the Limits of Love*. Translated by Patrick M. Clark and Annie Hounsokou. Washington, DC: Catholic University of America Press, 2016.
Pobee, John S. *Persecution and Martyrdom in the Theology of Paul*. Sheffield: JSOT, 1985.
Ricœur, Paul. *The Course of Recognition*. Translated by David Pellauer. Cambridge, MA: Harvard University Press, 2005.

———. *Oneself as Another*. Translated by Kathleen Blamey. Chicago: University of Chicago Press, 1994.
Stein, Edith. *Der Aufbau der Menschlichen Person*. Freiburg: Herder, 1994.
———. *Essays on Woman*. Translated by Freda Mary Oben. Washington, DC: ICS, 1996.
———. *La Estructura de la Persona Humana*. Translated by José Mardomingo. Madrid: Biblioteca de Autores Cristianos, 1998.
———. *Finite and Eternal Being: An Attempt at an Ascent to the Meaning of Being*. Translated by Kurt F. Reinhardt. Washington, DC: ICS, 2002.
———. *The Hidden Life: Hagiographic Essays, Meditations, Spiritual Texts*. Translated by Waltraut Stein. Washington, DC: ICS, 1992.
———. *Knowledge and Faith*. Translated by Walter Redmond. Washington, DC: ICS, 2000.
———. *Life in a Jewish Family*. Translated by Josephine Koeppel. Washington, DC: ICS, 1986.
———. *On the Problem of Empathy*. Translated by Waltraut Stein. Washington, DC: ICS, 1989.
———. *Philosophy of Psychology and the Humanities*. Translated by Mary Catherine Baseheart and Marianne Sawicki. Washington, DC: ICS, 2000.
———. *Potency and Act: Studies Toward a Philosophy of Being*. Translated by Walter Redmond. Washington, DC: ICS, 2009.
———. *The Science of the Cross*. Translated by Josephine Koeppel. Washington, DC: ICS, 2002.
———. *The Science of the Cross: A Study of St. John of the Cross*. Edited by L. Gelber and Romaeus Leuven. Translated by Hilda Graef. London: Burns and Oates, 1960.
———. *Self-Portrait in Letters: 1916–1942*. Edited by L. Gelber and Romaeus Leuven. Translated by Josephine Koeppel. Washington, DC: ICS, 1993.
———. *Self-Portrait in Letters: Letters to Roman Ingarden*. Translated by Hugh Candler Hunt. Washington, DC: ICS, 2014.
———. *Was ist der Mensch? Theologische Anthropologie*. Freiburg: Herder, 2005.
———. *Welt und Person: Beitrag zum Christlichen Wahrheitsstreben*. Freiburg: Herder, 1962.
Storer, Shawn. "*A Hidden Life* Hides Too Much of Franz Jägerstätter's Life." *Church Life Journal*, February 18, 2020. https://churchlifejournal.nd.edu/articles/a-hidden-life-hides-too-much-of-franz-jagerstatters-real-life/.
Tajra, Harry W. *The Martyrdom of St. Paul: Historical and Judicial Context, Traditions, and Legends*. Eugene, OR: Wipf and Stock, 1994.
Wallenfang, Donald. *Dialectical Anatomy of the Eucharist: An Étude in Phenomenology*. Eugene, OR: Cascade, 2017.
———. *Human and Divine Being: A Study on the Theological Anthropology of Edith Stein*. Eugene, OR: Cascade, 2017.

———. *Metaphysics: A Basic Introduction in a Christian Key*. Eugene, OR: Cascade, 2019.

———. and Megan Wallenfang. *Shoeless: Carmelite Spirituality in a Disquieted World*. Eugene, OR: Wipf and Stock, 2021.

Chapter 18

Authoritarianism and the Authoritarian Personality

Malick's Tragedy of Disobedience

DAVID BENJAMIN JOHNSON

Authority and authoritarianism figure prominently in Malick's later work. *The Thin Red Line*, for example, deals centrally with the authority and command structure of the military; *The Tree of Life* depicts a middle-class family dominated by an authoritarian father; *A Hidden Life* focuses on an Austrian man and woman resisting the authoritarianism of the Nazi total state. Yet even in the case of these manifestly authority-concerned films, scholarly attention to Malick's treatment of authority and authoritarianism has typically been fleeting, if given at all. I contend, however, that these themes appear centrally not only in Malick's later work but in his earliest feature films as well, and it is on these films, *Badlands* and *Days of Heaven*, that this chapter primarily focuses. These two films, I argue, present subtle but rich images of the *authoritarian personality*. They do so, moreover, with respect to the appearance of this personality not in the powerful and dominant, as we might expect, but rather in the largely powerless. These films, in other words, even as they depict relatively extraordinary events, attend to the phenomenon of mundane authoritarianism: the authoritarianism of life lived day to day, the authoritarianism of private desires and personal relationships, even the authoritarianism latent in disobedience.

Indeed, at the center of these films are depictions of what we might call *authoritarian disobedience*, a kind of pseudo-disobedience whose reactivity and irrationality result, in these films, in disaster and tragedy.[1]

The concept of an authoritarian personality or authoritarian character was initially developed in the 1940s and 1950s (developed explicitly, at any rate—one can find antecedents to this concept at least as far back as Freud) by thinkers associated with the Frankfurt Institute for Social Research. This concept, bringing together political philosophy and social psychology, aimed to characterize the pattern of interconnected desires, beliefs, behaviors, and emotions acting in and through individuals to render them susceptible, ready to submit, to the domination of demagogues, strongmen, and fascists. Though actual authoritarian political regimes do not appear in *Badlands* or *Days of Heaven*—indeed, do not appear in Malick's work until his most recent film at the time of this writing, *A Hidden Life*—the personality pattern that, according to this concept, underpins such regimes lies at the heart of these films. It is as if *Badlands* and *Days of Heaven* explore, in a kind of pre-theoretical way, the manifestation of the authoritarian personality in the absence of a large-scale authoritarian social movement into which it can be channeled. I argue, in other words, that Holly and Kit in *Badlands* and Abby and Bill in *Days of Heaven* are small-*a* authoritarians lacking a capital-*A* Authoritarianism.

To recognize the ways in which this personality appears in *Badlands* and *Days of Heaven* requires viewing these films through the lens of a critical-theoretical social psychology. This raises an important methodological question with which we should deal before going any further: are Malick's films at all amenable to psychological analysis? Is such analysis in any way fruitful for an understanding of his work? As many commentators have observed, Malick's characters offer little in the way of psychological depth, at least the kind of "depth" typical of much Hollywood cinema: his characters rarely give voice to their underlying motivations, anxieties, and desires in a way that would recognizably explain their actions, and when they do, these statements are often either dubious or, particularly in the later films, couched in a kind of metaphysical language.[2] The critical tendency to regard psychological characterization in Malick as insignificant finds perhaps its most emphatic expression in Pauline Kael's oft-remarked complaint that action in *Badlands* is opaque, unmotivated, and inexplicable. But while Kael's criticism is, as many have pointed out, plainly overstated, the observation on which it could be said to rest is not untrue: Malick is not a conventionally psychologistic filmmaker. Nevertheless, I think the kind of social psychology–grounded investigation I undertake here is not unfounded. While Malick's characters rarely articulate their motivations in the obvious and often clichéd ways typical of many movies, their actions, including what statements they make about themselves and others, cohere into patterns of behavior that express complexes of belief, affect, and drive—complexes that afford these characters the kind of psychological consistency that makes them recognizable as such and not, as Kael's remark would seem to imply, mere centers of more or less aleatory action. Malick's Kit and Holly are very different from, say, Resnais and Robbe-Grillet's A and X (and even A and X are not without psychological characterization). The motivational complexes expressed by Malick's characters, I contend, can be analyzed and can afford us important insights about the meaning and significance of Malick's work, in this case insights about his depiction of authoritarianism and disobedience. I am certainly not the first commentator to approach Malick in this way; Hannah Patterson, for example, has written compellingly about the search for identity as a motivating force for Kit and Holly in *Badlands*.[3]

We will begin with an examination of the critical-theoretical concept of the authoritarian personality. From there we will turn to *Badlands* and *Days of Heaven*, elucidating the forms under which this personality appears in these films, the ways in which it conditions relationships among the films' main characters, and the role it plays in the disastrous acts of seemingly paradoxical disobedience that ultimately lay these characters low. We will conclude with a brief consideration of the way authoritarianism and disobedience are figured at the other end of Malick's career thus far, in *A Hidden Life*, and the light this most recent film casts back on his earliest treatments of these phenomena.

The Authoritarian Personality

In the wake of Hitler's rise to power, scholars at the Institute for Social Research in Frankfurt (among, it goes without saying, many others) came to see as utterly exigent the task of explaining the relative ease with which fascist dictators had captured not only the institutions of power in Italy and Germany but also the enthusiastic support and adulation of masses of followers. Thinkers including Theodor Adorno, Max Horkheimer, Erich Fromm, Leo Löwenthal, Franz Neumann, and Herbert Marcuse rose to this task, drawing on political philosophy, sociology, history, aesthetics, and psychology to try to understand the contemporary authoritarian phenomenon. In 1936 Fromm, Marcuse, and Horkheimer published *A Study on Authority and the Family*, and by 1941 Fromm had developed an account of the complex of psychological factors inclining everyday people toward authoritarian social and political dynamisms, a complex he called "the authoritarian character." A year later Neumann published *Behemoth: The Structure and Practice of National Socialism*, and in 1949 Löwenthal, together with Norbert Guterman, published a study of American forms of proto-authoritarian agitation, *Prophets of Deceit*. The next year, in 1950, Adorno, Else Frenkel-Brunswik, Daniel Levinson, and R. Nevitt Sanford published their monumental—and controversial—clinical study of the psychology of authoritarianism, *The Authoritarian Personality*. Though these thinkers are far from homogeneous in their theories of the psychological sources of authoritarianism, they share enough in common to refer, in broad strokes, to a Frankfurt School critical-theoretical approach to the problem of the authoritarian personality. Over the next several paragraphs, I will adumbrate this approach, drawing principally on the work of Fromm and Adorno, with an eye toward laying the groundwork for an analysis of Malick's treatment of the themes of authoritarianism and disobedience.

In his 1941 book *Escape from Freedom*, Fromm names authoritarianism as one of the principal psychological "mechanisms" facilitating what he regards as the widespread contemporary propensity to shrink from the demands of freedom and to acquiesce to, or even support, "the Fascist system." He describes this mechanism as "the tendency to give up the independence of one's own individual self and to fuse one's self with somebody or something outside of oneself in order to acquire the strength which the individual self is lacking."[4] Fromm thus conceives of the impulse toward authoritarianism as rooted in an individual's perception of and inability to bear felt powerlessness and isolation. Because these feelings are experienced as threatening and intolerable, the individual seeks to escape from them by relinquishing the seemingly powerless individuality at their source and merging with some other or others through whom a sense of strength and security might be gained. Authoritarians, in short, flee from their unbearable freedom and independence toward union with something outside themselves.

Authoritarianism thus entails a kind of hierarchical partnership, or as Fromm puts it, symbiosis. For it to succeed as a mechanism of escape from freedom, it requires at least two parties: a party that merges into something bigger than itself and a party that incorporates the other. Authoritarianism, for Fromm, is thus composed of two superficially distinct but convergent and similarly motivated psychological drives: one toward submission and one toward domination. He characterizes authoritarianism, accordingly, as sadomasochistic. The masochistic drive predominates in those individuals who, to evade their feelings of individual powerlessness, attempt to annihilate their individuality by submitting to someone or something stronger than themselves. The sadistic drive predominates in those who, in flight from the same feelings of individual powerlessness, seek "to have complete mastery over another person."[5] Importantly for Fromm, though these two drives appear diametrically opposed, they spring from the same experience of intolerable powerlessness. It is this common source, together with the effective complementarity of the two drives that spring from it, that allows one to speak of sadism and masochism as constituting a single psychological defense mechanism.[6] Moreover, Fromm suggests, the two drives are often found in the same individual: "People are not sadistic or masochistic, but there is a constant oscillation between the active and the passive side of the symbiotic complex, so that it is often difficult to determine which side of it is operating at a given moment."[7] Fromm spells this idea out in a chapter on "the psychology of Nazism," which focuses largely on an analysis of Hitler. Hitler's sadism is obvious in his contempt for and wish to "exterminate" those he deemed weak or inferior, from the Jews and Roma to people who are queer or disabled, but Fromm points out that this sadism can also be found in Hitler's attitude toward the German masses themselves, "whom he despises and 'loves' in the typically sadistic manner" and whose will he understands himself to have broken through his oratory and propaganda."[8] Hitler's masochism is perhaps less obvious; Fromm detects this drive in his belief, attested by passages in *Mein Kampf*, that his rise to power was accomplished by "Fate" or "Nature," agencies to which he could only submit. Indeed, Fromm identifies this belief in something like fate or nature-cum-destiny as fundamental to the authoritarian character. "The feature common to all authoritarian thinking is the conviction that life is determined by forces outside of man's own self, his interest, his wishes. The only possible happiness lies in the submission to these forces."[9]

In *The Authoritarian Personality*, Adorno, authoring a chapter on the various types or "syndromes" of the eponymous personality, concurs with much of Fromm's analysis. Discussing what he calls the "Authoritarian Syndrome," Adorno invokes Fromm's account of sadomasochism to describe the authoritarian's simultaneous "blind belief in authority and readiness to attack those who are deemed weak and who are socially acceptable as 'victims.'"[10] Adorno explains the source of the sadomasochistic impulse in more explicitly Freudian terms than does Fromm (terms that, if we had more space, might inform an analysis of the family dynamic among the O'Briens in *The Tree of Life*):

> Love for the mother, in its primary form, comes under a severe taboo. The resulting hatred against the father is transformed by reaction-formation into love. . . . The transformation of hatred into love, the most difficult task an individual has to perform in his early development, never succeeds completely. In the psychodynamics of the "authoritarian character," part of the preceding aggressiveness is absorbed and turned into masochism, while another part is left over as sadism, which seeks an outlet in those with whom the subject does not identify himself: ultimately the outgroup.[11]

Here we see another way in which the simultaneity of sadism and masochism in one individual manifests itself concretely in the authoritarian: masochistic identification with and submission to the ingroup and sadistic vilification of the outgroup. Often accompanying this identification with the ingroup, Adorno writes, is a tendency toward conformism and conventionality.

The latter tendency, however, is not present in every instance of authoritarian personality; both Adorno and Fromm identify a variant of the personality that prominently features what appears to be the very antithesis of conformist conventionality, perhaps even the antithesis of authoritarianism itself. This is the compulsion to rebel indiscriminately, "to defy authority and to resent any kind of influence from 'above,'" all the while harboring a latent attraction to and willingness enthusiastically to obey authority under the right conditions.[12] Adorno regards this form of rebellious authoritarianism as a distinct syndrome—he calls it "The Rebel and the Psychopath"—and he again turns to psychoanalysis to explain its development: "Masochistic transference to authority may be kept down on the unconscious level while resistance takes place on the manifest level. This may lead to an irrational and blind hatred of *all* authority, with strong destructive connotations, accompanied by a secret readiness to 'capitulate' and to join hands with the 'hated' strong."[13] At the extreme, Adorno argues, this syndrome results in psychopathy, as embodied in the figure of the "tough guy." Such an authoritarian rebel is gripped by "the omnipotence fantasy of very early infancy. . . . Bodily strength and toughness—also in the sense of being able to 'take it'—are decisive."[14] This type of authoritarian personality, we may note, is well represented in film and television, sometimes critically or satirically but often approvingly; from Anakin Skywalker to Eric Cartman, from Will Smith's "bad boy" cop to Arnold Schwarzenegger's brutal, wisecracking ex-soldier, TV and movies are full of rebels ready to fall in line when push comes to shove.

Authoritarian Personality in *Badlands* and *Days of Heaven*

With the foregoing rough sketch of the critical-theoretical understanding of the authoritarian personality and some of its variations in hand, we may now turn to Malick's first two films, which, I argue, offer rich and ultimately tragic figurations of this personality. Each film centers on a sadomasochistic relationship that becomes the vehicle for a project of authoritarian rebellion, chiefly orchestrated by the predominantly sadistic member of the relationship. In each film, this project of rebellion results in mayhem, trauma, and the death of the sadist at the hands of the law. *Badlands* and *Days of Heaven*, in short, present a tragic vision of authoritarian disobedience.

At the heart of *Badlands* is the illicit sexual relationship between twenty-five-year-old Kit and fifteen-year-old Holly. This relationship is plainly sadomasochistic, in Fromm's sense. Hannah Patterson, without invoking the concept of sadomasochism explicitly, succinctly captures the dynamism it names: Kit and Holly, she writes, "may be drawn to each other, not through a conscious desire to change or reinvent, but because neither of them has any clear sense of self in the first place."[15] Holly is a schoolgirl, and like many teenagers she is awkward, self-conscious, and sexually anxious. Her mother has died and her father, with whom she has a strained relationship, has recently moved her from Texas to small-town South Dakota. She has no close friends. She is prone to belittling herself: she has neither, she says, "a lot of personality" nor "a lot to say." She is an ideal target for the predatory Kit—naive, pliant, unconfident, and yearning for such attention and companionship as can be construed as love.[16] Kit, on the other hand, is outwardly self-assured, violent, domineering, defiant, and somewhat preening; he prides himself on his resemblance, remarked repeatedly by others, to James Dean. At the same time, his employment is tenuous, and what jobs he manages to obtain are menial and low-status: at the beginning of the film he is a garbage collector, a position he very quickly loses; later he is hired at a feedlot, where he treats cattle with cruelty and contempt. It is suggested that he fought in Korea. His attraction to the underage Holly seems to be largely about finding someone he can control, and his murder of her father—which itself echoes the father's sadistic killing of Holly's dog—serves to trap her in the relationship, totalizing that control. In this way, Kit acquires his "symbiote," the powerless Holly, through whom the exercise of his sadism achieves its end, a sense of power and dominance that will compensate for his social status and provide him a means for self-aggrandizing action. Complementarily, Holly's masochism affords her an illusion of love into which she can disappear. In her voiceover she describes this love in rapturous, romantically self-annihilating terms—terms that are largely belied by the mundane relationship we see on-screen: "He wanted to die with me, and I dreamed of being lost forever in his arms." Later, speaking to the young woman whom Kit attempts to murder along with her boyfriend at Cato's house, Holly conveys the explicitly authoritarian character of the relationship: "He says 'frog,' I jump."

The relationship between Bill and Abby at the center of *Days of Heaven* is less blatantly sadomasochistic than the one between Kit and Holly, but it too bears hallmarks of the authoritarian character. Abby is dependent on Bill. After he assaults his boss in the factory where he works at the beginning of the film, she flees Chicago with him, adopting the life of a migrant farmworker to remain by his side. She manages to break away from him after marrying the farmer on whose land they find work, but when Bill kills the farmer in the film's climax, Abby returns to him, again taking flight across the country. But more than merely depending on Bill, Abby submits to his wishes, most notably his plot to obtain the terminally ill farmer's wealth through a sham marriage to Abby—a scheme she clearly finds repugnant. Again and again, her behavior toward Bill betrays a kind of hesitating masochism. Further, Abby is given to self-flagellation; though it is Bill and the farmer who are most responsible for the violence and calamity that erupt on the farm and lead to the farmer's death, "She blamed herself," Linda tells us in her voiceover: "She didn't care if she was happy or not. She just wanted to make up for what she did wrong." For his part, Bill is domineering, manipulative, and violent; like Kit his employment is precarious and his social status low. Though Malick shows us moments of genuine tenderness and care between Bill and Abby—moments the likes of which are almost totally absent from *Badlands*—the overall tenor of their relationship is one of unstable dominance and submission, with Bill largely controlling Abby and Abby reluctantly acceding to his control. This control reaches its apex, of course, in Bill's compelling Abby to marry the farmer, but we glimpse it in other moments as well: Bill's insistence, recounted by Linda, that he and Abby keep their romantic relationship a secret by pretending to be siblings, his mocking Abby for her self-pity as he tries to convince her to marry the farmer, the petulant anger he exhibits as Abby begins to pull away from him. But it is precisely his most audacious act of sadism that finally undermines the imperfect sadomasochism of their relationship: Abby's marriage to the farmer soon becomes a truly loving relationship that supplants her dependence on Bill. The evident equality and freedom that develop between Abby and the farmer (at least until the film's climax, when he wrathfully ties her to a column of his house) stand in stark contrast to the dependence and manipulation of her relationship with Bill, and it cannot be regarded as a coincidence that the weakening and eventual (though temporary) cessation of Bill's domination of Abby coincides with the development of her far more equitable relationship with the farmer.

These sadomasochistic relationships in *Badlands* and *Days of Heaven* function, we might say, as testing grounds and launchpads for acts of drastic disobedience. In the former film, this disobedience is manifestly authoritarian; Kit is a rebel in Fromm's and Adorno's sense of the term. The rejection of authority that seems to be expressed in his taboo relationship with Holly, murder spree, and cross-country flight from the police is belied by acts that testify to his deep attraction to authority. His emulation of James Dean, the archetypal "rebel without a cause," is emblematic in this regard. Not only does the very notion of a rebel without a cause suggest the irrational, helter-skelter pseudo-disobedience of the authoritarian rebel, but the fact that this figure constitutes a social type bearing a certain countercultural prestige points to the wish embedded in Kit's emulation of Dean to possess that prestige—a sort of cultural authority. It is this wish to be recognized, respected, and feared as a rebel that consciously motivates Kit's actions; when one of the police officers who finally catch him asks why he committed his crimes, he replies: "I don't know. I always wanted to be a criminal, I guess, just not this big a' one." Yet the glee he expresses at the attention he receives once caught seems to suggest, to the contrary, that he's quite happy to have been that big a' one.

Most remarkable, however, is Kit's deference to and respect for the police and National Guard who capture him. He likes the police and on some level is eager to submit to them. As we watch Kit shoot out the tire of his own car before surrendering to the cops, Holly wonders in voiceover about his reasons for giving himself up. "Was it despair?" she asks. I propose a different interpretation: Kit gives himself up because he desires sadomasochistic symbiosis. Now that Holly, his masochistic partner, has abandoned him, he needs a new partner to merge with. The police, and ultimately the penal apparatus of the state itself, constitute the perfect partner. But the roles will reverse: the sadist Kit now becomes the masochist in relation to the even more sadistic police. Kit admires their guns and their uniforms. The trappings and offices of authority appeal to him, particularly in their more rugged manifestations. We should recall here Adorno's observation that the rebel tends to have a fascination with strength and toughness—a feature further exhibited in the militaristic training exercises Kit performs while he and Holly are hiding out in the woods. Alongside Kit's attraction to police authority we must also place respect for the economic authority of the upper class. When he and Holly briefly invade a mansion and take its owner and maid captive, he treats his prisoners cordially, asks permission (simultaneously ironic and deferential) for the use of the house, and before leaving furnishes the rich man with an inventory of the things he's "borrowed." That Kit doesn't kill these captives, after he's killed or tried to kill nearly everyone else he and Holly have encountered—members of the lower or middle classes, all—further indicates his authoritarian respect for wealth.

Kit's disobedience, in short, is not driven by the kind of critical rejection of illegitimate authority that Fromm calls "humanistic conscience"; it expresses rather a displaced and barely latent desire for the authority he lacks and the submission he craves, and his adulation of the police suggests that this rebel without a cause would be more than prepared to adopt nearly any cause that might provide him an easy path to authority, prestige, symbiotic community, and release from the demands of independence. Moreover, his appreciative attitude to the authorities—his affable politeness to the rich man and to the cops, his apology for "any inconvenience" he's caused the police chief, his commendation of his capturers' performing "like a couple a' heroes"—testifies not only to his affinity for authority and the masochism lurking beneath his sadism, but also to a deep conventionalism underlying his seeming disobedience and nonconformism. Despite his brutality, Kit's values are largely middle-of-the-road, a fact most clearly exhibited in the anodyne and moralistic message he records on the rich man's Dictaphone, admonishing his imaginary audience to respect their parents and teachers and to consider the minority opinion while deferring to the majority. Malick himself, in a rare interview, remarks on this conventionalism, noting that Kit's rebel-without-a-cause act masks the fact that "he's more like an Eisenhower conservative."[17]

The character of the disobedience on view in *Days of Heaven* is more ambiguous than that of *Badlands*. Are Bill and Abby rebels? In the case of the latter, the answer is almost certainly negative. Abby does not display the kind of irrational reaction against authority characteristic of the rebel; nor does she appear to revere strength and toughness. Moreover, her disobedience goes only as far as agreeing to Bill's scheme to con the farmer, which she does reluctantly—the act of a masochist, not a rebel. The question of whether Bill is a rebel is more difficult to answer decisively. On the one hand, he evinces the rebel's reactive resentment of any influence from above. He assaults his boss at the factory, apparently killing him, seemingly for something as slight as a reprimand. Similarly, when the farm foreman docks Abby three dollars for unsatisfactory work, Bill appears on the verge of attacking him until Abby defuses the situation. Bill's truculence is not entirely directed against his superiors, however; when another farmworker crassly insinuates that he knows Bill and Abby are lovers and not siblings, Bill assaults him. But while this last act of violence might be taken to indicate the indiscriminate, rather than narrowly authority-targeted, character of Bill's aggressiveness, it should be noted that the source of his rage in this scene seems to be the other worker's flaunting of the fact that he knows something Bill does not want him to know. In other words, Bill is set off by the fact that this other worker has something over him. Thus, this assault too takes on the hue of a reaction against authority, here the authority of the possessor of knowledge.

On the other hand, Bill's aggression toward the farmer, which produces his most calculated act of disobedience, is more difficult to read. It is unclear to what extent he orchestrates the deception of the farmer because of his resentment at the authority the farmer represents and to what extent he does so simply because it affords him, Abby, and Linda an opportunity to escape their poverty. Clearly, the chance to inherit the farmer's wealth, to secure a stable and comfortable life, looms large in Bill's machinations. Linda's voiceover, however, suggests that his motivation is not purely material, that it is also driven by resentment and anxiety over his competence and social status. Bill, she says, "Was tired of livin' like the rest of 'em, nosin' around like a pig in a gutter. . . . He figured there must be somethin' wrong with 'im." Bill himself articulates this resentful anxiety in conversations with both the farmer and Abby. To the farmer, he admits to regarding himself as "not the smartest guy in the world" and laments the fact that he's "never gonna come up with the big score"; to an Abby incredulous at his proposed plot, he remonstrates, "As long as I can remember, people been giving me a hard time about one thing or another. Don't you start!" As Jon Baskin observes, "Bill, like Kit, is motivated by a desire to be significant in the traditional Western way, which means he acknowledges only the world of other men—the world where significance is measured by prosperity and fame."[18]

Abby's social status is also a source of anxiety for Bill, and this anxiety is refracted through the lens of his gendered and sexualized sadism toward her: "I hate," he says to her, "seeing you stooped over out there, them lookin' at your ass like you're a whore." This statement is particularly striking in light of the fact that what Bill is trying to convince Abby to do with this cri de coeur against her objectification—to marry the farmer in order to usurp his estate—amounts to something akin to a sort of secret prostitution with Bill as her pimp and the farmer as her unwitting john. Here Bill's sadism achieves its crowning moment of irrationality: he turns the specter of Abby's being looked at like a prostitute, together with his resulting sense of dishonor, into a prod to push her into becoming a quasi-prostitute. Put differently, he treats her as a whore so that others cannot do the same. But not only is his statement remarkable for the lucidity of its sadism; it also articulates his contempt for his fellow farmworkers—those pigs nosing around in the gutter, as Linda puts it, their minds full of dirty thoughts. Bill is driven by a need to distinguish himself from the low-class laborers around him, to prove that he is not one of them, and this need expresses itself more desperately, more cruelly, and more irrationally the clearer it becomes that he is exactly one of them. Bill is a self-hating proletarian desperate to join the bourgeoisie. The contrast between Bill's and Linda's behavior toward the other laborers is telling. Linda forms bonds, befriending a young woman, tap dancing with a fellow worker, grinning intently at a fiddle player; Bill, on the other hand, offers no indication, whether in word or in act, that he feels any sort of camaraderie, solidarity, or even warmth toward the others on the farm.

But his contempt does not stop at the class divide; he is contemptuous of the farmer as well. In the course of trying to convince Abby that their deception will be easy, he sneeringly predicts the farmer's imminent death:

"The man's got one foot on a banana peel, the other on a roller skate." The farmer is rich but weak—weak insofar as he is ill, insofar as he has no family, insofar as he has fallen for Abby, insofar as he has foolishly placed his trust in someone he has only just met. Bill, on the other hand, is strong and smart. Thus, the con is justified, and the farmer, like everyone else, deserves the aggression Bill metes out to him. Here we vividly see Bill's affinity, elucidated by Daniel Layman in the next chapter of this volume, with Thrasymachus, Socrates's proto-authoritarian interlocutor in Plato's *Republic*.

In all these ways, Bill seems to fit the profile of the authoritarian rebel. He strikes out against others' authority and influence wherever he encounters them; he despises weakness; he is motivated, at least in part, by contempt and resentment, both against those who possess what he wishes to possess (primarily the rich) and against those who remind him of what he wishes he didn't possess (the poor, the working class, the weak). The fundamental trait of the authoritarian rebel, however—a latent readiness to fall in line with authority—is not immediately apparent in his behavior. He does not, like Kit, fawn over the police, behave obsequiously toward the wealthy, conspicuously emulate established social types, or deliver conventionalist moral sermons. But in light of the lengths to which he will go, and will force others to go, to acquire not only the material comforts of wealth but also, importantly, its prestige and authority, we are justified in speculating that his rebelliousness hides an underlying authoritarian will. Indeed, the climax of the film, in which Bill leaps into action to help save the farm from the swarm of locusts despite his no longer being in the employ of the farmer, can be seen in this same light. While Bill's act may certainly be read naturalistically as one of altruism tinged with regret and desire for atonement, an effort to help the farmer, Abby, Linda, and the farmworkers in their emergency, it might also be read metaphorically or allusively. Many commentators have remarked on the biblical connotations suggested by the plague of locusts. I'd like to bring forward an authoritarian connotation: Bill and the farmworkers, under the command of the farmer, pull together in a project of exterminating vermin, first by driving them away, then by smoking or gassing them out, finally by casting them by the basketful into bonfires.[19] This effort, initially somewhat orderly but soon murky, chaotic, and violent, performed under cover of a kind of *Nacht und Nebel* that eerily resembles some of the archival footage of Nazi rallies with which *A Hidden Life* begins, culminates in the burning of the entire farm—a holocaust in the literal sense of the word. Now, I do not mean to imply that this reading—which, I will be the first to admit, is perhaps rather on the nose—exhausts the meaning of the film's climax or supplants alternative interpretations; it does neither of these things. But I do want to suggest that Bill's sudden spirit of collectivism, his abrupt expression of solidarity in this moment of crisis, his spontaneous participation in the *Ausrottung* of the vermin threatening the harvest and perhaps the very existence of the farm (the farm to which he now seems to feel some sort of allegiance or belonging or group-identificatory connection)—all this, I wish to say, testifies to the will to obedience lurking beneath Bill's disobedience, the authoritarianism within his rebelliousness.

I have so far said almost nothing about the character of Linda in *Days of Heaven*. In part this is because, as Baskin observes, Linda "plays absolutely no role in the plot of *Heaven*."[20] Further, she appears at first glance to have nothing to do with the theme of authoritarianism; she is a free and open spirit, utterly different from her taciturn and rebellious brother. As the literal voice of *Days of Heaven*, however, she frames the events of the film, provides them with a kind of overarching sense and coherence, and in so doing she articulates a final, important element of the film's engagement with the authoritarian personality: she expresses the sense of inexorability, of helplessness before destiny, that pervades the film's action. Early in the movie, as Malick shows us images of Bill, Abby, and Linda's flight from Chicago to Texas, Linda tells us in voice-over of the apocalyptic predictions related to her by "this guy named Ding-Dong": "The whole earth is goin' up in flames. Flames'll come out of here 'n there, 'n they'll just rise up. The mountains are gonna go up in big flames, the water's gonna rise in flames. There's gonna be creatures runnin' every which way, some of them burnt, half their wings burnin'. People are gonna be screamin' and hollerin' for help. See, the people that have been good, they're gonna go to Heaven 'n excape [sic] all that fire. But if you've been bad, God don't hear you, he don't even hear you talkin'." The world is inexorably marching toward a day of judgment that will be cataclysmic and merciless; the earth and its inhabitants are powerless against it. Later, over images of Bill, Abby, and Linda again fleeing, this time from the ruins of the farm, Linda relates her sense of both the cruelty and dreadful enchantment of the world, describing her fear of her friend Blackjack's ghost and her nonchalant assumption that the people she saw on the distant riverbanks "were probably callin' for help or somethin', or they were tryin' to bury somebody or something." Despite her generally playful disposition, Linda's world—and in a significant sense, the world of the film—is ruled by fate and brutality. We find a privileging of fate in *Badlands* as well, notably in Holly's explanation, again related in voiceover, of her decision not to run from Kit after he murders her father: "I felt that my destiny now lay with Kit, for better or for worse." The conviction that mysterious forces rule human life is, as we saw Fromm argue, "the feature common to all authoritarian thinking." To the authoritarian personality, the world is determined by largely inscrutable and irrational but irresistible powers, and indeed the worlds of these films, particularly of *Days of Heaven*, seem to be so determined: Ding-Dong's apocalyptic tableau is realized in the conflagration that destroys the farm. In this way, Malick presents us with a depiction not only of authoritarian characters but of the authoritarian weltanschauung itself.

A Hidden Life and the Tragedy of Disobedience

Disobedience in *Badlands* and *Days of Heaven* is at once authoritarian and catastrophic. Kit and Holly's disobedience results in the murder of at least five people and the execution of Kit (as well as, we may speculate, substantial trauma for Holly, though Malick does not show us this directly). Bill and Abby's disobedience results in two murders, Bill's death, a sense of unbearable guilt for Abby, the orphaning of Linda, and the destruction of the farm, including, presumably, the deaths of many of its nonhuman inhabitants. The catastrophic character of this disobedience is indissociable from its authoritarianism. Catastrophe in these films results from the irrationality, the compulsiveness, the resentment, and the repressed, paradoxical desire for both domination and submission that suffuses their characters' rebellion. In *Badlands* and *Days of Heaven*, in short, Malick presents a kind of tragic critique of the authoritarian personality.

As I noted at the outset, Malick's interest in the tragic dimensions of authoritarianism and disobedience persists in his later movies. In this persistence, however, there is also significant change. Nowhere is this more evident than in his most recent film at the time of this writing, *A Hidden Life*, with which we now conclude. By briefly examining *A Hidden Life*, we gain a sense not only of the ways Malick's treatment of the themes explored in this chapter have mutated over the course of his career but also of the broader stakes of his engagement with authoritarianism.

A Hidden Life is the first of Malick's films to depict a manifestly authoritarian political regime. As in *Badlands* and *Days of Heaven*, however,

Malick remains focused on the personal: we witness the authoritarianism of the Nazis in its destruction of the shared life of husband and wife Franz and Fani Jägerstätter. Again, a romantic relationship anchors Malick's investigation of authoritarianism and disobedience. Here, however, we find a major change from the early films: instead of the sadomasochism of Kit and Holly or Bill and Abby, Franz and Fani's relationship is one of equality, reciprocity, and true affection. Fani is not submissive or meek; Franz is not domineering or cruel. They do not manipulate or use one another; they discuss their desires and anxieties honestly, and they cherish and support each other and their children. Authoritarian personality patterns have completely disappeared from our central couple. We find these patterns instead among the film's more peripheral characters, most notably the mayor of Radegund, who exhibits not only the sadomasochistic, aggressive, and conventionalist components of the classic authoritarian personality but also the in-group/out-group dynamics to which we saw Adorno refer earlier, here expressed in the depressingly characteristic form of ethnocentrism and xenophobia.[21] Thus the disobedience at the heart of *A Hidden Life* no longer springs from the authoritarian personality; it is born, on the contrary, of the humanistic conscience in its resistance to illegitimate and irrational authority. By the same stroke, the tragedy of this disobedience is inverted: Franz is executed and Fani ostracized and widowed not because they commit destructive, murderous acts under the thrall of a perverse and irrational attraction to authority but because they refuse the demands of a state and society under the thrall of an actual, perverse, mass-murdering authority. If *Badlands* and *Days of Heaven* present an image of small-*a* authoritarians lacking a capital-*A* Authoritarianism, *A Hidden Life* presents one of capital-*A* Authoritarianism attempting to crush those who will not consent to be small-*a* authoritarians.

Thus, in *A Hidden Life* disobedience becomes heroic rather than foolish or pathological. Franz and Fani recognize the evil of Nazism and recognize in its authoritarianism the vehicle for that evil. They are confirmed in this knowledge by their religious faith, which tells them that God gave humanity free will so that individuals might reject wickedness and embrace the good, even when such an act might bring persecution down on the actor. Disobedience under such conditions becomes a holy act performed in the image of Christ—the "true Christ," as the church painter whom Franz visits says, not the Christ of so many official paintings, the comfortable and haloed King of Kings; rather, the suffering, fearful Christ, the Christ anguished at his forsakenness, Christ the persecuted disobeyer.

Obedience then becomes temptation, and like Jesus in the wilderness, Franz will be tempted, not by Satan but by a silver-tongued Nazi interrogator. Franz and Fani seem intuitively to understand Fromm's assertion, which brings together invocations of Greek myth, Judaic cosmogony, Christian messianism, fascism, and the nuclear arms race that would begin only a few years after Franz's execution: "Human history began with an act of disobedience; and it is not unlikely that it will be terminated by an act of obedience."[22] Even in the religiosity that comforts them in their time of suffering, however, Franz and Fani must contend with authoritarianism. The clergymen from whom Franz seeks counsel—first his local priest, later the Bishop of Salzburg—are cowardly and circumspect, and their advice evinces a kind of timid, barely moral pragmatism. The bishop ultimately toes the Pauline line on authority: "You have a duty to the fatherland. The Church tells you so. Do you know the words of the Apostle? 'Let every man be subject to the powers placed over him.' " Thus is sanctified a craven, un- or anti-Christlike submission and obedience to the evilest of earthly authorities. The spirit of the true Christ, the disobedient Christ, is not to be found in the Catholic hierarchy but rather in the humanistic conscience of the individual.

This emphasis on the spiritual dimension of Franz and Fani's disobedient conscience ultimately bespeaks the underlying principle of Malick's tragic orientation to authoritarianism and disobedience, one whose presence in the early films becomes clearer in retrospect. Authoritarianism, in Malick's work, is a threat to the human not only politically, because of its illegitimacy, its anti-democratic nature, or its massification of a populace; authoritarianism is most fundamentally threatening to humanity because of the moral and spiritual danger with which it confronts the individual. This spiritual hazard constitutes the overriding concern of Malick's treatment of authoritarianism across his career, from *Badlands* to *A Hidden Life*. Whether he is focusing on the manipulative and domineering perversion of love that is authoritarian sadomasochism, the irrationally reactive and ultimately bootlicking pseudo-disobedience of authoritarian rebellion, or the persecution and martyrdom of those who resist the demand for submission to an authoritarian society, Malick has depicted authoritarianism as fundamentally and tragically destructive to the individual, to the capacity for conscientious moral reasoning and free, autonomous action. The Nazis attempt to bind the free spirit of Franz and Fani, to demoralize and de-autonomize them; so too do the drives and affects of the authoritarian personality captivate Kit and Holly and Bill and Abby, clouding their reasoning, stunting their moral life, and rendering their behavior sociopathic. Fromm saw in the authoritarian personality a mechanism of the flight from freedom; for Malick it is the same. Authoritarianism in Malick's film is tragic, a spiritual cataclysm, because in it the freedom and conscience of the individual are destroyed.

Notes

1. Throughout this chapter I use the term "tragedy" in the loose, contemporary sense of an intensely sad and destructive event; I do not mean to invoke the classical sense of tragedy.

2. See, for example, Sinnerbrink, *Terrence Malick*, 25: Kit and Holly "are presented more as mythical or allegorical figures than as psychologically developed, concretely individuated characters." Similarly, in Michaels's *Terrence Malick*, 7: Malick's "protagonists, even when they are recognizable historical personages, like Kit (Starkweather) or Captain Smith, deliberately lack psychological depth, so much so that they are often barely recognizable as individuals."

3. Patterson, "Two Characters in Search of a Direction: Motivation and the Construction of Identity in *Badlands*."

4. Fromm, *Escape from Freedom*, 140.

5. Fromm, 155.

6. Fromm's understanding of authoritarianism as involving both a sadistic and a masochistic pole might be seen as an anticipation of the later social psychological distinction between an authoritarian personality and a "social dominance-oriented" personality. See, for example, Altemeyer, "Highly Dominating, Highly Authoritarian Personalities," 421–47.

7. Fromm, *Escape from Freedom*, 157.

8. Fromm, 220.

9. Fromm, 169.

10. Adorno et al., *The Authoritarian Personality*, 759.

11. Adorno et al., 759.

12. Fromm, *Escape from Freedom*, 167.

13. Adorno et al., 762.

14. Adorno et al., 763.

15. Patterson, "Two Characters in Search of a Direction," 32.

16. As Patterson points out, by the end of the film Holly has begun to throw off her masochism: "She may initially be led by [Kit] but ultimately she finds a way to assert herself and her will, separating from him and trying to take a firmer grasp of her own identity," 31.

17. Malick, "Malick on *Badlands*," interview by Beverly Walker, 82.

18. Baskin, "The Perspective of Terrence Malick."
19. See Sinnerbrink, *Terrence Malick*, 32; also Mottram, "All Things Shining: The Struggle for Wholeness, Redemption and Transcendence in the Films of Terrence Malick," 18–19.
20. Baskin, "The Perspective of Terrence Malick."
21. On the link between authoritarian personality and ethnocentrism, see Adorno et al., 57–150.
22. Fromm, *On Disobedience*, 1.

Bibliography

Adorno, Theodor, Else Frenkel-Brunswik, Daniel J. Levinson, and R. Nevitt Sanford. *The Authoritarian Personality*. New York: Verso, 2019.
Altemeyer, Bob. "Highly Dominating, Highly Authoritarian Personalities." *Journal of Social Psychology* 144, no. 4 (2004): 421–47.
Baskin, Jon. "The Perspective of Terrence Malick." *Point*, April 4, 2010. https://thepointmag.com/criticism/the-perspective-of-terrence-malick/.
Fromm, Erich. *Escape from Freedom*. New York: Holt and Company, 1941.
———. *On Disobedience*. New York: Harper Perennial Modern Thought, 1981.
Malick, Terrence. "Malick on *Badlands*." Interview by Beverly Walker. *Sight & Sound* 44, no. 2 (Spring 1975): 82–83.
Michaels, Lloyd. *Terrence Malick*. Chicago: University of Illinois Press, 2009.
Mottram, Ron. "All Things Shining: The Struggle for Wholeness, Redemption and Transcendence in the Films of Terrence Malick." In *The Cinema of Terrence Malick: Poetic Visions of America*. 2nd ed., edited by Hannah Patterson, 14–26. New York: Wallflower Press, 2007.
Patterson, Hannah. "Two Characters in Search of a Direction: Motivation and the Construction of Identity in *Badlands*." In *The Cinema of Terrence Malick: Poetic Visions of America*. 2nd ed., edited by Hannah Patterson, 27–39. New York: Wallflower Press, 2007.
Sinnerbrink, Robert. *Terrence Malick: Filmmaker and Philosopher*. New York: Bloomsbury, 2019.

Chapter 19

"But I Am Free!"

Malick on Freedom and Transcendence

DANIEL LAYMAN

Introduction: Freedom and Alienation

Terrence Malick is a consummate student and critic of human interiority. Nearly all his films focus squarely on the spiritual and psychological travails of human beings and their intimate relationships, and almost nowhere in his oeuvre do we encounter even an extended series of scenes, let alone an entire film, whose primary point or interest is economic or political. It may then come as a surprise that I have chosen to devote an entire chapter to the concept of liberty in three of Malick's most important films: *Badlands*, *Days of Heaven*, and *A Hidden Life*. The problem of human liberty, after all, is the problem of how human beings can live lives that are at once social and independent, constrained yet autonomous. In looking for a treatment of liberty in Malick's films, do we foist upon Malick concerns that are, despite their interest and importance, foreign to his artistic point of view?

This concern is, I think, a serious one. Nonetheless, I do not believe that a study of liberty in Malick is a fool's errand, let alone violent toward the filmmaker's aims and intentions. To be sure, it would be foolish at best to grope around in Malick's body of work for a political doctrine of liberty, or indeed for any political doctrine at all. But a productive investigation into Malick's treatment of liberty need not amount to such a goose chase, for the problem of human freedom that troubles Malick is not a political problem at all, at least not in the first instance. To the contrary, Malick's problem of unfreedom is the paradigmatically modern—and deeply interior—problem of alienation. This is neither the classical metaphysical problem of how the will can be free in the midst of a deterministic universe nor the classical political problem of how a citizen can be free in the face of political and economic power, but it is rather the classic moral—or, perhaps, spiritual—problem of how the person-as-subject can be free from forces that threaten to put them at odds with themselves so that they are never really at home in the world. This problem of subjective freedom is a serious one, and characteristic of modernity; as Susan Sontag puts the point, "Most serious thought in our time struggles with the feeling of homelessness."[1] Nevertheless, the problem is vexingly difficult to formulate precisely. It will therefore be useful, before turning our attention to any of Malick's films, to tighten our grip on the problem of unfreedom as alienation by considering how two important modern thinkers have motivated, framed, and pursued it.

Although worries about alienation no doubt preceded him, Karl Marx's treatment of the concept of "estranged labor" in his 1844 fragments defined a framework that would structure nearly all subsequent treatments of alienation and its potential remedies. Marx introduces estrangement as a necessary consequence of the wage relationship between workers and capitalists that is (partially) constitutive of capitalism. His concern is not merely that wage relationships are unfair and harmful to workers, although he harbors these worries as well. Rather, he argues that insofar as the wage relationship is one of estrangement, persons who must work on another's capital to survive invest themselves in their product only to confront themselves in that product as a hostile, alien force subject to the capitalist's will rather than to their own. In this way, the laborers lose themselves, and that is the fundamental unfreedom endemic to capitalism. Marx's language on this point is powerful: "The worker is related to the product of his labor as to an alien object. . . . The more the worker exerts himself, the more powerful becomes the alien objective world which he fashions against himself, the poorer he and his inner world become, the less there is that belongs to him."[2]

It is worth pausing for a moment over Marx's description of the worker's alienation as an impoverishment of his inner world. Although

Marx offers an unambiguously political-economic analysis of the circumstances of alienation, we see here that the phenomenon of alienation per se is nevertheless an inner, spiritual condition that rends the alienated person's subjectivity. The worker, as an alienated subject, experiences being in the world as doubled back against itself and, consequently, as barren, washed-out, and inhospitable. Whether or not this kind of spiritual sickness is baked into capitalist economic relations as Marx supposed, it clearly need not be restricted to those economic circumstances. Indeed, as we will shortly observe, intellectuals after Marx came to see alienation as the paradigmatic struggle of the modern subject, not just within relationships of production but in every dimension of social and private life. The modern subject as such struggles to be at home with themselves.

Although Marx diagnoses alienation as a capitalistic illness, he does not date its first appearance to the rise of that mode of production at the close of the eighteenth century. To the contrary, religion delivered the framework of alienated subjectivity ready-made to capitalist bosses. Marx continues the passage we considered previously: "It is the same with religion. The more man attributes to God, the less he retains in himself."[3] As we will later discuss in detail, Malick directly opposes Marx on this point; indeed, one way to read *A Hidden Life* is as a protracted attempt to turn Marx's claim on its head.

To broaden our view of alienation as a characteristically modern kind of unfreedom, let's turn now from Marx to Kafka. In *The Metamorphosis*, the protagonist, Gregor Samsa, famously finds himself transformed in the night into a giant insect. One imagines that in the event of undergoing such a shocking and unfortunate change, the natural response would be panic and terror; after all, Gregor's whole person has been swallowed up in inexplicable monstrosity. But all Gregor can think of is how to proceed with the routine of work and family obligations without getting into trouble or upsetting the quotidian order of interactions that defines the horizons of his existence. Gregor is, in effect, so deeply alienated from himself that even his own total transformation hardly matters; since he has long ago ceased to experience himself as anything but a cog in the various machines of which he has found himself a part, the only thing that matters to him about his transformation is whether he will be able to carry on as such a cog despite it. Just as Marx's laborers are swallowed up and sundered from themselves within the wage relationship in particular, Kafka's Samson has been ripped out of himself by the general impersonality, fungibility, and mechanism of his life. Kafka drives home the twofold, self-opposed character of Samson's subjectivity when, early in the novella, Samson reflects on his own post-transformation voice: "It was clearly and unmistakably his earlier voice, but in it was intermingled, as if from below, an irrepressibly painful squeaking which left the words positively distinct only in the first moment and distorted them in the reverberation, so that one didn't know if one had heard correctly."[4] The reader can only smile wryly here, as there can be no doubt that it didn't take a metamorphosis for Samson to experience his own voice as painful, distorted, and indistinct.

The thesis I will pursue in the remainder is that Malick offers in three films—the early *Badlands* and *Days of Heaven* and the later *A Hidden Life*—a three-step meditation on the problem of alienation and avenues toward freedom in the face of it. First, in *Badlands*, Malick considers and rejects the possibility of transcending alienation through violent confrontation with a world that refuses to hear or see us for who we really are (or think we are). Second, in *Days of Heaven*, Malick sketches a strategy dialectically opposed to the first: the way to achieve subjective freedom is to supplant, by guile or violence as necessary, those in positions of social and economic power. Finally, in *A Hidden Life*, Malick sketches—and ultimately endorses—a radical proposal that completely transcends the first two: freedom from alienation awaits, not in any form of rebellion or conquest, but in accepting absolutely the terms of existence on which a loving God created us for himself and for one another.

Badlands: "Ring the Bell"

"I guess I always wanted to be a criminal." So explains Kit (Martin Sheen), Malick's protagonist in *Badlands*, when asked upon his ultimate arrest why he ran off with his teenage girlfriend, Holly (Sissy Spacek), on a crime spree that spanned several states and piled up more than a handful of bodies. The arresting officer who poses the question understandably fails to make much sense of Kit's answer. After all, what kind of explanation is that for a sudden plunge from life as a small-town laborer into a months-long spree of murder, kidnapping, and terror?

Badlands opens, somewhat inauspiciously, with a garbage route. We meet Kit—twenty-five, rootless, and devilishly handsome (a dead ringer for James Dean, everyone agrees)—and his coworker, Cato (Ramon Bieri), as they make their way through the dusty alleys of Fort Dupree, South

Dakota, slinging the community's refuse into the back of their boss's rickety truck. After a few stops, Kit announces that he's done for the day, not because the route is finished but because he feels like it. As he wanders off, he encounters Holly, fifteen years old and practicing her majorette routine in the lush yard she shares with her father, a widowed sign painter. Kit has never seen Holly before, but he immediately invites her out for a walk. "What for?" Holly asks. "I guess I just have some things to say," Kit replies. Walk they do, but despite Kit's professed need to unburden himself of what is within him, his initial conversation with Holly fails to escape the most perfunctory small talk. These opening scenes offer the viewer a first glimpse into Kit's curious spiritual condition, which will inform so much of the action to come: Kit is, in a deep but ill-defined sense, trapped within himself. He feels that he has something important to do or say with or to those around him, that there is something of ultimate significance inside himself. But he cannot express—to himself or to others—what that is. As a result, he simply drifts through a world that is increasingly alien to him and to which he feels less and less connection.

Kit and Holly's romance quickly blooms, and Holly's father (Warren Oates) is understandably incensed once he catches wind of it. Kit, perhaps buoyed by his budding connection to another person, decides to approach her father directly and explain to him how deeply he cares for her and how much he respects her. When her father dismisses him out of hand and tells him never to show his face again, we see something snap—or, perhaps, harden—inside Kit. No longer does he hold out hope that he will be able to make peace with himself and the world, and express outwardly all that he has to say. He will, in a significant turn of phrase he uses later in the film, need to "really ring the bell"; that is, his only hope for freedom from the listless alienation that plagues him to is to make noise—loud, abrasive, and ultimately violent noise. Holly's father's act of rejection seems to confirm for him that the world can't (or won't) see or hear him. So, he will make the world hear him however he can, even if through violence and chaos.

Despite this hardening, Kit importantly does not at this point disconnect fully either from the need for human closeness or from respect for morality. After Kit kills Holly's father, burns down his house with his body inside, and runs away with Holly into the wilderness, he seeks something like homelife with Holly and attempts to explain his choices morally. As he and Holly build their camp, we see Kit come alive, taking pride and pleasure in the physical and emotional foundations he is laying with her.

For once, it is almost as though he feels himself finally at home, seen and heard by another person in a spirit of genuine closeness. Moreover, after Kit shoots and kills (to Holly's horror) the posse men who storm their camp, he doesn't just shrug his shoulders or claim to be somehow beyond morality. Rather, he explains (perhaps somewhat feebly) that the killings were alright because the victims were bounty hunters without honor. Kit's cognitive and emotional line to the moral and social world he is fleeing has not snapped, however much it may have frayed.

Things change, though, as life on the lam drags on and the manhunt for Kit and Holly intensifies. As the film's action (and Kit's desperation) mounts, Kit's killings become less and less explicable (even, it seems, to him, let alone to Holly), and his moral justifications become more and more forced. As the bodies pile up and his certain capture draws near, all that remains of Kit's emotional life is the desire to blaze out as a famous criminal on the way to the electric chair. In some of the film's most disconcerting scenes, Kit chats familiarly with the officers overseeing his arrest and confession, taking obvious and enormous pleasure in one deputy's wry remark that he is a "unique individual." This, of course, is not a compliment; the deputy's point is that he is uniquely deranged. But this doesn't matter to Kit. Others have finally seen him, even if only as a pitiable lunatic, and this is all the relief from alienation that is still comprehensible to him from the depths of his spiritual sickness. We know, though, that Kit has failed to attain even a taste of the real freedom he craves. Indeed, as the film closes with Holly, in her capacity as narrator, relating Kit's death in the electric chair six months later, we know that Kit died in absolute confinement, held fast until his last breath by the terrifying vacancy and incoherence of his subjectivity no less than by his manacles. As we will consider below, Kit's execution stands in important contrast to the very different (in terms of its meaning to the victim) execution that concludes the action of *A Hidden Life*.

Kit, I have suggested, tries to free himself from the alienation that confines him through an attempt to create a world of his own, an attempt that collapses into wanton violence. To better understand Kit's spiral and its significance for our theme of subjective liberty and confinement, it will be useful to introduce as a foil Rodion Raskolnikov, Dostoevsky's alienated young murderer from *Crime and Punishment*. Kit's and Raskolnikov's profiles and narrative arcs are superficially very similar. Both are young men troubled by a kind of deeply felt homelessness in their social and moral worlds who seek to liberate themselves through rebellion in the form of murder. Moreover, both cling to the love of a young woman—Kit to Holly and Raskolnikov to Sonya—as they sink ever deeper into violence and desperation. Their psychological profiles, however, differ importantly and yield different motivations for their crimes. Understanding these differences will help us better grasp what Kit's descent shows us about subjective unfreedom through alienation.

As we noted earlier, *Badlands* opens with Kit drifting listlessly through work and life; far from being agitated, he is relaxed to the point of disconnection with everything and everyone around him. He experiences the world as unhearing and incomprehensible, but his response is to check out; he doesn't seem to know what exactly it is he wants to say, and he can't work up much of a response to the distant world around him until he meets Holly and begins to "ring the bell" with his crime spree. Kit's motivation for murder is thus not an intellectual one, at least not in the sense of being attributable to an articulable doctrine or ideology. He hardly knows what or why he thinks or feels, and for all his crime and perverse satisfaction at finally being recognized for it, he never makes any progress on this front; his own beliefs and motivations are, throughout the film, fundamentally opaque to him. Raskolnikov, by contrast, experiences himself as confined by a much more intellectual form of alienation from his world. Dostoevsky's character cannot accept that he is a member of a moral community governed by norms that subject him no less than others to standards not his own. He feels that his life can have significance for him, and that he will be at home in the world, only if he transcends morality by radically violating it. Only then will he become, as Nietzsche would later say, a superman, free from the chains that bind the pitiable, slavish horde of humanity. It is from this perverse set of premises (through which Dostoevsky meant to capture the essence of the Russian nihilism that he so detested) that Raskolnikov viciously slays the pawnbroker and her sister. Raskolnikov doesn't want to "ring the bell" so much as he wants to remake himself according to what he perceives as the demands of a very definite intellectual doctrine.

Kit's transformation into, as Holly puts it, "the most trigger-happy person [she] had ever met," is, in an important sense, more terrifying than Raskolnikov's insofar as its grounds are much less articulable, if no less strongly felt. This difference between the characters' motivations generates a further important difference between their narrative arcs after they have committed their crimes. Since Raskolnikov's alienation is intellectual, there is always the possibility that he might find ultimate liberation by accepting a contrary doctrine, and this possibility, which is ultimately realized by his conversion to Christianity under Sonya's guidance, generates much of the novel's narrative tension. In Kit's case, it is clear from the beginning that such redemption is not a real possibility, as Kit doesn't understand his own feelings of confinement and alienation well enough for a rival understanding to take root and replace them. We thus know from the beginning that Kit is almost certainly doomed; there is no mechanism available for his potential liberation or salvation, and he ultimately finds neither on his way to the electric chair.

Days of Heaven: "A Big Score"

Kit's futile pursuit of agential freedom in *Badlands* comprises two distinct phases. In the first, he seeks to overcome his alienation through emotional closeness to Holly. He courts her openly and even takes the uncomfortable step of approaching her father to secure his blessing for the relationship. Only when her father rejects him does he begin his death spiral of increasingly desperate violence. Bill (Richard Gere), the male protagonist in *Days of Heaven*, also pursues—without success—liberty through two distinct phases of action. First, he seeks refuge from the burdens that afflict him—class-based bitterness and fear on account of an earlier crime—in a romantic relationship with Abby (Brooke Adams). But like Kit, there comes a turning point after which he takes up a different tack, one that spells doom not just for his life but also for any hope of the liberation he so desperately craves.

We meet Bill, much as we meet Kit, as he labors at a menial job. But whereas Kit seems to bear his trash-collection burdens lightly—indeed, he simply wanders off the job as soon as it suits him—Bill seethes with indignation as he shovels coal into an industrial furnace in the hardscrabble Chicago of 1916. An altercation with a foreman comes to blows, and Bill realizes at once that he has killed the man. Together with his sister, Linda (Linda Manz), and his lover Abby (he and Abby pose as siblings because, as Linda says in her capacity as voiceover narrator, "people talk"), he takes to the rails in seek of work. The trio lands at last in the Texas panhandle where he and Abby both engage as seasonal workers on a wheat farm owned by a terminally ill young man we know only as the farmer (Sam Shepard).

As life on the farm gets underway, Bill still struggles with anger at his economic situation, and he balks at the domination he suffers from the overseers on the farm. In one scene that drives home especially strongly the bosses' arbitrary power and Bill's resentment toward it, an overseer announces that Abby's pay will be docked significantly because she inadvertently wasted some of the wheat she had gathered. Rising in anger, Bill confronts his superior: "That's not fair!" The older man snarls: "Fine, you're fired. If you want to stay, then shut up and get back to work." Abby attempts to calm Bill down, but it is hard not to sympathize with his anger. For we see in Bill's relationship to his economic masters a dramatic illustration of the Marxian unfreedom we discussed earlier, which occurs insofar as the wage relationship subjects the worker's labor—and so the worker—to another's will. Bill cannot achieve inner freedom as an agent because, or at least partially because, he is an unfree worker in the Marxian sense. As Linda explains in a voiceover: "He was tired of living like the rest of 'em, nosing around like a pig." However, we notice as the action on the farm builds that although Abby works each day on the same terms and under the same conditions as Bill, she does not share his posture of anger and resentment. Rather, her attitude toward their work and general situation is marked by passive acceptance, at least until her relationship with the farmer begins. There is, to be sure, an additional struggle developing inside of Bill, one motivated by more than just the exploitative character of his economic position. Bill, unlike Abby, is convinced that the key to liberation—from work, from wandering, from alienation, and all the rest—is to turn the tables and end up on top. Bill, then, has—like Kit—a secondary thesis about what liberty means that comes into focus as his initial plans encounter resistance; whereas Kit turns away from Holly and toward nihilistic violence, Bill begins to see Abby not as a source of liberation through love but as a tool he can use to outdo the farmer and get on top. He convinces Abby to accept the farmer's romantic overtures and marry him with the secret intention of returning to their relationship, fortune in hand, after the farmer's imminent death. As Bill tells the farmer during a conversation after the latter's marriage to Abby, he had grown up thinking that he would one day devise a "big score" that would outdo everyone else and put them in their place. Until it all comes crashing down through a combination of Abby's genuine feelings for the farmer and the latter's discovery of their scheme (followed by Bill's murdering the farmer and his subsequent death by police shotgun), Bill sees his plot against the farmer as the biggest score of all.

We were able to clarify Kit's desperate gambit for freedom in *Badlands* by comparing him to another famous alienated young killer, Dostoevsky's Raskolnikov. It will likewise illuminate Bill's doomed bid for liberation to place him in conversation with a literary foil in the person of Thrasymachus, Socrates's principal challenger in the first book of Plato's *Republic*. Considering Plato's enraged sophist will at once clarify Bill's struggle and ultimate downfall and foreshadow Franz's very different pursuit of agential liberty in *A Hidden Life*.

Socrates's aim in the *Republic* is to uncover the nature of justice. As the dialectic among Socrates and his interlocutors proceeds, however, it becomes clear that to understand justice is also to understand freedom. For, according to Socrates, the just person is one whose soul is ruled by reason, and to be subject to such rule is to be free. This is not to say that a just person cannot be confined or fall under the yoke of various social, political, or economic tyrannies; such misfortunes are always in the offing, perhaps especially for those who will not resort to injustice to avoid them. Rather, it is to say that a just person is, in a sense deeper than tyranny's reach, absolutely free, or free from the evils that threaten to confine the soul within itself. Thus, justice is, as Glaucon puts the point in challenging Socrates to defend it, "the worst thing a soul can have in it," and why, in the Parable of the Cave, those who are far from the Good don't just stare at shadows but do so in chains.[5]

Socrates doesn't arrive at his doctrine of justice-cum-freedom without a fight. Early in the dialogue, as Socrates, Glaucon, Adeimantus, and Polemarchus are just beginning their investigation, Thrasymachus takes furious command of the dialectic, "hurl[ing] himself" at the other men "as if to tear [them] to pieces."[6] Justice, he declares, is foolishness, a kind of instruction manual for the simple and easily duped. Far from exemplifying freedom, the just can expect only oppression from those strong and crafty enough to "outdo" others and impose their wills on them.[7] Only the perfectly unjust, who ruthlessly outdo all others, are happy and free. By Thrasymachus's lights, there are only sheep and those who fatten them for slaughter. And who, apart from the weak or idiotic, would seek their freedom in the slaughterhouse?

Thrasymachus does not last long against Socrates; his rage and arrogance render him unable either to defend his position adequately or to follow Socrates's reasoning to a different one. But Glaucon quickly revives the nub of his challenge. Can it really be true that the just person is happier and freer than the wholly successful unjust person? If, like Gyges's ancestor, you had a magic ring that would let you get away with anything, wouldn't it serve your well-being and freedom alike to use it? The remainder of the *Republic* is devoted to answering this challenge.

There's no need to review the argument here, but it is worth recalling its conclusion: the unjust person is abjectly unfree because they are unable to pull themselves together to act toward what they judge to be worth doing. Their injustice is a kind of internal tyranny incompatible with liberty—or, at least, the sort of liberty worth caring about.

Bill does not enter the narrative of *Days of Heaven* in a Thrasymachean frame of mind. To the contrary, he initially seeks peace and freedom in his relationship with Abby. But as he becomes increasingly imbittered under the yoke of those who outdo him, his orientation begins to shift. Not only does outdoing his economic superiors start to look like a better route to liberation than anything available to him as a laborer, but much that was once sacred to him—including even Abby—loses all significance apart from the big score. Thus, when he becomes convinced that he can pull one over on the farmer by having Abby marry him and then making off with his money after his death, he goes for it. This is Bill's fateful moment, when he trades everything that really mattered to him for the empty promise of outdoing another. And, far from freeing him, from elevating him above a life of "nosing around like a pig," it lowers him far below that humble station. When he eventually succumbs to the sheriff's shotgun after murdering the farmer, he does so not as someone who has risen to freedom by outdoing others but as man utterly alone, bereaved not just of his decency but also of the relationship on which he had once placed his hopes.

In a moment we will turn to *A Hidden Life*, the last of the three films that concern us here. But first, by way of an interlude, it will be worthwhile to tarry a moment with one important feature of the Platonic conception of freedom as justice that Bill rejects in favor of the Thrasymachean conception of freedom as domination. Although Socrates emphatically rejects the idea that there is freedom in conquest over others, he does not propose any other sort of intersubjectivity as the seat of liberty. To be sure, he does cast a relationship in this role; it is only by pursuing and subsequently communing with the Good that a person can be fully just and so fully free. But the Good is not a person, at least not for Plato. It is beyond us, but in a way that transcends personality just as surely as it transcends human persons. This raises a tantalizing question: What if freedom is to be found in a relationship that is at once personal and transcendent? This question, I believe, lies at the heart of *A Hidden Life*. Moreover, I will contend that, in a departure from the mainly negative conclusions about liberty presented in *Badlands* and *Days of Heaven*,

Malick uses Franz (August Biehl), his struggle, and his death to answer it stridently, and indeed victoriously, in the affirmative.

A Hidden Life: "Everything I Need"

I began this chapter by noting that Malick's films tend to be apolitical. *A Hidden Life* is to some extent an exception to this rule. For the film's premise, which is based on real events that took place in Austria before and during the Second World War, is straightforwardly, terrifyingly political; after the Nazi Anschluss, a farmer named Franz Jäggerstätter refused to swear an oath of allegiance to Hitler and paid for his integrity with his life. It was a life well worth living, replete with faith, community, and love. But it was worth less to him than his soul, so he gave it up. Although this tragic story is obviously a chapter of political history, Malick is much less interested in the politics of Franz's situation than in his inner—indeed, *hidden*—life of spiritual struggle and ultimate redemption. That redemption is a liberation of the most profound kind, the very kind, in fact, that Kit and Bill seek but never find. Franz comes to affirm that even as he awaits the guillotine in a Nazi prison, he is as deeply, gloriously free as it is possible for a human person to be. This is because he is at peace in the knowledge of God's love for him, a love that vanquishes alienation and reveals that we all are, or at least can be, unassailably at home.

By way of first approach to Franz's spiritual journey, it will be useful to return for a moment to Kit and Bill. We encounter each of them in a condition of agitation and alienation; Kit listlessly goes through the motions of a trash-collection job, and Bill kills his factory boss in an angry fistfight before taking off on the lam. Each then comes tantalizingly close to peace—and, perhaps, freedom—in their relationships with Holly and Abby, respectively, before succumbing to a violent spiral that ends in death. By contrast, we meet Franz as a man at peace with himself, his family, and his community. He enjoys a loving marriage with his wife, Fani (Valerie Pachner), and a rich family life with her and their two daughters. He is on close terms with his supportive agricultural community, and he clearly takes deep pleasure in working his land. Moreover, he practices his Catholic faith seriously and reflectively, if not overly intellectually. We hear that he may have sown some wild oats as younger man, but those days are over. Franz is, in short, as free from alienation and at home in his world as any of us can reasonably hope to be. This peace is shattered by the Nazi Anschluss and subsequent military conscription of men living in the new Nazi Lebensraum. Franz receives the call, and as a member of the Reichswehr, he is eventually required to swear an oath of allegiance to Hitler and the Nazi Reich. As his family grows along with the gravity of the European situation, Franz refuses to swear the oath, despite the escalating penalties he faces for doing so. In addition to imprisonment and, eventually, looming execution, Franz, along with his family, faces rejection by his once-close community, which has been swept up in Nazi fervor, and even abandonment by the church, whose clergy urge him to relent and take the oath. It would thus seem that Franz is, as the film's narrative approaches its bloody end, utterly bereft of his liberty no less than his happiness, and that where once there had been a man free within himself and in his relations to others, there remains only an abject prisoner.

But this, Franz explains, is not the case. With his execution imminent, Franz, remarking on his apparently dire unfreedom, says, "But I am free! I have everything I need." On the face of it, this is absurd, if not delusional. Franz is, after all, languishing in dank prison, torn from the arms of his family, abandoned by his pastors, and staring down certain violent death. But Malick clearly believes in what Franz is saying and means for us to believe it as well. We thus face a question on which our whole understanding of the film turns: What grounds does Franz have, or at least believe that he has, for this seemingly fantastical assertion? To answer this question, it will be useful to turn once more to a literary foil, in this case, the imprisoned Boethius from the fifth-century *Consolations of Philosophy*. Like Franz, Boethius is a political prisoner facing death while seeking—and, in great measure, finding—consolation. Moreover, like Franz, Boethius finds internal liberation despite external confinement by reflecting on a goodness that transcends not just his situation but human woe altogether. But, as we shall see, the character of Franz's transcendent good is somewhat different from that of Boethius (and of Plato before him). Understanding how and why Franz differs from Boethius on this point will illuminate what we might not unreasonably call Malick's considered view on the nature of inner liberty. Boethius—both the historical person and the eponymous character in *Consolations*—was imprisoned at Pavia after falling afoul of ruling Roman elites. In *Consolations*, he receives a visit from the goddess Philosophy, who consoles him by directing his attention to God's sovereignty over the rational order of all creation. As the work opens, Boethius is distraught, and we read of him in the work's second verse passage (*Consolations* alternates between verse and prose):

> Alas! in what abyss his mind
> Is plunged, how wildly tossed!
> Still, still towards the outer night
> She sinks, her true light lost,
> As oft as, lashed tumultuously
> By earth-born blasts, care's waves rise high.
> Yet once he ranged the open heavens,
> The sun's bright pathway tracked;
> Watched how the cold moon waxed and waned;
> Nor rested, till there lacked
> To his wide ken no star that steers
> Amid the maze of circling spheres
> All this he knew—thus ever strove
> Deep Nature's lore to guess.
> Now, reft of reason's light, he lies,
> And bonds his neck oppress;
> While by the heavy load constrained,
> His eyes to this dull earth are chained.[8]

Boethius, in short, is in a bad way, at least as he judges matters in these lines. He was once a philosopher who turned his attention to the heavens and their secrets. But now he is cast down, seemingly irreparably severed from philosophy and languishing in a pit of despair. The goddess Philosophy, however, promptly proves him wrong in dramatic fashion; she appears to him immediately after he issues this lament, and she undertakes, for the remainder of the work, to console him. Her consolations are myriad and complex, and I cannot hope to detail them here. But they all share a common drift: Reason demonstrates that all of creation is subject to God's perfect providence. God knows all and does so from eternity, and we must trust that he has all creation well in hand, human beings very much included. To despair over such trifles as unjust imprisonment and execution is to doubt the ultimately rational—and so good—character of the universe of which each of us is only the tiniest part. Boethius (the author) puts these final words into the mouth of Philosophy:

> And all this being so, the freedom of man's will stands unshaken, and laws are not unrighteous, since their rewards and punishments are held forth to wills unbound by any necessity. God, who foreknoweth all things, still looks down from above, and the ever-present eternity of His vision concurs with the future

character of all our acts, and dispenseth to the good rewards, to the bad punishments. Our hopes and prayers also are not fixed on God in vain, and when they are rightly directed cannot fail of effect. Therefore, withstand vice, practise virtue, lift up your souls to right hopes, offer humble prayers to Heaven. Great is the necessity of righteousness laid upon you if ye will not hide it from yourselves, seeing that all your actions are done before the eyes of a Judge who seeth all things. (Cons. Phil. 5.6)

If, as I think reasonable, we understand Boethius (the character) as accepting this message and finding in it freedom and peace in the midst of confinement and looming execution, it is perhaps tempting to see in Boethius a close model of Franz. After all, Franz prays to God in his last days and unambiguously sees God as the source and ground of the profound liberation he experiences while awaiting his death. But whereas Philosophy comforts Boethius by arguing theology with him and thereby convincing him of rationally unassailable doctrines that cast his suffering in a different light, Franz at no point argues philosophical theology, whether with himself or with anyone else. Indeed, the viewer gets the strong impression that Franz is not a man who goes in for that sort of thing. To the contrary, Franz's spiritual passage from bondage to liberty seems to be entirely relational rather than metaphysical, at least if by "metaphysical" we mean concerned with specific metaphysical doctrine rather than with transcendence more generally. In reflecting on the depth and significance of his relationships to his family—relationships that will be permanently terminated, at least in their earthly forms, unless he relents and takes the oath—he comes to see that his relationship with God contains and transcends all that he stands to lose. Indeed, we see in the Catholic Franz a realization of the specifically Christian promise of limitless freedom through Christ and his resurrection. And so, I suggest, St. Paul, more than Boethius, is the author who captures most accurately the sense of liberty that Franz encounters and experiences so profoundly. We read in the letter to the Galatians: "Stand fast therefore in the liberty wherewith Christ hath made us free, and be not entangled again with the yoke of bondage" (Gal. 5:1).

This remark from St. Paul reads as something of a sheer command. One might reasonably ask in reply how exactly one might go about being "not entangled . . . with the yoke of bondage" under circumstances that, like Franz's, are characterized by abject, unjust, and mortal bondage. St. Paul offers something close to an answer in his letter to the Romans. His words there are perhaps our single best resource for understanding the thesis about freedom that Malick means to affirm through Franz:

> For ye have not received the spirit of bondage again to fear; but ye have received the Spirit of adoption, whereby we cry, Abba, Father. The Spirit itself beareth witness with our spirit, that we are the children of God: And if children, then heirs; heirs of God, and joint-heirs with Christ; if so be that we suffer with *him*, that we may be also glorified together. For I reckon that the sufferings of this present time *are* not worthy *to be compared* with the glory which shall be revealed in us. For the earnest expectation of the creature waiteth for the manifestation of the sons of God. For the creature was made subject to vanity, not willingly, but by reason of him who hath subjected *the same* in hope, Because the creature itself also shall be delivered from the bondage of corruption into the glorious liberty of the children of God. For we know that the whole creation groaneth and travaileth in pain together until now. And not only *they*, but ourselves also, which have the firstfruits of the Spirit, even we ourselves groan within ourselves, waiting for the adoption, *to wit*, the redemption of our body. For we are saved by hope: but hope that is seen is not hope: for what a man seeth, why doth he yet hope for? But if we hope for that we see not, *then* do we with patience wait for *it*. Likewise the Spirit also helpeth our infirmities: for we know not what we should pray for as we ought: but the Spirit itself maketh intercession for us with groanings which cannot be uttered. And he that searcheth the hearts knoweth what *is* the mind of the Spirit, because he maketh intercession for the saints according to *the will of* God. And we know that all things work together for good to them that love God, to them who are the called according to *his* purpose. (Rom. 8:15–28)

This, I believe, is the final resting place of Malick's dialectic of liberty. As we learned from the tragic narratives of Kit and Bill, there is no freedom from alienation to be found in either rebellion against the moral order or outdoing the powerful. But neither does true liberty await in the deepest and most meaningful temporal relationships of the kind that Kit and Bill seek with Holly and Abby, respectively, and that Franz enjoys with Fani and his daughters. Absolute freedom that permits a human being to come finally, truly home to themselves, and to remain there even in the face of death, is indeed to be found in a relationship with another person. That person is not anyone on earth, though, but rather the divine person of God as made known to us through Christ.

Conclusion: Abundant Liberty

We considered at the outset of this chapter Sontag's remark that struggle with alienation is a hallmark of serious modern thought. In making this suggestion, she is, I think, asserting a normative claim as well as a descriptive one; serious modern thought engages in this struggle because it constitutes a response to a problem that is, from a clear-eyed, modern point of view, insoluble. The best we can do, she seems to urge, is struggle with it as authentically and articulately as we can. Sontag is far from alone in this judgment; if anything, she speaks for a large majority of contemporary thinkers, especially in the world of arts and letters. If I am right about how to interpret the thematic arc that bends through *Badlands* and *Days of Heaven* to its conclusion in *A Hidden Life*, Malick's films offer a contrary thesis: freedom—indeed, final and complete freedom—is abundantly available to all of us, no matter our circumstances. Faced with this thesis, it is only reasonable to ask whether it is true. I, for one, have my doubts. Our purpose here, however, is not to interrogate this or any other philosophical doctrine but rather to discover whether and how Malick succeeds in illuminating a vision of liberty no less powerful than his portrayals of unfreedom and alienation. There can, I think, be little doubt that he does. To reckon fully with Malick's art and its meaning for us, one must contend with his startlingly spiritual—and provocatively contrarian—conception of human liberty.[9]

Notes

1. Sontag, *Against Interpretation and Other Essays*, 69.
2. Marx, *Selected Writings*, 60.
3. Marx, 60.
4. Kafka, *The Metamorphosis*, 9.
5. Plato, *Complete Works*, Republic 366e.

6. Plato, 336b
7. Plato, 349.
8. Boethius, *The Consolations of Philosophy*, 1.2.
9. I would like to thank Benjamin Bagley for helpful discussion of the ideas in this chapter.

Bibliography

Boethius, Anicius Manlius Severinus. *The Consolations of Philosophy*. Translated by H. R. James. Project Gutenberg, 2004.
Dostoevsky, Fyodor. *Crime and Punishment*. Translated by Jessie Coulson. New York: Oxford University Press, 1998.
Kafka, Franz. *The Metamorphosis*. Translated by Ian Johnston. Auckland: Floating Press, 2008.
Marx, Karl. *Selected Writings*. Edited by Lawrence H. Simon. Indianapolis: Hackett, 1994.
Plato. *Complete Works*. Edited by John M. Cooper. Indianapolis: Hackett, 1997.
Sontag, Susan. *Against Interpretation and Other Essays*. New York: Picador, 1965.

Contributors

Jussi Backman is an Academy of Finland senior research fellow at the University of Jyväskylä, Finland. His research fields include contemporary continental philosophy (phenomenology, philosophical hermeneutics, poststructuralism, recent continental realism), continental political theory and philosophy of religion, and ancient philosophy. His current research project is focused on the conceptual history of the concept of creativity. In addition to numerous articles, he is the author of *Complicated Presence: Heidegger and the Postmetaphysical Unity of Being* (SUNY Press, 2015) and *Omaisuus ja elämä: Heidegger ja Aristoteles kreikkalaisen ontologian rajalla* (2005), and coeditor (with Antonio Cimino) of *Bios and Polis: Biopolitics and Ancient Thought* and of special issues and an edited volume in Finnish.

Lee Braver is professor of philosophy at the University of South Florida. His main interests are continental philosophy (especially Heidegger and Derrida), Wittgenstein, realism, and the dialogue between continental and analytic philosophy. He is the author of *A Thing of This World: A History of Continental Anti-Realism* (2007), *Heidegger's Later Writings: A Reader's Guide* (2009), *Groundless Grounds: A Study of Wittgenstein and Heidegger* (2012), *Heidegger: Thinking of Being* (2014), and editor of *Division III of Being and Time: Heidegger's Unanswered Question of Being* (2015). He has written articles on aesthetics, analytic-continental dialogue, art history, Donald Davidson, Philip K. Dick, Dilthey, Hubert Dreyfus, entrepreneurship, Foucault, Gadamer, Gnosticism, Heidegger, the history of analytic philosophy, Kierkegaard, Levinas, John McDowell, Quentin Meillassoux, pedagogy, Putnam, Quine, robots, transgressive realism, unthinkability, and Wittgenstein.

Manuel "Mandel" Cabrera Jr. is assistant professor of philosophy at Yonsei University in Seoul, South Korea. His main areas of interest are the philosophy of religion and related topics, with work about and inspired by Spinoza, phenomenology, art, music, and literature.

David R. Cerbone is professor of philosophy and Woodburn fellow at West Virginia University. He is the author of *Understanding Phenomenology* (2006), *Heidegger: A Guide for the Perplexed* (2008), and *Existentialism: All That Matters* (2015), as well as numerous articles on Heidegger, Wittgenstein, and the phenomenological tradition. He is also coeditor (with Søren Overgaard and Komarine Romdenh-Romluc) of the Routledge Research in Phenomenology series.

Candace R. Craig is a veteran teacher of English, history, drama, and film studies at the secondary and college levels. She is the recipient of a grant from the National Endowment for the Humanities to study film adaptation of nineteenth-century literature. In her spare time, she is an independent scholar, creative writer, and freelance editor. She has published several classroom literary guides and her creative nonfiction has appeared in such journals as *The Hopper* and *US Represented*. Her published stories form part of an ongoing autobiographical project on growing up in the rust belt. She is the author, with James D. Reid, of *Agency and Imagination in the Films of David Lynch: Philosophical Perspectives* (2019) and is currently working on a book on philosophical and poetic resonances in several films of Terrence Malick.

Steven DeLay is a research fellow at the Global Center for Advanced Studies. He is the author of *Faint Not: Twelve Brief Meditations on the Word of God* (2022), *In the Spirit: A Phenomenology of Faith* (2022), *Before God: Exercises in Subjectivity* (2020), and *Phenomenology in France: A Philosophical and Theological Introduction* (2019). His works of fiction include *Elijah Newman Died Today: A Novella* (2023) and *Everything* (2022). He is also the editor of the forthcoming *Finding Meaning: Philosophy in Crisis* based on the online series of essays, "Finding Meaning," at Richard Marshall's *3:16 AM*.

Naomi Fisher is assistant professor of philosophy at Loyola University Chicago. Her research focuses on Kant and German Idealism and Romanticism, specifically the relationship between nature, freedom, and rationality

Contributors | 395

in Kant's critical philosophy and in Schelling's philosophy of nature. She also has interests in the history of philosophy more generally, as well as philosophy of science, philosophy of religion, and ethics. She is currently working on a manuscript on the influence of Plato and Neoplatonism in Schelling's early philosophy.

Rico Gutschmidt is assistant professor at the University of Konstanz. He has published on skepticism (ancient and modern), Heidegger, Wittgenstein, Cavell, philosophy of religion, negative theology, and the philosophy of physics. His current research concerns philosophical reasoning as transformative experience.

Keith Jacobs is professor of sociology at the University of Tasmania. He has an extensive track record with over seventy journal articles, and his recent books include the following: coeditor (with Jeff Malpas) of *Experience and Representation: Contemporary Perspectives on Migration in Australia*, coeditor (with Jeff Malpas) of *Ocean to Outback: Cosmopolitanism in Contemporary Australia Housing* (2010), and coeditor (again with Jeff Malpas) of *Towards a Philosophy of the City: Interdisciplinary and Transcultural Perspectives* (2019). He is also the author (with Rowland Atkinson) of *House, Home and Society* (2016), and the author (again with Rowland Atkinson) of *Neoliberal Housing Policy: An International Perspective and Housing What Do We Know and What Can We Do* (2019). Jacobs is a member of the editorial board of *Housing Studies* and the international advisory boards of *Housing Theory and Society* and *International Journal of Housing Policy*.

David B. Johnson is lecturer in the department of liberal arts at the School of the Art Institute of Chicago. His research focuses on the intersection of aesthetics, philosophy of film, critical theory, and recent French philosophy. His work has appeared in journals such *Deleuze Studies, Cinema: A Journal of Philosophy and the Moving Image*, and *The Sublime: From Antiquity to the Present* (2012).

Katerina Koci is a postdoctoral researcher at the Institute for Human Sciences in Vienna, Austria, and a laureate of the Lise Meitner Fellowship funded by Austrian Science Fund (FWF) for the project entitled *Woman without a Name: Gender Identity in Sacrificial Stories*. After defending her doctoral dissertation from KU Leuven, Belgium, in 2017, Koci held a fellowship at Charles University, Prague. She is the author of *The Land without Promise: The Roots and Afterlife of One Biblical Allusion* (2021).

Martin Koci is a postdoctoral research fellow at the Institute for Philosophy at the University of Vienna, Austria. He is the author of *Thinking Faith after Christianity: A Theological Reading of Jan Poatocka's Phenomenological Philosophy* (SUNY Press, 2021) and coeditor (with Jason Alvis) of *Transforming the Theological Turn: Phenomenology with Emmanuel Falque* (2019) and the forthcoming *God and Phenomenology: Thinking with Jean-Yves Lacoste*.

Daniel Layman is assistant professor of philosophy at Davidson College, where he teaches and writes about liberalism, early modern philosophy, and the relationships between them. In addition to a number of articles on figures such as Locke and Boyle and contemporary political theory, he is the author of *Locke Among the Radicals: Liberty and Property in the Nineteenth Century* (2020).

Jonathan Lee is professor of philosophy at Colorado College, where he has taught for nearly thirty years. While working extensively in ancient Greek philosophy and contemporary French philosophy, he has also written and published widely on contemporary music and sound art, film, visual art, poetry, and photography. The author of *Jacques Lacan* (1991) and editor of *I Am Because We Are: Readings in Africana Philosophy* (2016), his works have appeared in *Writings About John Cage* (1993), *Journal of Modern Greek Studies*, *The Cambridge History of Philosophy, 1945–2015* (2019), and *Exposure Magazine*.

James Lorenz is lecturer in philosophy of religion at York St John University. His research is broadly in the field of modern systematic theology, with a particular focus on religion and the arts, specifically cinema. His doctoral thesis engages with film-phenomenology (via Maurice Merleau-Ponty and Vivian Sobchack) in order to explore the theological concepts that emerge from the films and writings of Andrei Tarkovsky.

Jeff Malpas is research professor in philosophy at the University of Tasmania. He works across a wide range of topics in contemporary thought but is best known for his work on the philosophy of place and space, twentieth-century German philosophy, and contemporary hermeneutics and philosophy of language. Much of his work is interdisciplinary in character connecting philosophy with art, architecture, film studies, and geography, among other disciplines. His most recent books are *Heidegger and the Place of Thinking* (2012), the edited collections *The Place of Landscape* (2011), *Dialogues with Davidson* (2011), and (with Norelle Lickiss) *Perspectives on Human Suffering* (2012). He is also the author of *Place and Experience* (1999), *Heidegger's Topology* (2006), and has edited many other volumes, and has written more than one hundred articles that have appeared in various journals and collections.

Joel Mayward is assistant professor of Christian ministries, theology and the arts at George Fox University in Oregon, where he is also a faculty fellow in the Honors Program. Mayward serves as the theology editor for *The Other Journal*, an interdisciplinary academic journal of theology and culture, and publishes widely as a professional freelance film critic. The author of three Christian ministry books, he is completing two academic monographs on philosophical theology and cinema: *The Dardenne Brothers' Cinematic Parables: Integrating Theology, Philosophy, and Film* and *Theology and Christopher Nolan: Transcending Time and Narrative*.

James D. Reid is professor of philosophy at the Metropolitan State University of Denver. He has taught ethics and the history of philosophy at Chicago (where he won a Wayne C. Booth Graduate Student Prize for Excellence in Teaching), Colorado College, the College of William and Mary, and the United States Air Force Academy. His research is interdisciplinary, drawing from philosophical, artistic, and scientific sources and devoted to problems in axiology and the theory of meaning and the challenges of finding fitting ways of expressing the importance of what we care about. He has published numerous articles and book chapters on various philosophical issues in Kant and his successors in the nineteenth and twentieth centuries. He received a grant from the National Endowment for the Humanities to support a translation of Heidegger's *Die Frage nach dem Ding* (2018). He coedited Thoreau's *Importance for Philosophy* (2012) and is the author of *Being Here Is Glorious: On Rilke, Poetry, and Philosophy* (2015), *Heidegger's Moral Ontology* (2018), and (with Candace R. Craig) *Agency and Imagination in the Films of David Lynch: Philosophical Perspectives* (2019). His current projects include a monograph on the German philosophical poet Novalis and a book-length interpretation of Rilke's "Sonnets to Orpheus." He hopes in the coming years to revisit a long-standing project on freedom and nature in Kant's critical philosophy.

Fred Rush is professor of philosophy at the University of Notre Dame. He is the author of *Irony and Idealism* (2016) and *On Architecture* (2009). He is the editor of *The Cambridge Companion to Critical Theory* (2004), a coeditor of *Philosophy of Sculpture* (2021), and for several years also edited the *Internationales Jahrbuch des deutschen Idealismus*. He has just completed a book called *Film's Experience*.

Steven Rybin is associate professor of film studies at Minnesota State University, Mankato, where he is also codirector of the Film and Media Studies Program. He is the author of *Geraldine Chaplin: The Gift of Film Performance* (2020), *Gestures of Love: Romancing Performance in Classical Hollywood Cinema* (SUNY Press, 2017), and *Michael Mann: Crime Auteur* (2013). He is also editor of *The Cinema of Hal Hartley: Flirting with Formalism* (2016), coeditor (with Murray Pomerance) of *Hamlet Lives in Hollywood: John Barrymore and the Acting Tradition Onscreen* (2017), and coeditor (with Will Scheibel) of *Lonely Places, Dangerous Ground: Nicholas Ray in American Cinema* (SUNY Press, 2014). He is currently writing a book on film style in widescreen cinema.

Robert Sinnerbrink is associate professor in philosophy and former Australian research council Future fellow at Macquarie University, Sydney. He is the author of *Terrence Malick: Filmmaker and Philosopher* (2019), *Cinematic Ethics: Exploring Ethical Experience through Film* (2016), *New Philosophies of Film: Thinking Images* (2011), *Understanding Hegelianism* (2007/2014), and editor of *Critique Today* (2006). He is a member of the editorial board of the journals *Film-Philosophy*, *Film and Philosophy*, and *Projections: The Journal of Movies and Mind*. He has published numerous articles on the relationship between film and philosophy in journals such as the *Australasian Philosophical Review*, *Angelaki*, *Conversations: The Journal of Cavellian Studies*, *Film-Philosophy*, *Necsus: European Journal of Media Studies*, *Projections: The Journal of Movies and Mind*, *Post-Script*, *Screen*, *Screening the Past*, and *SubStance*.

Matthew Strohl is professor of philosophy at the University of Montana. He is the author of *Why It's Okay to Love Bad Movies* (2021) and specializes in film, philosophy of art, and classical philosophy.

Enrico Terrone is Juan de la Cierva postdoctoral fellow at the LOGOS Research Group, University of Barcelona. He works on philosophical issues concerning aesthetics, ontology, and technology. His main area of research is philosophy of film. He has published papers in journals such as *British Journal of Aesthetics*, *Journal of Aesthetics and Art Criticism*, *Erkenntis*, and *Ergo*. His books include *Cinema and Ontology* (2019), *Filosofia dell'ingegneria* (2019), *Filosofia del film* (2014), and *Filosofia delle serie Tv* (2012).

Donald Wallenfang is a Secular Discalced Carmelite, professor of theology and philosophy, and lay formator at the Institute for Lay Ministry, at Sacred Heart Major Seminary. His articles have appeared in *Philosophy and Theology*, *Logos: A Journal of Catholic Thought and Culture*, *The International Journal of Religion in Spirituality and Society*, *Listening: Journal of Communication Ethics*, *Religion, Culture*, and *Pacifica*, and in other book compilations. He is the author of *Metaphysics: A Basic Introduction in a Christian Key* (2019), *Phenomenology: A Basic Introduction in the Light of Jesus Christ* (2019), *Dialectical Anatomy of the Eucharist: An Étude in Phenomenology* (2017), and *Human and Divine Being: A Study on the Theological Anthropology of Edith Stein* (2017). He specializes in Catholic theology and philosophy, Carmelite spirituality, phenomenology, and metaphysics. His research concentrates on the work of Edith Stein, Emmanuel Levinas, Paul Ricœur, Jean-Luc Marion, the Carmelite saints, and the new evangelizations.

Index

Adorno, Theodor, 357, 359–60
Arendt, Hannah, 75, 131
Aristotle, 130, 267
Arnheim, Rudolf, 4, 9, 18n14
Art, 2; film as, 5, 11, 232; of living, 31, 42; photography and, 3–4; mimesis and, 4; narrative and, 47
Augustine, 29, 130, 202, 313
Authenticity, 15, 16; acting and being, 258–60; integration of, 30, 291, 327; *Knight of Cups* and, 27

Bach, Johann Sebastian, 73, 206–207, 257
Barnett, Christopher, 40, 44n40, 142n31
Bazin, André, 6; montage and, 211; philosophy and, 9; power of cinema, 203; realism of, 7, 9–10, 15, 241, 247, 219n18
Beauty, 1; call of 11–12; desire and, 242; embodiment and, 29; form of, 284; goodness and, 129, 148–49, 151, 154; life and, 69; love and, 120; nature and, 25, 36, 40, 51, 68, 99, 120, 127, 153, 157, 160n8, 180, 191, 241; search for, 267–70; truth and, 2–3, 253
Benjamin, Walter, 180, 191n10

Bergman, Ingmar, 179, 245
Bergson, Henri, 199–201, 211
Berlioz, Hector, 38, 43n37, 78–80
Blumenberg, Hans, 93–94
Boethius, 387–89
Brakhage, Stan, 7
Bresson, Robert, 179, 270
Bunyan, John, 29, 281, 303–305
Byron, George Gordon, 179, 191

Camacho, Paul, 253n1, 271–72
Carroll, Noël, 7, 8, 18n13
Caruana, John, 98
Cavell, Stanley, Bazin and, 6, 18n16, 85n2, 275n7; Malick and, 68, 97, 135, 222
Cézanne, Paul, 7
Chrétien, Jean-Louis, 11
Classical film theory, 4; art and 9; Deleuze and 204–205; philosophy and, 12
Conscience, 32, 34–35, 139, 324, 343, 349, 364, 372

Damasio, Antonio, 221
Day, Dorothy, 339, 343, 349
Dean, James, 51, 362, 378
Deleuze, Gilles, 14, 197, 201–206
Derrida, Jacques, 311, 325

401

Descartes, René, 14, 221, 233, 239
Dick, Philip K., 21n34, 310, 316n7
Dostoevsky, Fyodor, 13; freedom and, 154; influence of, 267–68, 380–81, 383; memory in, 147–50; morality and, 71
Dreyfus, Hubert, 9, 135, 233
Dürer, Albrecht, 186
Dyer, Jay, 19n16

Ebert, Roger, 68, 161n20, 226
Eden, 66, 81, 126–27, 138, 156, 302
Eisenstein, Sergei, 5
Emerson, Ralph Waldo, 85n4
Epicureanism, 32

Freud, Sigmund, 68, 186, 191n6, 356, 360
Fromm, Erich, 357–60, 369, 372

Gnosticism, 16, 21n34; evil and, 130, 300–304; story of the pearl in, 29, 281, 284, 304
Godard, Jean-Luc, 179, 186
Goodness, 12, 118, 123, 129, 133, 148, 158, 292, 384
Górecki, Henryk, 270–73
Grace, 36, 60; embodied, 250, 252, 261, 263, 267; gift of, 270, 271, 273; source of, 156; way of, 39, 66, 72, 74, 84, 100, 109, 106, 120, 125n15, 138, 148, 242, 293–94, 300

Hadot, Pierre, 12, 31–32, 42
Hegel, G. W. F., 2, 3; beauty in, 17n6; ethical life in, 34; German Idealism and, 134
Heidegger, Martin, 2; being-in-the-world and, 64; everydayness in, 6, 9, 309, 325; German idealism and, 134; Meister Eckhart and, 41, 91, 95; Nazism in, 16, 64, 344–45; poetry and, 97; technology and, 8; world in, 9
Henry, Michel, 10, 17n6
Herzog, Werner, 7
Hildebrand, Dietrich von, 1, 11
Hitchcock, Alfred, 18n10
Hobbes, Thomas, 221
Hopper, Edward, 185, 188
Horkheimer, Max, 357–58
Husserl, Edmund, 4, 6, 19n23, 135

Innocence, 128; childhood, 154, 158 161n17; lost, 228–29; primeval, 133; state of, 156, 228, 267, 322

Job, 36, 57–60, 65–66, 75, 115, 117–20, 136
Joy, beauty and, 1, 151, 181, 273; emotion of, 5, 63, 99, 257; Job and, 36, 57, 65, 117, 151, 312; life and, 36; suffering and, 40, 128, 134, 140, 338, 347; vision of, 34, 190, 270, 302

Kant, Immanuel, 2, 17n6, 68, 69, 131
Kearney, Richard, 100–101
Kendall, Stuart, 192n12
Kierkegaard, Søren, 9, 10, 16, 21n35; aesthetic life, 76; indirect communication of, 97; love and, 320–25; recollection in, 149; "weightless trilogy" and, 28, 241, 280
Krishek, Sharon, 322
Kubrick, Stanley, 78, 87n19, 311

Lacoste, Jean-Yves, 20n23
Language, 8; ineffability and, 10; in film, 166, 169, 223; metaphysical,

356; ordinary, 221; origins of, 176n6; Malick on, 97
Leibniz, G. W., 77, 129, 131
Levinas, Emmanuel, 345, 349
Love, 16; attention and, 242–47, 252; beauty and, 122, 127; death and, 82; grace and, 66, 74, 120, 138, 151; Plato and, 281, 283, 285, 288, 293; self-understanding and, 28, 190, 238–41, 247, 253, 293
Löwenthal, Leo, 357
Lubezki, Emmanuel, 38, 238, 248, 250

Marcuse, Herbert, 357–58
Marion, Jean-Luc, 14, 237–41
Marx, Karl, 376–77
Masochism, 253, 363, 370, 372n6
Merleau-Ponty, Maurice, 7, 244
Milton, John, 288, 290
Montage, 5, 10, 37, 59, 180, 198, 205–11, 250
Mozart, 73
Mulhall, Stephen, 9, 97
Mystery, 10; cosmic, 115; existence and, 13, 119, 217; Heidegger on, 107–109; of the world, 14, 123; suffering and, 117–19

Nagel, Thomas, 311
Negative theology, 92–94
Neumann, Franz, 357
Nicholas of Cusa, 93
Nietzsche, Friedrich, 2; aesthetics in, 40, 74; eternal return, 314; moral nihilism in, 69, 75, 84; suffering and art in, 17n10, 129, 299, 309
Nostalgia, 111–13, 124n9, 128, 136

Patočka, Jan, 326–27
Patterson, Hannah, 357, 361, 372n16
Pattison, George, 19n21, 142n31

Paul (Saint), 389–90
Perception, 5; disembodied, 231; normal vision of, 6, 9, 206; world of, 6, 9–10
Perkins, V. F., 10
Pippin, Robert B., 9, 17n6n10, 25, 26, 227
Plato, 1; allegory of the cave, 19n16; art and, 3; beauty in, 11, 307; evil in, 130, 304; love in, 253, 283; memory in, 148–51; myth of eros, 280, 283; philosophy as a way of life in, 32
Plotinus, 32, 94
Proust, Marcel, 215

Rilke, Rainer Maria, 81, 88n22
Romano, Claude, 19n23
Rossouw, Martin, 26
Rousseau, Jean-Jacques, 138
Ryle, Gilbert, 9; ghost in the machine and, 14, 221, 233; Malick and, 221

Schelling, F. W. J., 13, 129, 131–32
Schiller, Friedrich, 3
Schmitt, Carl, 186
Schopenhauer, Arthur, 2, 17n10
Scott, Ridley, 21n34
Sinnerbrink, Robert, Heidegger and, 92; influence of, 9, 13, 26, 40, 244, 280; transformative experience in Malick, 98–100
Sobchak, Vivian, 244
Socrates, 283, 287, 367, 384
Sontag, Susan, 179–80, 185–86
Stein, Edith, 16, 340, 345–47
Stoicism, 31

Taylor, Charles, 19n18
Teuber, Andrea, 8

404 | Index

Texas, 128, 158, 172, 230, 250, 382
Theodicy, 119, 131, 136
Theresa of Avila, 346
Tillich, Paul, 97
Tugendhat, Ernst, 20n23

Voiceover, 14; as film technique, 165; as inscription, 172–75; cosmos and, 53; narration with, 185, 214, 223–25, 233; non-diegetic, 29, 174; quotations of, 27
Voltaire, 131

Weil, Simone, 14, 241–44
Wittgenstein, Ludwig, 9, 10, 91, 122, 320

Zimmer, Hans, 229